Conflict of the Heart

Lucie Pagé

Translated by Marion Boers

Published in 2003 in Southern Africa by
David Philip Publishers,
an imprint of New Africa Books (Pty) Ltd,
99 Garfield Road, Claremont 7700, South Africa

First published in Canada in 2001 by Libre Expression

ISBN 0 86486 619 4

Set in Bembo 11 on 13.5pt
Typesetting by Charlene Bate
Cover photo by Elaine Cosser
Printed and bound by Paarl Print

To Léandre;
to Jay, who has given me love and peace, Kami and Shanti;
to my parents, Pierre and Louise, who have always encouraged
me to strive for the best.

To Wendy

I wish you lots of passion
in your life because with
it, everything is possible!

Lucie Pagé

22/08/14

pagedumonde@gmail.com

Contents

C'est blessant
Vivre en noir et blanc
Quand t'as le coeur
Rempli de couleurs

Serge FIORI

Acknowledgements

This book would not have been written were it not for the invaluable support of my friend and colleague, the author and journalist Luc Chartrand, who spent days and weeks reading and correcting my manuscript and months and years encouraging me. I owe a debt of gratitude to my dear friend Louise Sarrasin, who was always there with her pen, her ears and her heart to help me along the difficult paths of the writer's jungle. Thank you to my mother, Louise Grondin, for always being there for her children, without judging. Thank you to my friend Marc Cossette, for the constant vigilance of his internal grammar books and dictionaries and for his friendship seven days a week. Thank you to my dear friend Jacques Larue-Langlois, who for twenty years supported and assisted me in my projects and who in the course of this book spent a great deal of time correcting and advising me on my writing. Jacques unfortunately did not live long enough to see the finished product, but certainly long enough to bequeath me a great richness of life. Thank you to Fannie Morin from the publishers *Éditions Libre Expression* for her support, her corrections and her confidence in me. Thank you to Sharon Hughes from New Africa Books, for her incredible warmth, and for being there each step of the way; to Marion Boers also for her patience in translating the subtleties of my Québécois French. Thank you, finally, to my husband, Jay Naidoo, for his patience, his support, his constant encouragement and, especially, his limitless love.

Prologue

In 1990 I went to South Africa as a reporter for Radio–Québec's television programme, *Nord-Sud*. I had to prepare about ten documentaries describing the period of transition in which South Africa found itself on the release of Nelson Mandela, who had been freed from prison a few months before, on 11 February 1990.

I spent five weeks in South Africa. It was the first time I had been away from my son for so long. Thirty-five 'beddy-byes' exactly ... I had prepared a small envelope for him containing a short story and a surprise for each evening. Five weeks away is a long time, especially for a mother.

Léandre was then four years old. A good-natured little boy, curious, alert, and happy I think, despite his parents' separation. He had gotten used to a life of joint custody between his father and myself. He had two of everything: friends, bedrooms, toys. Two lives. Like so many children who are victims of our restless, modern relationships.

In the plane on the way back to Montreal, I was no longer thinking about the five most thrilling weeks of my journalistic career, but about my little darling on the other side of the world. And the closer I got, the more eager I became to snuggle into my little routine with Léandre – seven beddy-byes that nothing in the world could disturb.

Eight months after my return, I sold up and stored my belongings in friends' basements, garages and attics. I left for South Africa once more, this time to stay. My son was to join me in six months' time. His father and I had agreed on the only possible compromise: custody divided between two continents. An impractical, absurd arrangement perhaps, but one that seemed the fairest for Léandre and for us.

'In a hundred and eighty beddy-byes, Mama?'

'Yes, my sweetheart.'

'That's a long time, isn't it?'

'Yes, my sweetheart. But I will phone you every week. I will send you lovely stories, and surprises, and photos.'

Léandre was crying. He clung to my neck as though this was a final farewell. His embrace was choking me, literally. 'What have I done?' I asked myself. Together, his father and I had to tear his tense little arms from my neck. I rushed down the stairs as fast as I could, blinded by my tears. The cries and sobs of my son followed me into the street.

1

The interview

27 October 1990, 22:58: 'It's a wrap!' cries Patricio Henriquez, the producer of *Nord-Sud*, a Canadian documentary programme, also in charge of the Radio–Québec team with which I've come to make documentaries in South Africa. We're in the lobby of Jamieson's Bar, a jazz club in central Johannesburg, shooting a documentary on the history of jazz in South Africa with the group the African Jazz Pioneers, who are giving a concert here later this evening. Jamieson's Bar is situated in a dark and smoky basement, but the crowd inside is mixed and in good spirits. Here, apartheid doesn't exist.

We have to stop filming because at eleven precisely Patricio has to start paying the technical team double rates and our budget is tight. Just as we're about to leave, a tall thin man with Indian features comes in with a few others. As he emerges through clouds of smoke, I recognise him and cry out: 'You're Jay Naidoo!'

Earlier in the day, while we were filming in Soweto, this man had managed to silence a crowd of fifty thousand people that had gathered in Orlando Stadium. It was a celebration of the founding of the ANC Youth League. The stadium was filled to bursting point with young activists who were all worked up.

It is impossible to forget that scene. Tens of thousands of young people were chanting freedom songs and toyi-toyiing. Gold, green and black, the colours of the ANC, symbolising the riches beneath the earth, in the earth itself, and in the people, floated everywhere in all forms: flags, hats, jackets, jerseys, shields, scarves.

The *Nord-Sud* team was cordoned off, near the stage, with hundreds of other journalists. Heroes of the anti-apartheid struggle took the stage one after another to speak. The stars of the day were Walter Sisulu, Nelson Mandela's companion in the struggle and in prison, and Joe Slovo, General Secretary of the Communist Party, a white South African who said 'we' when talking about blacks. But the crowd was restless and certain groups were singing during the speeches.

And then a man dressed in an ordinary pair of jeans and a red silk shirt came onto the stage. The crowd stood up and roared. But as soon as he started speaking, a silence fell on the stadium. This man knew how to make himself heard.

I couldn't talk because the camera was rolling. So I wrote 'Who is this Indian guy?' in my notebook and passed it to our researcher, Marie-Hélène Bonin, also from Quebec but in the country a year already. The notebook was returned to me with the reply, 'Jay Naidoo, General Secretary of COSATU.' I passed the notebook to Marie-Hélène once again: 'I'd like to interview him.'

That evening, in the lobby of Jamieson's Bar, I had forgotten this request until I came face to face with Jay Naidoo himself.

'I want to interview you!' I cry out.

He looks at me, exasperated.

'Not another journalist! My first evening out to a bar in one and a half years and here I am, being bothered by a reporter! I'm sorry, I'm not available.'

Before disappearing into the crowd, he exchanges a casual greeting with Marie-Hélène. They seem to know one another … I leave my team and plunge after Jay Naidoo. I find him sitting at a table with a group of his friends. I plump myself down on the few centimetres that are still free at the end of the bench.

Holding out my business card, I start explaining to Jay Naidoo who I am and what I'm doing in South Africa, as briefly as possible because he doesn't look at all interested. I almost have to shout because the music is so loud. Marie-Hélène, who has followed me, taps me on the shoulder and whispers in my ear: 'Be careful of Jay Naidoo, he's a womaniser!' I reply that I don't give a damn, that all I want is to ask him for an interview. I'm still giving Mr Naidoo my story when Patricio, the producer, cuts in.

'We have to go, Lucie. I can't pay the guys overtime.'

'But I have Jay Naidoo with me! Just let me organise the interview and I'll come.'

'We can't wait. It's late and we have a heavy day tomorrow.'

'Five minutes. Give me five minutes.'

'I'm sorry, Lucie. We have to go.'

'In that case, go. I'm staying.'

Patricio glares at me and leaves, furious.

How will I get back to the hotel? I've heard that taxis don't venture into this part of town at night, because it is too dangerous. I will soon find out. Right now, I just want to get the interview.

I resume my monologue, but this time it's Jay Naidoo who interrupts me.

'Listen! You may stay, but on one condition: we don't talk about politics or work. It's my first free evening in a long time. I'm escorting fellow trade unionists from Scandinavia and I'd like them to have a good time. In fact I'd like to enjoy myself for a few hours.'

'No problem.'

But I told myself I would end up persuading him to give me an interview before we left in two weeks' time. Then I'd be able to sleep.

Just a few minutes later, Jay turns his back on his colleagues and becomes more and more talkative. We ramble from one subject to another, talking about everything and nothing, about his desire to laugh, his need to cry – without being able to do either. The conversation quickly becomes intimate. We talk a lot about our mothers, because his has just passed away. 'There are so many things that I would have liked to say to her, do for her,' Jay confides. His regrets and his pain, without the comfort of tears, move me. It feels as though this stranger has become a good friend in just a few minutes.

We let ourselves go on the dance floor to the rhythm of the African Jazz Pioneers. When we've had enough, we sit at the bar, where Jay points to various bottles of spirits. His emotions are trapped in bottles of different colours and shapes, like those over there. 'But,' he says, 'knowing how to repress one's emotions is one of the laws of survival for an activist in South Africa.'

It's two thirty in the morning. I haven't dared break our 'pact'. I haven't spoken about the interview, about politics, or about work …

'I have to go, Jay. I've got a hard day's work ahead of me.'

'How are you going to get back to your hotel?'

'By taxi.'

'Are you nuts? You'll never get a taxi. I'll walk with you.'

'No. I'm sure I'll be fine. After all, the hotel isn't very far away.'

'Here, the level of danger has nothing to do with the distance. I insist. 'Let's go. Anyway, I'm also tired.'

Deep in conversation we walk through the dark streets of Johannesburg, forgetting about the possible risk of talking out loud in such a nonchalant way, as one does in broad daylight in the streets of Montreal. We soon branch off into a pedestrian road. All the businesses are barricaded behind heavy metal shutters, which slide open and closed like the folds of an accordion. The little red lights of the alarm systems blink inside the shops.

An almost gloomy silence reigns in the streets when, out of nowhere, a group of five youths springs up in front of us. They've been hiding, apparently waiting for the first passers-by. One of them holds a knife to my throat. Another grabs me by the arm. They want our money, our jewellery, our watches. Our lives? Jay immediately goes onto the offensive, placing himself between them and me. He orders them to leave us alone, without any hesitation that might reveal fear. Then, fortunately, one of them recognises him. He apologises on behalf of the others and they all flee.

Turning to me, Jay also apologises, as though he feels responsible for the incident. He explains that there is still so much to do to rebuild this country where the youth are enraged and no longer recognise the value of life. He wants to change this, he says. It's his goal to give South Africa a new face. Is this the rhetoric of a politician or the sincere conviction of a wise man? I've only spent a few hours with Jay Naidoo, but, for some unknown reason, I already know that he is fundamentally honest and genuine.

We finally reach the hotel. I cannot let him leave without asking him for an interview. I take a deep breath and ask the question that has been on my lips for hours.

'Of course,' he says simply. 'Here's my secretary's number. Call him and he'll organise something.'

We look at each another, embarrassed by the silence that has suddenly fallen between us. How does one say goodbye after such a lovely evening? I feel like a stranger and a friend at the same time. This man is attractive, physically attractive, but he also seems deeply spiritual to me. Finally I break the ice and wish him goodnight. We embrace. A simple kiss on the mouth. But it lasts a second longer than an ordinary kiss. Just a second.

The following Monday I call Jay's secretary. Jay isn't in, so I leave a message, together with my pager number. On Tuesday, and the days after, it's the same story. We eventually abandon the idea of an interview with him and do some research, planning to find another spokesperson for the unions. But on Sunday, while we're in the middle of a shoot, my pager rings.

'Goodness! It's Jay Naidoo! Perhaps he's agreed to give us an interview.'

'Call him immediately,' Marie-Hélène suggests.

On the other end of the line Jay says nothing about the interview. Instead, he invites me to dinner at his place. I don't hide my surprise very well.

'Dinner? What kind of dinner?'

'A small simple meal at home. I'll be doing the cooking. What do you say?'

I have to accept. As an orator, this man is unrivalled. I have to have him in my documentary. Marie-Hélène repeats her warning: 'Be careful, he's a womaniser!'

Jay has given me vague directions to his house. But the taxi-driver gets lost, saying he hardly ever comes into this part of town. I'm afraid. Anything that moves is a target. In this run-down suburb, the houses are dreary, dilapidated, crammed together. The unlit streets are deserted. Nothing I have read about this country prepares me for the total silence, the dull calm that weighs on the city as night falls. I have read articles about the violence, the blood, the battles between different factions, the public benches reserved for whites, and the childhood diseases that black children die of. But nothing about the petrifying silence of Johannesburg when darkness descends on the city. Where does the war hide at night?

After numerous detours we reach our destination. Jay Naidoo lives in a house hidden behind a high, faded wall – only the red tiles of the roof are visible. Everything is locked, the entrance gate, the two doors to the internal courtyard and the front door to the house. I hear the keys turning in the locks, one by one. Jay comes to open the door to the courtyard for me. He welcomes me without much enthusiasm. I'm the annoying journalist come to disturb his private life. Is this odd behaviour shyness? He introduces me to Colette, the owner of the house in which he rents a room. She's about to leave for dinner with friends. Has Jay asked her if he can have the house to himself this evening? I think of Marie-Hélène's warning. I haven't had good luck with men. Bosses, colleagues, friends, even a doctor has assaulted me. But, curiously, I feel quite safe with this Jay Naidoo.

He has prepared everything himself. Chicken curry, dhal and rice, dishes that are very familiar to me, that I cook myself, ever since my visit to India four years ago. Jay dishes up for himself and invites me to do the same, then goes and sits in front of the TV! Annoyed, I'm about to make a rather cutting remark when he invites me to come and sit with him on the couch, explaining that the news hour is sacred to him. We watch reports of new atrocities, new deaths. Every evening there is a rundown of political assassinations, of victims of the confrontations between rival groups or with the police. This is the everyday reality …

After the broadcast, Jay is agitated. Distressed. He talks with passion. He asks questions and, without waiting for a reply, declares that what's lacking in this country, on this continent, on this planet, is respect for the dignity of every living being. I listen to him. I want this passion in my documentary. Then suddenly, out of the blue, he asks me to follow him to his room. Marie-Hélène … He explains that his hi-fi is there and that he feels like listening to some good music.

The room is small, littered with hundreds of books and CDs. He puts on Edith Piaf. So this was how he intends to seduce a 'French lady'! The conversation starts to wander. We're sitting on the floor. Then, with a calculated but very gentle gesture, he takes my face in his hands and kisses me. Nothing else exists.

Marie-Hélène was right …

❖   ❖   ❖

Six o'clock in the morning. I must leave! I feel guilty. My team, the shoot … Just imagine what would happen if they found out that I had slept with someone that we wanted to interview? Jay tells me not to panic, that he'll drop me off at the hotel. He's so calm. He laughs. Getting out of the car, I beg him to give me an appointment for our shoot. There is no way I can return from this 'business' dinner without the promise of an interview! He opens his diary, turns the blackened pages and finds a thirty-minute gap.

At half past six I shower quickly in my hotel room. I've only slept a few hours, but I feel wonderful! We're going to meet again this evening.

After a heavy day of filming, I have dinner with my colleagues. Then we each retire to our rooms, which are all next to each other. I wait a few minutes for everyone to disappear and then quietly leave, taking care to hang the 'Do not disturb' sign on my door handle.

I take a taxi to meet Jay. He's waiting for me. We go to the cinema in a rich area of town – Rosebank. I've spent the day in the black townships on the outskirts of Johannesburg, filming reports on another reality of this country. The contrast is shocking. Here, the cinema seats are ultra comfortable, the toilets are spotlessly clean. The shopping centre in which the cinema is situated is luxurious. Silver and gold glitters in the shop windows and around women's necks. Jay is the only black person in the movie house. This becomes the subject of our conversation. Despite his Indian ancestry, Jay considers himself black. He explains that all activists are considered 'black', even though the law of racial classification, the Population Registration Act, identifies them as blacks, coloureds or Indians.

After the movie, we go back to his place where, for another night, I let myself enjoy only the present moment. It seems like the first time in my life that I can surrender myself in this way, especially with a man I hardly know!

We get up at six in the morning. Jay once again drops me behind the hotel. I am back in my room at seven this time. I remove the 'Do not disturb' sign and dive into the shower. Half an hour later I go down to breakfast.

'Where have you been?' demands Patricio.

'What do you mean, where have I been? I've been here!'

'I knocked on your door at six-thirty, but you weren't there,' he says in a dry, accusatory tone, which he's in the habit of using with me.

'Oh! I couldn't sleep this morning. I went for a walk around the centre of town,' I reply, feeling my face redden.

'We had to go and film at the station!'

'But you never told me that!'

'No, I only decided this morning, and you were nowhere to be found.'

'I'm sorry.'

I keep quiet, so that I don't have to tell any more lies. I'm ashamed of what I've done. But at the same time I'm happy.

The following morning we go to the COSATU headquarters, in the city centre, for the interview with Jay. We're told to wait in a tiny room, where we start putting up our equipment. Sipho, the big boss's secretary, comes to find me: 'Comrade Naidoo would like to see you.'

Jay's office is small, modest and tidy. There's only one file open on his desk, which he closes as soon as I enter. I feel uneasy. I sit on the chair in front of his simple wooden desk. I feel paralysed by the ambiguity of the situation. He smiles, even laughs. He touches my foot under the table as we speak. We plan the interview and then go and join the team.

During the interview I forget the nights we've spent together and settle into my role as a journalist. Nothing exists except my work. It's the same for him. He's the trade unionist and passionate activist I listened to in Orlando Stadium in Soweto on 27 October 1990. Jay is a born speaker. I could listen to him for hours, but I have to end the interview. He gets up as soon as it's over and greets the whole team. The handshake he gives me is very professional. No one would see anything in it. I'm relieved that the job is done! Tonight we will resume our clandestine love affair.

At the end of the day the members of the team go out to dinner together, but I pretend to be tired and say I'm going to bed. After they leave, I meet Jay in an Indian restaurant in Yeoville, one of the few areas in Johannesburg that stays alive late into the night. Drugs and sex are always on sale here. But the small Asian restaurant we enter soon makes us forget the commotion outside. It's a warm, modest room. The small tables are covered with simple floral designs, a rose and a candle on each table. The smell of incense completes the romantic setting. Jay has chosen well. And as if that's not enough, the Edith Piaf song he played the other evening to seduce me echoes around the restaurant. Surprised, I accuse Jay of plotting with the proprietor, whom he knows vaguely. But he swears that he has nothing to do with this coincidence!

Jay speaks very softly. I have to listen hard to hear him. As we eat, we talk about our lives. He has difficulty coming up with memories that aren't political.

'When I was four years old,' he tells me, 'the government forced my family to move because we didn't belong to the right racial group. The whites wanted to give the suburb we lived in to coloureds. I will never forget it. It was the 'bulldozer' policy: whole districts were razed to clear the area. The whites just took the areas they liked.'

I ask him about Gandhi, who lived in South Africa for twenty-one years before returning to India, which he went on to liberate. But Jay doesn't identify with the Indian leader at all. For him, calling oneself an Indian means confirming the racial segregation imposed by apartheid laws. It means accepting the racist regime. The anti-apartheid activists are fighting for a country without differences, where being South African – whatever the colour of your skin – means the same thing for everyone.

'I am not Indian. I am South African. A black South African!'

The tone in which he affirms his identity leaves no room for contradiction.

'But you are so Indian in your ways!'

'What do you mean, I am so *Indian*?'

'The way you eat, think and act – these are all permeated by India.'

On that day, 7 November 1990, I initiated Jay into his Indian ancestry. Jay was part of a third generation of Indians born in South Africa. But it took him years to accept that he could be both South African and Indian. I did not insist too much. Rather, I tried to listen, to comprehend what it meant to be a black South African and to have been pursued by the police for years. Every person who actively resisted apartheid was a target for the government and Jay, as a trade union leader, had been one of the most important targets. He told me how for two years he had changed his place of residence constantly, to avoid prison. Two years spent running, day and night; to be able to continue working, fighting; disguised as a lawyer, an accountant or a doctor – in a jacket and tie, shaving off his moustache and beard, not to look like a fiery activist and trade unionist.

I listen to him carefully. I try to understand what it means to give up one's life for the cause. Finally I ask him where he finds the time for a personal life, a love life.

'I can't have any relationships,' he replies. 'My work takes up ninety-five per cent of my time. And the five per cent that remains is for sleeping.'

That night I, too, don't sleep much. When I get back to the hotel, I remove the small 'Do not disturb' sign almost mechanically. I am exhausted. I am starting to feel the effects of my double life. It will be over in a few days.

The next day we're filming in Soweto, in a hostel for black mineworkers. Hundreds of men – poor, hopeless, full of rage, drunk – are crammed into frightful cement constructions. The stench reaches right into the kitchens. It appears that white women are a rare sight, rarely daring to enter the 'territory' of a hostel.

In the struggle against the government, these male enclaves have become political fiefdoms, controlled by different parties – ANC, Inkatha – and their armed factions. Each hostel forms a fortress in the low-level civil war being waged by the various factions for control of the townships.

In the hostel that we're in, Inkatha is in control. I conduct a short interview with the local leader, who is drunk and aggressive. Then, walking along the building, I come across a man sharpening an axe. One of many weapons. Rather naively, I make a remark about the violence, pronouncing the three letters that are taboo here: ANC. The man leaps off his stool, grabs me around the neck and holds the still warm blade of his axe to it, saying, 'No one utters that word here!' I freeze. He sits down again and doesn't say another word.

Fifteen minutes later I receive a message on my pager: confirmation for an interview with Nelson Mandela! I can't believe it. After months of effort, the head of the ANC has finally agreed to receive us. I prefer not to think about what could happen to me if the man with the axe reads this message …

On the last morning of our shoot we pack our cases before leaving for Soweto, because the interview with Nelson Mandela will take place just two hours before our departure for the airport. The Mandela couple's home is a contrast to those around it in this part of Soweto.

The house is spacious, with numerous security systems, ranging from barbed wire and electric fencing to a team of armed guards. Nelson Mandela comes out onto the terrace of the courtyard where we are waiting for him. He has a frank smile and gives a warm and energetic handshake. He greets all the members of the team in the same way, making no distinction between the producer – the head of the team – and the soundman. He takes time to ask about our general well-being and our country and then invites us to sit down under an umbrella. I begin the interview by saying to him, 'You have spent the equivalent of my lifetime in prison.' He starts. But it's true: I'm twenty-eight years old and he has just spent twenty-seven years behind bars …

No doubt journalists have been asking him the same questions for months: 'How is the country doing? What are the main challenges now? Why the increase in violence? When will we see the great day of "One person, one vote"?' Nonetheless, Nelson Mandela plays the game with grace. He is a skilled speaker and his lucidity is a whip to one's conscience. His calm takes one by surprise, because he is so intense. Mandela is a sedate man. He harbours no desire for vengeance. He has had to negotiate with the very same people who kept him in prison for all those years. During his twenty-seven years of imprisonment he familiarised himself with the culture and history of the Afrikaners, devouring large numbers of books on these subjects. He learnt their language and attempted to understand what made the heart of this people beat. It takes a certain greatness of spirit to understand and respect one's oppressor.

We're all spellbound by his words, simply by his presence. He gives off an energy, inexplicable but almost tangible. For the whole team this meeting remains a precious moment spent in the company of one of the living legends of the twentieth century.

I leave South Africa feeling dazzled by its people, by its different cultures, by the magic of the freedom songs. And I take with me the memory of a time of great happiness: the hours spent on the sly with Jay. I would never see him again. At least, that's what I told myself every minute that I spent together with him. I had consciously and voluntarily made a stone of my heart during our nights of love. This morning I was ready for the goodbyes. Happy, even. Because the memory of these precious moments, of my sweet secret, would make me smile my whole life long.

At six in the morning, in the street behind my hotel, Jay dropped me off for the last time. He squeezed my hands in his and said, quite simply: 'It was beautiful. It was good. Thank you.' And I replied, 'I wish you a beautiful life!' Closing the car door, I never expected to see him again.

2

To go or to stay?

It's my birthday, 29 November 1990, already dark in Montreal when I get home from work. Winter is around the corner and I'm thinking about getting out my warm clothes and making the windows draught-proof. To think that a few weeks ago I was in the middle of a South African spring.

I relive my trip to South Africa on a daily basis, because every day I'm editing the material we gathered there. Watching the scenes we shot with Jay, my heart skips a beat. His speech in front of the crowd at Orlando Stadium sends shivers down my spine every time I watch it.

When I enter my apartment on des Écores Street, in the suburb of Rosemont, I find a message from Jay on the answering machine. He wishes me a happy twenty-ninth birthday. He says he really enjoyed the time we spent together and wishes me luck with my projects.

I call him back the next morning. We talk for a long time. And then a crazy idea pops into my head. I blurt it out without thinking of the consequences:

'What are you doing for the Christmas holidays?'

'I don't know yet. What about you?'

'I'm going to visit my mother in the Québecois Arctic. She teaches Inuit children there. Would you like to come?'

'Where?'

'To Umiujaq, at the North Pole! Would you like to come?'

We laugh.

He will come.

On New Year's Eve we meet again in Umiujaq. The Inuit village, on the coast of Hudson Bay, has a population of about two hundred and fifty. The sea is frozen, the waves magically suspended in mid-air. The little cluster of houses buzzes with the sound of snowmobiles whizzing by. They drive all over the place because there are no roads.

At midnight we let off rifle shots in the snow to mark the start of the year 1991. Jay jumps. The sound is familiar to him, but doesn't generally form part of festivities …

We go fishing on the ice, make excursions on snowmobiles and dog sleds, we go skiing and tobogganing on snow dunes. We have a whale of a time together. Everything is pure, white, beautiful.

Jay and I fall in love in the snow, at fifty degrees below zero …

In the warmth of my mother's apartment, Jay asks me, 'Why don't you come and live with me in South Africa?'

'You must be crazy! I have joint custody of my son. It's impossible!'

'Of course.'

There we were, caught up in an impossible love affair. Jay couldn't leave South Africa, because he was an important part of the anti-apartheid machinery. He had a mission to accomplish, although I didn't yet understand all the implications. Personally, I felt I couldn't take the risk of leaving everything for a man, for love …

But I torture myself. What if this is my chance to realise my dream of becoming a foreign correspondent? For a long time I've wanted to live this adventure, to practise my profession and discover an entire country, to expose myself to another culture, to a different reality. As a child, I already knew that I wanted to travel and accomplish a mission, without knowing exactly how to manifest this aspiration. After obtaining my degree in journalism, I went off to Asia for a year, with rucksack on back and mike in hand. In the course of my travels I found myself in Beijing, China, asking for a bed from Jean-François Lépine, Radio–Canada's foreign correspondent at the time. He really impressed me – his journalistic discipline and dynamism in all situations. He talked about the highs of working as a foreign correspondent. Everything fell into place for me: this is what I wanted to do … become a foreign correspondent. And here was an opportunity to realise a precious dream. South Africa had seduced me. I could easily see myself living there, for a year or two.

But no, it was impossible. Léandre …

❖ ❖ ❖

Valentine's Day 1991. The relations between trade unions in South Africa and America – the AFL-CIO (American Federation of Labour – Congress of Industrial Organisations) – have altered course after years of discord. Jay Naidoo has in fact spent some time in Miami with a mandate to build relations with the American federation. What the leaders of the AFL-CIO don't know is that Jay Naidoo has other ideas besides international trade union cooperation when he accepts the trip to the United States. 'To think that international trade union relations changed because I wanted to see you!' he would tell me one day.

We meet in New York. Our love is still strong, even though I sometimes wish it would fade … So that I didn't have to make impossible decisions …

'I have a surprise for you.'

'What?' I ask, intrigued.

'We have to go there on foot. Come.'

We walk for a long time in Central Park, in the heart of Manhattan. It's cold. Our ears are freezing and I want to know what's in the package Jay is carrying.

'Wait. The moment isn't right. Everything has to be perfect,' he says.

Finally, we arrive at Strawberry Fields Park and sit under a tree beneath John Lennon's old apartment.

Jay takes out a book, a collection of poems by Pablo Neruda, the romantic Chilean poet – as passionate and gentle as the man who starts reading to me. He reads two, three, four poems, some passionately, some gently, always with expressive hand movements. I am seduced, but perplexed.

Then, from a small crumpled paper bag, he takes a ring of dubious quality.

'Lucie, will you marry me?'

My mouth falls open. All I can say is, 'I'll think about it.'

Then it's Jay's turn to be stunned. He hasn't expected this reaction.

'You are the only woman I have asked to marry me. You are the only woman whose parents I have met.'

I have no doubts about his love. But I have to have a life of my own. I can't imagine abandoning everything in order to follow a man.

'Jay, I won't go to your country unless I can work there. I'll have to find out a few things from here first.'

❖ ❖ ❖

I offer my services as a foreign correspondent. Everywhere the answer is more or less the same, 'With Nelson Mandela's release there is certainly a need for news material from South Africa, but …'

I meet Gilles Le Bigot, in charge of choosing foreign correspondents for Radio–Canada. He already has a French correspondent in South Africa – Ariane Bonzon. But she's thinking of leaving Johannesburg 'soon'. When she leaves, he'll give me a chance …

The more crucial question concerns Léandre. How can I carry out this plan *with* my son? The solution would be simple if I could take him with me. But his father would no doubt oppose this. Would joint custody be possible between two continents? First I have to discuss it with Léandre. I need to see how he reacts.

'What would you say about one hundred and eighty beddy-byes with Papa, then one hundred and eighty beddy-byes with Mama, instead of seven beddy-byes with him and seven beddy-byes with me, like we're doing now?'

'One hundred and eighty, that's a lot, isn't it?'

Silence. His big brown eyes question mine. He's worried.

'Mama, how much is that, one hundred and eighty beddy-byes?'

I count out loud to a hundred and eighty. Léandre sits and stares. From that moment, he comes to sleep with me at night, something he has never done before. I feel awful. Can I live without my son for six months?

My friends tell me to go for it. My mother too. My father asks me to think carefully …

I have to make a decision. To go or to stay? To live or to forget my dream? To forget Jay?

After four months of insomnia I sit up in bed one night and say, 'If I don't do it now, I'll never do it! And anyway, I can always come back!'

I organise a huge garage sale. My mother and friends support me in every way, but keep checking how I feel. They're worried. 'Are you really sure?' Yes, yes.

But on the first of July 1991, standing alone in the middle of my empty apartment, I'm not so sure. Léandre … For months now we've been talking about my departure. 'One hundred and eighty beddy-byes, Mama, that's a lot, isn't it?' Too late to go back …

Neither one of us really knows what kind of adventure I'm dragging us into.

Léandre, my love, Léandre. When your eyes fixed on mine, surprised, afraid, I melted. I cried, for days and nights. The choice I made was the most difficult one of my life.

3

State of shock

My dictionaries and my clothes are going round the carousel at Jan Smuts Airport in Johannesburg. My knees are trembling. Like a robot, I take my bags and put them on a trolley. I feel nothing. My brain is muddled, my body numb. I've just left Léandre. I am in a state of shock.

I get in the red lane – yes, I have something to declare! It's too heavy to carry and it makes me feel ill. But the customs officer tells me I don't have to declare my troubles, it's quite legal to bring them in with me.

I also arrive with a 'disability'. I'm not deaf, dumb, one-armed or paraplegic. I'm suffering from chronic shame. When I look at myself in the mirror, I feel uncomfortable. I don't feel up to anything. Low self-esteem affects many people, especially women …

I have always pretended to be strong, up to anything. And I am soon to learn that in South Africa pretending to be strong can sometimes save your life. But at night, alone in my bed, I become the other person, the one who doubts. She and I inhabit the same body: one of us smiles and jokes, the other wants to hide under the carpet. And then one of the worst feelings adds itself to the handicap: that of being a bad mother. Because what kind of mother would leave her child on the other side of the world to follow a dream?

Jay is waiting for me at the airport. He has no idea how I feel, what it means to leave one's child behind. He welcomes me with Nisha, his sister, and Sagaren, his brother-in-law. They are all smiles. They knew nothing of the storm brewing inside me …

4

Guilty

A week after my arrival, I find myself sitting in the public gallery of a law court. There are four black defendants and one white judge. Jay is sitting in the dock …

'Everything will be okay,' he assured me.

'But is it possible that you could be sent to prison?'

'Yes, it's possible.'

He replied casually, as though there were no harm in spending several years in prison. I was soon to learn that in South Africa people proudly include their years in prison on their curriculum vitae. 'Three years in prison? Is that all? I spent twelve years there!' I had already heard at a function. Or, 'See that chap over there, he has spent fifteen years in prison!' said as though he were someone important. And then people seem to sympathise with those who have never been to prison, 'No prison time? Oh, that's a pity, a bit of a gap in your CV!'

This pride comes from the days of the 1952 Defiance Campaign, which baptised a new generation of ANC leaders – Nelson Mandela, Walter Sisulu, Oliver Tambo, James Moroka and several others. Four years earlier, in 1948, the Afrikaner National Party of Daniel Malan had taken power and introduced a series of reforms to help create a white paradise at the southern tip of Africa. After his election, Prime Minister Malan declared, 'Today, South Africa belongs to us once more.' Afrikaner nationalism had just triumphed, forty-six years after its defeat in the war between the English and the Boers. A series of laws aimed at maintaining and reinforcing racial segregation was adopted and formed the basis of the policy that became known as apartheid.

One of the first laws passed by Malan's government was the Group Areas Act, a pillar of apartheid, which allocated specific geographical residential areas to different racial groups. The appropriation of land was crucial to apartheid. In this way, through various laws governing land, the Nationalist government made eighty-seven per cent of South Africa's land available to eleven per cent of the population – the whites. The remaining thirteen per cent was divided into ten bantustans for the ten so-called Bantu groups – the blacks. The geographical layout of some of these bantustans, like that of KwaZulu, the area reserved for the Zulus, resembled a leopard skin, allocating the blacks scattered pockets of land, like so many islands in an archipelago. In general, they were among the least fertile regions in the country.

It was in order to escape the misery of the bantustans that black men came to the cities to find work, often in the gold or diamond mines. This is how the townships grew up around the white towns. The men who lived there were only allowed into the white towns at certain times of the day and during certain periods of the year, and then they had to have their passes with them.

In 1952 the ANC, influenced by Gandhi, advocated passive resistance against the most iniquitous laws, starting with the 'pass laws', which required blacks to carry a permit or 'pass' in order to move between their places of residence and their places of work. To many, these were the most humiliating of all the laws, because the police would stop them in the street to check that they were permitted to move around – in their own country!

Those participating in the Defiance Campaign refused to carry their passes, defied other laws forbidding membership of the Communist Party, organised large peaceful demonstrations, did not keep the curfew, turned their noses up at the rules regulating public places by going to spots reserved for whites, and so on. 'Do not resist. Allow yourself to be arrested.' This was their slogan. Over eight thousand people were arrested. The success of this mobilising campaign confirmed the leadership of Nelson Mandela, who, before and during the operation, travelled all over the country, to set up and support the ANC.

Mandela writes in his autobiography, *Long Walk to Freedom*, 'From the Defiance Campaign onward, going to prison became a badge of honour among Africans'.

But in my own case this type of pride was difficult to accept. And when Jay calmly announced to me that he might have to go to prison – 'Not for long, only two or three years' – I panicked. Two or three years was an eternity. Why beg me to come to this country if he'd be sitting in a prison cell?

I know, however, that, for Jay Naidoo, saving his country is a full-time job. It's his sole mission. When his eyes are open, he works. When his eyes are closed, he dreams of a country to be born.

In his capacity as general secretary of COSATU, Jay is one of the regime's special targets. For years, COSATU had spearheaded anti-apartheid activities in the country. The reason for this is that although the ANC, the Communist Party and many other anti-apartheid organisations were banned between 1960 and 1990, the trade unions had managed to win the right to exist.

In 1979, in order to appease the international community, President P W Botha legalised them. From that date, the trade unions became a pillar of the anti-apartheid movement. In 1985, hundreds of thousands of workers from different trade unions were regrouped to form COSATU, electing as their head a South African of Indian origin, Jay Naidoo. It was he who led the organisation when, sporadically, it plunged the country into general strikes, leading to significant economic losses for the country, but moving the black majority slowly towards liberation.

Jay's court appearance is therefore an event, and I have to push my way through an excited crowd to get a seat in the courtroom. Hundreds of people crowd outside, chanting pro-COSATU and anti-apartheid slogans. Inside, the courtroom is about to burst and the police officers are very nervous. But in the dock, Jay displays an air of perfect calm: legs crossed, reading a newspaper. He doesn't lift his eyes once during the whole session.

The 'crime' of which he is accused goes back to 1990. He and his team had noticed a man equipped with a walkie-talkie outside the COSATU offices. Things looked suspicious. Several of their colleagues had been assassinated, their head office had been bombed more than once and there were fears that such events might be repeated. There were also fears of police intervention against COSATU (suspicions that proved to be well-founded). They therefore went out to ask the intruder what he was doing. He refused to answer, but Jay suspected him of being a member of the death squads. After making a citizen's arrest, Jay and his colleagues found a photograph of one of Jay's colleagues in one of the suspect's pockets (Geraldine Fraser-Moleketi, who became the Minister of Welfare and Population Development under Nelson Mandela). They led the man into the building and Jay called the police, informing them that they were detaining someone they believed was a member of the death squads.

Two hours later, Jay gave a press conference to expose the facts. When he went to fetch the suspect to display him to the media representatives, he was caught unawares. The COSATU employees who had been guarding the man had undressed him completely! Then they had slapped him around a bit. Jay exploded with rage. 'What the devil are you doing with this man? Put his clothes back on!' He then led the man in front of the journalists so that he could answer their questions. The man categorically denied being a member of the security forces and refused to answer any questions. (It was later confirmed that he was in fact a police officer on a 'mission'.)

In the meantime, fifty policemen armed with automatic rifles had surrounded the COSATU offices. After the press conference, Jay and three colleagues (among them Sydney Mufamadi, who became Minister of Safety and Security under Nelson Mandela) were arrested and taken to the police station. To detain a police officer was already a grave offence. To confine him illegally, take all his clothes off and slap him around was disastrous!

The four accused were promised freedom in exchange for the names of those who had beaten up the policeman. They all refused to speak. In this way Jay and his comrades came to be accused of kidnapping and assault and battery.

At his trial, then, Jay read his newspaper, which seemed like an arrogant way of saying to the judge, 'I don't give a damn about your justice.' But essentially it was because he did not know where to look. At the judge? At me? At the defence attorney? At the state prosecutor? That day he read every single line of the newspaper, even the sports section. And when Jay reads the sports section of the paper, something is wrong.

'Jay Naidoo, accused number one, guilty of kidnapping and of assault and battery. Accused number two, guilty. Accused number three, guilty,' the sentence echoes. It was in exactly this tone, in this way, that so many years of the life of Nelson Mandela and his colleagues were stolen. 'Accused number four, guilty,' the judge says once more. (On appeal, the charge of assault and battery against Jay was withdrawn, and in the year 2000 his criminal record was erased by the Truth and Reconciliation Commission, which granted him amnesty.)

As the magistrate unfolds the sheet of paper giving the sentence, I tremble. The entire courtroom, except Jay, have their eyes riveted on the judge. At last, the sentence is delivered, 'Three years in prison, suspended.' Jay doesn't move a muscle. I have no idea what this means, I only catch the words 'three years'. I am in shock.

Jay comes out laughing. Across the cheering crowd he shouts to me, 'Don't worry. We can go home now. Everything has worked out fine.'

'What do you mean everything has worked out fine?'

'I am free. I must simply not commit a crime for three years.'

Easy to say, in a country where equality and justice are illegal.

5

Who is going to buy the 'special shampoo'?

I collapse on Jay's bed and cry. I cry for hours, days, even weeks. I want to see Léandre, immediately. I regret my decision. After months of reasoned planning, I'm discovering the reality of my emotions. As far as work is concerned, nothing is working out. I'll have to wait another five months before the Radio–Canada correspondent leaves the country, before I can hope to take her place. I began negotiations with a production house, but these have fallen through for financial reasons.

Jay's landlady, Colette Tilley, lives in Judith's Paarl, a stone's throw from Bezuidenhout Valley – or Bez Valley as people call it – and from Kensington; both officially white suburbs, but in fact fairly mixed. These three suburbs form a large valley. Bez Valley occupies one side of the mountain and Kensington the other. Judith's Paarl is situated at the bottom. Large trees and a few palms barely manage to cheer things up. The houses press up against one another and the nearer you get to the centre, the smaller and more tumbled-down they become. In the noisy streets, there are large numbers of children. Here, the people are poor.

But even among underprivileged whites there are black domestic workers. They live behind the houses of whites, in dismal hovels, hasty cement constructions erected in the backyards. The occupants cram in, sometimes fifteen to twenty in one room a few metres square, with no window. These shacks are the unofficial homes of blacks. Most domestic workers are women. Officially, they should live in the bantustans assigned to them, but because they can't find work there, they move to the towns to work for white families. Members of their own family, friends, cousins and acquaintances from their village often live with them. In the miserable rooms where these people live, the beds rest on bricks. This is a common custom, which serves as protection against the *tokolosh*, small spirits described in some regions as mischievous little imps and in others as creatures that possess an eye in the middle of their forehead or on their chin. It is to prevent these wicked creatures from casting a bad spell on the unsuspecting sleeper that beds are raised.

In order to clear my head, I adopt a routine. I walk six or seven kilometres a day, crossing the valley to buy envelopes, stamps and little surprises for my son. Each day I make my journey with only one thought in my head: the letter or package that I will send to Léandre. I look for little things that will amuse him: African stickers, coloured beans that turn into animal-shaped sponges when you soak them in water, books and games. Every day I go for a walk to feel closer to my son. His absence is torture; it's a pain between my heart and stomach, quite unbearable. Only walking relieves it for a few moments.

The domestic workers who sit on the red earth on the side of the road while taking their break look at me inquisitively. Some laugh. Is it so odd to see a white person walking alone in the street? I must admit, on all my walks, I never saw any other white woman doing the same thing. The domestic workers examine me from head to toe. I try, as well as I can, to smile, but I am too unsettled by all the changes in my life, and too depressed.

I arrived during the South African winter, but I had felt less cold in the snowy Canadian winter! It does not snow in Johannesburg, but you freeze. At night, the mercury often drops below zero. The only time that I saw snow fall here, everyone ran out into the streets to admire the flakes. It was in the middle of the day, in July. Homeless people sheltering under cardboard or corrugated iron often die of exposure.

Johannesburg is located at one thousand and six hundred metres above sea level. On a winter's day you need to stay in the sun. In the shade you freeze. In fact, I have never felt this cold before. People constantly say, 'You're a Canadian, what are you complaining about? You come from a cold country!' And I retort, 'Yes, but in Canada we don't freeze *inside* our houses!'

The houses of whites are neither insulated nor heated, except by small electric heaters on wheels that you move from room to room.

The richer people have underfloor heating, but this is not the case at Colette's. Always shivering, I curse the openings that I find in nearly all the rooms, high up in the corners – small rectangular grids with holes for ventilation. It occurs to me that they're more useful to let geckos in – those small climbing lizards with suction cups on their feet. They are always welcome, because they eat the mosquitoes and other harmful insects.

Johannesburg is also a cold city because of its dry, dusty and concrete-filled environment. It is surrounded by hills of fine dust, the residue from the gold mines, that rise up around the skyscrapers of the city centre. There are no expanses of water, there is no sound of running water.

While I kill time, Jay works seven days a week, as he has for the past seventeen years. But faced with my despondency, he takes three days off – Friday, Saturday and Sunday! We head out for the Eastern Transvaal, towards a town called Machadodorp. Three hours by road from Johannesburg, passing through the Drakensberg, the magnificent chain of mountains that crosses the country in the east, from north to south.

We travel at one hundred and forty kilometres an hour along the best highways I have ever seen: two, three or four lanes wide, a flat, smooth roadway, with small yellow and red reflectors along the edges. But everything changes when we enter a bantustan: the road breaks up and you drive into potholes … After Machadodorp there are only about forty kilometres to go, but the state of the road means that we take a good hour to reach the farm that friends have lent us for the weekend.

The spot seems to come straight out of a fairytale. Surrounded by three small artificial lakes filled with trout, the farm lies in the heart of a pine forest, far away from any form of civilisation. The main house is perched on the side of the hill. Majestic and silent.

We are alone … almost. There is a family that looks after the cows and chickens and cleans the house. They live on the hill above the house, behind some trees, a few minutes by foot, without running water or electricity. The six or seven children each have their daily task, according to their sex. The girls carry buckets of water on their heads; the boys, less skilful but stronger, carry wood on their backs. The older ones help their parents look after the farm, the younger ones leave early in the morning for school. Their clothes take on the colour of the long road that they travel every morning and every evening.

The house has six bedrooms, a huge lounge with a magnificent foyer and a verandah with an unimpeded view. I drink in the silence like champagne, a delight after Johannesburg and after the daily news about violence. Are we really in the same country? I realise for the first time that in South Africa it is possible to skirt around the misery and the violence while you live in a parallel reality. Ninety-eight per cent of whites have never set foot in a black township!

We choose the best bedroom. A queen-sized bed, windows looking out over the mountain, an en-suite bathroom. The perfect spot for a honeymoon!

Jay and I set about getting to know one another, discovering one another. Like two adolescents. It's exciting. We don't know much about what the other likes or doesn't like. I, for instance, like to do the washing-up before going to bed. I like to start the morning with a clean kitchen. 'But you don't need to do the washing-up. Someone will come and do it in the morning,' says Jay. It doesn't matter. I like to do the dishes; it relaxes me.

We walk through the forest around the lakes. Then we stretch out on the lawn to have a snack. Suddenly, I felt a prickling in my pubic hair. I take a look. Horrors! Lice? I have never seen lice, but I'm certain that's what they are. I tell Jay, who panics and pulls down his trousers immediately: he also has them! They're moving around everywhere. I, who have sworn that nothing will make me get back onto the road to go shopping, change my mind in less than ten seconds.

On the bumpy road, we cross our fingers and hope that the local pharmacy will have the right insecticide shampoo. When we reach our destination, a lively discussion takes place in the car. Who's going to buy the 'special shampoo'?

'It's your country. You go.'

'You found them first. You go.'

'No, you must go.'

'I can't. Can you imagine what will happen if someone recognises me and decides to call the press? "Jay Naidoo has lice!" That would certainly sell newspapers!'

'But if you were on your own, you would go!'

It's a long debate, a prelude to numerous discussions that we would have over the years, in all sorts of situations. But that day, for the first time, I had a taste of the real consequences of being married to a public figure. You have to think of everything, down to the smallest detail. You have to pay attention all the time. Later, something just as awkward would happen in Cape Town. I was given a false one-hundred-rand note when I bought something on the street. Unknowingly, I passed it on to Jay, who used it to pay for some petrol. The police traced it to him through his registration number and the story made the headlines. Jay had to explain himself before the National Assembly.

So I'm the one who goes to buy the shampoo …

Back at the farm, Jay goes to look for the farmer who looks after the house, takes him to the bedroom, pulls back the sheets and tells him that they have to be changed because they are full of bugs. I don't know what language this man speaks, but he doesn't know a word of English. His body slightly bent, his hands cupped together as a sign of respect for the *Master*, he shakes his head to indicate that he doesn't understand. Jay addresses him in Zulu, but he maintains the same questioning air. He hasn't understood a word. Eventually, I put the sheets in the bath.

We don't sleep in that bedroom. I spend a long time examining the sheets on the other beds before I lie down on one of them. Jay is already sleeping …

We laughed like crazy later on. In spite of everything we'd had a wonderful weekend – the only intimate weekend that we would enjoy, without children, without work, for the next eleven years.

6

Madiba magic

I'm tired of the valley. I've been crossing it daily for almost a month, tears in my eyes, present and card for Léandre in my hand. I have to snap out of it. Get out. Do the groundwork for the radio reports that I will eventually do for Radio–Canada. But for this, I have to go beyond the valley – something not advisable on foot.

The public transport system in Johannesburg leaves a lot to be desired. There are few buses and their routes are limited. Only a couple of buses a day travel between Judith's Paarl and the city centre; the red double-decker buses remind me of London. In spring, in October and November, they brush against the magnificent flowering jacarandas, leaving a carpet of violet-blue petals on the road.

Black people use another, unofficial, transport system. Why invest in a system of public transport, the authorities no doubt said to themselves, when 'everybody' has a motor car, if not two or three? 'Everybody' of course refers to the whites. The blacks use kombis or mini vans, each more dented than the next. Up to twenty persons can cram into these rattletraps, sometimes more. Millions commute each day between the black township and the white town, some of whom then polish the cars of white people. It is hell driving on the wide roads because of the thousands of kombis that stop wherever it suits them or drive at top speed without ever indicating.

I'm afraid to drive. I've never driven on the left or changed gears with my left hand. And here you do everything on the left! You walk, go up and down stairs on the left. I spent the first few months bumping into people on the pavement!

I choose the double-decker buses and quickly get into the habit of climbing up to the top in order to see better. I get out in the centre and wander about everywhere to familiarise myself with the city. I use the opportunity to locate the offices of the political parties and various social organisations, production houses.

One day, coming home from the office, Jay informs me that we've been invited to a meal with the leader of the ANC, Nelson Mandela. 'Do you want to come?' What a question!

The meeting place is in a working-class suburb of Johannesburg, in the 'lower' part of town, where I notice large numbers of factories with broken windows. It's also the tailors' district. Here, in the gloom of the workshops, they create clothing full of colour and life. In fact Nelson Mandela's tailor also lives here, and it's in his house that we are dining. His name is Yusuf Surtee, and he is a prosperous Indian businessman. He has invited several well-known persons, among them Jay Naidoo and Omar Motani. Omar, also of Indian origin but of the Muslim faith, is a great friend of Jay's.

The 'Chief' hasn't arrived yet, Yusuf Surtee announces as we enter. He invites us to sit down in the small lounge. In the minuscule kitchen, his wife is busy putting the last touches to a special meal: she scatters coriander leaves on the dahl, a thick lentil soup, as well as on the mutton and vegetable curry; then mint leaves on the raita, a cucumber and yoghurt sauce that takes some of the heat out of the strong Indian spices in the savoury dishes.

Standing near the window, on the first floor, I notice two cars stopping in front of the building. It's Mandela.

As he enters he seems larger than life again. It's true that he's almost two metres tall, but it is something else. A special aura emanates from his person. Today, leaving behind my role as a journalist and all it implies of critical distance and the effort to remain objective, I give myself up voluntarily to his charm.

After hugging me, his giant hands (the hands of a boxer) grip mine. He tells me he remembers our first meeting well and asks for news of the *Nord-Sud* team. All eyes are on us. In fact, when Mandela speaks, everyone listens. Some are surprised to learn that I am not *only* Jay's partner, but that I have a profession, something that never ceases to amaze many South Africans …

During the process of negotiation after Mandela's release, an expression was born: *Madiba magic*. 'Madiba', a term of respect, is the name that Mandela's most intimate friends use to address him. In fact it's his clan name, which belongs to the Thembu people of the Xhosa nation. Chief Thembu ruled a people of the Xhosa nation in the eighteenth century. As for the word 'magic', it refers to Mandela's gift of rallying even the most extreme parties around a common goal. Mandela headed a negotiated revolution.

The Madiba magic is at work before my eyes. Mandela goes around the room greeting the guests; each religiously observes his movements. He and Jay embrace. Jay has only admiration for his leader, 'I will remain at his side however long he remains active in politics,' he says. Mandela is the living symbol of the struggle in which Jay has participated all his life. The admiration is reciprocal. Mandela sees in Jay a young, courageous, honest and reliable deputy. 'We need you' is a phrase that often rings in Jay's ears.

That day I realised that with Nelson Mandela I could never be both a journalist and a member of his friendly circle at the same time. Seeing him over the years in official and casual situations, I would never mix the two. I would never try to benefit from a social meeting to obtain information or even an appointment for an interview. I did the same as everyone else and directed my requests to his press service … even if it meant the answer might be no!

Among the guests, I am the only woman, the only person under thirty, the only white, the only non-South African. We talk about everything and nothing, but in South Africa even 'nothing' is political and touches every aspect of life. During meetings like this, with Mandela or with others, the stories that I hear teach me more than any university course could do. In a way, they constitute my initiation into South African life and the history of the country.

Nelson Mandela talks a lot and is a master storyteller – and he certainly has some stories! He tells them calmly, pausing at appropriate moments. He also listens well and asks pertinent questions. His head movements indicate what does and doesn't correspond with his values. He never has to lift a finger in order to have his say. The tone of his voice always brings silence.

I believe that Nelson Mandela's destiny was fully mapped out in advance. Like that of Gandhi. The latter once said, 'I was born in India, but I was made in South Africa.' The unique character of this country, of its history and its political regime awakened aspirations and a sense of human justice, and, through this, elevated men and women above their station in life. Because it is in the absence, the negation or the deprivation of the most fundamental rights that the greatest energies appear.

Nelson Mandela is set on bringing about justice and equality. I will never be able to see him merely as a politician. Mandela is rather a political *activist*. His lack of political experience could even put him in awkward situations. Like the day he declared it might be an idea to drop the voting age to fourteen. He was reprimanded by the ANC, who determined that, at this age, individuals are still children.

Before meeting Nelson Mandela, and a number of other South African activists, I had never understood that one could risk one's life, or even lay it down, for the common good. It was only in the company of these people that I would fully realise the extent of their engagement and devotion. The best activists have one thing in common: they are led by their hearts.

One of the best known and, in my view, the most memorable quotations by Nelson Mandela remains this extract from his defence speech at the time of his trial, at the end of which, in 1964, he was condemned to life imprisonment with hard labour, when he was already serving a five-year prison sentence from 1962. He was to repeat these phrases with the same fervour in the speech he gave on the day of his release, 11 February 1990:

> *'I have fought against white domination and I have fought against black domination. I have cherished the ideal of a democratic and free society in which all persons live together in harmony and with equal opportunities. It is an ideal which I hope to live for and to achieve. But if needs be, it is an ideal for which I am prepared to die.'*

I asked Jay if he was prepared to die for the cause. Without hesitation, he replied, 'Absolutely. But I hope to live!' His response sent shivers down my spine. The liberation of a country is a very serious business.

7

Madness

I have a knife planted in the middle of my heart. I think about Léandre every day, every hour, every minute. It's making me ill.

Colette tries to console me. She quickly becomes a dear friend. I like women who get things done, who are energetic and determined. Colette is all these things. With her white skin, she has chanted anti-apartheid slogans with the black masses. She accepted work as Jay's secretary in an office that could have exploded at any time – two bombs had already gone off there ... She is no longer his secretary, but she and Jay remain friends.

Colette has never been idle. When she fell pregnant, in her mid-thirties, her boyfriend left her. So she raised her son Duncan on her own. She is always ready to help others. She looks after Spongi, the daughter of her former domestic worker, raising her like her own child, learning her language, Xhosa, which she now speaks fluently. Her house is open to all who need it. Her kitchen, for example, is a real community hotspot. Esther (her present domestic worker), Esther's family and friends all come to prepare their food in her house, because there is no kitchen in the room behind the house.

Colette is always broke. The little she has, she offers to others. Her home is modestly furnished with tired couches, worn tables and creaky beds. But the atmosphere is always good.

Colette senses my distress. I'm really beginning to regret my decision to pack my bags and turn the page on my 'former life'. Not a single day passes without tears. Jay is upset and doesn't know what to do.

One evening, at the beginning of September 1991, I crack. My sobs shake me from head to toe. I can't stop, my life flows by in a flood of tears. Jay and Colette feel powerless. They stroke my back to comfort me, but it does no good. I've never cried this much in my whole life. After five hours of sobbing, I still can't get out of the abyss. I'm finished. I want to die or see Léandre. Immediately. Jay is worried. He feels responsible for my condition. With a drawn face he says, very quietly, very gently, 'Lucie, go back to Quebec. This isn't working. It won't work. We can write to one another. We can see one another. But it's obvious that you can't stay.' Then, after a few seconds, he adds, in a strangled voice, 'I love you so much.'

This time I collapse. I cry even more, if that's possible. My whole body wants to dissolve into tears. Go back? See Léandre? Yes! That's what I want! But it also means admitting defeat. And I love Jay. My gut tells me he's the one, my great love. Léandre or Jay? This choice is my lot from now on. The two loves of my life. I cry. I howl. I want to die. It hurts too much.

For the first time I feel as though I might really be going crazy. I satisfy all the criteria in my dictionary: *Lack of judgement, common sense and reason.* I have left Léandre, my son, my own flesh and blood, on the other side of the world … *a violent, irrational passion that drives one mad* … Jay, I love you to the point of madness. Was it youthful folly to bury the only life I know, mine, the one that truly kept me alive? *A folly: a foolish or extravagant idea, utterance, action.* One of her crazy ideas. Yes, it's another crazy idea of mine. I can hear my father's voice, 'Lucie, can't you lead an *ordinary* life for a while?' I will try, Papa! I promise! *To commit a folly: an impulsive act, escapade, prank* … yes, fate must be playing a prank on me. I'm insane … there is no other way to describe it.

I've just been catapulted against a wall of reality: I have to make a choice between the two loves of my life. My son wins, obviously. I pack my bags. Jay encourages me. He can't bear to see me this way any longer. I fall asleep, my two suitcases filled with my dictionaries and clothes under the bed.

The next morning my eyes are red and puffy. If only I could do a story. Just one, to salvage something, to make this defeat less crushing. I can't go back without a story. Lady Luck smiles: the Radio–Canada correspondent is on holiday and a major event is about to take place. I am the replacement!

On 14 September 1991, I find myself sitting in the same room as the President of South Africa, Frederik de Klerk, the leader of the ANC, Nelson Mandela, and the head of Inkatha, Mangosuthu Buthelezi – the heads of the three most important political parties in the country. Something to shake me up a bit ...

8

Peace accord

The political violence has spread like wildfire since the unbanning of the anti-apartheid organisations in February 1990. It takes its toll in victims every day. The war between the ANC and Inkatha has spilled over from KwaZulu and spread through the townships in the Johannesburg metropolitan area.

Furthermore, Inkathagate – the scandal that erupted only two months ago, revealing collusion between the security forces and Inkatha (the government had financed 'anti-ANC programmes' undertaken by the Zulu party) – has only intensified the violence. The birth of a new country is not possible in this climate.

The leaders of the three most important political parties have gathered to sign the National Peace Accord. This agreement, which will be ratified by twenty-four political parties, binds them to abide by a code of conduct prohibiting provocation and intimidation in the townships and regulating the behaviour of members of the security forces.

Mandela and De Klerk remind me of an old couple who can't settle on a divorce. A historical union, even if everything is against it. Although they are working together to bring about a peaceful transition, their viewpoints often oppose each other. De Klerk would like to negotiate a lasting sharing of power between blacks and whites. He hopes to retain some sort of veto for whites. Mandela, on the other hand, advocates democracy by a simple majority, 'One person, one vote'.

Although De Klerk has freed Mandela, moral conviction isn't the reason. The country has been sinking into economic stagnation, smothered by international sanctions and paralysed by workers' strikes.

Buthelezi is torn between his two counterparts. He appears jealous of Mandela and his influence over the people. His own authority was legitimised by his bloodline: he was the uncle of the king of the Zulus, Goodwill Zwelithini, and his mother had been the granddaughter of King Cetshwayo. He has studied at the University of Fort Hare in the Ciskei, like other well-known figures in the struggle, including Mandela.

Mangosuthu Buthelezi has been the leader of the bantustan of KwaZulu since 1970. The ANC had even supported him in this role, believing that this would give them an ally within the bantustan system. In 1975 Buthelezi revived Inkatha, a cultural organisation established in 1922–1923, taking over the symbols and anthem of the ANC, of which he was a member. But in 1979 he left the ANC because he refused to accept the authority of the leadership in exile or to support the armed struggle and economic sanctions against the country. Inkatha then appeared as a rival of the ANC and the conflict between the two organisations began … Inkatha became a formidable power base, from which Buthelezi knew how to profit. He has always favoured a multiracial democracy and a free market economy.

Relations deteriorated further after the establishment of the United Democratic Front in 1983, the most significant anti-apartheid organisation inside the country. From August 1985, violent clashes over the control of territory in KwaZulu erupted between Inkatha and the United Democratic Front, an ally of the ANC. In 1989 Inkatha, on the one hand, and the ANC and the United Democratic Front, on the other hand, engaged in a small-scale civil war. A short time afterwards, in 1990, Inkatha announced that it was transforming itself into a political party and opened its ranks to all to form the Inkatha Freedom Party. At that moment, the Witwatersrand exploded in a new conflagration of violence between Inkatha and the comrades – supporters of the ANC and the UDF. The armed factions of Inkatha and the ANC surrendered themselves to continuous guerrilla war for control of the townships and KwaZulu.

Because the violence is tearing the country apart, the three leaders have no choice but to sign a peace accord. But how can they pass on the call to end hostilities to their followers? This is the question that they now have to answer.

On the day the agreement is ratified, I prepare my report in the hotel room where the signing session has taken place. My energy is back and I feel as though I am, at last, approaching my goal of becoming a foreign correspondent.

Sitting on the edge of the bed, about to call in my first radio news report to Montreal, I suddenly get the jitters ... but everything goes smoothly. Putting down the receiver, infinitely relieved, I feel liberated and almost euphoric. My first news report.

When I get back to Colette's, I unpack my bags.

9

Anti-apartheid separatist

Finally the work takes off! I start writing articles for the Montreal daily, *La Presse*. André Pratte, chief editor for international news, gives me the following subject: the perception that the whites have of the changes taking place in their country.

It's 1992. In general, whites are afraid. Some are convinced that vengeance from blacks is inevitable. Others simply fear the emergence of a black government and believe that the country will sink into stagnation or anarchy.

When, in 1990, Frederik de Klerk announced Mandela's release and legalised the anti-apartheid movements and parties, a number of members of parliament gave up their seats and slammed the doors of parliament behind them. The following year, within the National Party, which was leading the country, even the most liberal members felt that De Klerk was moving too fast and that he had 'given' too much to the black majority. Many Afrikaners considered him a traitor, some even held his initials up to ridicule: F W stood for 'Farewell Whites'.

His predecessor as president, Pieter Willem Botha, an authoritarian leader, had remained faithful to the policy of apartheid. Under his leadership, the country was no longer governed by the Cabinet of Ministers, but by a State Security Council, made up of senior representatives of the army, the security forces, the police and the justice department. This was to become known as the era of the Securocrats.

When Botha was forced to resign, for health reasons, in 1989, there were two candidates tipped to succeed him: Barend du Plessis, a protégé of Botha, close to the Securocrats and regarded as fairly liberal, and Frederik de Klerk, the hard-liner, the conservative. De Klerk was victorious by only eight votes, 69 to 61. Hence the surprise at the actions of this 'conservative' in February 1990. However, as conservative as he may have appeared, De Klerk felt that Botha had been using illegal methods to govern. As a result, his first action on taking power in September 1989 was to abolish the State Security Council and replace the military regime with a civil government.

The mandate of the National Party was thus to reform the policy of apartheid. Nothing was working any longer and the economy was collapsing. A survey indicated that seventy per cent of the white population was in favour of reform. But De Klerk had caused a shockwave that no one had expected by announcing the progressive abolition of one thousand and two hundred pages of legislation that governed black lives. Even the most liberal did not believe that he would touch the three pillars of apartheid: the laws that governed separate living areas, the division of land and population registration or racial classification.

From the moment these radical reforms were announced, the De Klerk government tried to negotiate a transitional constitution with the ANC, with a view to ensuring general elections. At the same time De Klerk wanted to salvage something for the whites. He envisaged two chambers in Parliament: a lower chamber and an upper chamber. The members of the former would be elected on the principle of one person, one vote. Those in the second chamber, a type of Senate as in Canada or the United States, would represent the minorities and would have a right of veto, allowing them to help establish a balance between the policies of the majority and the rights of the minorities.

'White politicians simply do not believe that a black government can govern the country efficiently,' asserted the political scientist Hennie Kotze of the University of Stellenbosch in the Cape, where all the major Afrikaner leaders studied. In fact, for a number of them a black government was synonymous with inefficiency and corruption.

Having set the process of reform in motion, De Klerk lost control of the country. Increasingly, the transition was determined by various significant community figures, by the trade unions, by the ANC and its allies and by a wide variety of other organisations. It was this loss of control that shook certain members of the Cabinet. Within the ranks of the National Party there was a desire to negotiate, but not at any price. 'Reform Yes – Surrender No,' they cried. Realising that De Klerk would probably be the last white president in the history of the country, the Nationalists wanted to ensure that they would occupy an important place in any future government, a place that would guarantee them real power-sharing.

Resistance came from the Afrikaners, who represented fifty-seven per cent of the white population. Only half of them supported De Klerk. The other half supported the Conservative Party; they were largely working-class people and farmers who did not want to see their country pass into the hands of the 'kaffirs'. These Afrikaners didn't want to listen to ideas about reform. In fact they wanted to strengthen apartheid.

Certain right-wing extremist movements had even established their own 'armies'. Eugene Terre'Blanche, head of the AWB, the Afrikaner Resistance Movement, warned that they would never allow a black government to lead the country. 'They will have to face our canons,' Terre'Blanche raged.

I interviewed this man on two occasions. The second time, while the guys were putting away their equipment after the interview, he stood in front of the AWB flag, which contains an emblem resembling a Nazi swastika, and quietly confided, 'Blacks have tiny brains this size.' As he said it, he closed his enormous fist and brandished it as if he was going to hit someone. He had in fact already done this on more than one occasion and would later be imprisoned for paralysing a black man.

Terre'Blanche perhaps felt free to say what he wanted because I had a white skin. People would often assume these liberties on first meeting me. When I went to a children's party with Colette, the hostess asked me what I was doing in South Africa. I told her about my professional projects, adding that I had met a South African with whom I was now sharing my life. She asked, 'Is he English or Afrikaans-speaking?' because for her it was inconceivable that my partner might not be white. Without thinking, I responded 'English-speaking' (because although Jay's parents' mother tongue is Tamil, his first language is English). For the hostess this would mean white and 'British'. I wanted to know what she thought of the new developments in South Africa. 'The blacks are not capable of much,' she declared without scruple, 'especially not governing a country!' In public, or beyond her garden, this woman would never see herself as racist.

My nationality also caused a lot of curiosity. And I was received differently depending on whether I introduced myself as Canadian or Québecois. I would provoke questions if I identified myself through my language and my culture. The first question was always, 'Are you for or against the independence of Quebec?' Without placing myself in either camp, I would always reply that even those supporting the independence of Quebec had supported the anti-apartheid struggle. Anti-apartheid literally means *anti-separation*. Isn't that a marvellous oxymoron: anti-apartheid separatist?

However, I was in for a surprise when I interviewed Robert van Tonder, leader of the Afrikaner Boerestaat Party, even more right-wing than Eugene Terre'Blanche's AWB. 'My idol is René Lévesque!' he kept exclaiming, repeating Lévesque's words 'This land belongs to us'. My colleagues had warned me that Van Tonder very rarely granted interviews. But when I called him and introduced myself as a journalist from Quebec, he was quite warm towards me.

The fact that I was Québecois attracted spontaneous sympathy from people on the extreme right. This was because these nationalists liked to use the example of Quebec to demonstrate the legitimacy of sovereign or separatist aspirations. A leader of the Conservative Party, Fanie Jacobs, told me, 'We are almost in the same situation as the Québecois in Canada, in the sense that we do not wish to be forced to live in a unitary state. I think that in a unitary state the principle of 'One person, one vote' would lead to chaos. The Québecois understand my position, because they have the same problems. I have been a professor of international law, so I know the situation of the Québecois very well and I often use this example to explain our situation. The Conservative Party wants self-determination for the Afrikaners, who form a people in the same way as the Germans, the Italians, the French or the Québecois do. And we believe that international law recognises this self-determination.'

The comparison does not work, however, because, unlike the Québecois, the Afrikaners are nowhere in the majority in South Africa. One day, a rich, white press magnate praised for his anti-apartheid positions and his support for ANC projects, told me that the Cape should be declared a white region and given to the Afrikaners. I asked him what would become of the several million blacks living in Khayelitsha, the township outside Cape Town. His reply, 'Khayelitsha doesn't feature on any map. They could just be relocated.' The apartheid 'bulldozer' approach was rearing its head once more.

This is the Afrikaner problem. They have everything except a country. And some are determined to obtain this country, by any means.

10

Bez Valley

Jay bought a house shortly before my arrival in South Africa, even though it was still illegal for us to live in the same suburb, let alone the same house. But our new home would not be free until October and, coincidentally, the Group Areas Act was repealed shortly before we moved in.

On the day of my arrival, Jay and I visited the house together with Nisha and her husband Sagaren. Entering it, I burst into tears. After travelling for thirty-two hours, this was the last thing that I needed: a dump. The house literally stank like shit. Nisha asked Jay if it was too late to stop the sale. 'Yes, too late,' he replied.

Jay is an impulsive person, like me – he didn't look at the interior before buying! He had chosen it because of a hundred-year-old chestnut tree on the property. A magnificent, solid specimen.

The house isn't far from Colette's home in Bez Valley, a rather poor suburb by white standards, but well-off enough compared to black areas. In spite of the filth and the dilapidation, the position is magnificent, perched on the hillside, overlooking the valley.

At the foot of the chestnut tree lies a large neglected swimming pool, fifty years old, full of slimy green water. The perfect ecosystem for frogs! I will clean it, because my favourite sport is swimming.

I will never allow Jay to choose a house on his own again! But it must be said that he had found a real bargain. The land and the view are well worth the price he had paid.

The pathway that leads to the garage is lined with fruit trees. I can fill my basket with peaches, mulberries, nectarines, dates, plums, apples, granadillas, avocados. On the lower level of the plot, two metres above the road, weeds are sprouting on the tennis court, which is as old as the swimming pool and also in a state of disrepair. Above the house, on a slope, there is a row of almond trees and a tired vine that still manages to produce a few grapes. From up there it's possible to take in the whole valley at a glance: the trees rising like little islands, above a sea of tiled roofs, like so many scales of a fish: ochre, black, grey and green.

Since the racial laws are still in effect, the estate agent has had to obtain consent from the neighbours for a 'non-white' person to move into their suburb. How humiliating! But Bez Valley is a suburb where Chinese, Japanese, blacks, Indians, coloureds and whites live side by side without friction.

Four months after our first visit to the house, we enter it for the first time as the owners. It's still dirty. And, to crown it all, there's no kitchen. Just a small sink in a corner. The walls have cracks. The bath *might* once have been white. Maggots crawl around in the dustbins and among the rat droppings. Outside there's an old toilet, which has been blocked for years. I cannot find the words to describe the shocking condition of this toilet, intended for the use of the former domestic workers, a worn-out old couple who still live here. The owner left, leaving these people behind. They live above the garage, at the other end of the property, in a dirty, gloomy room. When I enter it, the stench rushes up my nose and I feel like vomiting. It's dark. There are no windows, no water, no electricity. Rat droppings carpet the cement floor.

The man and his wife used to work twelve hours a day for the former owner. The wife cleaned the house, although she clearly hadn't done so for some time. Growing old there, they had simply stayed on, as 'parasites' of the 'Master', who allowed them to continue living in the hovel at the other end of his property.

When we take possession of the house, the old people beg us to keep them on. They want to work for us. I can't see what they would be able to do, and anyway for me there's no question of engaging domestic help, especially when they have to live in these conditions! We don't have the money either. I pity them, but I can't allow them to stay in that filthy room. Sending them away breaks my heart.

I start a thorough clean-up. While Jay works, I go to the house and spend eight to ten hours a day washing, sand-papering, painting, tearing down, rebuilding, scrubbing, polishing, sweeping, hammering, screwing and plastering. While working I discover the original plans for the house hidden in a hole in a wall, drawn up in 1928 and dated on the day of my birthday. Is this fate?

A month later, our new home is hardly recognisable. Even the chimney has been repainted. Jay climbs the roof with great difficulty to paint it pink, my favourite colour.

I hire a pump to empty the greater part of the swamp from the swimming pool, but even the pump can't cope in the end. There is too much rubbish and debris, as well as frogs and dead birds. I end up emptying the pool by hand. I spend a week at this task, after which I am ill for a month! But I am soon to discover that, lying in the shade all day, the water is so cold that the pool is practically unusable.

We still don't have a kitchen. Jay employs two handymen from Soweto to put one in. They are illiterate, but old hands at construction work. When they arrive on Monday morning, Jay has already left for work. I welcome them and offer them a cup of tea and a peanut butter sandwich, which they devour immediately. Then I explain what has to be done: take down this wall here, build another one there. The two look vacantly. Is it my accent? I thought I had spoken clearly enough. Finally one of them asks me, 'Where's the Master?' That word again! I reply that my husband has gone to work. I use the term *husband* even though Jay and I are not married. Living together doesn't appear to go down well in South Africa. Besides, Jay talks regularly about marriage – but I still don't feel ready to seal this transatlantic destiny. I ask the workmen if the orders absolutely have to come from the *man of the house*, but all I obtain in reply is laughter. I assure them that my husband is in agreement and beg them to start working, but they won't budge.

'We want to see the Master.'

'The Master is not here. He's only coming back tonight. Please start!'

'No, we want to see him.'

So the two men remain seated on the steps all day long! I come out several times to tell them to start working, but get nowhere. I'm beside myself, but can't get them to move. I can't call Jay because the phone hasn't been installed yet.

When Jay comes home, at around six, he asks the men why they haven't started the work. In front of me, as though I don't exist they reply, 'What do you want us to do?' I remain calm. Jay simply repeats what I have already told them that morning. 'Yes, Master.'

I discover that the problem of sexism in South Africa is far more serious than I could have imagined. And the situation of black women is far worse than mine, since they are victims of both racism and sexism ...

11

Depression

I'm not eating. It's weeks since I've done any cooking. Jay forces me to swallow something from time to time, even if it's just a crust of bread. I spend my days on the couch looking outside, without seeing or hearing anything. I have never been in such a state. I have to gather all my energy just to run a bath.

Jay looks at me, helplessly. 'Go and spend a few weeks in Canada to see Léandre.' But the Radio–Canada correspondent will be leaving the country soon and I don't want to miss my chance of replacing her.

I find myself in the office of Judy, a psychotherapist. Judy works at the Family Life Centre, where they offer all kinds of therapy, from marriage counselling to psychological support for people who are HIV positive. It's 29 November 1991, my thirtieth birthday. Colette, who herself has an appointment with Judy, has given me her place.

'Why did you come to South Africa?'

'I wanted to do some international reporting on South Africa for my country.'

'And are you?'

'Not really. But it shouldn't be much longer. I should soon be taking the place of the current correspondent.'

'So what's the matter? What is making you cry?'

'Léandre – that's my son. My love, my little sweetheart, whom I've left on the other side of the planet.'

'Why don't you go back?'

'There's Jay.'

What's keeping me here is not only a professional dream. It's more than that. I am also here because I am in love with a man. But this doesn't seem reason enough to abandon my son on another continent. I am consumed with guilt and shame simply thinking about it. I explain to Judy that leaving SA to return home seems as difficult to me as staying here. But what is one supposed to do when you have a son on one continent and a spouse on another? Even if Jay has promised that he'll come to Canada 'one day', I know he can't leave now.

Judy decides to send me to see a psychiatrist immediately so that he can put me on Prozac. It's urgent, she says to me. Leaving her office, I break down on hearing her diagnosis: severe depression. I have always thought of myself as a 'strong woman', capable of anything. I thought I could take whatever life served up, whether it was physical or mental, that life continued in spite of the obstacles, that it was possible to function normally despite the circumstances.

The staff at the Family Life Centre have to come and bring me in from outside, under a tree. I'm losing it, I don't know where my car is; in any case, I can't drive. I don't think I can even spell my name.

Judy's diagnosis echoes in my head, 'I suspect that you have been living in a state of depression for at least ten years.'

I start taking Prozac on the same day. I've never heard of the drug, but I'm assured that it will restore me to a condition in which I can function.

12

Rape

'More than a thousand women are raped every day in South Africa,' I learn from an article in the excellent weekly newspaper, the *Weekly Mail*. I read that one in two women will be raped in the course of her life in this country. One thousand and thirty-eight rapes are committed each day. I take out my calculator: more than forty-three rapes an hour! It's the highest rate of rape in the world, but 'one in two women' – surely that's an exaggeration?

Something inside me spurs me into motion. I grab the telephone and make about twenty calls to various organisations – government, university, independent, feminist. Apart from the government services, all the organisations confirm the statistics in the *Weekly Mail*. One in two women will be raped in the course of her life. I can hardly believe it.

This means that a rape is committed every eighty-three seconds. The police do not deny these figures. According to several surveys and investigations, only one in twenty women reports her rape to the police.

I call the SABC (South African Broadcasting Corporation) to find out if I can view reports prepared on the subject. I am told there are none. Rape, sexual aggression, marital violence – these subjects don't exist for the SABC. Why? Because they are a 'black' problem. In fact, ninety-five per cent of rape victims are black.

I call the people I know at VNS (Video News Services). VNS had been a real fly in the ointment for the apartheid regime in the domain of television. They had filmed and broadcast very subversive images. Without them, the world would not have seen a quarter of the images of South Africa that were broadcast over the previous ten years.

I share my 'discovery' with Jeremy Nathan, co-director of the company with whom I have worked while shooting with *Nord-Sud*. I propose a documentary. 'Write a synopsis,' he replies, 'and we'll see what we can do.' I borrow Jay's laptop computer. He can manage without it, he tells me, whereas I am handicapped without a keyboard.

I start my research. I make calls, accumulating statistics and theories on the high rape rate. I ask everyone I speak to whether a documentary on the subject would be useful.

'Absolutely! We need it now! We needed it yesterday!'

'Would you be able to contribute to the financing of such a documentary?'

'No. We survive on subsidies ourselves.'

I receive the same response everywhere, even from Heather Reganass, the director of the National Institute for the Prevention of Crime and the Rehabilitation of Offenders. She is enthusiastic about my video project, but her organisation isn't able to participate financially. However, she does provide me with very valuable information.

I start editing my synopsis. For two days I write. A rape every eighty-three seconds. I watch the second hand of my awful yellow, battery-operated clock hanging in our charming new kitchen, and every time eighty-three seconds pass, I imagine the pain. A scream that no one can hear. That no one wants to hear. And then, silence. For life. And every eighty-three seconds another scream joins the silence. Victims of their gender, one thousand and thirty-eight women are raped every day, twice as many as in the whole of the United States.

South African feminists have worked out a theory of rape for the national context. According to Heather Reganass, the scale of the phenomenon is closely linked to the political system, 'It's the result of forty years of apartheid. It's an extension of the violence, and it forms a part of everything that is going wrong in this country. The country is governed by violence. The people respond with violence.' Mary Mabaso, a great woman who organised the first march against rape in Soweto in 1989, expressed a similar opinion, 'To the extent that rape is a problem that is concentrated in the black townships and since, by comparison, it occurs far less in the white communities, it seems to be clearly linked to apartheid.'

It's an interesting theory. Could it mean that large numbers of black men, deprived for so long of a sense of power over their own lives, respond with violence against women? Because rape is above all an act of power.

In South African society, governed for decades by an ultra-conservative administration, perceptions about rape have not evolved. Everyone, whether victims or members of the judiciary, maintains a mentality that industrialised societies shed almost a quarter of a century ago. Rape is still viewed, by the victims and by others, as a shameful 'illness'. One suffers it, and that's that. The law only fuels the attitude.

I come across an edifying article in the *Weekly Mail*: a man, no longer living with his wife but still married to her, is accused of rape. His lawyer defends him by arguing that 'since they are still legally married, the husband has *right of access* to his wife. It was therefore legal for him to force his wife to have sexual relations with him.' The marital exemption that protects a husband against prosecution for rape is a principle that was established in England in 1773 and is known as Hale's Rule. South Africa still applies it. Rape, with a licence, is legal!

A terrifying phenomenon is on the increase: gang-rape or *jackrolling* in township slang. A 'sport' that young men in particular take to without scruple, almost openly. Jackrollers believe that by forcing a woman to have sexual relations they are doing her a favour rather than committing a crime. The rise in this phenomenon seems closely linked to the political crisis. Law and order are collapsing everywhere. You get the impression that the strait-jacket constraining the population has just burst open, giving free rein to all forms of savagery and violence.

I am bent on producing my documentary, but I need money, a lot of money. In a country where illiteracy is the lot of almost half the population, the power of the image increases tenfold. I want the camera to go where silence has concealed the truth, where women stifle their cries, strangled by shame. I want to show where, why and how rape is committed. But above all I want to create an instrument to break down the wall of silence, to tell women, 'You have the right to scream out your anger. And even if the law offers scant protection, you have the right to cry out against injustice.'

In the synopsis that I present to various bodies, enterprises, government and non-governmental organisations in an effort to find funding for the video production, I argue that if this documentary 'can save just one woman from rape, just one, it will have achieved its objective – to reduce the violence against women.' And I end with the following footnote, 'While you have been reading this text, two women have been raped.'

Two days later I go to VNS. Jeremy Nathan isn't in, but I see his colleague and co-director of the firm, Lawrence. He reads the synopsis in front of me, then places it on top of a pile of papers on the corner of his desk and thanks me. He'll see what he can do.

I look at him, disbelievingly, frustrated. I realise that he isn't going to give my project another thought. He's a guy and these stories bore him to tears ... I leave, furious.

But I have my doubts, as usual. Is it the subject that doesn't interest him or could it be that my synopsis was poorly written and inadequate?

I return home completely discouraged, and fall into my old routine: crying and waiting for Jay.

13

Omar

Our friend Omar Motani is a South African of Indian origin like Jay. He looks white though, which means that during the apartheid years he was able to walk along beaches reserved for whites with a pretty woman on his arm, without being arrested and thrown into prison!

Omar, born on 2 November 1933, doesn't belong to any group; he's a self-made man. He started making furniture in his backyard. Today he heads an empire and owns six furniture-manufacturing factories. He takes me to visit the one in Pretoria. 'We repainted the walls of the workers' toilets in warm colours. And the workers' staffroom has large windows, like those in our offices.' Turning off the lights of the enormous room in which leather and material are stacked, he says, 'I like to make the working environment as pleasant as possible.'

Omar almost always has a cigarette between his fingers – except when he plays tennis! Even at fifty-eight years of age, he manages to leave his younger opponents breathless every Sunday. Omar turns women's heads: he is good-looking, always dressed in a distinguished manner, and his body reflects his physical condition. He is extremely polite, especially with women, who feel 'special' in his presence. He charms them, in a perfectly natural manner. 'A woman in my company never lights her own cigarette, never fills her glass, never opens a door.' Omar likes to laugh and to make others laugh. His sense of humour is his best asset. I laughed so much with him. Stretched out on his enormous bed, we talk for hours, sometimes all night long. Omar is also genuinely humble. He's a good friend of Nelson Mandela, but you have to meet him fifty times or more before he mentions this privileged relationship with the great man.

If Omar comes to your house and you invite him to sit down on your sofa or on one of your kitchen chairs, he'll take ten minutes to sit down. He'll talk to you, a cigarette between his lips, as he examines the furniture, evaluates its comfort, the quality of its stitching, its base and its cloth. He'll sit down in the middle, then on the side, without bringing up the subject of furniture. He'll hop discreetly from one piece of furniture to another, raise his eyebrows, mutter and then continue the conversation as though he were thinking of nothing else.

Omar, the capitalist, got to know Jay, the socialist, shortly before the release of Nelson Mandela. This Naidoo, Indian and trade unionist, intrigued him, so he asked to meet him. Omar thought Jay had a lively spirit and wanted to get to know the man behind the media image – that of the 'demonic being'. He has the devil's eyes, people used to say of Jay.

Their meeting took place at the Carlton Centre, an enormous hotel, the highest building in the city, right in the centre of Johannesburg. Jay agreed to see him because he needed allies in the business world.

They established a relationship of trust almost immediately, they both now claim. The hours passed and, as their conversation continued, Jay cancelled his appointments for the afternoon. They talked about everything, cured all South Africa's ills, presented all the solutions. They talked about life, death, joy, pain and suffering.

From this meeting an unexpected friendship was born between two men who could not be more different: the one a Hindu and a trade union leader, the other a Muslim and capitalist, twenty years older than the first. This relationship would never cease to amaze the business and political community in South Africa. Jay and Omar are soulmates, as they say. When they are together, I often see Omar put his arm around Jay's neck and affectionately slap his cheek with the other hand.

On leaving the hotel, Omar offered Jay a lift. The two men went down to the underground parking garage, but Omar couldn't remember where he had parked his car. They searched for it, going up and down the three or four levels of the parking garage, laughing. The parking attendants, who recognised Jay in passing, shouted, 'Viva COSATU, viva!' 'Actually,' asked Jay, 'what kind of car have you got?

What colour is it?' Omar hesitated, then replied in a low voice, 'It's a Rolls Royce … gold.' Jay was flabbergasted. And when two attendants approached them, only too happy to help Comrade Naidoo find his car, he didn't know how to answer their questions regarding the vehicle. In the end he muttered a vague explanation. Omar then remembered that he had parked his Rolls Royce in another parking garage …

I first met Omar only a few days after my arrival in South Africa. On the way to his house for dinner, Jay warned me, 'Don't be surprised at the people around him. He has servants.' I had never seen so many domestic helpers in one house: gardeners, cooks, housemaids … That evening, at the large rectangular glass table in the dining-room, I sat down at the place that would remain mine for years to come – second to the right from Omar's throne. We got on well immediately. In the course of the evening he asked me whether I had accepted Jay's marriage proposal. 'It's a big decision for me, Omar. I am thinking about it.'

One evening, seated on the soft couch in Omar's room, Jay once again broached the subject of marriage, as he had done regularly for weeks. 'I promise you a garden of roses, with plenty of thorns, of course, because there will be difficult times, but there will always be the roses – beautiful, large, pure, enchanting, passionate. Will you marry me?' When I say yes, he jumps for joy and wants to get started immediately. We decide to get married in December, which is only three weeks away, on Omar's tennis court! The timing is perfect, because Léandre is coming over with my mother. I explain to Jay and Omar that there can be no marriage without my mother there.

Omar is already in a state. 'A wedding in three weeks?! The invitations! The food! The tables, the chairs, the tablecloths, the flowers, the serviettes! Three weeks? The music! The priest! The marquee! We have to have a marquee. It's the rainy season.'

Jay and Omar draw up the guest list. I only have two people I wish to invite: Léandre and Louise. But for Jay it's more complicated. First of all, Indians, whether they are Hindus or Muslims, do not know what an intimate reception is. And if Jay invites one person, he has to invite four hundred! Soon it's five hundred, and on the day of the wedding six hundred people gather on Omar's property to attend the wedding of a famous son of the South African Indian community and the anti-apartheid struggle!

14

First wedding: South Africa

Two days before the ceremony, Léandre arrives with his grandmother … and his father!

The latter wants to see for himself the country in which he is going to leave his son for six months. I would have done the same thing. I would have gone to the other side of the world to make sure that the full moon filled my child's dreams with sonatas and not bogey-men armed with AK-47s. But as for going to my ex's wedding …

I had even written him a long letter begging him to trust me, promising never to put Léandre's life in danger and assuring him that despite the political violence, everyday life in South Africa was tolerable. It made no difference.

On the day of their arrival I count the hours and minutes. Léandre's room is in tip-top shape. Not a speck of dust anywhere. Each object has been carefully chosen and placed. I have spent a month scraping, re-plastering, painting, cleaning, polishing and decorating the room, which is the most spacious in the whole house.

We go to the airport well before the flight is due. I can't wait at home any longer. Sagaren, Jay's brother-in-law, accompanies us. He works for South African Airways and his office is at the airport. Louise, my mother, almost didn't make it. There's been a storm in Umiujaq, her point of departure, for several days, and a number of flights had been cancelled. When I hear about the weather conditions, I tell Omar again that I can't get married if my mother isn't there. He looks at me as if to say, 'Do you think that I am going to cancel a reception for five hundred people?', but he realises that I am very serious.

The plane finally lands. A little more patience. It takes a good half hour to collect one's luggage and go through customs. Then, the sliding doors open and the passengers start to come through …

I haven't seen Léandre for six months. Since he's almost five years old, this represents ten per cent of his life!

The sliding doors open less often. The end of my wait is approaching. But no familiar face appears, neither Léandre's, nor his grandmother's, nor his father's. And then, nothing more. The doors remain closed.

Suddenly, I'm jumping over the safety barriers that prevent access to the section for travellers. Jay and Sagaren try to hold me back, but nothing is going to stop me, nothing! I run towards the large opaque glass doors and try to open them by pulling with all my might. A security guard approaches … and then the doors open to let another passenger through. I have a few seconds to see inside. There they are! They're near the carousel, which is now empty. One of their bags is missing! That's all it is! I catch a glimpse of Léandre, sitting on a luggage trolley, so beautiful, fresh and innocent.

Finally they come through. I don't know how to receive them. The atmosphere is calmer than anticipated. Léandre's father drives back to the house with Sagaren and Jay. Léandre, Louise and I travel in another car. This gives me fifteen minutes to re-establish contact with my son privately. Not much time, fifteen minutes, but so precious.

Léandre spends the whole day exploring his home for the next one hundred and eighty beddy-byes. He touches everything, rummages through everything. He comes to kiss and hug me all the time, saying 'I love you, Mama, I am so happy to see you', with such affection that I still savour the moment today.

❊ ❊ ❊

Only a few clouds threaten on the wedding day. But according to Hindu tradition, a little rain blesses the ceremony.

Finding a wedding dress is a nightmare. Why spend a lot of money on a garment that I'll only wear once? I visit the fabric shops at the Oriental Plaza. The Indian shops have a good range of fabric at reasonable prices, as well as huge pattern books. But because trains three metres long and veils six metres long are not my style, I eventually opt for a fairly modest dress – for a maid of honour! There's a little lace along the edge, which falls to mid-calf.

Jay has borrowed a very elegant beige suit, in the style of Nehru. He even borrows the buttons from a friend's outfit so that he can sew them onto his for the wedding.

Léandre doesn't really understand what's happening. He's wearing an Indian outfit in the Punjabi style. The long white silk shirt reaches his knees and the pants are drawn in around the ankle.

We all went to buy Léandre's clothes together, with his father. People recognised Jay in every shop at the Oriental Plaza. They asked about our marriage plans. Jay did the introductions. 'This is my future wife, my son, my mother-in-law and, um … young Léandre's father.' People didn't quite know how to react. We all laughed, as the absurdity of the situation hit us.

I assured my ex that he didn't have to attend the celebration, but that he was welcome. He accepted the invitation …

They roll out the red carpet for us. Omar welcomes me outside his home and opens the car door for me. There are people everywhere. Half of Mandela's future cabinet is here! People are feverish with excitement.

I would very much have liked my father to be part of the ceremony, but, having spent almost half his life involved in aviation as a navigator in the Canadian armed forces, he can't stand flying any more. He also hates crowds and would have felt uncomfortable here. So it is the person who had adopted me from the first moment, welcoming me into his large family, who acts as my 'father' – Omar. He has eight children, four boys and four girls, and a dozen grandchildren. His three youngest daughters are the children of Hajira, his current wife. They are all here to welcome us.

I let the wave carry me along and abandon myself to the photo session, although my smile feels forced. Jay, on the other hand, is ecstatic. He is meeting up with all his friends, colleagues and comrades, people who have risked their lives with him in political and trade union activities. I am soon lost in a whirlwind of introductions, encounters and congratulations.

Then, like a wave coming to find the sandcastles on the beach, the atmosphere is suddenly calm. The energy of the crowd has changed. I lean back to see what's happening. Then I hear that distinctive tone, from a man who never needs to raise his voice. 'Hello! How're you?' Nelson Mandela has just arrived.

Mandela asks about my child, as he does every time we meet. 'Léandre? He is here! Come and meet him.'

'How're you, little one?' Léandre is not an easy name if you're not French. Some say Leo, Leon or Lee-ander, but rarely Léandre. 'How old are you?' Léandre has heard people talk about this wise man, but at this moment, he's just another grown-up asking questions in a strange language. He doesn't understand anything and hides behind my dress.

'You look very elegant today,' Mandela compliments me before they drag him off. People flock around him. Many are filming him or taking photos. No one uses a flash though, because everyone knows that his eyes were damaged during thirteen years of hard labour in the blinding glare of the limestone quarry on Robben Island.

The marquee on the tennis court is overflowing. The Indian musicians are tuning their tablas and sitars. Tables for ten have been carefully arranged and simply decorated: flowers, small serviettes attractively folded, Indian condiments. The table of honour seats twenty, and includes my mother, Omar, Nelson Mandela and several heads of the ANC, among them Walter and Albertina Sisulu, Oliver Tambo and his wife, Adelaide. Around the property crowds of curious onlookers have gathered, scaling the walls to catch a glimpse of the celebrities gathered for the event.

Oliver Tambo expressed himself with difficulty after a stroke in 1989. He was seventy-four years old and his gestures had lost their assurance. He had led the ANC for three decades. Forced into exile, he directed the movement against apartheid and the military operations of Umkhonto we Sizwe, the armed wing of the movement, during the long years of Mandela's imprisonment.

A modest and discreet man, Walter Sisulu was not well known abroad, particularly to us Canadians. He spent more than twenty-six years of his life in prison. His wife Albertina was arrested, detained, banned and harassed for twenty-four years. Their eight children (three of whom were adopted) and one of their grandchildren suffered from or fled the South African system of 'justice'. Walter remembered how Albertina had wanted to buy some furniture when the couple were married in 1944. He told her that it was pointless because he would not be there to pay it off. 'I knew that I was going to spend my life in prison,' he said, 'I thought I was going to die there.'

Léandre takes his place at my side, while his father sits at the other end of the table of honour. Omar walks proudly, whispering in my ear that he is glad that I am Jay's chosen one.

A few minutes later, Nelson Mandela says the same thing to the crowd. When he gets up to deliver his speech, everyone falls silent. He is the only guest wearing a rather informal outfit – a white summer shirt with a pair of casual trousers. 'I enquired about the dress code for this occasion,' he begins. 'They told me that Jay Naidoo had a very relaxed style and that casual dress would be suitable, but I see that I've made a mistake.' Then he tells a long story about Jay, a man he admires, who has devoted his life to the cause. 'Women all over the world have had their eye on this handsome young man. I see that Lucie has won the contest.' I find this allusion to a contest a little out of place. But if it is tactless, it only proves that he is human.

Then Albertina, the wife of Walter Sisulu, Ma Sisulu to her familiars and a really gifted speech-maker, gets up and heads straight for the podium at a pace that doesn't reflect her seventy-five years. Her first words are a cold shower: 'Lucie, Jay is already married.' Forced laughter from the audience, then silence. She knows how to speak, how to weigh her words. 'Yes, you are his second wife. His first wife is the country, the struggle, the cause. Your greatest apprenticeship will be learning to live with this situation.' She turns to look straight at me, directing six hundred pairs of eyes towards me.

Laughter fills the silence. I force a smile. Through clenched teeth I whisper to Jay, 'What is she talking about? Is she mad?' Jay tries to calm me, 'I have only one wife and that's you ...' But I don't appreciate Albertina's remark in the least. To the extent that I don't hear the rest of her speech!

Yet, Albertina was right. And if I had to give a speech for such a wedding today, I would repeat what she said. Her words couldn't have been more appropriate. I had no idea, at that moment, how pertinent her message would be – she knew what she was talking about. She, who had had no interest in politics before meeting Walter in 1942, had quickly rallied to the struggle for equal rights.

'My husband never forced me to become his political shadow,' she would tell me one day. 'And just as he never forced me to become politically involved, he never stopped me from doing so either.' In time, she began her own political career, but as the mother of a family, she had more obstacles to overcome. 'Once, the ANC forbade me to participate in an event because other members of the family were already involved. Someone had to look after the children ...' However, she did not miss the march of twenty thousand women to Pretoria in 1956, to protest against the pass laws; nor did she fail to defy the new pass laws in 1958, which resulted in her arrest and detention for six weeks while awaiting trial. She was breastfeeding her ten-month-old daughter at the time. 'They would not allow me to have her with me. That hurt me.' At the trial she was declared innocent. Her lawyer's name was Nelson Mandela ...

Albertina spent seventeen years under house arrest, from 1964 to 1981, completely isolated from society: the banning order reduced her to silence; contact with her husband was rare and difficult. She stuck it out, almost miraculously, torn between eight children, prison bars, her love for a great man ... and a country in transformation. Between 1982 and 1985 Albertina Sisulu spent almost two years in prison. In 1983, while she was behind bars, she was nominated as president of the United Democratic Front for the Transvaal region. Although Winnie Mandela is known as the 'Mother of the nation', there are many who silently accord Albertina Sisulu this title.

Walter, who became a dear friend, confided in me one day, 'Without Albertina I would never have been able to do what I did. She is the backbone of my life and my family.'

Of all the speeches made on my wedding day, my mother's would remain the most memorable. For years, people kept referring to it, 'I was at your wedding in Johannesburg. I loved your mother's speech! What a woman!'

It's not only what Louise says that charms people, it's her way of saying it. Everywhere she goes, she leaves her mark. People remember her. Yet, when people talk about this speech today, she is embarrassed. She denies being an exceptional woman and constantly denigrates herself. It's not hard to see where my problems with confidence come from …

Louise gets up, shaking like a leaf. But she is a woman of the stage, an artist, a pianist, a comedienne, and the crowd stimulates her as much as it terrorises her. Without notes, without sheets of paper, but with her piercing eyes, keen mind and expressive hands, Loulou knows how to communicate.

First she describes Jay's arrival at the little village of Umiujaq, on Hudson Bay. 'I told my Inuit pupils that someone from South Africa had just arrived. Since they only knew Mandela's name, they asked, 'Is Mandela here?' I replied that no, the visitor's name was Jay. So the children started chanting: 'Jay Mandela is here! Jay Mandela is here!' Nelson Mandela laughed heartily.

Like me, Louise suffers from a certain naivety. For example, it did not occur to her that it might not be the right thing to talk about Québecois nationalism in the presence of the Canadian Ambassador … She introduced the subject by saying that, living near the North Pole, she had not been able to buy a 'proper' wedding gift, like a toaster. But, knowing how much I loved my country and how much I was missing it, she had found something else. From her plastic shopping bag she then took out and unfolded an enormous flag with four large fleurs-de-lys – the flag of Quebec! The Canadian Ambassador, seated among the guests, was no doubt rather put out by this. But it was not over yet! Her bag contained other treasures!

Loulou is a knitter. She had therefore knitted us a wedding present – blue mittens with large white fleurs-de-lys on them. She gave me a pair, then one to Jay, all the while talking about Québecois identity. Then she took out a third pair of mittens, which she had knitted specially for Nelson Mandela! Silence descended on the audience as she moved towards his place in the centre of the table to give them to him. He embraced her and thanked her. Then he slipped his hands into the mittens, stood up, slowly drew up his body, raised his arms high in the air, and turned from right to left, like a president who has just won an election, showing off the front and the back of the mittens, to cries of 'Hurrah!' and 'Viva!' from the guests. Louise had fascinated the audience gathered under the marquee in a way that would have filled the Québecois nationalist René Lévesque with satisfaction! The Canadian Ambassador, I was told, found it less amusing: he got up and left.

This 'diplomatic incident' ended up on the pages of the Québecois magazine *L'actualité*, which published a photograph of Nelson Mandela with his fleur-de-lys mittens a few months later. But the article provoked another 'diplomatic incident' between my friend Luc Chartrand, the journalist who had written it, and my mother. The photograph appeared under the heading 'Long live free Phentex'. Phentex is a synthetic brand of wool, which Louise, who proudly knitted with pure wool, absolutely abhorred. Despite Luc's repeated apologies, my mother bore him a grudge for some time.

As for the idea that Nelson Mandela might support separatism, in any form, this was obviously not true. All his battles had been fought *against* apartheid, against separatism. Perhaps right-wing Afrikaners and nationalistic Zulus supported the idea of separatism, but certainly not anyone in the ANC.

The speeches end, and it's time for the ceremony. Suddenly, the heavens open. It absolutely pours, but only for a few minutes. Jay thinks his mother has just blessed us.

Two priests officiate. One is Catholic and French, Father Emmanuel Lafont, a good friend, and the subject of one of my *Nord-Sud* broadcasts. This remarkable priest lives in Soweto. It takes a great deal of courage for a white man to live in Soweto. He has taken the trouble to learn several African languages. From time to time I go to mass on a Sunday morning in Soweto, when my batteries need recharging. In his cassock and sandals Emmanuel Lafont causes a stir at St Philip's Church. You forget his small stature when he raises his arms to embrace the faithful. The congregation dances and sings songs that stir the depths of my soul with their power and depth.

Emmanuel lifts his head high and looks at Jay in anticipation. No, Jay does not have a ring. No matter, Emmanuel isn't offended. Jay and I kiss one another after saying 'I do'.

Next, the Hindu ceremony begins. The priest assumes a serious expression. A yellow dot on his forehead, his feet bare, his robe reaching to the ground, he arrives with a collection of sacred objects: incense, camphor, water, fruit, some blessed milk, fire, and two exquisite garlands woven from blessed flowers, which we have to place around our necks and exchange three times. This ceremony, a bit longer than the first one, has a greater significance for Jay and his family. His six brothers and sisters have tears in their eyes. Jay, the youngest in the family, is the last to marry. The last, at the age of thirty-seven (he would celebrate his birthday the following week, on 20 December), to finally 'settle down'. 'My mother would so much have wanted to be present at my wedding!' He can't stop thinking about her all day. He was very close to his mother. She was the one who taught him the values of equality and justice. When her children invited friends home, blacks, whites or Indians, she always gave them something to eat, even her own portion. 'The greatest influence in my life was my mother,' Jay said. He felt her absence very keenly. Jay's two sisters, Nisha and Dimes, and his four brothers, Logie, Pat, Iyaloo and Popeye, would say the same.

I was warmly welcomed into Jay's family. Our visits to his sisters and brothers are always friendly and lively. Delicious, spicy food is always in abundance. Sometimes the women drape a sari around me, leaving my navel exposed, and draw a bindi on my forehead. Not that they ever expect me to abandon my culture. They accept me as I am, with my jeans and T-shirts, with my language, my culture and my spirit. The Naidoo family is united, a true nucleus of life. This is part of the Indian culture. From now on, I am one of them. Even at gatherings of thirty, forty or fifty people where I am always the only white, no one would ever allude to my 'difference'.

The Hindu ceremony is complex. Jay's eldest sister, Dimes, the 'mother' of the family, the one who thinks of everything, organises everything, recites the appropriate prayers, the one who always has a small dish ready in the freezer for an unexpected visit, is very familiar with this ritual. Although Dimes may be serious, she exhibits a great openness of spirit and is prepared to try everything. She would never divorce, though. That is not done in her culture. Marriage is sacred. And today she conveys this fundamental value as she guides us through the ceremony together with the Indian priest.

Once the religious ceremony is complete, it is time to celebrate. The Indian musicians put away their sitars and tablas to make way for the African Jazz Pioneers, the group that got Jay and me dancing the evening we first met.

And does the party start! Six hundred people sing and dance the toyi-toyi as they come, in turns, to congratulate us.

Around nine in the evening, I have had enough. I sit with Léandre asleep in my arms. I only have one wish – to leave. But Jay protests that it's much too early and that people will think it rude, especially since they've travelled all this way to see us. But I still want to curl up at home with Léandre and listen to *Cinquième Saison* by Harmonium (a French Canadian music group) with a nice beer. Too much has happened in the last forty-eight hours. I'm exhausted. And then, like my father, I don't like crowds.

Louise, Léandre and his father leave. Jay and I stay a while longer. Then I insist: I am physically and mentally exhausted. Eventually, we also leave the festivities, even though Jay would like to spend the night celebrating. If I had been in the company of six hundred friends, people I had grown up with, studied with, made love with, cried and risked my life with, I would no doubt have wanted to stay. But that was not the case.

In the car on the way home, suddenly realising that we haven't signed anything, I ask Jay if we are properly married. Jay hesitates and then replies that no, we are not. What?! This entire circus for nothing? We aren't married?

'It wasn't a waste,' says Jay. 'It was for our pleasure.' That's all very well, but six hundred people got together and the marriage was not valid?

I learn that neither of the two religious ceremonies make our union official in the eyes of the law. Despite hundreds of thousands of believers in this country, the Hindu religion isn't recognised by the South African state. As for Father Lafont, his permit only allows him to marry people in black areas, in Soweto. And we are officially in the 'white' city of Johannesburg.

❊ ❊ ❊

All night long Jay has visions of his mother and even talks out loud to her, as if they are having a conversation. It feels as though his mother is talking to me through him. He has never recovered from her death. When she passed away, he was on a business trip in Europe. They brought the news to him during one of his speeches. He jumped onto the next plane. The family was going to wait for him for the funeral, which usually takes place within twenty-four hours of the death. But there was a misunderstanding. When Jay arrived at the airport, his sister Dimes was weeping bitterly, not only for the death of their mother, but because Jay had missed the funeral, which had taken place without him. He was utterly crushed by this. To this day he still regrets not being able to be there. And he would have liked his mother, more than anyone in the world, to have been with us at the celebration.

Bakkium Chetty, Jay's mother, was born on 11 December 1913 in Newcastle, the daughter of an Indian merchant. Both her parents were born in South Africa. Only Jay's great-grandmother was born in India. She was a courageous woman who travelled halfway around the world looking for a better life. She came from the state of Tamil-Nadu and left India for Africa with her daughter in 1865. Jay would often speak of his great-grandmother's immense courage in his political speeches, trying to incite people to action.

Jay's relationship with his father was more complex. When Jay was born, his father, born in 1898, was fifty-seven years old, a compulsive gambler. He lost all the family's money at the races, including the inheritance from Jay's maternal grandfather, and the savings intended for the education of the seven children. Only Pat, the eldest, realised his dream of becoming a doctor. Things were also spoilt by the introduction of apartheid. Jay's father died when Jay was seventeen. Jay didn't make peace with him. 'He took me into his arms only once,' he told me, 'when I burnt my leg at the age of five or six.' But a few years after we were married, Jay went to Dundee, his father's birthplace, to meet people in the village who still remembered him. He made peace with his father, at last.

His mother remained by far the most significant, the most influential person in his life. She gave birth to Jay, at home, at the age of forty-two. She breastfed him for four years and adored him for thirty-five. Jay was thirty-six years old when I met him …

I held him in my arms all night long while he held back his sobs. He did not cry. He smothered his emotions. Jay still has not worked through his mother's death.

15

Group honeymoon

Omar has lent us a mini-bus for our honeymoon … which seats five: Jay, myself, my mother, Léandre and … his father!

The presence of Léandre's father puts me on tenterhooks. We have to avoid scenes, discussions and tears in front of Léandre. Easy to say …

My former life, the life I have left behind, catches hold of me, ensnares me once more. Walking on eggshells all day long, I no longer know where to draw the line between common politeness, necessary in the circumstances, and giving in to another's moods.

I have always been afraid of my ex, a fear similar to that which I felt as a small child when my father raised his voice. Now I say 'yes' to another man in my ex's presence, consumed by guilt. I feel cold towards my new husband, unsettled by the presence of the old one. I wait for Léandre to fall asleep before crying my eyes out. I have to spend three unbearable weeks raging internally, without the power to change anything about a situation that seems completely absurd whenever I introduce 'my family' as though this set-up is normal for us.

Our honeymoon becomes a laughing matter. Somehow the story reaches the ears of the press. In the second week of January 1992, the *Weekly Mail's* Krisjan Lemmer, a columnist with a dark sense of humour, includes the following snippet in his weekly gossip column: 'Many stones have been thrown at Cosatu's Jay Naidoo recently, but if any man has set an example of reconciliation to the rest of the country, it is certainly him. Following his recent wedding in Houghton, the honeymoon party set off – Naidoo, his bride, the bride's mother and the bride's ex-husband.' He forgot 'and the bride's son'.

Finally the day arrives. Léandre and I are driving his dad to the airport, where he'll leave for Quebec. Léandre is upset. I can still feel his arms around my neck when I left Quebec. It haunts me. I am afraid of a similar scene, this time with his father. But everything goes smoothly. Léandre sheds a few tears, and so does his father. They remain calm. The scenario has been planned and discussed for a long time.

I feel awkward with Léandre. It is the first time we have been alone together since he arrived in South Africa. After six months' separation, I find him at once changed and the same. How should I comfort him? I know that his father's departure is painful for him. I feel his grief, but I don't know how to comfort him, cheer him.

We get into the car. Mechanically, I hand my parking ticket to the attendant. Léandre is sitting beside me – I make an exception today, because usually I put children in the back seat. There's such a heavy silence in the car that the ring of the cash register outside resonates inside the car. I caress Léandre with my left hand between gear changes, searching for words. And then, all of a sudden, I jump! Léandre is banging on the window, beating hard with his fists. He's shouting and screaming as he hits the glass, 'Why did you come to Africa? Why did you come to Africa, Mama?'

He shouts through his sobs. My heart sinks. I feel his despair as though he's just transmitted a hundred thousand volts! Then guilt overwhelms me. It will remain, like an indelible tattoo, on my heart for years to come. Perhaps for my entire life. Who knows?

I try to comfort him. 'You will talk to him every week. We will write to him, send him drawings, write him stories, make him presents. We will do lots of nice things.'

But he continues to hit the glass. Bang! Bang! Bang! 'Why, Mama?'

'I know it's hard. I understand.' Seeing him like this is torture. 'I love you, Léandre. I'm sorry, Léandre. But you'll see, our life together will be rich. And we will keep your father close to our hearts every day. I love you, Léandre.'

Bang! Bang! Bang! I can feel the knocking in my head. I feel sick, I want to throw up. Making a child suffer like this! *Bang! Bang! Bang!*

✣ ✣ ✣

At home that evening, Jay and I celebrate our real honeymoon, alone with Léandre. Louise has also left. We spend a long time in one another's arms, on the couch, chatting, laughing and showing our love for one another. We swim, even though the water is cold. We snuggle up in Léandre's bed for a few minutes, time for a short story, for kisses and hugs. *Bang! Bang! Bang!* I am still suffering. It was Léandre's fist beating against the window that ushered us into our new life. *Bang! Bang! Bang!* Léandre has woken me up. I have to give meaning to my life again.

16

The colour of learning

Our family life is taking form, marked by daily rituals: bathing Léandre and preparing meals because there is a child in the house. We have to settle down to a routine because children feel better when they have a frame of reference and set limits. This return to 'normal' does me enormous good. I don't skip meals any more. I cook with inspiration and I try new recipes, combining ingredients and styles of cooking from all over. I was cooking Indian food long before I met Jay. In India, in Nepal and elsewhere in Asia, I was seduced by the spices, especially chilli. Apparently chilli is addictive. If Jay goes four or five days without it, he'll empty the kitchen cupboard for anything with a bite, pouncing on anything that will burn his tongue. The spices are divine. They lift the spirits. Like the colours of autumn ...

I haven't seen autumn this year. I miss it terribly. A few years later, when I get into the habit of going back to Quebec every summer, Marie-France Bazzo, a radio presenter on Radio–Canada, invites me onto her show, *Indicatif présent*. During the interview, she asks me what I miss most about Quebec. Without hesitating, I reply 'The smell of Quebec, especially the fragrances of autumn'.

She looks at me as if I am completely crazy! I think she expects something more profound, intellectual, philosophical. Nevertheless, after eight years in South Africa, it's really the odour of damp wood, freshly covered with leaves, that I miss. And the colours. They transport me. I adore walking in the forest, hearing the crunch of leaves, breathing the fresh, healthy air. When I fill my lungs with the freshness of the late autumn, my sweetest memories come back to me. I smile at life. Breathing like this refocuses me.

I find that autumn is the right season for reflection. It allows me to work through the year's projects, to give my dreams some shape, to put aside my utopian ideas, to analyse the risks involved in the projects that I intend to take on during the year and the obstacles I will have to face.

❧ ❧ ❧

Léandre doesn't speak a word of English and Jay not a word of French. Through me, Jay announces that he and Léandre are each going to teach the other their language. It's a deal! The two get on marvellously. When they met for the first time, a year ago in Quebec, Léandre spontaneously jumped into Jay's arms. Taken aback at first, Jay quickly returned the embrace with equal fervour. Jay had never had a child, but he adored them. He brought Léandre up like his own son. For years afterwards, even as an adolescent, Léandre would spend hours sitting on Jay's knees talking about everything, from Julius Caesar to the latest *Star Wars*, from telecommunications in Africa to Pokémons. They played and laughed a lot together.

Jay had never had to deal with the numerous daily tasks involved in bringing up a child. At Colette's he had played with her son Duncan, but never went as far as giving him a bath, seeing that he brushed his teeth or preparing meals for him. Adapting to this reality with Léandre would require a certain amount of time from him. He would discover that the presence of a child sets the tone for a household.

Our outings are transformed. Nowadays, we go to the zoo or to the park, because Léandre is here. A child allows us to discover a world we might otherwise neglect.

Before his arrival, I had booked a place for Léandre at Smarties Nursery School, right next to our home in Bez Valley. I had sent him some photos of the area, the playground, the games and the children. Even though he could have stayed at home with me all day, I thought it preferable for him to have a social life, to familiarise himself with the country, with children his own age.

On the first morning at the nursery school there is drama, and the same scene recurs every morning for two long months. Léandre doesn't want to go there. He clings to my neck …

Bang! Bang! Bang! Why did you come to Africa, Mama?

Every morning this phrase echoes in my head. Léandre spends his days in the office of the nursery school with 'teacher', instead of playing outside with the others. He draws, plays with the paperclips, throws rubbish into the bin. In the afternoon, when I come to fetch him, the contrast between the two cultures is striking. Léandre is immaculate; his friends from the Rainbow Nation have dirty legs and muddy T-shirts – red with Johannesburg soil.

Léandre still speaks no English, let alone Zulu or Xhosa. The teacher is very patient with him, because she's sensitive to his situation. She often reassures me, 'Don't worry. It will come. We mustn't push. We must let it happen on its own.'

Despite Léandre and Jay's monolingualism, there is still a lot of communication between them at home. When he wants to ask Jay a question (for example, 'Do you want to play Lego with me?'), he asks me how to say it. I translate the phrase for him and he repeats each word after me, looking Jay right in the eyes. 'Do – you – want – to – play – Lego – with – me?' He never asks me to speak directly to Jay on his behalf. He wants to learn how to formulate his requests by himself. This requires patience, but it's stimulating. We know that, sooner or later, he will know how to express himself with ease.

One day, entering the nursery school office, I notice that Léandre doesn't have red eyes. Instead, he is red from head to toe! He has been playing outside! The principal smiles, 'He played with his friends today. And he spoke his first words of English!' Léandre is in a good mood. 'I played on the swing. Come and see!' I go out into the yard with him. He jumps onto the ladder and then runs to the slide. He shows me the sandbox filled with red sand where he has built sandcastles.

When Jay gets home that evening, Léandre speaks to him in English.

'Do you want to play with me?' he asks.

'Do I want to play with you? Of course I want to play with you! How was your day at school?'

'Fine! I swing.'

From that moment onward, like a flash of lightning in a blue sky, Léandre starts to speak English. Two months after his arrival in South Africa, the words tumble out of him; during this short period of time he has absorbed everything in silence. He no longer needs me to communicate with Jay. He speaks well enough to converse and to develop his day-to-day vocabulary gradually.

From the moment that Léandre was able to communicate in English, he was always eager to go to nursery school. This is one of the riches he gained from his African experience: Léandre speaks a perfect English, tinged with a South African Durban-Indian accent!

And Jay? He learnt two words of French, which he repeats to each of us every day: *je t'aime* (I love you).

17

Seventy-second minutes

On the work front, everything happens at once. Ariane Bonzon, the Radio–Canada correspondent, has left the country and I officially take over as from January 1992; the daily newspaper *La Presse* regularly buys articles from me; I start working on the synopsis for the rape documentary again – it's been sitting on the corner of my desk, haunting me. My days are full!

On the way to the nursery school, I stop to buy the three newspapers that I read almost daily: the *Star*, the *Business Day* and the *Sowetan*. Every Friday morning I also buy a copy of the *Weekly Mail*, which I *devour*. It is a newspaper that 'dares', that risks censure by publishing articles that denounce government laws and that give anti-apartheid movements the right to speak. Later renamed the *Mail & Guardian*, this weekly continues to take issue with the government ... the new ANC government.

Almost all the media are in white hands and practise conservative journalism. The press agencies are controlled. The president has a direct line to the newsroom. Television is completely controlled by the government. The SABC is not a public broadcaster, but a state broadcaster. There is a difference. It has two channels – one for whites, one for blacks. On the 'white' channel, which I watch not because I am white, but because I do not understand the African languages, the news appears alternately in English and in Afrikaans, one night in English, the next in Afrikaans. On the seventh day, the Lord's Day, Afrikaans prevails. This is more than a symbol.

Historically, the majority of Afrikaners have always considered themselves a people chosen by God to dominate the 'inferior' races. Everything is dictated to them by God and the Bible, which they naturally interpret in accordance with their interests. You cannot understand apartheid without taking this religious dimension into account. It is their faith and their destiny that led the Afrikaners to develop a political system that would have been unimaginable anywhere else in the world.

Television only came to South Africa in 1976. Very Calvinistic, white society saw this as a medium inspired by Satan and delayed its implementation as long as possible. Jay was twenty-two years old when television became a part of his life!

Apart from the SABC there is only one other television channel in South Africa: M–Net. This channel is not allowed to broadcast news; it only offers films and sport.

When I send my CV to M–Net, I am called in for an interview. 'Are you bilingual?' I am asked. 'Yes, I'm actually trilingual. I speak French, English and Spanish.' The man looks at me, stupefied. By 'bilingual' he means 'Do you know English and Afrikaans?'. 'And I have taken Zulu lessons,' I add naively. Big mistake. He replies dryly that I should come back and see him when I can speak Afrikaans. 'You have no future without this language,' he concludes. It is actually Zulu that I find more interesting. I think this is natural, because it is the most widely spoken language in South Africa, with eight million Zulus in the country. And once you have learned Zulu, Xhosa comes fairly easily, just as Spanish comes easily for someone who speaks French.

It took me four months to learn how to pronounce the clicks of the Zulu language. To pronounce the c sound you click your tongue against the back of your front teeth, as if you're scolding a naughty child. To pronounce the q sound you click your tongue right in the centre of the palate, as if you're imitating the cork of a champagne bottle popping. The x, as in 'Xhosa', is the most difficult click to pronounce. You have to click both sides of the tongue between the teeth. This is easier to do if you smile a little. It's like the sound you make when you give a horse the command to move forward. The letter itself is relatively easy to pronounce; the difficult part is incorporating the click into the word without separating the sounds. In four months I learned to say the essentials, like 'Hello', 'How are you', 'Thank you', 'Sit down', 'Go to sleep', 'I am not working'. That's all. To make more progress I would have needed a more methodical approach, a teacher who could explain the grammar to me, and perseverance, of course. But the few words and phrases that I do know make life a lot easier work-wise. The welcome is always warmer.

I also listen to the radio a great deal, moving rapidly between two stations: the SABC or government radio station and '702', a private radio station devoted almost entirely to phone-in programmes. Obviously a large proportion of the calls come from whites, since they have telephones. But over the years, particularly after 1994, the audience becomes more and more black. All subjects, especially political subjects, are discussed. Racism, sexism and violence are the 'hot topics', as are rape and paedophilia. The radio station causes an uproar when one of its presenters spends three hours discussing the latter subject. A paedophile calls in – remaining anonymous, of course. The presenter keeps him on the line and carries out an excellent off-the-cuff interview that reveals a great deal about the mind of this type of person. Extracts from the interview are broadcast over and over again. This story leads to discussions about journalists and the role of the media in society. Should they reveal their sources, pass information on to the police when this could lead to arrests or convictions? For example, should they supply the telephone number of the paedophile who has admitted to his crimes over the air? Large numbers of journalists have been prosecuted and imprisoned for their little notebooks. Some have even been tortured. Radio 702 has never been afraid to bring up this type of debate, which is still unusual in South Africa at this time.

I work hard, learning the ropes, during my first few months as the correspondent for Radio–Canada. When the technician at the other end of the phone tells me to start recording, I panic every time. As usual I feel awkward, because I don't quite know my way about the job yet.

When you work in radio, you have to create pictures with sound. During my three years in Bez Valley, whenever I wanted to send an excerpt from an interview, the sound of a frenzied crowd, anything, I would pull the telephone plug out of the wall, find the two little screws and connect them to my cassette recorder with 'crocodile clips'. Jean-François Lépine taught me this trick while he was a Radio–Canada correspondent in China.

My immediate boss is Gilles Le Bigot, the international news assigner in Radio–Canada's newsroom in Montreal. Quite a person! He is the brother of Joël Le Bigot, the well-known radio presenter. Gilles is never content to view reality in terms of the journalistic cliché – a coin with two sides. Rather, he sees it as a prism, which offers a variety of colours and perspectives depending on the viewpoint – black, white, grey … 'But have you seen the pale pink tinged with orangey-green down there? It would perhaps be interesting to consider this new angle, but be careful not to confuse the listener, Lucie.' The listener only hears what you say once. Radio doesn't allow the listener to go back as the newspaper does. The information has to be clear from the outset. This is not easy, especially when you have to present a new participant in current affairs in order to describe events happening far away. If, for example, the Pan Africanist Congress sets off a bomb, how do you explain, in a few seconds, the party, its policy and place in the political arena, the attack and its consequences? You have to be able to provide this information in seventy seconds. This is the challenge you face as a foreign news correspondent … I love it!

Gilles talks a lot, but he always has something valuable to add. Except when everything is clear, but then nothing is ever perfectly clear. Gilles can get to the heart of a matter and ask all the relevant questions in one minute, using only a few phrases. As I gain experience and knowledge, our discussions become richer and richer. I suggest a new angle and immediately he asks the right question. Gilles is my ally as a colleague and will remain a friend for life. We work together as a team. Gilles is also a language expert who tirelessly corrects the errors of his French correspondents, without ridicule and without any pretension.

When you only have seventy seconds to tell a story, each word is loaded with meaning. This is the challenge of preparing radio pieces, the challenge that excites me, under the pressure of time limits, or the famous deadline. Watching the minutes tick by when you have to produce something creates enormous stress, but it's also an adrenalin rush.

From time to time Gilles announces a news story that he's picked up before me from a press release. 'Oh, really? I didn't listen to the last news bulletin.' It becomes an obsession to listen to all news bulletins. Every hour, from the time I get up until the time I go to bed, I have to listen to the news. In case Gilles phones me.

The equipment I have for producing news is a joke. I only have my radio-cassette player, always ready to record, my newspapers, my telephone and my old computer. No Internet, not in 1992. No money. No printer. No cellular phone.

Radio–Canada paid me eighty dollars per report. I stayed on the same fee for eight years … In the end it cost me money to work. I spent a fortune on newspapers and magazines, parking, fuel, office equipment and air tickets for flights between Johannesburg and Cape Town. If Radio–Canada had at least reimbursed me for the price of a subscription to a daily newspaper or a press agency …

But what was the alternative – to say no? To say no and risk my position as a freelancer? To say no when this was exactly what I wanted to do with my life? I said no once. Only once in eight years. 'It will have to wait. It has just been announced that a bomb has exploded and, according to the radio report, it's next to the French School that my children attend. I want to go and check that they are still alive. I will call you afterwards.' The person on the other end of the line seemed a little taken aback. 'Yes, yes, go and see. Don't worry about the report.' My children were safe and sound. I did the report that evening, after the little ones were in bed.

I paid to realise a dream. My work gave me immense pleasure, which I still savour today, but I was exploited. I knew that. Gilles knew it. Everyone at Radio–Canada knew it. The worst was that some people thought that Radio–Canada correspondents abroad got rich!

Nonetheless, corresponding for my country allowed me to stay in touch with my language and my culture. Radio–Canada was my umbilical cord. The public broadcaster had definitely replaced the Prozac!

18

One hundred and eighty beddy-byes ... and then?

The problem of Léandre's custody was getting complicated. His father and I had agreed that for the first two years we would alternate every six months. One hundred and eighty beddy-byes each. After that we would evaluate the situation. But after just three months, the communication between Bez Valley and the suburb of Rosemont in Montreal starts to sour. Our 'divorce' – even though we were never married – has not been settled. I become aware of this as we exchange letters. And it's still the era of snail mail! Email has not yet made its spectacular breakthrough. It can therefore take a month to get an answer to one question. This is hard on the nerves.

'Three people's lives have been turned upside down and spoilt because of a decision made by one of them,' Léandre's father writes. 'We are all suffering because of your move.'

'You understand the word suffering in terms of distance. One can be two millimetres away from someone and still suffer,' I retort.

Our letters are harsh. Pages and pages of acrimony and despair on both sides. 'Didn't we talk about working abroad for a year or two when we were together? Must divorce imply the death of all our dreams as well?'

Soon my ex is openly questioning our agreement. I put myself in his shoes. What would I have done if he had left for the other side of the planet with my son? In my letters I try very hard to convince him that

I am the best mother in the world, that even if I move to the moon this will not remove my right or my duty to have my son with me. I'm also trying to convince myself of this fact as I write.

Bang! Bang! Bang! Why did you come to Africa, Mama?

As I have promised Léandre, I keep his father's presence alive in the house. Léandre hangs his photo on the wall and makes drawings for him that we go to post together. We also buy his birthday present together. Respect for my son's relationship with his father is sacred for me. Léandre adores his Papa. It makes him happy to love his father. If I do not give him the freedom to express this love, it will backfire on me.

But what is the solution when both parents want to have him for the school year and only let him go for the Christmas and summer holidays? 'There is no question of me having him only at Christmas and for the summer!' his father yelled at me over the phone. For my part, I am determined to give my son what I have to give him while he is still very young. There is no question of my not finding him at my side in the morning. I know he needs me. I can feel it in his hugs, in his drawings, in his tender words at night before he goes to sleep, with his arms around my neck. A child needs his mother. And a mother does not sleep well if she is not giving what she has to give to her child. If she does not, it gets stuck and accumulates. It forms tumours in the subconscious. It has to get out, just as milk, in swollen breasts, must be drunk.

I know. It is my fault. I am the one who has come to the other side of the world. Who will give in? Will we need lawyers and judges? Will we be the actors in those awful stories of custody battles? I try to persuade myself that common sense will prevail, that the father of my son believes me when I tell him I have no desire to destroy his relationship with his son. But I know that our initial pact is over. Someone will have to give in.

19

Parched

I am looking for a hundred thousand rand, the sum I need to make my documentary on rape. I have to stop expecting things to land in my lap. The producer, Jeremy Nathan of VNS, helps me to work out a budget. In TV I have always worked with large organisations in which I never had to worry about the pennies. With Jeremy, I learn to calculate everything that has to appear in the budget for the production of a video.

I have sent my synopsis on rape to dozens of governmental and non-governmental organisations, embassies, movements, trade unions. Despite all my efforts over six months, I still haven't found a penny.

Everything changes at a dinner at the Canadian Embassy. There I meet Jerry Kramer, in charge of special projects at the embassy. I talk to him about my idea. He's really taken with it. And he holds the strings of an important purse – that of CIDA (Canadian International Development Agency). He asks to see my synopsis. When I see him again a few days later, he only needs two minutes to look through it. 'I will give you fifty thousand rand for this project,' he says to me, lifting his eyes from the document. I can't believe it! That's half the budget!

CIDA's participation changes everything. It gives my initiative credibility. Soon after, KAGISO Trust, a group of non-governmental organisations, also gives me fifty thousand rand. I can start my documentary at last.

My quest begins in the townships. I am looking for women who have been raped and who are prepared to talk about it openly on screen. Because the main message I want to get across is, 'Talk about it'. I need black women because ninety-five per cent of rape victims in this country are black. Almost every day, I go to Soweto, to Alexandra, or to Orange Farm, an informal settlement on the outskirts of Johannesburg.

My search lasts three months. In the meantime I rummage through the archives of the *Star* newspaper and the public library in central Johannesburg. Less than a year ago this library was reserved for whites. Since the abolition of the Public Amenities Act, which controlled access to public places, the library has started to charge an entrance fee. Very few blacks can afford this. Economic apartheid is far more subtle, but just as effective.

Time passes. I have the money, I have recruited the production team, but I'm still missing the essential ingredient: two female rape survivors. And yet there is no shortage of these women in the country.

I place an advertisement in the newspaper: LOOKING FOR WOMEN PREPARED TO TALK ABOUT THEIR EXPERIENCE OF RAPE IN FRONT OF THE CAMERA FOR A DOCUMEN-TARY ON THE SUBJECT. CALL THE FOLLOWING NUMBER AND ASK TO SPEAK TO 'MARIE'.

The morning after the advert appears, the phone rings. It's a man's voice.

'Is this Marie?'

I have used the name Marie (my second name) to avoid problems and to be able to identify the object of the call immediately. It is a 'white' name and I also have a white accent.

'Yes, this is Marie.'

'What gives you the right to make a video about what you call rape? Why are you interfering? You whites, you don't know what you are talking about! You call it rape, but it's actually a favour to women!'

I can't believe my ears. He hangs up on me.

'Marie? Are you Marie? I am going to find you. I am going to rape you and I am going to kill you. Believe me! You have just declared war on men!'

I replace the receiver, shaken. But ten thousand times more deter-mined! Kill me because I am making a film on one of the worst problems faced by women in South Africa? This call strengthens my resolve. That's exactly what I need to keep going, a death threat!

For a few weeks I receive only threatening and insulting calls. These calls encourage me to break the wall of silence that protects this devastating 'custom', as these men call it. Custom! Because it's the custom to rape a woman, to exploit her, one has to accept it? When I express my indignation, I am accused of lacking respect for African customs. I am accused of being racist.

Time passes and I begin to despair. In a country where a rape occurs every eighty-three seconds, I am not able to find two victims who want to talk about it.

Three months or ninety-five thousand rapes later, Mary Mabaso calls me. I had put a poster up on her noticeboard during one of my visits to Soweto. She heads a religious organisation that teaches women sewing and various artistic techniques. She tells me that she thinks she's found someone, a young girl of sixteen, the victim of a gang rape. A quarter of all rapes in South Africa are gang rapes.

I go to see Mary in Soweto. I borrow a wreck of a car that will hardly stand up to a rape, let alone a bullet, even with the doors locked. I head for a far corner of the township. As usual, I lose my way, which is dangerous in Soweto. There is no question of stopping on the side of the road to consult a map of the town. Definitely not a good idea. A white woman lost in the streets of Soweto will inevitably attract trouble. If she is raped, the judge will conclude she has provoked it! It's difficult to find your way when there are no street names in a 'town' of several million inhabitants, as my directions testify: 'Turn left at the wreck of the double-decker bus, turn right at the brown building with the missing windows, continue straight past the place where a dozen people were killed last week. You will see the blood stains.'

I discover Soweto through its major landmarks: the squatter camps, the churches, the wrecks and the police stations. I am in a state, sweating from the fear and the heat. The sun is beating down on the dusty roads without trees and I have to keep the car windows closed. I discover Soweto nervously, but curiously.

Soweto is a large, multifaceted town of several million inhabitants – no one knows the exact number – a patchwork made up of relatively habitable sections, where the black middle-class lives, and of shanty towns, or squatter camps. There one finds people who smile easily, solidly attached to life, but also savage bands ready to kill for a motor car or less. Mountains of waste litter the streets, which are filled with smoke from the charcoal burning for cooking and heating. Four out of five houses in Soweto do not have electricity. An enormous city, plunged into darkness when evening falls, is something you would never see in white areas. Many of Soweto's inhabitants do not have running water either.

The toilets will remain engraved on my memory. One day, in a squatter camp, I really needed to go to the toilet. Nine children were living under one corrugated iron roof. Where did they relieve themselves? In the veld. If you were prepared to walk for ten minutes there were also disease-infected pit toilets. I chose the walk. With both feet in the piss and the shit, I urinated with my eyes closed, splashing myself up to the elbows. I felt like vomiting.

I eventually arrive at Mary Mabaso's sweating, with a burning thirst. I had forgotten my bottle of water.

Mary informs me that the name of the teenager who has been raped by a group of young men is Christina. The incident occurred about a year ago and she is still traumatised, as is her mother. I can also meet the mother now, if I wish, says Mary. She works as a cleaner in a community centre in Soweto. I agree, but before leaving I would like to quench my thirst.

'May I have some water?'

'There is no water. The water was cut off in this suburb today.'

'A Coke? Some juice? Anything.'

Nothing. There is nothing to drink. My thirst begins to distract me. In fact, I cannot remember ever being this thirsty. My throat is dry, my mouth furry.

On our way to Christina's mother, we stop at a centre for abandoned children that is about to be opened. The press is there. Also a crowd of dignitaries, among them Walter and Albertina Sisulu.

The two of them recognise me. Albertina takes me in her arms. The words she uttered at my wedding come back to me often, 'Jay is already married. You are his second wife.' I didn't appreciate it at the time, but I am becoming more and more aware of how right she is!

My thirst is tearing at my throat. Hugging me, Albertina seems to draw the last drops of water from my body. She hugs me warmly like a big African mama, squeezing hard. But all I can think of is my thirst. Here too, the water has been cut off. Probably because the people have not paid their bills, a form of protest organised by the civic organisations. The thirst for liberty takes its toll in physical thirst.

I hug Walter, who asks about the family, about Jay and about Léandre. He takes my hands and looks me in the eye, 'Come and have tea with me when you can.'

One hour later, Mary and I head for another suburb to go and see Christina's mother and obtain her permission for her daughter to participate in my documentary. There's water running here! I ask for a glass of water. The head of the centre sends an employee to fetch some water for all of us. I see her clean the glasses one by one, without hurrying. I see the tap running. I have a mad desire to go and douse my head, my tongue, my palate and my neck under the tap. Water suddenly appears very precious to me. I imagine the millions of women in the rural areas who do not have access to water and have to walk for hours and hours to fetch a bucket of water. In hot, dry areas. In areas where thirst is a daily preoccupation. Cleanliness obviously becomes of secondary importance. Or even unimportant. If these mothers had access to clean water, it would be possible to save the lives of eighty of the one hundred children who die of diarrhoea each day in South Africa. Water – the source of life. The source of death as well. I don't ever want to be as thirsty as I was that day. It makes you ill! It darkens your spirits. Nothing is clear any more. Nothing matters any more.

In South Africa ninety-nine per cent of whites have access to potable water in their homes, compared to thirteen per cent of blacks.

The employee arrives with the water, a jug and three empty glasses, turned upside down, spotless, without a trace of dirt, on a silver-plated tray. She approaches slowly and I have to keep from pouncing on her. She puts down the tray. I watch her pour water into one of the glasses. I want to swallow the whole jug. She takes the glass full of fresh water and hands it to me. I drain it in one gulp. Empty. But I've hardly slaked my thirst. I can no longer be polite. I get up, take the jug, fill my glass and again empty it in one gulp. I repeat this procedure once more. When the third glass is empty, I breathe deeply. I feel better. My body is still thirsty, but my throat is no longer burning. Then I notice that Mary and Christina's mother are staring at me, their eyes as big as saucers. I pretend it's nothing, sit down and resume the role of journalist. Parched, at last, for information …

20

Christina and Rose

Christina, a poor but model pupil, had been raped on her way to church one evening. She was the 'perfect' victim for a documentary. On the way to church, eight young men pursued her and then took turns to rape her, holding a knife to her throat.

I explain to her mother why it is important for Christina to tell her story in front of the camera. Journalists have always used the 'public interest' argument to persuade people to talk. We always put ourselves in a slightly ambiguous position, because even though these testimonies often do serve the collective interest, they also serve the professional interests of the journalist, always on the lookout for sensational information. But this time I am convinced that a documentary will be useful and will help to prevent rape, perhaps to save lives, to give women power and a voice. I beg Mary to convey my request correctly. I have spent months searching for a Christina.

Her mother seems a bit confused to me. I think she sees me as a lifeline. A year down the line nothing has yet been done to find the guilty parties. She thinks I can help her with the investigation. This is not my objective. But I offer – promise, in fact – to look after Christina. I always keep my promises. After filming a re-enactment of a visit to the doctor, for example, Christina goes for a real examination. They discover that she has been suffering from a vaginal infection for a year since the rape. The damage is extensive. I pay for the medication to treat the infections. I take chicken, bread and litres of fizzy drinks every time I visit her in the miserable shack without water, electricity or a toilet.

In the developing world people sometimes expect to receive a lot of money when they see a television crew arriving. I explain to Christina's mother that I do not have a film budget. The food and my sincerity will have to suffice.

I would like to find another victim. I need at least two to support the purpose of the documentary.

Some weeks later, a friend of a friend calls me. Her name is Rose and she has been raped, although she has never spoken about it. This type of secret kills you slowly. Now she wants to break the silence. Her silence. She tells me about the circumstances of the attack.

Rose was at home one Sunday afternoon. Someone rang the doorbell. It was an old friend, so she invited him in and offered him a cup of tea. After only a few minutes, he threw himself on her. Certainly not from sexual desire, she said, because he had difficulty achieving an erection. The rape was first and foremost a manifestation of power.

Rose never reported the crime. Who would believe her, anyway? And in South Africa who cares if a black woman is raped?

It's another story if the victim is white and the aggressor black. This happened in Yeoville, a Johannesburg suburb just next to Bez Valley, which is alive until late at night and where a woman is never really safe. The day after the rape, an identikit of the man was displayed everywhere, on the front page of the newspapers and on the TV news. When black women are attacked, nothing is done. Being born female *and* black in South Africa is to be born the lowest of the low.

An ANC leader shocked me one day. After receiving a call in front of me, he put down the receiver slowly, looked at me and said,

'My wife has had a baby. It's terrible!'

'What's terrible? Is the baby dead?'

'No, no, it's a girl.'

The struggle of women in South Africa has been eclipsed by the other, more important, more 'noble', more 'worthy' struggle, that against apartheid. Now that the wall of apartheid is crumbling, we're discovering how much women suffer. In South Africa you read the worst kind of suffering on the faces of women.

21

Every eighty-three seconds ...

Ready? Set? Action!

It's evening in the streets of Soweto. We're re-enacting the rape scene with Christina. It's a big shoot and we've spent four hours preparing, mostly to get the lighting right. We light a fire in a big blue rubbish bin and we shoot Christina attempting to flee her attackers, all armed with knives. Christina played by Christina. This is how the film will start.

The shoot will last two weeks. While I work, I search for a good title. A title that will shock, something short, that says everything. Brian Tilley, my cameraman, finds one. As luck would have it, he works at VNS and is Colette's brother. 'But the title is right under your nose! There's a rape every eighty-three seconds. That's your title: Every eighty-three seconds ...'

After the shoot I shut myself up for two weeks with the videotape and my papers in the cold, humid office that I've set up at home. Jeremy Nathan has installed an editing suite in it. This equipment allows me to cut the documentary and assemble it temporarily on another tape, in preparation for the final edit, which will be entrusted to Shelley Wells, an excellent editor (I insisted that a woman do the job). We spend an intense week working together.

Then we have to prepare for the launch of the documentary. I have to give a speech in front of three hundred and fifty people. I don't sleep. For a whole week I write, rewrite, correct, improve and refine my speech. One of my weaknesses is shyness. At school, if I had to give an oral presentation, I'd have diarrhoea for days. And now I have to get up on a stage in front of hundreds of people to present my film. I'm terrified.

The room at the Market Theatre is full. It's been offered to us free of charge, in support of women's rights. Jay is there and the crowd is pressing around him. Since I never talk about our relationship in the context of my work, this evening we're not introduced as 'Jay Naidoo and his wife', but as 'Lucie Pagé and her husband'. A woman we were introduced to in this way later addressed Jay as 'Mr Pagé'!

There's nothing on the stage. Not even a lectern. I feel completely naked. I didn't know what it was like to have three hundred and fifty pairs of eyes on you! Very nervous at first, I gain confidence as I read my two sheets of paper, the words I've reflected on for so long. At the end of the screening, people are applauding on their feet. And then they present me with an enormous bouquet of flowers. Just like in the movies!

The videotape is very much in demand. Organisations, schools, women's centres, trade unions and even the police use it. The film is broadcast a few times on the SABC – on the 'black' channel. All the profits go to women's centres.

A year later, a group of women from Johannesburg organised a march in the city. Every eighty-three seconds thousands of women blew their whistles at the same time. I took part in the march, but no one knew who I was …

Oddly enough, after my documentary four of the eight young men who had raped Christina were arrested. But a few days before their court appearance all charges were dropped. The files had been 'lost' – in other words someone had been bought off.

Christina and her mother called me. They begged me to help them. But what more could I do?

I do not know what has become of Christina.

22

The blue square

I'm unsure about something and I want to check it out. In April 1992, during the edit of the documentary, I take a pregnancy test. As the small square on the tester turns blue, I turn white. I feel like fainting.

'Lucie, what's the matter?' asks Shelley, the editor. 'You look as though you've seen a ghost!'

'I must go. I have to leave. I'm pregnant. I'm pregnant …'

I grab the car keys and run. It's dark and I'm very nervous about driving in Johannesburg at night. I reverse down the driveway and hit the metal gate at the entrance with full force.

Pregnant? Pregnant! The half-hour journey to Bez Valley seems to take all night. At every red light I take out the little tube with the blue-stained square. Perhaps I saw wrong. No, it's still blue. Pregnant? But I've used a gadget that is highly regarded, a kind of electronic thermometer that indicates a green light for 'no ovulation' or a red one for 'danger of fertilisation'. With all the stupid letters passing between Africa and Canada about Léandre's custody, perhaps my ova have jumped the lights?

Pregnant! I press the remote to open the garage door. I'm still in shock. I climb the steps as I did Mount Gokyo in Nepal, short of oxygen, dazed. I run towards the house. I have to talk to Jay. I need to know his reaction.

I finally get there. It's Léandre's bed-time and Jay is reading him a book, stretched out beside him on the bed. 'Back already?' they say in unison. I told them I'd be working half the night.

I sit down on the bed. I don't know how to announce my news. Jay can see I'm troubled. 'What's the matter? You look pale.'

My throat tight, I finally let it out, softly, 'You are going to be a father at Christmas time.'

Complete silence. Two seconds. Three seconds, then, 'What?' 'You're going to be a father at Christmas time.' He leaps up in one bound, like Tigger in *Winnie-the-Pooh*, and takes me in his arms. He jumps for joy. He laughs. He picks up Léandre, who doesn't really understood what's happening. He tells him he's going to have a brother or a sister. They're overjoyed! Léandre is thrilled. Jay is laughing. We're still laughing at midnight.

✳ ✳ ✳

Jay brings up a sensitive subject, and not for the first time.

Since I'm pregnant and since I'm working full-time, producing my documentary, writing articles and preparing news reports for Radio–Canada, we could hire a domestic worker, he suggests, at least to help me with the cleaning and washing.

Since I work at home, it's natural for me to do more of the household tasks than Jay. In addition, I like tidiness. My home has to be clean and tidy at all times. I like people to feel comfortable there and I don't feel comfortable in a mess. And I've always done 'my' cleaning myself.

'Out of the question,' I retort. 'I can look after my house by myself.'

By myself or with Jay, who always does his share when he's at home. But he was brought up with a domestic worker. This is normal in South Africa. Among whites it's unusual not to see a domestic worker in the kitchen. Among Indians, the second most 'privileged' group, it's also customary to have a domestic worker. Those who don't are accused of depriving the poorest, the most impoverished, of a job.

'I don't want anyone else living in our house!'

'But we could renovate the room above the garage, install running water and electricity. The domestic worker could live there.'

The idea of becoming a white 'Madam' with her black 'servant', even at a good salary, is repulsive to me. My Québecois upbringing undoubtedly has something to do with it. Almost all Québecois who go to live in the South feel reluctant to hire a domestic. They get used to it, of course, as do all those who profit from this 'privilege'. But this practice is foreign to their culture, contrary to the Europeans.

Jay accepts my stubborn refusal. No domestic worker. That's the end of it.

23

The last white vote

The whites are worried. President Frederik de Klerk is worried. It's two years since he freed Nelson Mandela and nobody really knows where the process of transition is leading. The blacks want one thing: one person, one vote. The same demand, repeated constantly. The whites are afraid. They want to retain greater control over their destiny.

De Klerk wants the last word. He announces a referendum in which three-quarters of the population of the country will not be able to participate. Another white vote! The president wants to gauge the opinion of white South Africans on the apartheid reforms he initiated two years earlier. He wants to silence the critics who say that he doesn't have a mandate to change the country from top to bottom. He wants to neutralise the official opposition once and for all: the Conservative Party claims that he no longer represents the majority of whites and accuses him of moving too far, too quickly.

The blacks don't appreciate the referendum at all. The ANC obviously rejects the principle of a racial referendum, but can't encourage a boycott because the question that whites must answer on 17 March 1992 is: 'Do you support the continuation of the reform process, which the State President began on 2 February 1990, which aims to establish a new constitution through negotiation?'

A victory of the YES vote would give the government a green light to negotiate the details of this 'new' South Africa. A NO majority would spell 'suicide for South Africa', De Klerk warns. Mandela and the ANC, their backs against the wall in the face of political realism, have no choice but to accept this referendum.

Bez Valley has taken on a different appearance. Johannesburg has changed. The whole country has changed! You can't find a single telephone pole without a poster for the YES or NO camp. The referendum has propelled the country into transition. From now on the word 'transition' is at the heart of all political thinking. The result of the vote will determine whether the process of transition is irreversible or not. If the answer is YES, the transition will be guided by a new body established a few months ago. Codesa (Convention for a Democratic South Africa), which represents nineteen political parties, has the task of negotiating a new constitution, precisely to ensure that the process is irreversible.

President de Klerk has taken a bold risk, putting not only his head, but the future of his country, on the block. If he wins the YES vote, his mandate will be as clear as ever and Codesa will finally be able to get on with its work. If it's NO, he has promised to resign. 'I will accept your verdict,' he said. This would inevitably mean white general elections, victory for the Conservative Party and most probably … civil war. But one wonders whether without this referendum the risk of chaos wouldn't be greater still.

De Klerk is a clever strategist. The progressive whites who boycotted the elections during the years of apartheid, or those who voted against the National Party in that period, against the party that had installed the apartheid regime that had 'legalised' racism, should, this time, vote *for* him.

De Klerk knows how to ally himself with practically the whole population by holding this referendum to marginalise the extreme right, who constitute the main obstacle to the transition. The vast majority of the population cannot vote in the referendum; the most they can do is participate in the National Party's campaign in favour of a YES vote.

If the Conservative Party wins the referendum and then the elections, they promise to ban all black trade unions. They don't advocate a return to 'grand apartheid', but would maintain the concept at the heart of all their legislation. The army and police would resume a central role. They would create an 'ethnic' committee (they would ask

Nelson Mandela to participate in it as the head of the Xhosa state rather than as the head of the ANC). The country would be divided into ethnic territories and no doubt you'd need some type of 'passport' to enter white territory.

De Klerk plays the game well. He conducts a 'negative' campaign that focuses on the dangers of a NO victory rather than a campaign that focuses on the advantages of a YES win. The National Party plays all its cards: saying no in the referendum, says yes to sanctions and international isolation. This would result in the complete destruction of the economy. It would be to commit an act of extreme violence against the state. Even the sports argument is invoked. Vote no in the referendum, or the country will no longer be able to participate in international sports competitions. This is what worries people, what they talk about in letters from readers in the newspaper, on phone-in shows, in the streets. Not the fate of Codesa, but the fate of sport.

On 17 March 1992 eighty per cent of the white electorate vote. The YES vote wins with sixty-eight comma seven per cent of the vote. The whites have said no to apartheid.

This is the last white vote in the history of the country.

24

Second wedding: Quebec

Today, all I can think about is Quebec. I'll be resuming my old life for two and a half months. I'm hoping that this pilgrimage will allow me to reclaim my *joie de vivre* and that I'll have the courage to find solutions to my situation. I don't want to live so torn up inside. I seek reconciliation. I want to laugh as I've always laughed. It feels as though I haven't laughed in a year!

Léandre, who has just spent six months in South Africa, is going home with me. For the next six months he'll stay in Quebec. I can't let this separation get me down because I am carrying another child. Your unborn child feels everything that you feel.

The atmosphere between myself and Léandre's father has deteriorated a lot. We're still talking, though with difficulty. I'm still hoping I can fix things.

I am naive.

In one year everything has changed. I've suffered a depression, I've done some reporting, I've produced an important documentary on rape, I (almost) got married, I've fallen pregnant, and I've initiated a battle for the custody of my son. Above all, obviously, I've cried. I wasn't aware that a human being could cry so many tears for such a long time.

Léandre can't wait to see his father. I try to savour every single moment with him. I spend the twenty-hour flight playing with him, telling him stories, listening to him and watching him sleep.

Jay and I will get married in Quebec, this summer. For real this time! Martine Boisjoly and André Ouellet, old friends of mine, have offered their house in Lanoraie for the wedding celebration. They've also offered me a room for the summer, since Jay is still in South Africa and will only come over for the wedding, towards the end of August. The house overlooks the Saint Lawrence River. In the dining room, which is completely surrounded by glass windows, you can hear the waves washing up to the shore from the ships.

As soon as I arrive I get in touch with my friends. I want to see everyone I know, to remind myself that there's another me, that she exists in more than my memories.

I make the necessary arrangements for the wedding. I dread going to the Joliette courthouse. Will the declaration that I want to marry an African give rise to questions charged with innuendos? Not at all. The official is very cooperative. He explains everything that I need to do and assures me that he'll speed up the process, in view of the short period we have available.

I invite people to the wedding over the phone. I would really like Léandre to be with us, but I'm scared stiff that his father will again be keen to attend the ceremony. My son will therefore miss this beautiful celebration, so simple and unique, and I will always regret that. I should have found the courage to confront my ex.

On 22 August, the day of the wedding, the sky is exactly the same as it was in Johannesburg on 14 December 1991. A few clouds floating in the sky, some threatening rain. Perhaps even today too we'll have our blessing from heaven.

I wear the same dress as last year. Five months of pregnancy stretch the material to the limits of the acceptable.

Our very dear friend Omar joins us. Jay has chosen him as best man. Mine is my father, this time able to play his proper role! It warms my heart, holding onto the arm of Pierre (or Pierrot, as he is known to his grandchildren). I advance down the short aisle in the neon-lit court-house. The judge conducting the ceremony has an engaging smile. No sign of racial prejudice in her look. It almost surprises me, relieves me. The week before, walking hand-in-hand with Jay in the streets of Montreal, I heard racist remarks. As one might hear in London or Boston, but, curiously, almost never in South Africa, where the practice of racism is more subtle.

When we come out onto the steps of the courthouse, Martine

throws confetti, like in the movies. I enjoy this. At the same time, it starts to rain. Once again, Jay says his mother is blessing us …

We celebrate our union at Lanoraie. There aren't six hundred people this time, only forty-two. My parents, who have been divorced for fifteen years, meet for the first time in many years. My father is with his wife, Suzanne Bernatchez, whom I like very much. The presence of my sister Anne is a wonderful gift. She is three years younger than me and we've called her 'Baby Anne' half her life, until she really got annoyed about it!

I have another, younger sister, named Tanya. My parents adopted her when she was only four months old. She is in fact my first cousin, the daughter of my father's sister, Diane Pagé, who let herself die when she stopped taking insulin for diabetes. Tanya was nine years old when she died. Tanya was born after a one-night affair between my aunt, who was then sixteen, and a Trinidadian from the merchant navy, who disembarked at Montreal with pillowcases full of drugs. At her birth Tanya developed a dependency on LSD, because her mother had taken it while pregnant. She was immediately given a blood transfusion. When she came to us, at the age of four months, the paediatrician said she was suffering from serious depression … Tanya had meningitis at the age of four and encephalitis twice, at six and at seven. Eventually she also started to suffer from epilepsy. Tanya lived with us for twelve years. Then her delinquency, which had become unmanageable, drove her to hospitals and clinics until she reached maturity. She went looking for her father and finally found him at the age of eighteen, when he raped her …

My brother Gérard, reserved and more-shy-than-is-possible, gets busy roasting the lamb on the spit that Uncle Daniel, my father's brother, has provided. Daniel doesn't attend the festivities. He doesn't like weddings. Or rather, he does not like gatherings. He is a Pagé, and doesn't like groups of more than two people. Succeeding in getting my father to the reception has been a major achievement. He never attends festivities. But he couldn't miss his daughter's wedding, the first in the family!

I would very much have liked Eva, my godmother, my maternal grandmother, to be there. I've spent a lot of time with her from a young age. I saw her every summer. I stayed with her when I was working at the Lac-Mégantic summer camp. But she is ill and 'lives' in the hospital in this town in the Cantons-de-l'Est region. She suffers from light delirium and incoherence, but she always recognises me. We hold hands. I tell her stories. Jay and I went to see her. Despite the language barrier, Jay and Eva spoke to one another, with smiles, with looks, with their hands. She could not imagine where he came from nor what life was like on the other side of the world, but she agreed with my 'choice'. 'You have a real man here,' she said to me.

Our union raised many questions. I still don't know the answers. How can two people, from completely different cultures and languages, with different customs and histories, different races and religions – celebrate a *union*? It's love that we celebrate, Jay and I were one from the first moment we met. The moments we spend together are always passionate. The subjects we talk about seem inexhaustible. We have discussions and debates on every aspect of life. Everywhere, all the time, on the phone, in person, we talk, we discuss subjects that inspire us. I have never, to this day, had any 'dead time' with Jay. Never.

At the age of eighteen, Jay came within a hair's breadth of dying. Struck by a rare disease, sarcoidosis, which attacks the lungs and the eyes in particular, he almost didn't make it. Between one and five per cent of people who get this disease die of it. Everyone feared the worst, because he was suffering from tuberculosis at the same time.

The doctors did two biopsies. The two scars on his neck and his eyes, which often fill with blood, always remind me of this story. The doctors informed the family that they would have to operate, but that they did not know whether he would pull through. Jay's mother and sister summoned Mrs Patel, a wise old Hindu, so that she could pray and ask the heavens to help the young man on his deathbed. She arrived with incense, fire, water, little silver trays, fruit, milk and a coconut. Jay was only half conscious in his hospital bed. Right in the middle of the prayer, the priestess stopped. She said with a smile, 'This child is not going to die. He has the spirit of a mahatma, a leader of the people.' At which she gathered up her belongings and left the room!

❖   ❖   ❖

Omar and Jay went cycling in the small roads of Lanoraie. One day they were thirsty and stopped at the corner shop. While Jay held the door open, Omar dragged the bicycles in, with great difficulty and a lot of noise. The few customers at the counter and the cashier stared at them, their mouths hanging open.

'What are you doing?' shouted the cashier.

They replied, in English, that they didn't want the bicycles to be stolen.

'But who would steal your bicycles?' asked the cashier, taken aback.

But it was the two friends who were most surprised ...

In South Africa theft is rife. The small lamps that Omar had placed in front of his house had been stolen a few days after they were installed. People steal everything that it is possible to steal. And sometimes, when bystanders get in the way, they're eliminated.

Jay and Omar could not believe that one could live so peacefully.

You can feel autumn in the air. The beginning of September meant it was time to return to South Africa. I was surprised how much I missed the autumn. I had to go away to realise how dear it was to me. As with so many things, so many people.

I left with Jay. There aren't words to express my happiness.

I left without Léandre. There aren't words to express my sorrow ...

25

Possession

Every day I go down the road to fetch the post. The slope is harder and harder to walk up as I make my way back to the house. At seven months, I slow down and lose my breath. The pregnancy aggravates my low blood pressure. I get dizzy easily, and if I don't sit down immediately, I faint.

Today, finally, I receive a letter from Léandre's father. It's over a month since I sent him a copy of the agreement reached during the summer, so that he could sign it and send it back. Léandre will start school next year, in September 1993, and we have to agree where he will go. Obviously we both want him with us. It will be a hard battle.

During my stay in Quebec my ex and I had a meal at a restaurant and agreed on custody for the coming year. We would make the arrangements for the following years during this period. Our meeting was calm and polite. The atmosphere was more serene than usual and I left feeling peaceful and at ease. Léandre would return at the beginning of December, in time for the birth of his brother or sister.

Breathless, I sit down at the kitchen table to open the letter. Reading the first few words, even though I'm sitting down, I feel dizzy. His letter no longer resembles our agreement. He says that he's thought about the proposals I made in August, that he doesn't agree, and that he's therefore sending me a new 'agreement'. The more I read, the more I tremble. He wants to keep Léandre and only grant me restricted custody rights. In terms of the new proposal, I would only see my son next summer, in almost a year, and then only for a few weeks! If I sign the agreement, his father states, he will let Léandre come and see me for two weeks at Christmas. Otherwise, he'll keep him.

My head is spinning. All of a sudden I feel as though I'm flying through space, as though someone has pushed me from the tenth floor of the Johannesburg police building. Many people have fallen from there ... I'm falling, falling. I reread the words, through my tears, to make sure I have read them correctly.

I'm completely overwhelmed. I phone Jay. 'I'm coming,' he says, cancelling all his appointments. He had sensed my distress.

When he arrives, I'm still in tears.

'What can I do?'

'Calm down,' he says. 'There are solutions to every problem. We just have to find them.'

'But he's the one who has Léandre at the moment!'

'I know. But it will all work out. You'll see.'

These words don't really comfort me. The more I analyse the situation, the more I lose confidence. What judge would send a child to the other side of the world, to a violent country, when he was living calmly in Montreal, attending a lovely nursery school where he spends his days making beautiful drawings?

❖   ❖   ❖

'But you are his mother!' says Peter Harris, a lawyer friend of Jay's. No one can take that away from you! And mothers have rights.'

'But how can we get his father to honour the agreement that we made? He even denies there was an agreement! I have no proof, it was all verbal.'

'Why did you not put it on paper?'

'I suggested that, but he said he was too busy and we would do it in a letter in September.'

Peter looks at me, incredulous. For a lawyer, this is probably the most stupid thing one can do in a situation like mine. He comforts me, but explains calmly that the current 'possession' of the child lies in the father's favour. The courts are usually reluctant to remove a child from its environment. For that to happen, the environment has to be harmful. Nonetheless, as his mother, I still have rights. It's a question of knowing whether I would be accorded visiting rights or custody rights.

I feel hopeless.

I decide to make my ex admit that we had an agreement. I prepare my cassette recorder and phone him. The conversation is long and stormy. We shout at each other. He ends up admitting that we had an agreement, but that he had no intention of honouring it. He doesn't know I'm recording our conversation, which I continue to do for three years. War requires the tactics of war!

Wednesday, 18 November 1992. I go to my weekly appointment with the midwife, who assures me everything is fine. But, she adds, the baby is still high up. She wouldn't be surprised if the baby was born a little late. In this case the baby would be due shortly before Christmas. Perfect, that will give us even more reason to celebrate, I say to myself. If only I could be sure that Léandre will be here!

Thursday, 19 November. Léandre's father sends me another agreement. If I sign it, he will put Léandre on the plane in two weeks' time, as arranged. However, his proposal is completely unacceptable. I can't resign myself to it. According to my lawyer, his father is holding my son hostage. In his letter he says he fears I'll steal his son from him. So he's doing it first!

Saturday, 21 November. The fax machine rings. I dread this now, because since we got this machine, only two months ago, it spits out nonsense, accusations, lies. I go to look at the two-page letter that has just come through.

Barely halfway through the letter I collapse. He's going to keep Léandre! He refuses to negotiate! I panic. A contraction grips my belly before I can finish the letter. I continue reading the letter. Jay is there. I translate it for him through my tears. I sink to the bottom of the pit. My body weighs a ton. I'm going to faint. I am shaking from my sobs and, more and more severely, from my contractions. Nonetheless it's too early.

'Come on, let's go to the hospital!' cries Jay. 'Let's call the midwife! The suitcase isn't ready! What must we do?'

'First let me write a letter. Let me write one last letter. So that he sends the agreement and I can sign it. I want to sign the agreement at once. I want to see Léandre. I want Léandre. I'm not ready to have this baby!'

I write as quickly as I can on the computer, between two contractions, through my tears. Even if someone had told me the end of the world was coming, I would have continued writing that letter, before everything collapsed.

But the baby can't bear the shock. It wants to come out. Immediately!

26

Kami

It's almost midnight. I can't bear it any more. The contractions are so strong. Sitting on the edge of the bed, I have my arms wrapped around Jay's neck, who is on his knees in front of me, supporting me, my weight, talking to me, pampering me during strong contractions.

'Stop thinking about him. Think about the baby. Think about the baby that's coming. It is our baby, my darling. *Our* baby!'

Another contraction. Then Jay excuses himself. He has to get up for a minute, he says.

'No, I need you! Don't go!'

'Just wait. I'm going to look for a cushion. My knees are hurting.'

I burst out laughing. He has sore knees! He realises the contrast between his pain and mine. We laugh, until the next contraction; it does me an enormous amount of good.

Liz Harding, the midwife, is very calm. Jay tells her about the recent events. Yes, she says, an emotional shock can bring on delivery, but now we have to deal with the situation.

At midnight on 22 November 1992, Liz urges me to push. I assume a half-sitting position on the bed, with lots of cushions behind my back. I'm too tired to move. No, I don't want any medication, I already feel dazed from recent events. I don't have the energy to push any more, but I surrender to her urging and coaxing, 'Come on, Lucie! It's almost over!'

One, two, three pushes and, at thirty-seven minutes past midnight, the baby arrives. Very small ... too small ... too early. But he has made it, a boy! I know his name is Kami. He told me at Martine's house, this past summer in Quebec.

I was lying down in bed, poring over a book of Indian names, Asian Indian and American Indian names, all with a special meaning, thousands of them. First I drew up a list of some girls' names. Then, in the boys' section, going through the *Ks*, my eyes suddenly fell, involuntarily, on 'Kami'. I froze when I saw this name. It was about ten in the evening. The window in my bedroom was wide open and it was hot. Martine and André were asleep in front of the television in the lounge. I shivered when I read 'Kami', I don't know why. Then I read the meaning: *Black Hindu god of love*. Kami means love.

And now he is born, my Kami.

Jay is beaming. He picks up his son and doesn't lose his proud smile for the next hour. A son! A boy!

Kami, my little Kami. You're the one who paid for my suffering and I am dreadfully sorry for that. You were the greatest victim in all the bickering about custody.

Kami, my beautiful Kami. If I could, I would start all over again, just to be able to give you nine calm months of pregnancy and a birth to celebrate. Kami, my little Kami, you are so tiny. Two kilos and a few grams is very small. Three words: 'I'm keeping Léandre' robbed you of your right to finish your reign in my womb. Three words destroyed me and it was me, in that state, that you were fleeing. I'll never be able to erase a feeling of regret, even with years of therapy. I love you, Kami, I love you so much, but you were born in anger, fear and despair. Will you forgive me one day?

27

Breakdown

Kami has just been born, and Jay leaves. He has to attend a conference in Vancouver and will try to bring Léandre back with him.

Léandre's father claims that there's too much violence in South Africa. From my bed, I try to negotiate with him – in letters, faxes and recorded conversations.

The argument about violence in South Africa is a trap. I can't deny it, because I witness it every day in my work. But I also knew that distance distorts the perception, and seen from Canada, the situation appears far worse than it actually is.

Provided that you live in the 'right' neighbourhood, it's still possible to shelter your children from this violence. To a large extent, life in a white suburb is organised in order to achieve this objective. Thanks to alarm systems and security guards, the life of a white child in Johannesburg is not much more dangerous than that of a child in New York, for example.

My opinion doesn't seem to count. So I call the Canadian High Commissioner. He composes a letter stating that when a country becomes too violent a warning is issued to Canadian citizens, but that at present no warning is necessary in South Africa.

I'm alone at home with Kami. I don't know whether Jay will succeeded in getting Léandre. I think of my godmother, Eva, whom I adore. I miss her. I'm keen for her to meet her new great-grandson! Unfortunately, at the moment, he is ill. He's over his jaundice at least. But he vomits a lot, every time he drinks milk. It seems to be something more than the usual regurgitation by a small baby.

The telephone rings. It's my mother, wishing me a happy thirty-first birthday. She asks about the health of her new grandson, but I don't go into the details, because I don't want to worry her. I ask her how Eva, her mother, is. She hasn't been very well of late. I feel like ringing the hospital. Since my last visit, with Jay, she's told everybody about my 'African prince'. She really believes that Jay is a fairytale prince.

I repeat the question, because I haven't received an answer.

'How is Granny?'

Granny has just died, just a few hours ago. She died today, on my birthday. She died before I could say goodbye, hold her hands one last time, just for a few minutes.

I put down the phone, shattered by the news. So shattered in fact that I have no milk for two days.

I'm afraid I won't be able to breastfeed. The doctor prescribes Eglynol, a rather unorthodox treatment, banned in Canada, but good; an anti-depressant that stimulates the production of milk as a side effect. I can benefit from both effects.

I have no further news of Léandre and it drives me crazy. Kami continues to bring up; the problem gets worse. I call the midwife, who rushes over. No, she says, it's not normal, he must go to hospital.

At the hospital, they tear my little one away from me and he disappears behind a door for an hour. A nurse comes to see me while he's being examined.

'You really should have come earlier!' she accuses.

'What's the matter? Is it serious?'

'A good mother would have come earlier!'

'But I'm here now! I have come! Everyone told me it was normal, that he was only regurgitating.'

'It may be too late.'

'What are you saying?'

'The jaundice may have reached the brain. We are doing tests right now.'

A good mother would have come earlier. I wonder why this woman feels the need to spew her bile all over me in this way. The accusation touches my deepest being. As though I needed another catalyst for the guilt I already feel.

Friends tried to reason with me later on. They explained that this woman had seen the colour of Kami's skin, read the father's name in the file and simply betrayed her prejudice about racial marriages. It happened more than once. For example, when another nurse realised I was Jay's wife, she purposely inserted the needle in the wrong spot on my arm three times while taking blood. My arm was black and blue for a month. Today it's Kami getting jabbed by needles while I get stabbed!

Kami reappears after an hour, his head bandaged. They've taken blood through the fontanelle. Apparently mothers aren't allowed to see this.

He doesn't have jaundice. They have to run other tests. They give me an appointment for the next day. I phone Jay, at my brother Gérard's home in Montreal. Gérard was supposed to accompany Léandre to South Africa at the beginning of December because Jay did not want to leave me alone in case the baby came. My brother had renewed his passport and booked his plane ticket. Then at the last minute everything was cancelled because I had given birth. Gérard took the change in plan in his stride, doing everything he could to help us. We did not make his life easy.

Jay used his time in Montreal to meet my new lawyer in Quebec, Luc Deshaies. I had called my friend Claude Marcil during the November catastrophe, asking him to find the best custody lawyer, regardless of the cost. Claude was my mentor. I could call him from China or from the moon, night or day, three hundred and sixty-five days a year. He was one of the best researchers in Quebec. Claude knows everything. And when he doesn't know, he knows how to find out in the shortest possible time.

He recommended Mr Deshaies, of Lafleur, Brown and Associates in Montreal. A reserved, conscientious man, even if he doesn't show his emotions. When Léandre's father received a letter from this lawyer, he realised that I was serious and he agreed to let Léandre come. Obviously he didn't want to look ridiculous by forcing me to sign an agreement under duress, so he agreed to negotiate. But I would only believe it when Léandre was in my arms!

Kami is really ill. He still can't keeping anything down. His weight is below the critical threshold. He weighs only a kilo and a half. I return to the hospital. They force-feed him a white liquid. He screams, he cries, he howls. They put him into a big machine.

'Don't you have a dummy, for heaven's sake?'

'No, he doesn't like dummies.'

I've tried. Kami cries all the time, as though he has stomach ache all the time. Obviously he's suffering, if he vomits like this. Did I pass on my own nervous tension to him, that knot in the stomach? You can't see it on X-rays, but it's there. I dread the possibility; it's irrational, but I can't help it.

The diagnosis: Kami has an under-developed oesophageal opening. There is a kind of flap that is supposed to open only to let food in. But Kami's is elastic, so soft that it is almost useless; it lets most of the contents of the stomach escape. Only a small amount of milk reaches the intestines to be absorbed. This is why he's getting thinner.

There is no operation for this condition. Only time will improve things. It will take two years before he stops vomiting and regurgitating. He has to sleep sitting up, be fed like this, rocked like this, and comforted all the time because he cries so much.

Kami is now ten days old. Jay and Léandre are arriving tomorrow. I don't feel well. I'm breastfeeding. All of a sudden he vomits. This time the contents of his stomach fly straight onto the wall, one and a half metres away! I call 'Foxy', a great friend of Omar's, also our warm-hearted GP. He's always been there for us; one evening when Léandre burnt himself, he rushed over faster than an ambulance.

Foxy's real name is Ebrahim Asvat. Some people suspect that Winnie Mandela allegedly had his brother, Abu-Baker Asvat, assassinated. Abu-Baker was a doctor like his brother, a political militant and a friend of Winnie Mandela. She had established a group of young men, the Mandela United Football Club, who served as her bodyguards and who sowed chaos in Soweto, as well as committing crimes. At the end of 1988 the members of this club locked up four activists from a church in Soweto, suspecting that they were police informers. Winnie Mandela also accused the priest from the small church of sexually abusing these young men. Among them was Stompie Seipei, who was fourteen years old. Winnie called her friend Abu-Baker to examine the adolescent. She wanted a medical report proving her allegations. But the doctor refused to corroborate Winnie's version. Instead, he stated that the young Stompie had been savagely beaten, even tortured, and that he had also suffered brain damage. The following day Stompie had been found dead in the veld, near Winnie's home. A month later, on 27 January 1989, Abu-Baker Asvat was assassinated by two men who later claimed they had been paid by Winnie to commit the crime. There were a lot of irregularities in the police investigation. Winnie was eventually found guilty of kidnapping and complicity in the torture of Stompie Seipei. Her six-year prison sentence was commuted, on appeal, to a fine of fifteen thousand rand. This was probably the straw that broke the camel's back in the Mandela marriage. Nelson and Winnie finally divorced. Foxy is still waiting for justice to be served regarding his brother …

Foxy arrived at the house accompanied by Omar and started to examine both Kami and me. When he had finished, he looked at me with a concerned air. 'It is not the little one I am worried about, it's you. You are not well. You are drawn and pale, too pale. And you are also running a temperature.' He suspected an infection of the uterus. But Foxy was too intimate a friend and would certainly not dare to give me a gynaecological examination. He recommended that I go to see another doctor.

The following morning I don't want to think about my misfortunes, but about Léandre and Jay. They're arriving in an hour!

I'm over-excited. I strap Kami into his car-seat and leave for the airport. The car is making an odd noise. It occurs to me that I might have to take it to the garage.

On the highway, seven kilometres from the airport, the car starts to vibrate and shudder violently. The needle on the radiator gauge is in the red zone and smoke starts pouring out of the bonnet! If only I can make it to the airport.

I don't. Two kilometres further, the engine dies. Having driven the car to death, I let it roll onto the side of the road, where it comes to a complete halt. There's not only smoke coming out of the bonnet, there's a fire raging underneath it! Flames are escaping everywhere. I jump out of the vehicle, unstrap Kami from the back seat and pull him out as quickly as I can. Then I run. I wave at passing cars to stop. A taxi pulls up almost immediately.

I open the back door and warn the driver that I'm Jay Naidoo's wife, that he shouldn't take advantage of me. 'Take me to the airport at once and I will pay you!' Jay Naidoo's wife? He is honoured, he says, 'I'll take you there immediately, madam!'

We leave the burning car behind us. It's the first time I've used my husband's name to ask for something.

Léandre and Jay come through the doors. At last! They're here. All of a sudden I feel relief. The tears flow. My legs fold under me. I collapse.

I only got up again ten days later, after another stay in hospital. I was suffering from a serious infection of the uterus and from mastitis in my left breast. I was also anaemic and running a temperature of forty degrees. My body had managed to hold up up to that point. Now it needed to be looked after.

28

When love hurts

Oh no! Not more women!

'I am very sorry,' I say on the phone. 'I can't make another film on women's rights. I am too busy, sorry.'

My documentary on rape had repercussions that I hadn't expected. Now I'm receiving calls from women's groups, organisations that fight crime and rehabilitate criminals. They want me to tackle another serious problem: domestic violence. In fact, women are beaten and even raped, on a daily basis. However, I don't want to be 'labelled' a feminist film director.

NICRO (the National Institute against Crime and for the Rehabilitation of Offenders), the executive producer of my film on rape, is very persistent. Naomi Hill, the NICRO representative in Cape Town, calls me several times to convince me to make another video. Finally I give in. I tell her I'll do some preliminary research and get back to her.

This is how, between reporting for Radio–Canada, the custody battle for Léandre and the care involved in looking after a newborn baby, I embark on a project that will take me into the bedrooms of South African women.

At the end of the day my research is more extensive than I had anticipated. Once again I wrote a synopsis to obtain funding to produce a thirty-minute documentary.

Everyone knows that South African society is violent. Recent studies have revealed that homes don't escape this violence. At least one in six women in South Africa is beaten by her partner. Some put the figure at one in four. And others simply say that all the statistics under-estimate the situation, that the walls of homes hide disturbing realities on a large scale.

Over and above these figures, the South African reality is unique. Violence is more 'accepted' here than it is anywhere else. And domestic violence is criticised even less than rape. It is a 'protected' crime.

Why do men beat their wives? Is there a typical profile for a wife-beater? Is this form of violence a 'chronic illness'? One study has shown that more than eighty per cent of violent men were sexually abused. How can we break this vicious cycle of violence? These are some of the angles I want to pursue.

My experience in producing the video on rape stands me in good stead. This time, in two ticks, I plan the documentary, draw up a detailed budget and solicit financial support from various organisations. I need one hundred and forty thousand rand. And, in two ticks again, the money comes in! The Canadian government (which has always supported me in my production efforts in South Africa), a Japanese non-governmental organisation and some Swedish trade unions provide the funding. As with the previous video, I cede authorial rights to NICRO, who will use them to finance projects for the advancement of women in South Africa.

This time the subject is multi-ethnic, because domestic violence affects all races. Unlike rape, which often occurs in the wake of attacks in poorly lit streets, which attract the wrong type of people in poor areas, domestic violence is just as likely to take place behind the security gates of Sandton or Rivonia – the smart areas – as it is in the corru-gated-iron shacks of Alexandra or Soweto. I meet one victim, a white woman named Michelle Bruce. Michelle is beautiful, incredibly beautiful. In the eighties she was elected Miss South Africa. She is also an intelligent and dynamic woman. She was beaten for years and ended up in hospital on more than one occasion. Finally she managed to get out and, since she wants to speak out against marital violence, she gives me an interview that proves riveting.

I decided to ask the women I was interviewing to address the camera directly as I ask them the final question, 'What would you like to say to battered women?' Michelle's eyes bore into the screen as she declared, 'Your whole body belongs to you, from head to toe, inside and outside, and no one, no one has the right to rape you in any way, mentally or physically. You must always remember that you can get out of your situation. You have a mouth, you have a brain, say what you have to say and leave! Because it is your life, only yours, and life is far too short. To spend it continually being humiliated and beaten is simply not a life!'

Another woman who appears in my documentary is Zuleiga, a Muslim woman from Cape Town. Her husband has been raping her almost every day for more than a decade. Sometimes he sodomises her. Always by force. He threatens his wife with death if she says anything to anyone, if she complains. He is serious, because he has already tried to kill her a few years ago. Zuleiga is therefore the only woman in the documentary to speak in the dark, under a false name. After the interview, she will catch a plane to return to her hell with this man. This is one of the issues that I deal with in this documentary: why do women return to a violent environment? Financial dependence and the hope that they may be able to change their husbands are the main reasons.

I did everything that I could to give Zuleiga the means and the courage to get out. I gave her the telephone numbers of women who could help her. She finally took refuge in a centre for battered women, but her husband found her there. He arrived armed and took her home. I do not know whether she will have the courage to dare to defy him again.

Dare – that was the message from Rookmin, an Indian woman from Natal that I go to visit. Half her face and neck are covered with scars. Her husband missed the aorta by only a few millimetres. He stabbed her numerous times in her ear, her head and her neck. In one of her arms, in her hands and her fingers. He slaughtered his wife in front of his daughters. He got one year in prison. Less than a cattle thief! 'What message do you have for abused women?' Rookmin does not hear. I have to repeat the question. She is deaf in one ear now.

Rookmin's two daughters are still traumatised. The eldest, Sumita, at twelve years of age, understands the problem so well that she is not only traumatised by her father, but equally terrified of all men. I want her on camera. Her mother hesitates. 'Breaking the ice is always difficult, but that's how to reveal the problem. It is the only way to find solutions that will put an end to the problem.' She agrees.

Sumita's eyes are deep and sad, even when she smiles. Her father often beats her. 'I like to go to bed before he gets home in the evening,' she says, starting to cry. I feel distraught. I let the silence speak. And then she fills it. 'We are used to being afraid of him.' Sumita doesn't believe that her father is to blame. 'At least,' she adds, 'that's what the judge said. I learnt that it's because of alcohol. Apparently this is an illness that cannot be cured.'

I also meet two black women. One of the myths about domestic violence is that it's only rife in rural areas, among poor, illiterate women. I have to dispel this myth. The two black women I've chosen come from totally different backgrounds. There's Dinah, an old woman from a rural area, poor, illiterate and without any social power, and Joyce, a city-dweller, educated, a trade union representative at her workplace.

After three months of research I find two men who beat their wives and who are prepared to tell their stories. They come to my place. Neither will be identified. One will have his back to the camera, the other will be in shadow, and both will have fictitious names. But the things they say present another view of violence.

'James' is rehabilitated. Divorced, but rehabilitated. He says, 'It was like a competition for me. She would stay late at the office and I would have to take care of the children. So I would beat her for that, to make her pay for following a career.' He'd had to summon up all his courage to come and talk to me. 'I have two university degrees, I am a university professor, I travel all over, even overseas, where I speak at conferences. I am well known, but I am not prepared to show my face on camera, not right now at any rate. Because when I look at myself in the mirror, I see a monster.'

Trevor is also rehabilitated. He says he was also a victim of circumstances, 'just as whites are victims of their own laws in South Africa'. Trevor explains, 'We would argue. One thing would lead to the next until there was poison in the air. Until the only way out was to shut her up by hitting her.' Trevor did not understand what made him beat his wife. 'I would never see the disaster coming. While it was happening, everything was black. And afterwards, I felt like a dog. And I felt alone. Completely alone.' He went to therapy … after his divorce. He ended the interview by saying, 'Society tries to sweep this problem under the carpet. And yet violence against women is the worst social problem.'

The stories of these men were striking. 'James' came to the launch of the video. He congratulated me. He was on his own. He left without attending the reception.

I found a pearl of a person who acted as my right hand during the production of the documentary: Anchu Padayachee, director of the Advice Desk for Abused Women, the largest help centre for battered women in KwaZulu and Natal. Anchu suggested the title for the documentary: *When Love Hurts*.

I made use of a nanny during filming, so that I could continue breastfeeding Kami. The nanny looked after him between feeds. He fed every three hours, day and night! His oesophageal problem prevented him from swallowing very much at any one time.

One day I was busy feeding Kami when a man came to find me for an interview. I told him, with Kami discreetly at my breast, that I would be with him in two minutes, that my son would soon be finished feeding. He flew off the handle.

'Where is your boss?'

'I don't have a boss. I am the producer and director of this film.'

'But you must have a superior to whom you report?'

'No, I am the head of the team.'

'Since when does a boss breastfeed a baby during working hours?'

I had not wanted to wean Kami for two weeks of filming. It is hard to find the balance between being a mother and a professional … It is not unusual for people to accuse you of being a bad mother because you work while breastfeeding, or accuse you of being incompetent because you breastfeed while working!

Almost four hundred people attended the launch of the video in Johannesburg. The Market Theatre again offered us their auditorium. Jay carried Kami in his arms and Léandre on his back.

The auditorium was full. Among those attending were representatives of women's organisations, obviously, of anti-crime organisations, of NGOs, of various governments – South African, Canadian and others – ambassadors, heads of companies, trade union representatives – including the general secretary of the Congress of South African Trade Unions, this evening in the role of the director's husband, but also examining the documentary with a professional eye.

'Did you know that you are likely to get a more severe sentence if you steal some sheep than if you beat and mutilate your wife?'

My introduction to the subject surprised more than one person. I continued, 'If a murder occurs in a house, it's a crime. If someone is attacked and beaten by a stranger at home, it's a crime. If a stranger threatens to kill you, it's a crime. If a stranger rapes you, in your home, in your bed, it's a crime.' And then I leave my notes aside. I look at all the eyes fixed on me. After a short pause, I ask, 'Why do these crimes become acceptable when they are committed by a lover? Why does love give one the right to resort to violence against one's spouse?' I let the silence speak before the audience breaks into applause.

I add that South Africa still has a long way to go in eliminating this other apartheid, that divides women from men. Then I ask the audience to think of the problem in reverse, to imagine what would happen if more than a thousand men were raped every day, if hundreds of thousands of others, even millions, were beaten, ill-treated, brutalised and raped every day! 'And if, in addition, these men were white?… Do you really believe for an instant that they would fold their arms as they are doing now?'

Some women in the audience cried 'Viva!'

❈   ❈   ❈

Five years after producing this documentary, I find myself in the company of Ela Gandhi, the granddaughter of Mahatma Gandhi, who has become an ANC member of parliament in South Africa. She also deals with women's issues and is recognised worldwide as one of the leading experts in the field. We're travelling by car towards KwaZulu-Natal, sitting at the back while Jay drives.

In the course of the conversation, Ela mentions that she wants to open a new centre for women in Phoenix, an Indian suburb near Durban. She tells me about a woman who has been beaten and mutilated, and who almost died before she escaped her marriage. This woman, she explains, has told her story in a video documentary that Ela is using everywhere to raise consciousness about violence against women. I ask her what the documentary is called. *When Love Hurts*, she answered. She's talking about my video! When I tell her that I am the director, she takes my hand, looks me straight in the eye and says, 'Thank you, from the bottom of my heart'. Not even a Gemini Award (a Canadian television award) could have given me such joy!

29

Post-scriptum on rape

In 1993 my videos receive special mention at the Southern African Film Festival, which is held in Harare, Zimbabwe, that year. I am invited to chair a debate on the documentary *When Love Hurts.*

At the end of the first day the organisers hold a banquet. I am having a drink when a good-looking African man approaches me, speaking a magnificent French – how I love the West African accent! He is himself a well-known director. He has heard about my documentary and we exchange our points of view on the cause of women in South Africa, on their triple struggle – against sexism, against apartheid and against cheap labour. He insists on calling this exploitation of women a 'crime'. Then the tone of the conversation changes. Am I married? Yes. Do I have children? Yes. And you? Yes, yes.

The discussion takes an unexpected turn. 'You are very pretty.' What does one say? Thank you? I smile inanely. He continues. He likes my body. He would like to sleep with me, tonight. I stare at him, incredulous. I repeat that I am married, happily married. 'I like married women,' he replies with a mischievous glint in his eyes. 'When women say no,' he continues, 'it's because they like to be begged.'

Oh no! This time it is too much! I lose my temper. People turn to look as I raise my voice. He grips my arm and says that he will sleep with me tonight, that it will be good. Softly, calmly and with a smile, I ask him to please hold my glass for a moment. Then I take to my heels and run! Why didn't I ask for help at that moment? I do not know. It was an immediate, instinctive reaction.

Outside I run fast, down the small paths, between the buildings of the campus where the festival is being held. I get lost. All the dormitories look the same. He is there, behind me. I can hear his footsteps. Eventually I find my dormitory and rush into the hallway. As I run I look for my room key in my bag. As nervous as I am, I put the key into the lock without trembling. I open the door, close it immediately and lock it. I am out of breath. I am afraid. I wait. I don't turn on the light, because there is a small window above the door.

A minute later I hear what I fear – the man's footsteps. He doesn't know which room I am in. He knocks at each door, calling my name. I hide under the bed. I hear him approaching, banging on each door with his fist, on each side of the corridor. Then mine starts to shake under his blows.

It is because I have made a film on violence against women that he is so taken with me! I represent an even more attractive challenge in his eyes. I am certain of it. Running has left me completely out of breath, but I stop breathing, somehow. I am paralysed. He knocks on the door next to mine, then the next. He is furious. He shouts, 'I will have you!'

I tremble until midnight. There is no telephone in my room and I am too afraid to go out. What if he is there, waiting for me?

I've escaped like this once before, down a path between buildings. I was twelve years old, living in Ottawa …

It was nine in the evening. The shops had just closed and I was returning to Algonquin College, where my mother worked. It was dark. The car park was enormous. A man in a pickup truck stopped next to me, pointed a rifle at me and told me to get into his vehicle. I screamed. He was surprised by how loud my voice was. I ran away fast! I entered my mother's office as white as a sheet. I did not need to say a word, she knew. She called the police. I told them everything, but I don't think they took me seriously.

A week later, a young girl my age was found, raped and shot with a rifle in the head, in the same suburb where my own unfortunate incident had occurred. At the police station, looking through photos of criminals, I identified the man who had threatened me. He was arrested shortly afterwards. He was indeed the man who had killed the young girl. He died of liver failure in prison seven years later. I celebrated the event.

When I was seventeen, my boyfriend forced me to have sex. Today I know this is rape. When I was twenty-seven, a well-known Radio–Canada journalist attacked me at home. One of my buttons came off as he tried to pull my blouse off by force. I pushed him down the stairs of my small flat.

Around the same time, and for a period of two years, I was constantly harassed by one of my bosses in a TV production studio in Montreal. For two years I was scared to go to work, because sometimes, as I sat at my editing desk, he would stand behind me and press his penis against my back. He would say, 'Are you afraid of me? Are you afraid of losing your job if you report me?' Yes, I was afraid. I even called a male friend one evening, because I was alone with him and I was afraid he would rape me.

All my life I have rejected sexual advances. Very recently, an attendant at a drycleaner squeezed my hand while giving me my change, and said, 'I can do another type of cleaning if you wish – for free.' Colleagues at work, some of whom have become friends, as well as lecturers at college and university, sometimes tried their luck with a little too much ardour. I also had a boss, in a record shop, who took pleasure in forcing his tongue into my mouth, and touching my backside and breasts, whenever he could catch me by surprise. When a woman raises her voice in situations like this, some men say, 'Be careful of her, she will take you to court just for looking at her.' I never raised my voice. I always ran.

Perhaps my videos were my way of expressing anger against men who have an unhealthy power relationship with women. My mother was raped three times in her life! The first time, she was only seven years old ... A 'family friend' also sexually assaulted one of my sisters. Another put his fingers in my vagina when I was only nine years old. My mother reported the incident to the police, but they did absolutely nothing ...

All women have similar stories to tell. And that evening, there I was, under a bed in Zimbabwe, still trembling. I was sick of it.

The next morning I went to tell the person in charge of all the guests about the incident. She was stunned. 'But he is so well known!' 'That has nothing to do with it,' I retorted.

I cancelled all my workshops and demanded that someone take me to the airport so that I could return, immediately, to South Africa. I laid a complaint with the festival organisers. But not with the police. I did not have the courage for that. I was too afraid. Plus, who would they have believed – the well-known director or the young unknown?

The almost cynical irony of the situation was that the main message of both my documentaries was, 'Speak out! Denounce your attacker!' I was afraid of this man. Afraid that he would find me one day. I wanted to disappear.

30

Elizabeth

Léandre has been with me for six months. His father has finally agreed to respect the agreement we made in Quebec the previous summer, but only after my lawyer's intervention. Besides, his arguments about the violence in South Africa weren't solid. And most of all, Léandre has his heart set on coming. So he has started pre-school at the French School in Johannesburg, in January 1993.

Kami has been bouncing around on my back since birth in a baby carrier that I bought in Guilin, in the south of China. The baby is supported by a sort of flap that you fasten by crossing two long straps of material, each about three metres in length, over your back or stomach. He's fine. He hardly ever cries when I carry him around like this. And it's comfortable for me, because his weight is evenly distributed over my shoulders, unlike the African method, where you strap the baby on your back with a towel tied over your breasts; you need big breasts for this method to be comfortable.

I read my papers while walking up and down to pacify Kami. I rock him while I work on the computer. Not ideal for concentrating, but better than leaving him to cry in his cot.

These days I'm preparing the groundwork for a documentary series that Claude Charron and his team are coming to film for the current affairs programme *Le Match de la vie*. I'm still doing radio pieces for Radio–Canada news. I take care of my two sons and of the house, and the discussions relating to custody of Léandre continue to take up a lot of my time. All this forms part of my 'job description' as a mother and working woman.

One day Jay comes home at midday, while I'm struggling to edit my radio text. I immediately dump Kami in his arms and shut myself in my office for two hours, the time it takes to write and send the story to Radio–Canada.

When I return to the lounge, Jay once again suggests that we employ a domestic worker. Since Kami's birth, he has become more insistent. 'We need somebody to help you, Lucie. Someone to look after Kami when you're working. She'll be a nanny rather than a domestic worker.' I think about it. Yes, perhaps I do need someone to look after Kami. It would give me the chance to work in peace. It will give me a few hours between feeds to work efficiently.

Finally I agree, after almost two years of endless discussion! I think I was resisting the idea of being a white boss, which threatens the image of myself as the 'enemy of exploiters'.

Quite quickly, I find five candidates. To evaluate them, each comes to work for a day. I ask them only to look after Kami. But all of them, without exception, start cleaning the minute they set foot in the house. Well, perhaps a little assistance with the cleaning would not be such a bad thing …

Elizabeth stands out from the rest. At the end of the day, the house is spotless, the washing is done and Kami is purring. So I choose Elizabeth. Now I have a domestic worker – or rather a nanny. I don't look back. What a pleasure to lock myself in my office and work undisturbed while the housework gets done without me!

Elizabeth is a Venda woman. She is twenty-eight years old and has three boys. She has been doing housework all her life. Her children live in the bantustan of Venda, with her mother. She sees her sons twice a year, sometimes three times, like millions of other women in South Africa. Black children often don't live in a nuclear family set-up, because their parents have to live a long way away in order to work. They are generally brought up by their grandparents.

I've cried so much because of Léandre's absence, but I'm living side by side with a mother who hardly ever sees her children. When I speak to her about it, her eyes fill with tears. I tell myself that I have nothing to complain about. Millions of domestic workers live separated from their children, right here, in their own country. They're being torn apart, not because they are trying to realise a dream, like me, but because they are living a nightmare, apartheid.

Elizabeth's husband works in a shop that laminates photographs and earns a thousand rand a month. It's a good salary for a black man (Jay makes just under two thousand as general secretary for the largest trade union in the country!) except that Elizabeth's husband keeps the money for himself and his mistresses … Elizabeth and her husband live together in a tiny house in Tembisa, a township on the outskirts of Johannesburg, where poverty and violence are so rife that it is not unusual to find dead bodies in the street.

Elizabeth has to travel more than an hour, every morning and evening, to come and work for us. She very much wants to come and live in the 'dump' above the garage at the bottom of the garden. But I tell her it's out of the question, that no human being could live there. I get the impression that she doesn't understand, that she thinks I want to prevent her from living on the property. But in fact I would very much like to have a small clean, sunny room for her.

So we decide to renovate the rooms above the garage. We borrow the money we need to put in water and electricity, a shower and toilet, a kitchenette, a small lounge and a bedroom. It's small, but clean and well lit. I dig up some nice furniture at the flea market. This accommodation, Elizabeth announces, is a thousand times more comfortable than her home in Tembisa. 'Here at least I can go to the toilet and wash myself. I do not have water at home.' Her 'home' is a corrugated iron shelter.

Elizabeth is illiterate. She doesn't have an iron constitution either, but she knows how to look after a house and take care of a child. I start to spoil her. A friendly relationship develops between us. I lend her money, because she often needs a little more than her salary to cover the needs of her three children. Although she always promises to pay me back, she never does, but I forgive her. She has so little. 'Be careful,' Omar warns me. 'You should never develop personal relationships with your employees.' I ignore his warning and later pay the price.

Six months after she starts working with us, Elizabeth tells me she is pregnant. She cries. She doesn't want – can't keep the baby, she says, because she's barely managing to support her other three children. But above all she's afraid I will throw her out. I reassure her, explaining that I would never sack her because she was pregnant.

'Do you want to have an abortion?'

'Yes, that is what I want.'

'Are you certain?'

'Yes.'

I thought I was in Canada, where it was relatively easy to 'correct' a mistake and where you accept abortion as a necessary evil. In South Africa in the early 1990s, however, abortion is illegal. Only therapeutic abortions are allowed, including those justified by depression. Elizabeth spends her days thinking about this baby. She cries. She is angry. She doesn't want to keep it. A doctor will undoubtedly agree to an abortion, I tell her, because it's obvious she's depressed. I say I will help her.

In just a few days, I manage to find a hospital where abortions are performed. We need authorisation from three people: a general practitioner, a gynaecologist and a psychiatrist. At the end of the day it's the psychiatrist who will give the green light for the abortion. I accompany Elizabeth to the hospital each time and, obviously, I pay the bill.

First we see the general practitioner. After doing a scan to determine the age of the foetus, he informs Elizabeth that the abortion can take place within ten days. Then he sends her to see the gynaecologist, who concurs in just a few minutes. All we have to do is obtain the permission of the psychiatrist, a 'mere formality' the first doctor assures us.

The psychiatrist is a white man. I explain the situation to him and suggest that I be present during the consultation, as Elizabeth does not speak much English, although I am able to understand her. He doesn't respond, asking me to wait outside his office.

Just in case, I have brought a book with me, because a psychological evaluation usually takes at least an hour. However, I don't even have time to get to the second page before Elizabeth comes out. Five minutes. Just five minutes. So fast?

I go in to see the psychiatrist. He tells me, without even lifting his head from his papers, that Elizabeth cannot have an abortion. I can't believe my ears. I throw a fit in his office, but come up against total indifference.

I call the doctor who was supposed to perform the abortion, but he is powerless. He. cannot proceed with the abortion. He would risk losing his licence to practise medicine.

There is only one solution: for Elizabeth to go and have an abortion in Soweto. In the townships, this is a lucrative service. Hundreds of thousands of abortions are performed there each year. However, the death rate is very high. In addition there are repercussions for the majority of women – infections, handicaps, sterility, perforations of the uterus. Elizabeth would be risking her life having an abortion in Soweto. It's simply not possible. No, she has no choice but to have this baby.

Almost all the legal abortions performed in South Africa are performed on white women. They have the social power that allows them to control their lives. Even in a framework where it is illegal, abortions remain accessible to them.

Elizabeth abandoned her daughter with her mother in Venda when the little one was less than a year old. She sank into depression. She stopped singing while she did the housework. She stopped nursing Kami. She even stopped washing … That white doctor had held Elizabeth's destiny in his hands. That is what apartheid is all about.

A law abolishing restrictions on abortion was passed in October 1996. Too late for Elizabeth.

31

The Institute for the Advancement of Journalism

Allister Sparks offers me a job. Sparks is a well-known journalist, not just in South Africa but throughout the continent. A fifth-generation white South African, he fought the injustices of apartheid in his own way, with words. Allister was the editor-in-chief of the *Rand Daily Mail*. This newspaper was so critical of the regime, that it was shut down by the government in 1985.

Allister Sparks is also the author of the book *The Mind of South Africa*, a work considered essential reading on the political and social history of the country, and of *Tomorrow is Another Country: The Inside Story of South Africa's Road to Change*, a large-scale investigation into the secret negotiations initiated in prison between Nelson Mandela and the government of PW Botha, which eventually led to the 1994 elections. He has received several journalism prizes, proving that you can work with discipline and integrity as a journalist while opposing apartheid, even if you are married to an anti-apartheid activist. (His wife is the human rights campaigner, Sue Sparks.)

During my stay in South Africa I was often asked how I could claim to be objective when I was the wife of an ANC activist. My position against apartheid and racism never prevented me from doing my work with integrity. I see red when anyone insinuates that I might be biased, that, because Jay is a member of the ANC, I cannot practise my profession properly. I get angry when people confuse the wife and the journalist. It is an insult to my intelligence, my integrity and my professionalism.

Yes, I am against racism, against apartheid. Journalists from all countries have opinions. In Quebec, they vote for or against independence in a referendum and still continue their work. However, the matter is more nuanced in South Africa. For example, reports describing the ANC as a *victim* of circumstances often create feelings of uneasiness, especially in the West. The ANC received bad press for a long time, particularly in the American and British media, which looked askance at its links with the Communists and its black face, just as Afrikaners feared Communists and blacks in the form of *die rooi gevaar* and *die swart gevaar*.

People overseas wanted to support the struggle against racism, but they feared the arrival of a black government. If Nelson Mandela had had other allies besides the Communist Party, he would have received far more international support, especially if he had been white. Because of this prejudice, any journalist remarking on an ANC success could easily be accused of partiality. Being married to an ANC activist, I had to defend myself twice over. I believe that this increased the care that I took with my reporting.

Allister Sparks appears very capable of mastering the subtleties of the situation. He offers me a position at the Institute for the Advancement of Journalism, which is affiliated to the University of the Witwatersrand. It was established in June 1992 for the training and improvement of journalists, who would henceforth work in a free press.

Allister is constantly irritated by the poor quality of journalism in South Africa. Years of government censorship have paralysed the development of an independent press in favour of propaganda and media that are content to reproduce press releases from the military information service.

Allister Sparks needs someone, he says, to manage the electronic media section of the Institute. Television jargon, even in English – *frames, freezes, pan, tilt, fade-in, cross-mix* – is Greek to him. He is looking for someone who knows the language of radio and television to get this section on its feet and start training students in it. I know nothing about training, but he insists. I accept the position on condition that I can remain a correspondent for Radio–Canada.

Jacques Larue-Langlois, my radio broadcasting professor at the University of Quebec in Montreal, responds to my calls of distress. He sends by post course notes, outlines, ideas. I am happy that Allister has insisted. I will learn a great deal by teaching and I already know that this experience will become an excellent educational path for me.

It is Amina Frense, my immediate superior, who initiates me into the workings of the Institute. My first task is to organise one and two-month training programmes. Since this project has Australian funding, I collaborate with several journalists and directors from the Australian Broadcasting Corporation (ABC) who have just held training courses in South Africa.

Jim Revitt is our mainstay. He is an old hand at the ABC. He wears a pacemaker and listens to relaxation tapes in his free time. He is now a specialist in the training of journalists and directors. Jim teaches me how to structure a course.

The collaboration between Australia, Canada and South Africa proves a success. It's the start of an Australian network that brings me good friends, among them Denise Eriksen, Deborah Masters, Norman Taylor, Marion Wilkinson and Sue Spencer, whom I later visit in Australia in 1997.

Most of the journalists who attend my courses work for the SABC. When I advise them to go to Soweto, for example, to interview people, they are astonished. 'Why go and talk to a little old lady in Soweto?' I explain to them that this woman embodies the subject. 'She is the one who suffers the consequences of decisions made in high places. You need to talk to her to understand what is at stake. You need a face in the report, a human face, not only statistics and press releases!'

For journalists from the SABC in 1993, only interviews with members of the police or the government hold value. They are not used to testing the political discourse against reality. In my classroom, we hold great debates, often ideological debates more than debates about journalistic methodology. These journalists are also astonished to discover the amount of preparation necessary to produce a documentary. I bring the files I have used to prepare various documentaries to show them, as do the Australians. Practically every minute is detailed, practically every image is edited. I still meet trainees from that period and they all say to me that they remember my advice, especially that a journalist may never ask a question on camera without knowing the answer. This requires rigorous preliminary research and an anticipation of all possible answers.

As was to be expected, the transition towards the 'new South Africa' served as an excuse for certain blacks who wished to acquire privileges without making the effort to earn them. At the Institute, where for the moment all the lecturers are white, accusations of racism are thrown around on the slightest pretext. For example, an angry student accused me of being racist because I refused to give him a certificate at the end of the course. He had not attended eighty per cent of the lectures. He sat in his car all day long, except at lunchtime, when he came in to eat. Bad luck, I replied, my husband is black. His expression froze for a moment, then he retorted that I was racist 'at work'. He left, slamming the door behind him. His boss at the SABC, an agent in the military service responsible for news, laid a complaint. But all my colleagues and the director of the Institute supported me.

Unfortunately more and more of these shirkers would come to light, imagining that everything was owed to them because they were black.

32

Couple therapy

Friday mornings are sacred. For years, no matter what I am doing, at the Institute or reporting, I devote Friday mornings, from eight to nine, to my mental survival. I can get to the Family Life Centre with my eyes closed. I know that it's going to upset me, but I go. During this sacred hour I always broach the same subjects, cry the same tears, repeat the same words: 'Léandre', 'papa', 'Quebec', 'mama', 'roots', 'Jay', 'I'm afraid', 'how do you live on two continents at the same time?', 'cul-de-sac', 'go for it'. It really requires an incredible amount of energy to feel good about oneself!

Judy, my therapist, asks me questions. We talk about my youth in the English part of Canada and my education in an extremely strict environment (my father served in the Canadian armed forces for a long time) where nothing was ever 'good enough'. We try to understand why I feel fat, even in a body that weighs only fifty-seven kilos. I feel as though I take up too much space. I want to be very small, because that's how I see myself. I also feel that I never measure up, either in my work or with my friends. I feel obese physically and anorexic in my self-esteem.

The episode of Léandre is the last straw, bringing all my problems to the surface. This drama has deeply affected my relationships. It has become a daily preoccupation.

There is also a certain amount of back-stabbing going on at Radio–Canada at this time. A few individuals apply pressure to terminate my services because I am married to a leader of the ANC. 'Keep going, Lucie. Do your stories. I will worry about all that,' Gilles says to me repeatedly. One of my denigrators in the news service doesn't like me and tries to whip up some opposition. Eventually, she moves to another department and things calm down. I don't know whether the gossip has stopped, but I suspect that Gilles simply doesn't tell me about it because he knows how much it upsets me. He continues to reassure me, 'We would not keep you if you sent bad reports.' In a way the slander motivates me. I will show them what I am capable of, I say to myself. 'If only they knew that you don't give a damn about anything I tell you!' Jay sometimes comments laughingly. But he doesn't always laugh …

The upheaval sent ripples through our relationship.

Jay could do with some form of release for all the emotions he has accumulated. No doubt there are times when he'd like to yell at me or shake me to bring me to my senses. But he never does. My tears upset him. He feels responsible for my happiness, guilty about my unhappiness.

Jay and I bring together all the ingredients that could cause our marriage to fail. Everything that characterised us was different: nationality, culture, language, religion, skin colour, profession, country, continent, even hemisphere. And joint custody over two continents could end up undermining any couple's relationship. Jay promises regularly that one day he will come to live in Quebec, but he doesn't know when.

Jay exploded twice in our first eight years together. Twice he lost control. Completely! He punched the wall with his fists, two centimetres away from me, shouting at the top of his voice that he could not take it any longer, that he had had enough and that if I wanted to go back, I only had to leave. I still remember these outbursts vividly. I thought that he was going to hit me. But in a way I was relieved that he could explode like this. It reassured me that he was in fact human.

Because of the problems affecting our relationship, Jay and I go for counselling together. The first session with Judy goes well. Gradually, we start to deal with the real problems – how to manage the problem with Léandre in practical terms, for example. Soon we can't do without these sessions, where we're allowed to get things off our chest once in a while. Jay and I never refused to attend a joint meeting when the other requested it. I am convinced that without these sessions, which went on for eight years, Jay and I would no longer be together.

In 1995 I attended a different sort of counselling. The Canadian government established an assistance programme for Canadians in South Africa suffering from homesickness. It was my dear friend Marie-Hélène Bonin (who had been the researcher for the *Nord-Sud* documentaries) who called me one day to tell me the news.

'What, you mean I'm not the only one?'

'No! With you, there would be nine women. Are you interested?'

Of course I was interested. And as chance would have it, the meetings took place at the Family Life Centre. From then on, I went there twice a week.

Except for Marie-Hélène and myself, all the participants were English-speaking Canadians. All were married to, or at least living together with, a South African, in almost all cases a political activist, not an easy situation. We had several things in common: coloured children, violent or absent husbands (mine was always absent), broken family backgrounds, low financial resources, a fear of returning to Canada, a fear about remaining here. I suggested that we invite our husbands to our last meeting. Three-quarters of them came. Jay saw for himself that we were not the only ones with problems, that others were even worse off. A few years later only two of the nine women were still living with their South African husbands …

During my eight years of counselling, first with Judy, then with Nicki, then with Dr G, I cleaned, washed and ironed my experiences, my thoughts, my emotions, my concerns, my fears, my hurts. But this never lessened my love for my country. I missed it terribly.

One evening, between sobs, I asked Jay, 'Why weren't you born in Montreal? Why do you live on the other side of the world?'

'Because if I had been born in Montreal, we would never have met.'

33

Everyone at war with everyone else

The radio announces the discovery of another hit list with the names of ANC leaders. Jay's name is in fifth place.

The violence is a new element in my life. Jay's bullet-proof vest, which he carries around in his car but refuses to wear, haunts me. 'The spirit of my mother will protect us,' he says, as if that should be enough to reassure me.

South Africa is going up in flames. Violence is breaking out everywhere. It's 1993 and dozens are dying every day in conflict between supporters of Inkatha and supporters of the ANC/COSATU alliance in KwaZulu-Natal. The soldiers of Umkhonto we Sizwe, the armed wing of the ANC, are unhappy. Since the suspension of the armed struggle, they find themselves without work, without hope, above all without power, so they fight for the sake of fighting. De Klerk and Mandela are having difficulty talking to one another. Mangosuthu Buthelezi, the head of Inkatha, also the Chief Minister of KwaZulu, has burnt his bridges with both. Things are not looking good in South Africa.

Journalists from around the world are already starting to put out feelers to prepare for coverage of a civil war brewing. Some are palpably thirsting for blood to put on the front page. 'Perhaps one day we will say that things didn't go too badly under the whites,' one journalist writes …

Jay and I spend a few days in Natal with the boys, Omar and his three young daughters. We often go to rest at Omar's apartment at Umhlanga at the coast.

One evening, Jay and Omar go out to see someone. At eleven, they're still not back. They should have been back around nine. I am worried. In South Africa when you aren't back at the expected time, especially at night, it's a very bad omen.

We have already had a call, at four in the morning, from one of our female friends. Her husband, a high-placed trade unionist, had not yet come home. No doubt this meant that he'd been robbed, beaten or killed, and his wife was in a state. There are endless stories like this. Everyone has a horror story to tell. Jay had phoned the chief of police, friends and colleagues to try and find him. We contacted all the hospitals and clinics. Nothing. He finally arrived back at seven in the morning, drunk. The fact that he was back so late said everything. They got divorced.

Finally Jay and Omar arrived – at midnight! They had run out of petrol in a village that was an Inkatha rural stronghold! If Jay had been recognised, he might well have been dead. In 1986 Mangosuthu Buthelezi had arrived at a rally attended by tens of thousands of people with a coffin. There were two names on the coffin: Elijah Barayi and Jay Naidoo, president and general secretary of COSATU respectively.

'How could you be so stupid! Getting lost in an Inkatha stronghold with an empty tank!' I am furious. And relieved. Jay and Omar apologise a thousand times. They are only too familiar with this waiting and worrying, so often well-founded. How many friends had they themselves not waited for, and lost?

All sorts of wars are brewing in the country. The one between Inkatha and the ANC is the most clear and open. But there are also those between the Afrikaners and the English, between certain Afrikaners and other Afrikaners, between conservative whites and liberal whites, between Communists and fascists, between nationalists and supporters of a unitary state, between radicals and pacifists. The country seems to have reached a point where everyone is at war with everyone else.

The alliances are sometimes extremely varied, and even paradoxical. For example, a brand new 'Freedom Alliance' combines black nationalists and right-wing extremists who advocate a white state! The former want to retain power in certain bantustans, like Mangosuthu Buthelezi in KwaZulu; the latter have given them this power. Both groups are products of apartheid and believe they stand to lose a great deal if the ANC's proposal for a unitary state succeeds.

Every step, every important political agreement or stage is marked by a wave of violence. The announcement of the date of the next elections (27 April 1994), the creation of an executive transitional council, the adoption of an interim constitution, to mention only three events, each give rise to a wave of violence. Each time dozens of people are killed in cold blood, women, children, innocent people, it doesn't matter. The destabilisation of society is a strategic element in the chess game being played.

Up to the time of Mandela's release in 1990, the violence had been concentrated in the black areas. Almost all the victims of theft, murder, rape and vandalism were black. But the political liberalisation of the country and the ineffectiveness of the police force also liberate the forces of crime, which then move very quickly into the white areas.

The conflict between Inkatha and the ANC is complex. Inkatha is essentially a rural party. Mangosuthu Buthelezi has the support of the rural traditional chiefs who come to power by heredity, and not through elections. The ANC is a democratic party that wants to establish universal suffrage. The power of the chiefs, which Buthelezi would like to have written into the new constitution, represents a point of major disagreement between Inkatha and the ANC. This is one of the reasons that Buthelezi, for the time being, boycotts the negotiations and refuses to participate in any future elections.

Contrary to what is often reported in the media, here and abroad, this is not a 'tribal' struggle taking place between the Zulus and the Xhosas. Yes, Mandela is a Xhosa. And Buthelezi is a Zulu. But half the Zulus are ANC supporters. And the political violence is also instigated or fanned by the whites.

While Inkatha and the ANC battle it out, a conspiracy forms between Inkatha and the white government, which initially wants to establish a union with Inkatha in order to win black support and to form a strong enough opposition to prevent the ANC winning the elections. This collusion is eventually revealed by the media and ends officially, according to the government. Unofficially, however, members of the security forces of De Klerk's government continue to collaborate with Inkatha, supplying them with arms, among other things.

It's in this context that I go to do a report in a township in KwaZulu, Bambayi, near Durban. Jay 'lends' me his bodyguard. He doesn't want to see me walking on my own in dangerous areas. The atmosphere is tense. The bodies of victims of a gun battle the previous night have just been dispatched to the morgue.

As I interview a man from the ANC, with my microphone in the open, I notice military trucks followed by armoured tanks coming towards us. It's the South African army. The people I'm with start to get edgy. They are all ANC supporters.

Shots ring out. Government soldiers are assisted by men from Inkatha, I am told. The bodyguard snatches my equipment bag, grabs me and presses me to him, shielding me with his body. I protest in vain, insisting that I want to finish my interview, but he drags me to the car. 'I have my orders, and they are to protect you. I have no desire to be strangled by Comrade Naidoo!'

Situations like this have a tendency to multiply. It was not long after this that I ventured into Alexandra, the black township adjacent to the very rich white Johannesburg suburb of Sandton. I was covering a story. Turning at an intersection, I came face-to-face with three armed men. They stiffened and pointed their guns at me. I braked immediately. All four of us remained frozen for a second that seemed endless.

I don't know what took hold of me … To break the ice, to douse the fire, I smiled and waved at the men, which perplexed them. I wound down my window. The man in front came towards me, slowly, looking down the barrel of his gun, his finger on the trigger, his body leaning back a little, his knees slightly bent. Before he came too close, I shouted, 'I am from Canada! I'm lost! But what is happening? Who are you afraid of?'

Would Jay's name save my life today? Was I dealing with supporters of Inkatha or the ANC? The man replied, 'You are in danger here, madam. Inkatha attacked last night. Leave, madam, leave!' He signalled the others to lower their guns.

I did a U-turn and left. My leg jumped every time I had to press in the clutch, I was trembling so much.

'Your smile made all the difference,' Mahlape Sello, an expert on violence, told me later on. A smile is disarming, even to a soldier.

I had no need to run to the townships to taste danger. Just living with Jay was a risk in itself …

One day, I was alone at home with Léandre. As I was hanging up the washing on the line outside, I saw something move behind the trees on the hillside. Léandre was playing in the kitchen. I ducked under the line to go and see what was moving and came face-to-face with two armed men, one white, one black. (After having described their guns to an expert, I realised that they were AK-47s, the most commonly used assault rifles in the country.) They trained their guns on me, their fingers on the trigger. Without thinking, I cried, 'He's not here!', knowing full well that it was Jay they were looking for (he was in Nigeria for two weeks). Then I ran to the house. I snatched Léandre up and we went to hide under my desk in my office. Léandre had no idea what was going on. I whispered to him that we were pretending someone was breaking into the house. 'And what do you do when there are burglars? You hide and you call someone.' I grabbed the telephone and called for help.

A few days before that, I had noticed a white car that was often parked in front of our house. I had memorised the registration number, just in case.

I phoned Peter Harris, our lawyer friend. 'Don't move. I am coming. And whatever you do don't call the police!' he warned me. When he arrived, he made me sign a sworn statement describing what had happened. He left with the registration number of the suspicious car.

The registration number belonged to a police vehicle, he told me later. After that incident, the white car did not appear again.

If Jay had been home that day, I might well have been a widow today.

34

Chris Hani

At last, a family holiday! It's Easter 1993 and we're leaving for the game reserve, Jay, the two boys and I, with a colleague of Jay's, his wife and their four children. It's Jay's first safari: we're going to discover South Africa together. It's only in my company, for the first time, that Jay walks in parks, goes to cinemas, restaurants and tourist resorts. He wasn't allowed to before …

After a day in the car, we arrive at the Kruger National Park, where a jeep is waiting to take us on a night safari, the only way to admire lions in action – or rather lionesses, since they're the ones that hunt. Our guide warns us to remain seated, because he's driving close up to the lions. Indeed, a pride of lions passes only a metre away from us. The guide stops breathing. We all turn into statues. The lionesses give chase to a giraffe. We see everything in the powerful floodlights … It's fascinating!

The following morning I leave Jay in our thatched hut and go to breakfast with the children. Jay has some work to do. We're busy eating our eggs and cereal, when a waitress runs out of the kitchen shouting. She's just heard that Chris Hani, General Secretary of the Communist Party, has been assassinated. I can't believe my ears. Chris Hani is without a doubt the most popular man in South Africa after Nelson Mandela. I interviewed him only a few months before (without his knowing that I was married to a good friend of his).

The first thing that comes into my head is that if 'they' have managed to kill Chris Hani, at home in his driveway, 'they' could undoubtedly kill Jay. I run to the hut to tell Jay. As soon as I enter, he realises something is wrong.

'Chris has just been assassinated.'

'Not Chris Hani?'

'Yes, Chris Hani.'

His dark skin turns pale. He collapses on the bed.

'I am afraid for you, Jay! I am so afraid! If they can kill Chris, they can kill you too!'

'But Chris has just died! How can you even think about that?'

I keep quiet. Jay bursts into tears. I have never seen him cry before.

'I need to be alone.'

I leave him. How do you console someone who has lost someone close? Jay stays in the hut for two hours. Then he comes out and announces that he has to go back to Johannesburg.

We leave immediately. We drive without stopping, without saying a word. The children don't understand the gravity of the situation. Jay has lost a friend. South Africa has lost a great leader. Chris Hani had fallen to the bullets of Janusz Waluz, a Polish immigrant to South Africa, allied to the Conservative Party.

Born in 1943, Chris Martin Thembisile Hani became involved in the struggle for 'justice and human dignity' at the age of fourteen. When he went underground to train for Umkhonto we Sizwe, he not only carried ammunition and grenades in his backpack, but works by Shakespeare, a pen and some paper to write poems and stories. Said to be an outstanding soldier, he became one of the leaders of Umkhonto we Sizwe.

An activist, militant, poet, Communist, exceptional speaker, a tough soldier with a tender heart, he often said that he was ready to die for the cause. But he had always tried to avoid violence at all costs. It was largely due to him that the tripartite alliance (ANC, Communist Party, COSATU) survived during the most difficult moments of the negotiating process. His constant pleas for a peaceful solution and greater political tolerance were taken to heart.

On the morning of 10 April 1993 Chris Hani told his bodyguards they could take the Easter weekend off. He was not supposed to go out alone, but on that Saturday he had ignored warnings, putting his faith in life and fate as usual. He went to buy some bread and the newspaper at the store near his home. As he got out of his car, another car drove towards him. Waluz got out of it, lifted his pistol and fired four shots, at point-blank range. Waluz fled, but did not get very far. Chris Hani's neighbour, an Afrikaans woman, was driving past as the crime was committed. She had time to note the registration number of the vehicle leaving the area. She immediately called the police. Fifteen minutes later, Waluz was arrested ten kilometres from Hani's house, his shirt stained, the still-warm gun next to him.

The images of Chris, his head in a pool of blood, send shockwaves through South Africa. The majority of the population – white and black – are so angry that people fear a revolt, an immense bloodbath, chaos. The country literally goes up in flames.

On the day of the funeral the country is vandalised, by rage, anger and savagery. In all the cities, Cape Town, Durban, Johannesburg, Pietermaritzburg, East London and Port Elizabeth, protesters smash shop windows, loot and break everything that can be broken. Bombs explode everywhere. Seventy people die.

President De Klerk is completely powerless. In a second, his country has revolted, venting a rage that he has no way of controlling.

He appeals to Nelson Mandela, who addresses the nation live on television. He calls for calm. He speaks to the camera as a father might console a child. He is firm but gentle, emotional but rational. He tries to salvage something from the situation. 'It was an Afrikaner who reported the crime,' he stresses.

Hani's funeral is the most important in the country's history. The state television service broadcasts it live, the first time this honour has been accorded to 'an enemy of the state'.

35

Guess who's coming to dinner

Nelson Mandela is completely devastated by the death of Chris Hani. He still looks downcast two months after the assassination. But his welcome is always warm when we meet. 'We must get together for a chat one of these days,' he says each time. 'You must come over for dinner.' I accept with pleasure. How could I refuse? But where would he find the time to entertain us?

One day I suggest in turn that he come to our place for dinner. Without hesitating, he replies that he would be honoured.

We leave it at that. But my mind is set and I select a date: 7 December 1993, Loulou's birthday. My mother is coming over for a month at the beginning of December, together with Léandre, who has returned to Quebec to start his second year of primary school there. For two years Léandre has spent six months at a time on each continent. He completed his first year in six months at the French School in Johannesburg, because he already knew how to read and look up words in a dictionary at the age of five. We were now working in periods of a year. The latest agreement with his father, which is still 'temporary', stipulates that he'll spend his second year in Quebec and his third year here.

I would never get used to his absence. This year, however, I am very grateful for it. The violence, a few months away from the elections, seems to be getting worse by the day. Jay is a target. I want to spare Léandre all of this. His absence is the price I have to pay for peace of mind.

Loulou turns fifty-six on 7 December. I have a crazy idea to offer her a meal with Mandela as a gift. She admired him long before her daughter's South African experience. She kept up with the news from South Africa and boycotted all products from the country from the seventies on.

I tell Jay about my idea.

'He is very busy, you know.'

'But he was the one who suggested we should have a meal together. Every time I see him, he mentions it.'

'I'll ask him.'

A few days after Kami's first birthday, Jay announces that Mandela will come over on 6 December, because on the seventh he has to be in Oslo to receive the Nobel Prize for Peace for 1993 with Frederik de Klerk. This joint presentation of the prize has a made a lot of people angry in South Africa. They look at the problem from a different perspective: would a black president at the head of an oppressive government, which had committed violations of human rights, and even murdered whites, have been offered a Nobel Peace Prize? Nonetheless, Frederik de Klerk had freed Mandela and was voluntarily giving up his position …

On the day of his departure for Oslo, Mandela will come for lunch. He'll be with us from twelve to two. At last, I can plan the meal … I order a cake with the colours of Quebec and the ANC, blue and white on one half and yellow, black and green on the other. My mother, obviously, suspects nothing.

On the big day, Loulou lazes in bed reading. I go and tell her she has to get up and get ready.

'Get ready for what?'

'We have a surprise for you. We are giving you your birthday present today instead of tomorrow.'

'What is the surprise?'

'A private meal with Nelson Mandela.'

'What are you talking about?'

'I'm telling you that you are going to have lunch with Mandela, so get up and get a move on. He'll be here in three hours!'

Loulou looks at me in complete amazement, as though I'm having her on. She almost feels offended because you don't joke about such things.

'Stop it now. Don't be silly!'

'I'm telling you, he's coming to lunch!'

'Here?'

'Yes, here.'

'I don't believe you! It's not funny!'

For fifteen minutes – precious time when there is so much to organise – Loulou and I are practically having a row. She refuses to believe me. She thinks I'm playing a joke on her. I have always been the clown in the family and now I am paying the price. In the end I tell her I have to get the house ready, and if she really wants to meet Mandela tousled in her nightdress, it's up to her. I leave the room.

She comes to look for me.

'You are serious, aren't you?'

'Why do you think I went to fetch the video camera from the Institute yesterday? He is arriving at midday, so MOVE IT!'

Then the panic starts. She's finally realised that I am not joking.

The next two hours are completely crazy. I rush around making sure that everything will be ready on time. We have ordered an Indian meal, fruit – lots of fruit, because Mandela likes fresh fruit – and the famous cake. The only other guest is Omar.

At last everything is ready. Our quaint old house has a lot of charm. We've thought of everything, right down to the music that will accompany our meal.

As we wait, Loulou chain-smokes.

On the strike of twelve, a car arrives. Mandela is always on time. Seeing him, with his bodyguards, Louise murmurs, as though she still can't believe it, 'It's him, it's really him! It's really true!'

He comes in looking very relaxed, and sits down in the lounge. Kami is impossible to control at this age. He climbs onto Mandela's lap, grabs his glass of orange juice and takes a few large gulps. Mandela is incredible with children. He adores them. When he sees a child, he always stops to talk. This was what he missed most during his twenty-seven years in prison – contact with children. When he became president, he created the Nelson Mandela Children's Fund, a fund to assist children in need, and donated a third of his monthly salary to it. So Kami pulling on his trousers, drinking from his glass and making dirty marks on his clothes seems to give him great pleasure.

We all have our video cameras and our portable cameras, but no one dares to use them. I am embarrassed by my 'groupie' tendencies. But too bad! I can't let this moment pass without preserving the memory. I grab my camera and take some pictures.

I watch Mandela giving Kami some juice, then drinking himself, oblivious to the dirty marks. He wipes his trousers where Kami has dribbled on them ... There's such tenderness in his look and his gestures, such simplicity in his attitude. How can one not be touched by them?

Loulou sits next to him, living the moment like a dream. Even Jay, who knows Mandela so well, who has worked so closely with him, is nervous. I see the admiration in his eyes. Jay would do anything to support Mandela's cause.

As the elections approach – they are to take place in five months' time – we often hear the remark, 'If Mandela dies now, it will all be over.' I am convinced that a man with such a destiny cannot die before achieving what he is destined to achieve. He will live, I am sure of it, and he will take his place at the head of the country. I look at him, calmly sitting on our old couch, and I'm struck by the thought of what a heavy burden the destiny of an entire country must be for one man.

He is about to receive the Nobel Peace Prize with President De Klerk, but the responsibility for the peaceful nature of the transition really belongs to him alone. He has the moral authority to calm people.

The meal is ready and we take our seats. I have prepared a list of conversation topics, just in case. I needn't have worried! Nelson Mandela, at seventy-five years of age, has a lifetime of stories and he talks non-stop! One anecdote after another. Among the most memorable is that of his first day at work in the offices of attorneys Witkin, Sidelsky & Eidelman, a job he got thanks to Walter Sisulu.

'The first morning, a young white secretary took me aside and said to me, 'Nelson, we don't have any racial barriers here. We have even bought two new teacups for you and Gaur Radebe [the only other black employee in the office].' Now the reason that she had taken the trouble to buy two new cups was to prevent us, the two black employees, from drinking from the same cups as the others. I dropped a word in Gaur's ear and he immediately cottoned on. He told me to do whatever he did at teatime.'

Mandela picked up his glass and took a sip of water to draw out the suspense, then replaced it delicately and continued.

'At teatime, I let Gaur serve himself first. He pretended not to see the two new cups and took a 'normal' cup, poured some tea into it and slowly stirred in his milk and sugar with one of the 'communal' teaspoons. When my turn came, I did not know what to do. I did not want to alienate myself from my white colleagues on my first day at work, even if their little trick to force us to drink from different cups was evident. I hesitated, then said that I was not thirsty. I did not have any tea.'

A little smile played around his lips as he concluded.

'From then on, I had my tea by myself.'

That's Mandela: a man who avoids confrontation if he can, but who is nobody's fool …

Then it was time to give our gifts to our guest. More gifts! I wonder what goes through his mind when he receives them. Two people work for him full-time, just opening and listing all the gifts he receives from all over the world. Loulou offers two presents (which she has found at the last minute, in the house), which he unwraps with care. The first is an *inukshuit* (or *inukshuk*), a miniature replica of the stone statues of the human form that are scattered across the Arctic. They are markers, she explains to Mandela, to help the Inuits find their way in the white desert. He listens attentively, asking questions from time to time. He recalls an incident that happened among the Inuits. When he got out of his plane, during a stopover to refuel in the Canadian Great North, he heard people shouting his name and saw them pushing their hands through the railings to try and touch him.

'I was very surprised that these people, living on the other side of the planet in a white desert, knew who I was.'

The second present is a jar of maple syrup. A real Québecois gift! He is thrilled.

Louise has given her video camera to Léandre so that he can discreetly film the meal. What a surprise we got when we looked at the cassette: Léandre, who had not seen Kami for five months, had only taken a few pictures of Mandela. Most of the film was devoted to his brother's antics – something that really moved me …

Throughout the meal I feel rather annoyed. *Here I am sitting next to the man I have been trying to get an interview with for eighteen months; I have my portable microphone, a professional video camera, but ... But this is a* private lunch. I won't go back on the principles I adopted when I had agreed to share my life with Jay. One thing is certain, no one will ever be able to accuse me of using my husband for professional ends! And it certainly isn't because I haven't had enough opportunities.

He calls from time to time to speak to Jay, often around four or five in the morning, when he starts his day. Once when he called I did not even dare speak to him. Léandre answered the phone. 'Jay! Mandela wants to speak to you!' he shouted. Their conversation lasted about five minutes and then Mandela asked to speak to me. I sat there, frozen.

'He just wants to say hello,' Jay whispered to me, holding the telephone out towards me.

'No, I cannot. Tell him I am in the bath. Tell him I am changing Kami's nappy. Tell him I am not feeling well.'

'Lucie, stop being silly. He just wants to say hello!'

'Tell him I am in the bath.'

And while Jay tried to convince me to speak to Mandela, Mandela waited. I was making him wait.

'Lucie, take the telephone!' Jay insisted, throwing the receiver at me.

'No!'

And I threw it back to him.

I couldn't speak to him; I felt terribly shy.

Towards the end of the meal, I finally decide to use my camera. Mandela gives me a funny look, but I really need a few video images. It's stronger than me, I can't help it.

We serve the cake in the colours of the ANC and Quebec, covered in birthday candles. He is surprised. He says he never eats sweet things – he only has fruit for dessert – but that today he'll accept a little slice of the beautiful cake with pleasure.

It's two o'clock. Mandela has to leave us. He is catching a plane in a few hours and he has to prepare for the journey.

We walk with him to his car. On the way he stops at the little flat above the garage to greet Elizabeth. He asks her a few questions, laughs a little and shakes her hand warmly. Elizabeth has her head in the clouds for days!

And so do we!

36

Lessons in freedom

The first time I saw Jay on television, I was startled. 'With your tousled hair and your rumpled jacket, you look like someone hiding a grenade in his pocket. This is not the image to project if you want your message to be heard!'

By force of circumstance, and even almost unconsciously, I started to train Jay for television. Whenever I could record his interviews, we would watch them together and I would suggest improvements: clothing, hair, posture, body language …

Then I started to analyse the way in which he presented the content of his message and advise him on this: what information to give; how to say what he wanted to say even if the journalist did not ask the right questions; how to 'read' the journalist; how to say more with fewer words; how to prepare for an interview; how to put together short messages as one-liners (like the famous phrase aimed at the American people, 'Do not ask what your country can do for you, but rather what you can do for your country') and grabs (thirty-second messages).

In this way, over the months and years, I made a contribution to the way Jay faced the media. And, little by little, people commented on his 'new appeal'. 'What have you done?' they would ask him in relation to his new-found control of the media.

A few months before the elections, it was Jay's turn to panic when he saw his colleagues on TV. 'They all look like they could be hiding a grenade in their pockets! Couldn't you organise a little workshop on the media for them?'

'But I have never done anything like that. I wouldn't know what to say.'

'For three years you have been telling me what to do. And it's working! We need it so much. Especially with the elections around the corner!'

Jay had recently announced that he was leaving his position as General Secretary of COSATU in order to stand as an ANC candidate in the elections. Twenty of them were leaving COSATU – a severe blow for the organisation. At the time of its establishment in December 1985, the trade union confederation was described by white politicians as 'a barking dog with no bite'. How wrong they were! Jay was extremely popular; he was unanimously elected to the position of General Secretary, for three consecutive terms. Now he was preparing to play a role in government, and it was crucial for him and his team to know how to interact with the media.

The new democracy had brought freedom of the press, something unknown up to this point. In the past there was no awareness of this source of power, which had been completely subordinated to the government of the day. Microphones were pushed away because they were government weapons. Then, overnight, a group of apprentice politicians were forced to interact with an army of seasoned journalists from all over the world. Candidates across the political spectrum were taken by surprise. They had to learn how to tame the media and learn its rules.

I told Allister Sparks about the project. He was really taken with it! So I started putting together a document for the Institute for the Advancement of Journalism, a guide explaining how to handle the media. Sparks had often received requests for the Institute to offer such a course and now, a few months before the elections, the requests were streaming in from everywhere. Allister was not familiar with this subject so he gave me the task of developing a course for anyone who wanted to learn how to handle the media.

I spent a month preparing the course with video clips to illustrate what to do and what not to do. Extracts from interviews with Frederik de Klerk often featured among the examples of 'good' things to do. He had been trained by British specialists.

The training session lasted eight hours and started with a role-play of a press conference. The candidates – four or five per course – were placed in front of the camera, behind a long table. Allister and I played the role of the journalists. Afterwards, we analysed their performance on the videotape to advise them on how to present their messages.

It ended up being a sort of intensive journalism course for me. By observing Allister Sparks, who had been in the business for forty years, grilling these politicians, I refined my own interviewing techniques. It was during this course that I really broke down the wall of my shyness, because I had to be on stage for eight hours at a stretch!

In the end I trained more than two hundred and fifty politicians over a period of five years, including Nelson Mandela. The day before the big television debate between Mandela and De Klerk, the team from the Institute was called in to assist an American team who were coaching Mandela. I was given the role of a journalist. Four of the five questions I had prepared were put to him the next day by the three journalists hosting the actual television debate. Allister Sparks played President de Klerk in our role-play. He played De Klerk better than De Klerk himself! An enormous amount of knowledge was required to give a good performance as President De Klerk …

Mandela spent the day listening attentively, taking notes, accepting our criticism and trying to correct his 'media' faults: lengthy responses, a stiff body posture, sometimes a cold expression, a dry tone. He was a model pupil.

It was a tense debate, but Mandela surprised De Klerk, and the nation, when he held out his hand, saying, in front of millions of television viewers, 'Let us work together to build this magnificent country.' Even De Klerk admitted that Mandela had, in media terms, won the debate.

At the Institute we trained politicians from all parties: the ANC, the Freedom Front, the National Party, Inkatha, the Pan-Africanist Congress and other smaller parties. My own apprenticeship while training people from these parties was invaluable. I have never reported what was said in those classes, but I greatly enriched my understanding of the national political context. Oddly enough, this exercise allowed me to develop 'friendships' in very diverse camps on the South African political scene. I now get on very well with General Constand Viljoen, the leader of the Freedom Front, and his wife, and with Suzanne Vos, an

Inkatha leader. This woman, originally from Australia, joined the ranks of Inkatha because of its liberal economic policies. In the evening, over a drink, she is wonderful. Ironically she found herself elected to the opposition with the specific mission of criticising Jay's policies!

Paradoxically, I had to show the politicians how best to 'evade' journalists, or at least how to deliver their message in the most effective way, and to teach journalists to navigate the manoeuvring of politicians trying to get their message across without responding directly to their questions. I have seen interviews on television where I have trained both the journalist and the politician! These two tasks may seem contradictory, but in South Africa at this time, an apprenticeship in press freedom was a matter of national urgency.

37

KwaZulu

Fifty-three people died today, 28 March 1994. A month before the elections, this does not augur well! René Mailhot, a Radio–Canada journalist who has come to do some reporting for a current affairs radio programme, calls me from his hotel in central Johannesburg. 'Is this scene normal?' From high up in his hotel room he has seen tens of thousands of Inkatha supporters demonstrating in the streets, armed with spears and shields, some with firearms. They are demanding sovereignty for the Zulu people and shouting their opposition to the elections, which Inkatha has decided to boycott.

In actual fact, for a journalist who had just arrived in Johannesburg, this scene might have seemed 'normal', in view of the fact that the news presented about this country is always so bloody.

It was not normal. This incident was serious, very serious.

The police had ignored the warnings of the ANC, who feared the worst after learning that their headquarters lay directly in the path of the demonstration. Nelson Mandela had given the order to protect the building 'at all costs'. When the security guards saw the crowd of armed Zulus turn at the intersection and rush towards the building, they fired. Reports said that some of the shots could have been from party members. Eight people died in front of the ANC offices. Elsewhere, in the streets of the city, forty-five people lost their lives in the riots that followed.

During the next three weeks, three hundred people die.

People fear the worst is yet to come.

The violence probably constitutes the biggest obstacle to overcome before the elections. It could threaten or even prevent the elections from taking place. Peace efforts proliferate. But the violence continues.

Hoping to convince Inkatha to participate in the elections, Frederik de Klerk, Nelson Mandela and the head of Inkatha, Mangosuthu Buthelezi, hold a 'peace summit'.

They argue about the date of the elections: Buthelezi wants to delay it at all costs, to give him time to negotiate crucial elements; Mandela is categorical and defends 27 April 1994 as sacrosanct. A team of seven international mediators flies in, among them America's Henry Kissinger and Britain's Lord Carrington. But they swiftly leave again, because nobody can agree on the terms of their mandate.

It is in this climate that I leave for KwaZulu, the centre of the war zone between the ANC and Inkatha. I accompany two Québecois journalists: René Mailhot of Radio–Canada and Richard Hétu of the newspaper *La Presse*.

In Empangeni, which Inkatha controls, we climb to the second floor of a small, rather dark and gloomy building. At the end of a poorly lit corridor is a door carrying three large letters: IFP – Inkatha Freedom Party. Armed with mikes, recorders and notebooks, René, Richard and I enter. The reception area is full of people, the poor and the helpless, whose reasons for being here I cannot fathom. I tell the person in charge that we have come to see Mr Ben Ngubane, a top Inkatha official (who will become Minister of Arts, Culture, Science and Technology in Mandela's government). He looks at us, taken aback. 'That's impossible,' he retorts. 'He is three hundred kilometres away.'

Everything has been arranged, though. They send us to see the regional head of Inkatha. Entering his office (it's obvious that he has not been warned of our presence), we are dumbstruck. René Mailhot describes the scene well: 'Guys built like tanks with AK-47s hanging around their necks.' They are surprised and uneasy with our intrusion when their arms are so clearly in evidence. The head asks us to leave and then receives us a quarter of an hour later, after a 'clean-up'.

He is full of smiles during the interview. After answering a dozen questions, he tells us we can turn off our tape recorders. I don't know why, but when I press the stop button nothing happens. The cassette continues to turn and I do nothing to stop it. So I decide to record the conversation. And what a conversation! In a belligerent tone of voice, he tells us that Inkatha will vehemently oppose the holding of elections. Then he explains that he would choose his weapon over his wife at a drop of a hat. He can't go to bed without his weapon, but he can go to bed without his wife. Ha! He finds this very amusing, and laughs heartily. But he's said too much now. If he notices that my tape recorder is still on, his 'tanks' might reappear – they might be the last thing I experience. René has noticed what I have done; he is getting very jumpy. We leave.

I feel a little nervous on the rural roads in KwaZulu, even though I am with two men. We're familiar with the war in KwaZulu; we have been covering it for years, after all. What we need are bullet-proof vests!

Driving through the mountains and valleys, I realise that what I actually need is a camera. We take the Valley of a Thousand Hills route. The scenery is breathtaking! Are we really in KwaZulu? Where they kill children with an axe and grandmothers with an assegai? Where AK-47 fire rains down? I myself regularly give radio reports on the number of battles tearing KwaZulu apart. But the magnificence of the Valley of a Thousand Hills is not reflected in the news reports. This is the real Africa. Africa with its little thatched huts, wisps of smoke escaping through the roofs. Africa with children running barefoot over the ripples of the valley. The Africa of women bent low over their tools, tirelessly working the earth. It is beautiful. It is tranquil. It is simple. But the violence is invisible. The sorrow is invisible. You can't trace the fear in this landscape.

Another Québecois journalist who had passed through the region a few days before noticed the same thing,

'KwaZulu is a land abandoned by the outside world […] Everyone knew how likely it was to have your car stolen there, to be raped or killed. Not to mention the risk of finding yourself caught in the middle of a political skirmish.

'In spite of this, the countryside looks peaceful. Children wave at our car as it passes. Bare-breasted women walk nonchalantly along the side of the road, bundles of wood on their heads. Some wear rings around their legs, to below the knee. The car has to weave around cows lying in the middle of the road. A pastoral calm reigned in the region, one that did not tally with the apocalyptic images of the rebel province shown abroad.'

The journalist is my friend Luc Chartrand. He has come to prepare a pre-election report for the newspaper *L'actualité*. But he is also Paul Carpentier, the hero of the novel *Code Bezhenti*, which Luc was to write on his return from Africa. Paul, or Luc – take your pick – would experience some of his adventures in KwaZulu, which, at that moment at any rate, appeared so calm. 'It was not the first time that Paul realised how big the gap was between the media image and the reality,' Luc writes in *Code Bezhenti*.

❦ ❦ ❦

A second peace summit is organised. A week before the elections, Inkatha finally agrees to participate in them. A few days later, on 25 April, less than twenty-four hours before the handicapped and aged cast their vote and forty-eight hours before the general election, Parliament amends the Interim Constitution to give effect to the compromises reached with Inkatha: the recognition of the Zulu kingdom and protection of its monarchy, its laws and its constitutional role.

With this peace accord, the killings will surely stop. Mangosuthu Buthelezi has one week to mount his election campaign, one week to tell his followers to stop the boycott and to go and vote.

The elections are safe. What else can happen?

38

The bombs

A bomb explodes.

It is 24 April 1994, two days before the elections. Kami is playing by himself. I am sitting in the lounge, using these few hours of peace to prepare my files on the elections. I am reading piles of articles from all over while listening to the radio. Suddenly, a special bulletin is broadcast: a bomb has just exploded in front of the ANC headquarters, killing nine and injuring almost a hundred.

I am terribly worried: Jay had some appointments in town today, one of which was at the ANC offices ...

Some people have said they will do anything to prevent the elections from being held. Eugene Terre'Blanche, the leader of the Afrikaner Resistance Movement (Afrikaner Weerstandsbeweging – AWB), has said this more than once. Last year, he used tanks to smash down the enormous foyer windows of Johannesburg's World Trade Centre! His followers then urinated on the carpets, in front of the delegates who were gathered to negotiate the new constitution. But have they gone as far as setting off a bomb to sow panic before the elections?

Twenty minutes later, Jay calls me. He is shaken, but alive. He tells me that one of his colleagues has been killed ...

I grab the phone to get the details and immediately send a report off to Montreal. No one has claimed responsibility for the attack, but the suspicion falls directly on the extreme right. I write my report and send it, my stomach in a knot:

'Today is the last day of campaigning for the twenty-six political parties participating in the elections in South Africa. The president of the ANC, Mr Mandela, was in Durban, where more than two hundred thousand people gathered to listen to him one last time before the elections. Despite the resounding success of this mass rally, Mr Mandela hurried back to Johannesburg with a heavy heart. One of his colleagues and an election candidate was among the nine people killed today when a powerful explosion shook central Johannesburg just a few feet from the offices of the ANC. Witnesses said they saw two white men get out of a car and run off. The car exploded minutes later. Mr De Klerk has warned that the radical minorities who are trying to destabilise the process of democratisation in South Africa and to prevent the holding of elections will not succeed. The head of Inkatha, Mr Buthelezi, was in Soweto for his fourth and last day of electoral campaigning. He said that today's incident proves that it is impossible for the elections to be free and democratic. Some people have said that they will not go to vote because they are afraid.'

I am afraid of the violence too. I am afraid because Jay is a target, now more than ever. Fear is everywhere, but with it comes determination …

The following day, 25 April 1994, the last day before the start of the elections, the news is even more sombre. A series of explosions shakes the country. One explosion in Germiston, Johannesburg, kills ten people and injures at least thirty-six others – eight hundred metres from an ANC office. The police offer a reward of two million rand to anyone who can supply information that will lead to the arrest of the perpetrators who carried out the attack.

I prepare a retrospective report. I wish the bombs would stop. Deep within me, I would like to be able to announce good news, to say that the country is on its way, that a miracle has occurred, that everyone has gone to vote in peace and that South Africa will be an example for the rest of Africa. But no, I read my next sombre report with a shaky voice:

'Yesterday, you could read the despair in South Africa in the face of a mother who lost her three children in an explosion that shook central Johannesburg. During the night three other bombs went off across the country. One of these explosions damaged a polling station. And this morning several other bombs caused large amounts of damage. Witnesses saw bodies and cars ripped to pieces. This morning's bombs were placed at minibus taxi stops, the main form of transport for black workers. Hundreds of people crowd around these stops every morning: perfect targets for terrorists who want to prevent the elections. In two of today's explosions, witnesses say they saw white men running off just before the bombs exploded. People are shocked and disgusted. On one of the most popular radio stations in the country, which broadcasts phone-in programmes day and night, people are calling in to vent their anger and sadness, to say they are afraid to go and vote. No one has yet claimed responsibility for the attacks. People suspect the 'Third Force', a handful of people who want to prevent South Africa's democratisation. The elections begin tomorrow. South Africa is on the alert.'

The term 'Third Force' is now part of the South African vocabulary. The expression refers to a 'secret force' made up of conspirators from the extreme right, the police or the army trying, at any cost, to prevent the blacks from taking power. This Third Force is composed of people from within and outside the government. The term was also used in Chile before the conspirators overthrew the Allende government in 1973. The first force refers to the current government; the second to the opposition; and the third to individuals prepared to keep members of the first force in power by illegal means.

I am on the alert and I am hardly able to eat. Everything makes me nauseous. The attitude of many journalists sickens me. Some are in seventh heaven, as if their fortunes are increasing with the number of bombs.

As for me, when I go out in the morning I look under the car to see whether a bomb is hidden there. I check Jay's car especially. I look all around me, to make sure that there is no one suspicious in the area, for example sitting in a car doing nothing. When I do notice things like this from time to time, I know what to do: call the police. We have learned, among other things, that two men who were watching our house had close links with the extreme right.

Since Jay became a candidate in the elections, he has been assigned a bodyguard. The man given this job is Lucky, a scrawny chap barely a metre and a half in height! I inform him that a man sits in a van just outside our house, every evening between five-thirty and six-thirty. The writing on the vehicle indicates that it belongs to a Chinese restaurant.

Sometimes a woman sits with the man. I give the registration number to Lucky, who calls in the special police squad assigned to look after the security of political candidates. The investigation reveals that the vehicle has been registered in a town far from Johannesburg, in the name of another company, not a Chinese restaurant. When Lucky's efforts don't get very far, I decide to call the special squad myself and ask them to look into the matter properly. A few days later the police tell me that they have questioned the driver. He has told them he comes to see his mistress, who lives close by. He begs the police not to say anything, because both of them are married. This story of an extramarital adventure comforts me somewhat … I am becoming paranoid.

But 'Lucky' never gets to enjoy the 'new' South Africa. One morning he arrives at the house with a fever. He has a headache and is vomiting. I call his brother, who comes to fetch him. He dies of malaria a week later.

Léandre is not with me during this time. If he had been, his father would probably have come to fetch him, after listening to my reports. But I have another son here. And every evening when I come home, I pray that nothing has happened to Kami. If Jay is unfortunate enough to get back late, my stomach is in a knot. I am on my guard. I have dark rings under my eyes, because I am sleeping badly. But when I sit down and concentrate on writing a report, I forget everything … for an hour or two.

When I finish writing, reality bites. Fear literally invades me. I mumble and make language mistakes when I phone Montreal to read my texts. On one occasion I am in tears. I am sure the other side is wondering whether I am going to make it.

The big day is approaching. Mixed with the fear is excitement, the hope of finally seeing the birth of a new country. A country of colours – the Rainbow Nation, as Archbishop Desmond Tutu put it. It is this rainbow that will dominate tomorrow, whatever the result of the elections. Freedom is in the air. As if the people can't wait any longer. Everyone is ready. Everyone is afraid.

The bombs continue to explode. In Pretoria a bomb has exploded in a bar, killing two people. In the past two days, the series of bombs has killed twenty-one people and injured one hundred and thirty-three others. President De Klerk has called for calm and order and has increased security measures. The nine thousand polling stations are being guarded as from tonight. The main political leaders have tried to curb the fear and panic by broadcasting messages of encouragement and hope. Bombs or not, they say, we are all going to vote.

The country has gone to bed tonight, but I know that it is not sleeping. Seated at my bedroom window, I look at the lights of the city through the iron bars that are supposed to protect us. I have goose-pimples. I try to hear the last breath of apartheid. I can scarcely believe that I am here at a moment of such intensity.

Another bomb explodes. I jump, even though I am almost expecting it. Jay comes to join me. We try to work out where the sound came from. A few kilometres away at the most. I wait for the wailing of ambulances. Are there any dead?

If there are only a few dead, Radio–Canada will not be interested. When there are many bombs, many dead, routine sets in. The news is no longer new. But the fear that I feel always seems to be new to me.

This evening we are on the brink of a miracle or a civil war. It is as if the country is perfectly balanced on a fence, but a feather falling from the sky could topple everything.

39

The first black election

Jay left at six this morning. Everyone is fighting over him today, because it is the first of the three election days, reserved for the aged, handicapped or ill. Some areas of the country are experiencing serious logistical problems. No ballot papers, no invisible ink to identify those who have voted, no Inkatha stickers, which have to be added to every ballot paper. The Inkatha leader, Mangosuthu Buthelezi, has even called for the elections to be extended by a day in view of these problems. But the Independent Electoral Commission, while admitting they have been overwhelmed, deny that these problems will affect the validity of the elections. Tomorrow and Thursday, twenty-two million people will vote, eighteen million of them for the first time!

Jay has always known that he would experience this great day. He has often told me that he was always certain he would participate in the country's new government. He is about to realise his life's work. I am aware of the magnitude of what is happening for him now.

I start a marathon of reporting. I only have seventy seconds at a time to put it all across.

'Old people, some on crutches, other in wheelchairs, waited more than two hours to vote because the polling post had not yet received its ballot papers. In another region, five hours after the polling stations opened voters were still waiting for the arrival of the Inkatha stickers that have to be added to every ballot paper. One of the first people to cast a vote this morning, a man of seventy-one who was voting for the first time in his life, came out of the polling station jumping for joy.

"I have voted, I have voted," he repeated, laughing. Then he sighed and added, "Now I can die in peace." '

I was born with the right to vote. And I am only just beginning to understand what this means to those who have been deprived of it all their lives. Last week, in a shop, the people at the counter in front of me were negotiating monthly instalments to pay off the new pair of shoes they were buying to go and vote in!

'There were queues and queues today, some of them more than a kilometre long, in prisons, in hospitals and in community polling stations. A number of people waited the whole day before voting. One aged woman said, "Yes, it is long. Yes, I am hungry. But I have waited ninety-two years for this day." [...] And thousands of people have already settled down for the night, in front of the polling stations, to make sure that they do not miss this historic occasion.'

The machinery is in motion, as they say. The country is ready for the general elections tomorrow and the day after.

Jay and I have a second restless night. Neither of us can sleep. In fact I slept better the day before I got married, the day before my first live television presentation! We are up before the alarm goes off at five.

I obtain the right to vote only with the help of my marriage certificate (this right would be withdrawn at the following election – unless I was prepared to renounce my Canadian nationality!). The polling station I go to is situated in the local primary school. A white man tells me that after living with his domestic worker for fifteen years, he is only getting to know her for the first time today. For fifteen years he has worn the shirts that she has ironed impeccably, but today, for the first time, he is having a conversation with her as they wait in the queue together.

The people are feverish. Behind me, voter education is still taking place, at the last minute. A man draws a square in the sand with a stick. A black woman looks at it, frowning with concentration. 'There will be a square like this,' explains the man. 'You look for the photo of the person you would like to see at the head of this country, and you make a cross, like this, in the square, next to that photo.' And then, squatting down, he solemnly draws a cross in the sand.

In a country where more than forty per cent of people are illiterate, it has been necessary to simplify everything. Photos of the leaders appear on the ballot paper, with the name of their party. The woman takes the stick and in turn draws a cross in the square. The others approve and each one repeats the action.

The man in front of me has borrowed his brother's suit. He would never have believed, he tells me, that he would see this day in his lifetime. He is excited but patient. He is prepared to wait all day if necessary, but, like the others, he is going to make his cross.

Suddenly, the earth trembles beneath our feet. We all jump. For about ten seconds, the ground shakes. At first there is a general stupor. The people in the queue look at one another in silence. Another bomb! (I learned later that it exploded at Johannesburg's international airport, some twenty kilometres away. And we felt it!) The people in the queue are furious.

'They want to stop us from voting, to dissuade us, to make us afraid!'

'I am not moving from here. I am voting!' someone shouts.

'Yes, yes, me too!' cry others.

At that moment the queue becomes an instantaneous community, drawn together by the same hope, the same determination, no matter where their cross will be drawn.

What if a bomb has been put in our polling station? I realise that nothing will make me move; intimidation from extremists won't discourage me. Those around me feel the same; they do not hesitate to take the risk.

I read the pride, and the worry, in people's faces. Everyone examines the area; passing cars become suspect. Everyone tries to detect signs of a possible threat. But they all remain firm, even the elderly.

I eventually enter the polling station. I present my identity document. My hand is stamped with invisible ink. At last I am allowed to enter the booth. I unfold the ballot paper and look for his face among those that appear there. I make my cross with a hesitant hand. I have voted all my life, and here I am as moved as someone who has always hoped for this moment.

This morning, in front of the cameras, Nelson Mandela, all smiles, lifted his ballot paper with a precise movement, then inserted it into the slot in the ballot box in the same calm manner as he has negotiated the revolution in this country – carefully, reflectively and without any sudden movements. Then he said, 'I am happy that we have finally seen the day we have dreamed about, but also sad that our heroes had to make so many sacrifices for this dream.'

I spend the rest of the day in front of the television, which is broadcasting live from all over the country. I have turned on two radios and the television, and I go from one station to another. I am not hungry. I drink coffee, lots of coffee, and make notes madly. The police have confiscated a large quantity of arms and explosives. The majority of the men arrested are members of the AWB, Eugene Terre'Blanche's rightwing movement. The irony of his name never fails to amaze me.

Despite the problems, despite the long queues, everywhere people say that they have waited all their lives to vote, and they can therefore wait a few more hours. One old lady literally waited all her life. She died in the queue, overwhelmed by the heat. I sat frozen for several minutes after hearing this news on TV. I felt that I would have liked to be there to help her, to hold an umbrella over her head, to give her something to drink, to encourage her and say to her, 'You're almost there. A little longer, hold on, you're almost there.' But she is dead. I can still see her collapsing, the sun beating down on her.

There is so much confusion in some polling stations that we wonder whether the elections will be validated. Later it is discovered that certain officials have hidden millions of ballot papers in a warehouse, and that some of the chaos in black areas has been 'organised'.

I have written dozens of reports since the start of the elections. But I have not received any feedback from Montreal. 'Yes, Lucie.' 'Hello, Lucie.' 'An error here, Lucie.' 'Do this again, Lucie.' 'Bye, Lucie.' Yes, bye. Thanks for the encouragement.

As improbable as it sounds, I have no direct access to media releases from a press agency. I have been working for Radio–Canada for a number of years, three of them as a correspondent. CBC, the English network of Radio–Canada, has an office in Johannesburg. One day I go there to ask whether I can use a corner of the office during the elections to have access to media releases, which will help me prepare my reports more easily. 'The office is small,' the CBC correspondent tells me. I look at all the work areas and offices around me and I say, 'All right! Can I at least come in and read the press releases from time to time?' 'Our office is very small,' repeats my 'colleague'. I can't quite credit the extent of the rift between Radio–Canada and CBC, so I persist. And he replies, in a curt voice, 'Our offices are *too* small.' I have never set foot in the place again. I write my reports without access to media releases from the press agencies. For a journalist following current developments from hour to hour, this means ten times the work.

One piece of news keeps coming in: the rigging of the elections in certain parts of the country, particularly in KwaZulu-Natal. The ANC claims to have proof that Inkatha has established pirate polling stations. Members of Inkatha are said to have stolen some ballot papers and proceeded to hold their own vote. The Independent Electoral Commission is currently investigating these allegations.

In a 'normal' country they would have said, 'Stop everything. These elections have failed.' In certain ballot boxes, hundreds of ballot papers were found folded into one another. The elections have obviously been rigged in certain regions. But to declare them a failure would spark a civil war. In KwaZulu-Natal, cancelling the elections would have resulted in large-scale fighting. So it's necessary to hope for a reasonable failure! And this is what the Electoral Commission does. It evaluates the risk of chaos, considers the seriousness of the irregularities and concludes that it is better to live with the cheating.

Today television showed the oldest woman in the country, at the age of one hundred and eight, going to vote for the first time in her life. When she was asked to talk about her memories of the old South Africa, she replied, simply, 'When I was a small girl, I saw a shooting star.'

At dusk on the last day of voting, a wish has been realised. South Africa is finally turning the page on three hundred and fifty years of colonialism and oppression.

40

Victory

The vote is over. The political violence seems to want to give way to euphoria. To calm people as they wait for the results to be announced, the political leaders hastily organise various socio-cultural activities. The counting of the votes could take up to ten days!

I am restless. I am exhausted. I allow myself an outing to a restaurant, something I have not done for a long time. I like to go to the restaurant Ba Pita, in Yeoville, even if it does not look like much. It attracts punks, gays, artists, bikers, mixed couples, in fact everyone who is different or marginal. The music is loud. The food is simple and delicious.

I pick up a buzz from the people sitting at the tables in Ba Pita today. They have bet several hundred rand on the results. People are drinking to the new South Africa. Something has changed.

Whole communities of whites, especially Afrikaners, panicked as the elections drew closer. Companies selling baked beans and tinned tuna made a fortune before the elections, as people stocked up. They stocked up on everything they could. 'The Communists are coming! They will take everything, control everything!' they were saying. But this evening, in the restaurant in Rockey Street, the scene resembles a celebration after a World Cup cricket victory. A dozen ecstatic people are bending over a table where people are stacking their bets. They are laughing as they argue.

Another ten days until the results … Keeping the country in suspense like this is risky. The people want to see the new president.

Everyone knows that Mandela will be elected, but the country is becoming impatient, and impatience, in South Africa, is dangerous.

The counting of the votes is a huge and laborious operation. The ballot boxes from nine thousand polling stations have to be transported to eight hundred different counting stations. That is the first step. The second consists of checking that the number of ballots returned is the same as the number sent to that polling station (the ballot papers are counted three times, by three different people). Then the ballot papers are sorted. Each one has to be verified by independent observers. Finally, the votes, some fifteen, eighteen, twenty or twenty-three million of them – no one knows any more – will be counted.

The next few days will be a journalistic headache. What is there to say while the ballots are checked and rechecked?

It is torment in front of the computer. I go round in circles. I hardly go out. Everything is happening live in the different media. But in truth, nothing is happening. The president of the Independent Electoral Commission, Judge Johann Kriegler, is constantly bombarded with questions, attacked, accused of incompetence. The Commission admits, to some extent, a certain degree of incompetence. They had underestimated the magnitude of the elections!

Even though the political results of the elections are slow in coming, the social results are making themselves felt. In nine years, more than a hundred thousand South Africans have died violently. In the past week, there has been almost nothing to report. Even in KwaZulu-Natal, the police and the peace monitors are twiddling their thumbs.

The picture slowly becomes clear. The ANC has taken seven of the nine provinces; the National Party has taken the Western Cape and Inkatha has taken KwaZulu-Natal.

The National Party's victory in the Western Cape might seem astonishing at first glance. The population in this province is predominantly coloured. There are also large numbers of Afrikaners there; that they would vote for the National Party is understandable. However, that the coloureds should re-elect the party under which they had suffered so badly surprises even the ANC. It can be explained by the fact that the National Party followed a divide-and-rule policy, in which the coloured population were encouraged to see themselves as racially superior to the blacks.

Victims under apartheid, but less so than the blacks, the coloureds today feel excluded under the ANC government, which embodies the black majority. This is the reason that the coloureds rallied around the National Party, just as the Indians did in KwaZulu-Natal, because this party says that it represents the interests of the minorities.

During apartheid the skin of the coloureds was too dark. Now it is too light …

The Electoral Commission has not finished counting the votes, but the ANC decides to celebrate its victory. So much for bureaucracy … The people's impatience is too great. The partial results leave scarcely any doubt about a national victory for the ANC. The rest is merely statistics.

I decide to attend the ANC celebration. Jay is already there. It is late, but I will do my last report of the day after I have seen the celebration of the victory with my own eyes. Mandela should be there. I phone Omar to come and fetch me. We go to the centre of town, to the Carlton Hotel. There are police barricades everywhere, but Omar manages to convince the police to let us through.

Getting into the lift, I can already hear the celebration. In the function room, revellers are floating around like the hundreds of balloons in the colours of the ANC. I arrive at the same time as the man who is about to become president of the 'new' South Africa. The ANC is crying victory!

Mandela has the flu. He starts his speech, in front of dozens of national and international cameras, by saying that his doctor has forbidden him to get out of bed. 'Don't tell anyone you saw me here this evening,' he says. The crowd before him explodes with laughter. I drink a glass of rum and Coke. Then another. I dance with the crowd. I observe and I make notes, drunk with pleasure, drunk with the experience of this wonderful moment with people who have fought so long for this great day. It is one of the best parties I have ever attended.

I notice the American actor Danny Glover, an actor I like very much and who has invested part of his fortune in South Africa to support the anti-apartheid activists, particularly the trade unionists. He acts in *Lethal Weapon II*, among others. My favourite scene from the movie is that in which Glover goes into the South African embassy in the United States with a white friend, played by Mel Gibson. Gibson says to the embassy official that one of his friends wants to emigrate to South Africa. 'No problem,' says the official. When Danny Glover points to himself, there is a dismayed reaction. A black, emigrating to South Africa?!

Danny Glover is on the point of leaving. I corner Jay and literally drag him over to Glover. I get to within two metres of this great man and tell him I am a fan. He shakes my hand distractedly, looking for the exit. I withdraw my hand and say I would like to introduce my husband. He turns and notices Jay. His face lights up. He grabs him, hugs him repeatedly, showers him with accolades. Jay is his idol, he says. He has always wanted to meet him. He has followed his career in the trade unions since the beginning, in 1979. He encourages him, tells him to keep it up, that the work is only just starting.

Jay and I dance for a good two hours. But I have to go home and finish my work … I write my report:

'Without waiting for the final results, the country celebrated victory tonight. President De Klerk conceded defeat and congratulated the man who will take his place in a few days' time. Mr Mandela arrived dancing to give his victory speech. He had scarcely finished when hundreds of thousands of people streamed into the streets all over South Africa to celebrate. The sight was unbelievable. Blacks, whites, coloureds, Indians, people of all colours dancing, singing together, hugging people they didn't even know, literally crying for joy. In the city of Johannesburg the streets were packed; people were standing on the roofs of cars. Fireworks lit up the sky.'

I have never in my life seen so many happy people. Mad with joy. Hooters blaring throughout the country. Champagne, tears and laughter flowing.

A few days later, the Independent Electoral Commission announces the results, stating that the elections were free and fair. The ANC is the victor with 65,7% of the votes; the National Party gets 20,4%, Inkatha 10,5% and the Freedom Front 2,2%.

The eyes of the world are focussed on the head of the Commission, Judge Kriegler. He looks drawn. He has just accomplished an impossible task: organising two types of election at the same time (national and provincial) in a country that has never known democracy and where certain election organisers themselves were stocking up on tinned food, fearing the worst. Judge Kriegler closes his speech with the words, 'There is only one thing left for me to do. Sleep!'

That is what I do. That is what Jay does. That is what the country does. Sleep – after forty-eight years of apartheid, after years of insomnia.

41

The race against the crowd

At the Houses of Parliament in Cape Town it's complete chaos. Four hundred members of parliament are gathered in the hall to fill in forms, sign papers and receive their various passes. It is the first time that this venerable institution is opening its doors to blacks who are not cleaners or tea-ladies or shoe-shiners.

In about an hour's time, Nelson Mandela will inaugurate the work of the new parliament. Hundreds, no thousands, of journalists are crowded around the doors of the building.

The crowd inside parliament is not only black. It is also female! The struggle against apartheid perhaps eclipsed other struggles, but it did not destroy them.

'MPs, here. Wives, above,' the porter of the National Assembly shouts, on this the 9 May 1994, to the MPs who are shortly to take an oath. 'Above' refers to the balcony from which wives have always admired their MP husbands. And for decades the porter at parliament in Cape Town in South Africa has shouted this instruction with his eyes closed, 'Wives, above!'

Today the porter has woken up. Women, lots of women, are looking at him, examining him carefully, smiling at him and then passing him by as if he were a waxwork in a museum dedicated to South Africa's shameful history. Today, on the eve of Nelson Mandela's presidential inauguration, about a hundred women proudly come in and take a seat in the National Assembly. The porters' mouths are hanging open.

In the centre of the enormous hall, the great throne of the Speaker of the Assembly is empty. All around it sit the four hundred new members of parliament and, on the balcony, their wives or husbands. Among the MPs there are ex-prisoners who are to become Ministers and women, some of whom have been beaten and raped by their husbands or scorned by society, some of whom are leaving part of the hard South African reality behind them for the first time. All the people present, those from the extreme right, from the extreme left, from Inkatha, from the African National Congress, from the National Party, whites, blacks, Indians, coloureds, women, men, are looking at one another, observing one another, and saying, 'Here we have a more just picture of our society.' They are all waiting for the arrival of the new Speaker of the National Assembly.

She arrives ... in a sari. Frene Ginwala, a South African of Indian extraction, silences the Assembly with the awe she inspires rather than by traditional respect. For a 'black' woman to take up this position, up to now reserved for a white man, is quite a feat. Frene Ginwala, seated on this great chair, up to now the very symbol of racism, sexism and injustice, represents the fruit of the two struggles fought in South Africa: the political struggle and the women's struggle. However, in the same way that democracy is far more than simply having the right to vote, women's emancipation is far more than having a woman in a sari sitting in a place of honour.

Women in South Africa have a long way to go, a long way. But they have already made great progress. For example, they fought for a one-third representation within the National Assembly *and* within the Cabinet. The first battle was won within the ranks of the ANC: eighty of the two hundred and fifty-two ANC MPs are women. But at the point where the real power is yielded – within the Cabinet – they lost the battle: only two of the twenty-seven ministers are women. And the nine provincial premiers are all men.

Nonetheless, it's an important accomplishment. It's not yet possible to judge the success of the struggle for women's rights or even the struggle against racism in South Africa. The curtain is rising on the 'new' country and everyone expects quite a show.

I am sitting on the balcony. Not the one reserved for journalists, but the one for 'wives' – or rather 'spouses' of both sexes.

I am here as a journalist. The number of places available in the press gallery was far too small to accommodate all the international reporters who have come to participate in this event. I therefore took advantage of my new status as the wife of an MP – and soon to be wife of a Minister. From now on I will have to get used to this new double identity: 'Mrs Naidoo', wife of the Minister, and Lucie Pagé, journalist.

For the moment I am observing everything and making notes. The expressions on people's faces, the polished shoes, the saris and coloured scarves, the velvet of the cushioned seats. All around me are women, each one more smartly dressed than the next in her Sunday best, most of them wearing a hat reflecting their new status as a 'Minister's wife' or 'MP's wife', and men ill at ease, searching for the right stance in a balcony previously reserved only for women. I am wearing neither a hat nor a dress, preferring pants. Besides, I do not understand this custom of spouses wearing a hat to parliament. I feel a bit out of place here …

After a few minutes, an usher comes up to tell me that I am not allowed to write.

'And why am I not allowed to write?'

'It's the rule, madam.'

'But I have to write.'

'I'm sorry, madam, but then I will have to ask you to leave.'

There is silence in the hall. Mandela will be arriving any minute. And I defy this zealous usher. I need to take notes, because I have to send off a report in a couple of hours. I continue to write.

'Madam, I must ask you to put away your pen or to leave. That is the rule,' the man repeats, impatiently, in a tone that attracts the attention of the people around us.

'Please explain to me, my dear man (my children would have recognised this tone as a warning impending doom), where does this rule come from and why does it exist? I do not understand.'

'Madam, it's the rule.'

'Why does this rule exist?'

I notice that everyone is looking at us. This pen will help me record the historic event that is about to take place before my very eyes! I tell myself that I shall continue to write; he will have to throw me out by force. But all of a sudden I realise that it is Jay's reputation that will be damaged by a scene. Sadly, I put away my pen and my notebook. The usher smirks over his little victory. My pride is wounded.

I won't attend these special sessions of parliament again. I prefer to watch it on television, so that I can take notes. Because if I receive an invitation to attend a speech in the National Assembly or some other official event, it means there is something important to report!

The crowd falls silent. A silent vibration runs through the hall. Nelson Mandela makes his entrance. The emotion is too strong: parliament explodes into applause, cries, songs, tears. I shiver as though a bolt of lightning is coursing through me. It is an incredible moment, difficult to explain. I am already trying to find words for my report. Nelson Mandela walks at his usual pace, slow, sure, measured, calm, towards the lectern. His smile reflects his pride. His wrinkles reflect his struggle behind bars, the number of years he sacrificed for this country.

All eyes follow him to the front of the hall. Behind him, Frene Ginwala, from her chair, watches with admiration. This black man, this former prisoner long considered a Communist, a terrorist, takes the place up to now reserved for a white man. The gathering watching him so closely is multicoloured; the porters, the security guards and all the white staff watch him as if this is a dream, as if, at any moment, a movie director is going to shout 'Cut!' and bring them back to reality.

Former president FW de Klerk is seated next to Thabo Mbeki of the ANC. They are both deputy-presidents, as stipulated in the Interim Constitution. When the negotiations between the ANC and the National Party reached a stalemate, the head of the South African Communist Party, Joe Slovo (Minister of Housing in the Mandela government until his death on 6 January 1995), proposed what became known as the Sunset Clause, which provided for a sharing of power during the first term of the democratic government. This Government of National Unity would negotiate and approve the final post-apartheid constitution. The clause stipulated that any party that received more than twenty per cent of the vote would be given a deputy-presidential post and a ministerial post for five per cent of the votes. The National Party just managed to obtain twenty per cent of the vote and that is how Frederik de Klerk became deputy-president.

Nonetheless, it is still quite amazing that the former head of government should voluntarily take second place, in fact third place, because

Thabo Mbeki is the 'first' deputy-president. De Klerk is indisputably a man of courage. He freed Mandela, legalised his movement and ensured that this same man took power. I try to imagine what is passing through his mind at this moment, but I don't even know where to start.

Mandela begins his speech. I memorise the most beautiful images from it. 'Today we celebrate not the victory of a party, but a victory for all the people of South Africa,' he says. I would like to take out my pen and notebook, but I see out of the corner of my eye that the security guard who almost threw me out is getting ready to pounce.

Nelson Mandela finishes his speech, 'We have fought for a democratic constitution since the 1880s. We place our vision of a new constitutional order for South Africa on the table not as conquerors, prescribing to the conquered. We speak as fellow citizens to heal the wounds of the past with the intent of constructing a new order based on justice for all. This is the challenge that faces all South Africans today, and it is one to which I am certain we will all rise.'

It is past midday. I do not have a telephone to send my report, which anyway isn't even written yet. Cellular phones have only just become available a few weeks ago, but in any case I cannot afford one, and Radio–Canada does not want to pay for one either …

After the ceremony inside the parliamentary building, Mandela will deliver a speech to a crowd of several hundred thousand waiting outside, in the blazing sun, a kilometre away. I must also find the time to go there before sending my report.

I leave parliament to get there by bus. It's still chaotic. The streets are blocked, people are toyi-toyiing everywhere; kilometres of film are used as cameramen capture footage and people take photographs. Sitting in the bus, I make a few notes as I observe what is happening outside. Looking at people's faces, you would think that hundreds of thousands of them had won the lottery today.

There *he* is at last! The crowd goes mad. They cry, they laugh. Joy. Freedom. Total pleasure is reflected everywhere. Mandela knows how to address a crowd … Shivers pass repeatedly through my body, as if I have my finger stuck in an electric socket.

As soon as the final word has been spoken, I rush to a hotel room a friend has lent me so that I can call Montreal. I have thirty minutes. I jostle the security guards and force my way through the crowd of half a million people, clearing a path as I go. I think of Gilles Le Bigot, of what he will say if I am late. On days like this, when the eyes of the whole world are fixed on a political event of this magnitude, he absolutely has to have a report. These are the type of events that justify having a correspondent abroad. In three years I have never missed a deadline. I have never said no to Gilles. But here I am caught in a crowd, the crowd that is the subject of my story, which is also preventing me from getting through. I push forward, only to be pulled back. I am writing the story I will be reading in my head as I go. And I keep pushing. I have the police barricades to get past, the hotel to find …

Two o'clock strikes. The Radio–Canada news bulletin starts on the other side of the world. I am still caught in this enormous crowd. The streets are jammed. I squat down to pass between people's legs. It's easier, but there is also a greater danger of being crushed. I manage to move ten metres on all fours on the pavement. The news broadcast continues, without my story, without *the* news of the day. I panic. Every network on the planet has a live story. And Radio–Canada, which has put its trust in me for all these years, has nothing …

I finally reach the hotel. It is a quarter past two. I am out of breath. My knees are sore. I am drenched with sweat. I feel like crying. I slip in discreetly, without the hotel security guards noticing me, because I would have had to spend at least another five minutes convincing them I was allowed in.

Reaching the room, I throw everything onto the bed and snatch up the telephone, as if I am in a hurry to be scolded. And what a dressing down I get! Gilles is not happy. Not at all! He gives me hell. I feel like dropping everything, telling him he can find another fool to work for next to nothing, to fork out the one thousand two hundred rand it costs to fly from Johannesburg to Cape Town. Gilles chews me out and, silently, my defences give way. I start crying. He tells me that I could have prepared a report in advance, acting 'as if' the event had already taken place. A back-up report. I have never done that.

Gilles wants the report for the nine o'clock bulletin in Montreal. It is twenty-five past eight. With blurry eyes, a heart filled with shame and rage, I hang up. Writing in such a short time produces a stress that I abhor, but that I find stimulating. I have twenty-five minutes. My emotions weigh down on me and muddle my ideas. I feel like chucking it all in, leaving as a free person, in charge of my own life. To hell with Radio–Canada! To hell with Gilles Le Bigot! To hell with journalism! But then I remember Montreal.

'There was an extraordinary sight, this morning, in the parliamentary building in Cape Town. The very people who have protested and demonstrated in front of this building reserved for whites for three hundred and forty-two years, the men and women who suffered, were tortured and imprisoned, for the first time in their lives entered this parliament and took their seats in the National Assembly. Mr Mandela made his entry together with his two deputy-presidents, Thabo Mbeki and Frederik de Klerk. The four hundred members of the National Assembly elected Nelson Rolihlahla Mandela, the first democratic president elected in South Africa. Applause broke out when he embraced the head of Inkatha, Mr Buthelezi, and the leader of the extreme right, General Viljoen. Outside, hundreds of thousands of people were singing and dancing. From the same balcony on which he addressed the people after his release in February 1990, President Mandela declared, 'You want a new country? You shall have it! South Africa is celebrating not the victory of the ANC, but of the people.' The crowd shouted its joy. Never has this country seen so many happy faces. The presidential inauguration will take place tomorrow in Pretoria, in front of the largest gathering of heads of state ever seen in the world.'

I leave the hotel, relieved to have finished. But this relief does not diminish the feeling of shame and guilt that pervades me. I go and sit down on the hotel terrace and order a beer. There is happiness everywhere. People are celebrating, drinking and laughing. Balloons float in the sky. Beggars take advantage of the general exaltation to extract a few cents from people. But my eyes are clouded. I recognise some friends and I hide behind a menu. I don't want to see anyone. I would like to free myself of my skin, of my body, rise up into the air like those balloons and expire without feeling a thing. Poof! Just like that! In a flash. I did everything this morning to produce good work. But I missed my deadline. It is unacceptable to miss your deadline.

42

Never, never again

The presidential inauguration taking place in Pretoria the next day would be attended by princes, kings, prime ministers, presidents, all the international political top brass, from Fidel Castro to Yasser Arafat. Not to mention Whoopi Goldberg, Nelson Mandela's jailer and hundreds of special guests.

I call Gilles Le Bigot.

'Prepare a report immediately. Anticipate the news.'

'But, Gilles, I have to have been there first.'

'No, prepare something at once.'

Obviously I don't want another Cape Town disaster.

'I don't have a cellular phone. So I will have to stay at home in order to watch everything live.'

'Stay at home if you prefer, but we must have some stories.'

'But the emotion won't be in it.'

'We must have some stories.'

'I can't not go. I need a cell.'

'Then get yourself one.'

I get hold of one. At my own expense, of course … I simply cannot be in South Africa and not be present at the Union Buildings in Pretoria when Mandela lifts his hand to take the oath and finally becomes president.

I therefore write a story in advance to prevent a scene like yesterday's, then I go to bed, over-excited. I sleep badly, rewriting the text in my head the whole night.

Early the next morning Jay, Omar, Colette and I travel halfway from Johannesburg to Pretoria. It is not possible to go to the Union Buildings by car. The roads have been closed and only authorised buses are allowed through.

We get into one of the buses. Everyone is in their Sunday best. The excitement is tangible. Suddenly, I go pale. Jays asks me what's wrong. A catastrophe! I have left the cellular phone in the car!

Catastrophe of catastrophes! I have even given Gilles Le Bigot the telephone number so that he can call me, because it is still impossible to make a call overseas from South African cellphones without special authorisation, a password, a fat bank account and who knows what else!

I am seized by utter panic. In fact, during that journey, I experience every single state of mind possible: anger gives way to tears, then to fear, despair, and, finally, hope. I have to find another phone! Jay tries to calm me. But I sense that he is worried; he knows that the only reason I am present at today's historic event is that telephone! 'I will find you one. I promise,' he tells me. And I will find someone to call Gilles in Montreal and give him my new telephone number.

When we enter Pretoria, the tanks, the policemen, the roadblocks and the barbed wire remind us of recent history. The packed buses make their way, in single file, to the Union Buildings, the seat of government.

Today, Pretoria shines as never before. The crowds are already waiting. Balloons float in the sky. The new flag with its six colours – green, black and yellow (the ANC colours), and red, blue and white (the colours of the old flag, or almost, the red replacing the orange) – flutters everywhere in the crowd. This flag does not yet have a history: it is simply announcing a change.

I am privileged to be sitting with Jay, among the VIPs, a few steps from the stage. Further away, on the vast, grassy hillside, a hundred thousand people, or even more, are gathered, ready, with Mandela, to cross the fence into the land, they hope, of justice, liberty and equality.

Jay and I leave immediately to look for a phone. Mathapelo, Jay's secretary, has offered to help us. She comes back three minutes later, pointing towards Zwelinzima Vavi, the Deputy General Secretary of COSATU. He is standing up, talking on the phone! I go to meet him. I know him fairly well. He is young, around thirty-three or thirty-four. He isn't sure of his exact age. Like hundreds of thousands of Africans, he doesn't know his date of birth. He comes from a tiny village where there was no doctor and no birth register. A priest had selected for him, at random, 20 December, a date he does not celebrate. I ask him whether he needs his phone today, then, without waiting for his reply, I add that I need one very urgently. In fact, I say, his telephone would save me from the worst possible nightmare. He hesitates. And I go one step further. I drive the point home so well that he ends up giving me his phone as if it is a hot potato. I call Logie, Jay's brother, who undertakes to phone Gilles and give him the number of this telephone.

The dignitaries start to arrive. I have never seen so many bodyguards. There are more of them than there are guests! Seeing me arrive with Jay, Buthelezi gets up, with his entourage, to give us two seats. Jay greets him politely and they exchange a few words. Yesterday, Buthelezi was publicly wishing Jay were dead. Today, he offers him his seat. How times have changed …

Jay and I amuse ourselves by picking out the dignitaries among the security officers. I see, from behind, someone with a piece of black and white fabric on his head. Yasser Arafat. And over there is Hillary Clinton. And who is that man surrounded by a dozen bodyguards? He is hardly visible in the middle of such a human shield. It is Fidel Castro, the head of state who has, it seems, received the greatest number of death threats in the world. I look for Jean Chrétien, the Canadian prime minister. He has not come. What a pity. Especially since Canada has supported and encouraged the anti-apartheid struggle all these years.

I leave Jay and go and take refuge on a staircase inside the Union Buildings. I need a few minutes to write a new story. I have the feeling I am getting ready to describe the most important day in the history of this country. The words come easily to me:

'President Nelson Mandela, the first democratically elected president, is today receiving his full powers. Everywhere people are saying, "I am free, I am free. Long live free South Africa!" Hundreds of thousands of people are celebrating in the street and shouting victory. Happiness and peace abound today. Enemies are embracing one another, saying "Let's start again." South Africa is a new country, people have a new hope, the hope that never, never again will this country know the horrors of the past centuries. Yes, long live free South Africa!'

I read it through and ask myself whether I am not going a bit far. *Long live free South Africa*. No, I don't think so.

I would only learn much later that these words were the subject of a debate at Radio–Canada. Some saw in them an evocation of the words of Charles de Gaulle on the balcony of the Montreal city hall in 1967, 'Long live free Quebec.' But my report was eventually broadcast as it was.

As for me, it is the words *never, never again* that give me gooseflesh. I wrote them in my head last night, on my pillow, while trying to go to sleep. Today, I *see* them on black and white, Indian and coloured faces. I see pride and dignity on black faces, relief from the guilt that used to burden white shoulders. This is liberty … It is as if people have realised, all together, just today, how ridiculous apartheid was.

When Mandela mounts the stage, the barriers give way in the crowd. Everything explodes. The jubilation spills over to drench a global audience. The crowd is drunk with ecstasy.

Eventually the crowd quietens. I see shivers run down spines and shake shoulders, the same shiver that passes through me, despite the warm sunshine.

'I, Nelson Rolihlahla Mandela, do hereby swear to be faithful to the Republic of South Africa. […] So help me God.'

There is a standing ovation of course. Then an impressive air display takes everyone by surprise. Planes from the army, the SADF, the very institution that crushed any revolution over the years, fly overhead. The same men, in the same positions of command, are celebrating the man they themselves pursued and imprisoned.

In his speech, Mandela surprises me by using the same words I have used in my story. He says, 'Never, never and never again shall it be that this beautiful land will again experience the oppression of one by another and suffer the indignity of being the skunk of the world. Let freedom reign.'

Lunch is held at the official residence of former president De Klerk, with only the 'big names' from all over the world attending. No journalists. Although I accompany Jay, I do not cover the event, on principle. Outside, an enormous marquee has been erected. Inside it, I circulate among the celebrities. Jay and I take our places at a table next to Arafat's. And then I see Castro. I want to go and meet him. His name

From left to right: Léandre, Lucie, Jay, Kami, Shanti.

'Jay does not fear failure. He is living proof that it is possible to be humble and to have confidence in oneself at the same time.'

Lucie meets Nelson Mandela to film her first interview with the leader, in November 1990. Mandela had been released from prison only nine months before.

Jay giving a speech, in the early nineties. On his left, seated, is Govan Mbeki, chair of the Senate and father of Thabo Mbeki.

In Umiujaq, in the Québecois Great North, in January 1991. 'Jay and I fall in love in the snow, at fifty degrees below zero ...'

The couple's first home, in Bez Valley, renovated by Lucie, and the swimming pool, which Lucie cleared and emptied by hand.

Lucie and Jay's first wedding, December 1991. Nelson Mandela shows off the fleur-de-lys mittens knitted and given to him by Louise, Lucie's mother. On either side of Mandela sit Walter and Albertina Sisulu.

Lucie and Omar Motani, at the first wedding in December 1991. In the foreground is Omar's daughter, Yasmin.

Second wedding in Joliette, Quebec, in August 1992. 'Martine throws confetti, like in the movies. I enjoy this. At the same time, it starts to rain. Once again, Jay says his mother is blessing us ...'

In the company of Desmond Tutu, 10 May 1994, during Nelson Mandela's presidential inauguration.

Lucie and Jay with Fidel Castro during Nelson Mandela's presidential inauguration. In the foreground is Joe Slovo, General Secretary of the Communist Party, and his wife, Helena Dolny.

Robben Island, 1997. Lucie is recording a radio documentary in the prison in which Mandela served two-thirds of his sentence. She is sitting on Mandela's former bed – a commodity the famous prisoner was entitled to only during the very last years of his incarceration.

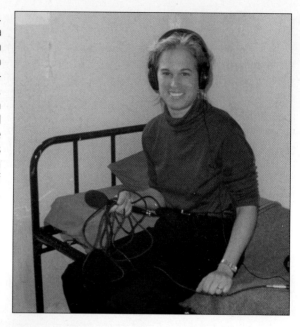

Lucie and Walter Sisulu, her neighbour in Cape Town. She often went for a stroll with the former ANC General Secretary and mentor of Nelson Mandela.

Jay and Terese, in 1994. Terese was later killed by a thief who stole her car.

The family, after Shanti's birth, in June 1995. Nisha, Jay's sister, performs a Hindu birth ritual.

Lucie's family at the third wedding, celebrated in India in 1998. 'A wedding in which we celebrate our love – intense, powerful, fiery – and we unite our destinies, this time more deeply conscious of our commitment to each other.'

'We saw beauty at Agra: the Taj Mahal. So grandiose and majestic that I can't find the words to describe what you feel before this tomb ...' From left to right: Nisha, Léandre, Kami, Jay, Louise, Lucie, Shanti.

On the back of a camel with Shanti, in the Thar Desert in India.

Jay, Kami and Shanti meet Fidel Castro in September 1998. Lucie stayed at home that day, to edit a radio report on … Castro's visit to South Africa!

In the heart of KwaZulu-Natal, at Nongoma, with the king of the Zulus, His Majesty Goodwill Zwelithini.

An Indian cultural celebration in Cape Town in 1999.

Jay's arrival at Cape Agulhas in South Africa, at the end of the African
Connection Rally in 1999.

Nelson Mandela and Kami, after the speech Mandela gave while holding Kami in his arms, after the child had run onto the podium.

Lucie and Jay with Graça Machel, Nelson Mandela's wife.

The famous photograph signed by Nelson Mandela.

Mandela and Louise, Lucie's mother, get ready to taste the cake decorated in the colours of Quebec and the ANC. December 1993.

was pronounced so often in our home by my father, who was fascinated by him. I would like to be able to tell my father I had shaken the hand of the Cuban head of state. I tug at Jay's arm and lead him towards Castro, who is surrounded by bodyguards. I make my way past outstretched arms and move between people to get to him. Here we are. Even though Castro speaks English, he never addresses anyone in that language. Jay is presented to him. I forget all my Spanish. I put out my hand to him, smiling warmly. Then he kisses Jay and embraces him. He knows Jay and congratulates him on his work in South Africa. I thrust my camera at a bodyguard and tell him to take a photo right away. I move in front of Castro. Click.

We are still choked with the morning's emotions. Jay especially. He keeps repeating to me that finally the last two decades of his life are taking on their full meaning. Mandela gives another speech. More emotion! It is almost too much, all in one day.

As we are leaving, I bump into Archbishop Desmond Tutu, 1984 Nobel Peace Prize winner and a fervent opponent of apartheid. I have never spoken to him. He is a lovely person. His good humour and his smile shine out of him. His hands are warm. As is his greeting. Click! Another photo memory.

It's over. Well almost. I have to do … one last story! I end it with 'Sekunjalo'. 'The time has come' to rebuild this country!

This report is the end of a cycle for me, that of the dizzying coverage of the final chapter in this 'long walk to freedom', to borrow Mandela's expression. The past few months have been an unbroken crescendo in which tension, fear, frenzy and amazement have succeeded one another.

However, I am left feeling a little bitter, definitely alone. I haven't received a single word or gesture of encouragement from Radio–Canada. Perhaps that is the price you pay for journalistic exile.

But four months later I receive a note the editor-in-chief of news at Radio–Canada, Mr Richard Sanche, wrote two days after the presidential inauguration. He thanks me for my reports on the end of the apartheid regime, 'The quality of your work, your knowledge of the subject and the visualisation of your reports allowed our listeners to 'live' this historic event.'

If you only knew, Mr Sanche, what a pleasure it was to cover this event …

43

Rivonia

A few days after the elections, Nelson Mandela phoned. Jay went to see him and Mandela informed him that he was going to be a minister. Jay was expecting a post of that nature, and he obviously accepted.

I, however, was not prepared for what was to come. Very soon, Jay made the headlines as 'Minister without Portfolio responsible for the Reconstruction and Development Programme in the Office of the President'. That was his official title! He was the only minister without an office or staff. He had to draw up his own job description. His role in fact was to work together with all the other ministers, because with the new government came new priorities, the main ones being development in rural areas and the provision of services for those without. Jay had to ensure that all the ministers worked together in the ANC's ambitious plan to reconstruct the country and develop its potential. I saw the preliminary draft of this 'Reconstruction and Development Programme' come to life on my kitchen table, written by Jay and his great friend and colleague, another Jay Naidoo, a story that requires a quick explanation ...

This other Jay Naidoo's name is in fact Jayendra Naidoo, while the full version of my husband's first name is Jayaseelan. The two men, of Tamil origin, both come from Durban (Jay Naidoos in Durban are like John Smiths in England) and have known one another for more than twenty years. They have always worked together, sometimes closely and sometimes at a distance. The media named them 'Big Jay' (for Jayaseelan, the head of COSATU) and 'Small Jay' or 'Baby Jay' or 'Jay Junior' (for

Jayendra, who had a less prominent position in the political hierarchy). (Physically, however, the opposite is true; my children have always called Jayendra 'Big Jay' because he is tall and broad-shouldered.)

The similarity of their names created some confusion in the media. For example, when Jayendra criticised Buthelezi and his party, Inkatha, the *New York Times* attributed the remark to my husband. On another occasion, Jayendra made a tongue-in-cheek suggestion that the swimming pools of the whites be taxed to finance some projects for blacks. My husband had to face the media and deny having said any such thing. In order to prevent these problems, Jayendra used his full name from then on.

In 1995 Jayendra married Liv Torres. Liv is white, like me, and was born in 1961, like me, in the snow, but in Norway. She has a daughter in joint custody between two continents, the same age as Léandre. Liv sold everything on the other side of the world in order to come here, like me ... And there you have it.

Our home in Bez Valley, which we share with the rats, is not up to scratch for receiving a minister's guests. For friends, it's fine. For the President, it's fine. But for VIPs, it's not good enough!

We decide to move. My friend Hugh Lewin, Deputy Director at the Institute for the Advancement of Journalism, and his wife Fiona, buy our house. Hugh is an author, journalist and political activist. He spent seven years in jail for planting a bomb during the armed struggle and wrote the book *Bandiet* about this experience. Hugh had to go into exile, first in London and later in Zimbabwe, to avoid persecution, perhaps death, certainly torture.

When Hugh and Fiona come to look at the house, it's love at first sight. Sold! Going outside, Léandre says to Hugh, in his lovely Durban-Indian English accent, 'Mama killed a rat this morning. Look! It's over there!' Very proud of his mother's exploits, he explains how I stood on the couch and killed the rat with the broomstick while he shouted 'Hit harder! You've got it! Hit it!' He also explains that this wasn't the first rat killing. I blush with embarrassment. Hugh looks towards the tennis court, where I've dumped the bodies of five or six dead rats at various times. Even the exterminators haven't been able to get rid of the rats. Hugh looks at me, surprised. But he doesn't say a word. He adores the house. Our friendship is in any case too good to bother about rats.

Léandre has done me a favour by exposing the only shameful secret of the house!

Jay and I are impulsive people. Now, impulsiveness is not advisable when you are buying a house, it seems. An estate agent takes us to see a house in Rivonia, a 'fairly wealthy suburb', fifteen kilometres from Johannesburg. We buy it on the spot. No doubt we are influenced by the fact that two of our close friends live within walking distance: Allister Sparks, my boss at the Institute, and his wife, Sue, with whom I can speak French.

The property is one acre. The children have more than enough space to play in, which is necessary because they can't leave the property to go and play with the neighbourhood children. The property is enclosed by a large, white cement wall, two and a half metres high. On top of the wall are steel spikes that have to be replaced with stronger ones, as security for a minister's home requires. Later, when we leave and rent out the house, we have to put up electric fencing. Even so, the new tenants get burgled on four occasions ...

Rivonia is the suburb where, in October 1961, in a relatively isolated house called 'Lilliesleaf Farm', Mandela established the headquarters from which he planned the clandestine operations of the ANC (banned only the previous year), and, specifically, the activities of its armed wing, Umkhonto we Sizwe. The farm had secretly been bought by the Communist Party and disguised as a riding school.

Nelson Mandela and the men who were to become his prison companions, Walter Sisulu, Ahmed Kathrada and Govan Mbeki (father of first deputy-president, Thabo Mbeki), here sketched a plan of attack that would mobilise troops, submarines and military aircraft from other countries. This rather over-ambitious project was named 'Operation Mayibuye'.

On 11 July 1963, a truck from a dry-cleaning firm arrived at Lilliesleaf Farm, releasing a pack of policemen and their dogs. Sisulu, Kathrada and Mbeki slipped out through a back window, but were soon caught (by this time Mandela had been in prison for one year, serving a five-year sentence for leaving the country illegally and inciting workers to strike). The police confiscated hundreds of documents, some written by Nelson Mandela, who they thus considered to be the head of Umkhonto we Sizwe. This was the start of the famous Rivonia Trial, which changed the course of South African history.

Mandela and his colleagues expected to receive the death sentence, so they were relieved at the sentence handed down. In June 1964, eight of the nine accused were condemned to life imprisonment with hard labour. It was on this occasion that Mandela pronounced one of the most famous phrases of his life, a phrase that he repeated when he came out of prison, 'This is an ideal which I hope to live for and to achieve. But if needs be, it is an ideal for which I am prepared to die.' Rivonia was henceforth inextricably bound up in the country's destiny.

And henceforth it would be part of mine ... As a suburb, Rivonia is welcoming. Lots of trees, a little river, and peace. At least for the moment.

It was while we were in the process of moving, while we were staying over at Omar's, that my third child was conceived, in October 1994. Expected time of arrival: 27 June 1995. I therefore arrive in Rivonia pregnant.

The house is two minutes by car from the French School (this proximity was our most important criterion during the search). I also spend wonderful times with Sue Sparks, who acts as my guide in the suburb, showing me the places where she meditates, next to the river, and telling me where to find the delicatessens, the post office, the pharmacy. Sue has lived in Rivonia for two decades. Her parents are of Swiss origin and have always spoken to her in French. Even though she has lived in South Africa all her life, she still speaks a very good French, without an English accent.

I often walk to visit Sue. It takes me a few minutes longer to get there, as my belly grows. During the summer, Sue and Allister eat outside on a little covered terrace, next to the kitchen. Kami and Léandre get on well with their son, Julian, who, at fourteen, is as tall as Jay. They have great fun throwing a ball as far as possible in the enormous garden, while the Sparks' two dogs fight to see who can bring it back.

Sue looks at everything in a positive light, including her cancer, which obstinately reappears, after long and short periods of remission. She is always smiling, even during the side-effects of chemotherapy. I admire her for her persistent, constant optimism, which has kept her alive – miraculously – for years.

It is Sue who comes to comfort me when a good friend of mine calls with news that completely shatters me. She has had her breast implants removed, because the silicone was running into her arms, back and chest. The implants had been fixed in place with metal pins, which have now bonded onto the bone!

My friend has phoned me just after having her breasts removed. The surgeon had had to scrape away at the bone for several hours in order to free the pins. The silicone has caused serious damage, leading to many problems, including chronic migraines. The doctor has managed to save the nipples.

Sue senses my distress and rushes over. She takes me in her arms and says:

'Come and look.'

'At what? Where?'

'Let's go into a bedroom, I want to show you something.'

I follow her into the boys' bedroom. She closes the door behind me. Then she unbuttons her blouse without saying a word.

I am staggered. Sue no longer has nipples. Her cancer has started in the breast, requiring the removal of first one, then the other breast. Her flat chest only has two big scars on it. The sight gives me another shock, but the message gets through. She communicates her solidarity, her compassion, her understanding. Sue does up her blouse and says, 'Lucie, come and smile at life. You can always do that. Come and smile with me.' We have a cup of tea. She calms me. Her words are like velvet to my soul.

Sue Sparks has always been a bit of a black sheep in the suburb, regularly the subject of gossip among the 'ladies' of the area. To them she is 'the white woman who welcomes blacks into her home and who works in the townships'. She laughs about it. Because the townships are her life. She is a missionary at heart.

It is from the townships that she draws her anecdotes. Sue loves telling the story of a blind couple. While she was working for the Black Sash, an organisation established by wealthy white women to silently protest against apartheid and to do their part in bringing comfort to the poor, she met a man who was single, poor and blind. She helped him obtain the papers entitling him to a government pension for handi-capped persons. Elsewhere Sue also knew a woman who was single, poor, albino and blind. She was extremely ugly, but exuded extraordi-nary warmth, explains Sue, who organised for the two blind people to meet. 'A current ran through our bodies when we shook hands,' they confided in Sue afterwards. 'They see only their internal beauty,' says Sue with a sigh. She attended their wedding. 'I helped two people find happiness.'

Sue makes it possible for many people to live happily. Like the time she spent the night in hospital with her son, who had asthma. She chatted for hours with a black woman who was very sad because her husband was suffering from a serious illness and had to have a big operation in London. She confided in Sue that she was unable to accompany him, to be at his side to hold his hand, because she did not have the money for the air fare. Sue, convinced of her integrity (her instinct was never wrong!) wrote her out a cheque straightaway. She only told Allister about this gesture a few years later!

'You know, Lucie, one day I am going to die of cancer,' she tells me. For years we talk about chemo, we celebrate the remissions and the fear of the cancer returning. But Sue accepts the illness. 'I have come to terms with the idea of dying. It's Allister and Julian who are not ready. But it's not going to happen right now!' she reassures me, laughing.

Sue receives a new treatment. The side-effects are tough. Sometimes I do some shopping for her or go and fetch her post. But she doesn't like losing her independence and relies on others only when she absolutely has to.

Sue Sparks has changed many people's lives, including mine. She teaches me to recognise happiness, even if it's only temporary.

44

Léandre

Léandre has been with me since September 1994, after finishing his second year of schooling in Quebec. His father and I have, once again, concluded a new agreement – on paper this time! But the bickering has started again, and it's worse than ever. We had agreed that Léandre would finish his primary schooling in South Africa, but the arrangement is brought into question once again. Why does Léandre's father have to wait until I'm pregnant to attack?

A few weeks after I return from Christmas in Quebec, my first in the snow since 1991, I receive a sworn statement stipulating the exact opposite of what we have agreed. He is now claiming custody, with visiting rights for me in Quebec.

My lawyer is not very encouraging, 'Agreements are worth nothing, because they can always be changed.'

We have scarcely moved to Rivonia before I take out my radio equipment to start recording my telephone calls with Léandre's father. He has lied in his statement and I want proof. I get him to confess the truth without much difficulty.

'Why did you lie?'

'Lucie, a person can say anything they like in a sworn statement.'

I have his confession on tape. For three years I have been collecting proof without his knowledge. I would not like to shame him by divulging it, because he is the father of my son and my son adores his father. But nothing will prevent me from preparing myself adequately, or from fighting to keep my son!

For three years, acrimonious exchanges, agreements made and rejected and lawyers' letters have formed part of my daily life. I carry the squabbling about Léandre's custody around with me all day long. It haunts me constantly. His father's words are vicious. So are mine.

We have reached the stage of psychological evaluations. The real war is starting. It is set for summer 1995, in Quebec. Since a psychologist from Quebec cannot come and do a family psychological evaluation of Léandre's South African living environment, my lawyer asks me to prepare a video portrait of the house and my son's immediate environment and to request a psychological evaluation *in situ* from a South African professional. I borrow a camera from the Institute and spend two weeks filming: the school, Léandre's friends, the family, his tennis and swimming lessons, the park, his bicycle, soccer with Jay, the trampoline in the yard with Kami. Even though the standard of living is high in Quebec, our African lifestyle is luxurious by comparison: a swimming-pool, a one-acre garden, four bedrooms, two lounges, four toilets ...

The psychological evaluation is more complicated though. I have to explain it to Léandre ...

'Your papa wants you to live with him, and I want you to live with me. So some people are going to ask us some questions to help the judge decide where you should go to school.'

'But I want to stay here!'

It comes out spontaneously. I take him in my arms and we cry together. He has just realised, at the age of only eight, the importance of the decision that is going to be made.

'I want to do primary school with you. Then, maybe when I'm twelve, I'd like to go and do my secondary school in Quebec.'

It is clear in his mind. He knows what he wants. And that is also what he repeats to the three psychologists he sees, who ask him his opinion in a hundred different ways.

His father is convinced of the opposite and is determined to get Léandre back for good from June 1995 – the month my baby is due ... Things become ugly. Our letters become more menacing. He demands another psychological evaluation, in addition to the 'neutral' one performed by a psychologist appointed by the court in Quebec (which costs me twenty-five thousand rand). In the end I pay for three psychological evaluations in order to comply with his demands. He, on the other hand, doesn't spend a penny ...

The psychologists, in South Africa and later in Quebec, two men and one woman, all come to the conclusion that it would be 'far more damaging for Léandre to be deprived of his mother than of his father at this young age'. But his father won't give up. He wants Léandre back.

Omar advises me to consult one of his lawyers, Norman Kades. Norman has a solid reputation and his services are expensive, although he makes an exception for me. 'She is a friend of the family,' Omar warns. 'Take care of her as though she were my own daughter.' Omar is respected. Norman is devoted.

I meet him in his offices in central Johannesburg. He makes me understand that I run the risk of losing Léandre, whatever the psychologists say, because the slightest thing can swing the balance in favour of life in a more peaceful country. 'Everything depends on the judge,' says the lawyer.

Kades advises me to use a bold strategy. He tries to convince me to keep Léandre here. South Africa has not signed The Hague Convention on the abduction of children. I could therefore keep him with me. Léandre's father and the Canadian government wouldn't be able to do anything ... as long as I don't set foot in my country of birth.

Norman's suggestion haunts me for some time. But never to be able to return to Canada, never to be able to sleep with a clear conscience because I had abducted a child – that would be a constant nightmare. I think I would die of guilt-induced cancer.

Whatever my decision, I must first appear before the court in Johannesburg in order to settle my legal custody status in terms of South African law. Here an unmarried father has no rights, so the judge grants me legal custody without any problem. This document is completely worthless in Canada, but the procedure puts pressure on Léandre's father.

I am six months pregnant. It seems as though history is repeating itself. It's even worse because I almost lose the baby. In fact, I do lose one. I should have twins, but one dies. I have an ultrasound and the doctor tells me, without my asking, that the foetus that has survived is a boy. How many babies will it cost me to have peace?

I write a desperate letter to Jay. I don't know how to talk to him any more. He is buried in his work and we are drifting apart. Even if he finds me obsessive about the custody affair, I have to fight and resolve it finally. If I fight in Canada, I risk losing not only Léandre, but Jay as well, because if I do not obtain exclusive custody of my son I have to live near him. Kami and the new baby risk being separated from their father for several years. If I keep Léandre in South Africa, his father will not give up the struggle ... 'A mother is always a mother,' I say to Jay in this letter. 'Léandre is my love. He is my son. He is my blood. You are my love. You may not be of my blood, but mine cannot flow without you. You are the love of my life. I feel caught. I need you. And at the same time I want to save you from this experience. I want to close the book on this nightmare. But I do not want to close it in the wrong way.'

The stress increases. I suffer as a result. I have difficulty walking. I am afraid of losing Léandre and this manifests itself in contractions. I have to take medication to stop them.

Even my therapist is worried. She knows that if I do not win custody of Léandre, I will have to return to Quebec with Kami and the baby I'm carrying. Jay will not be able to follow me, as he is too involved in the politics of the country. The prospect: a family torn apart ...

A glimmer of hope soon appears. Luc Deshaies, my lawyer in Quebec, sends me the judgement in a case that is very similar to ours, divided custody between Australia and Canada, in which the mother living in Australia won. There would therefore be a precedent, although no guarantee of victory, because South Africa is a far more dangerous country than Australia.

The uncertainty is killing me. I finally make a decision: I will go and fight in Quebec, at the risk of losing my case. It is the fairest thing to do. I owe it to my son.

45

Looking for friends

'I feel like I am on a waiting list.'

My therapist jumps.

'What are you trying to find here?'

'My life. My real life.'

'Your real life? Isn't this one real?'

'It's like a dream. It is as if in South Africa I am waiting for my life to start again. I am waiting to return to Quebec to be able to live fully.'

'And if you only return to Quebec in ten years' time?'

'I will go back before that!'

'*If*. I am saying *if*. And even if it was next week, why waste your days waiting when you can live in the present?'

I don't know how to reply.

'Why don't you have any friends? Why don't you have a social life?'

'Because my time is too taken up by my children and my work.'

'That isn't a valid reason. Don't you think that you avoid making friends because you are afraid of engaging in any relationship that might oblige you to make a life here?'

I remain silent.

'Lucie? Are you afraid to take the steps that will make South Africa your new home?'

You usually meet new people through work. Now with Jay's new job, I have had to resign from the Institute for Journalism. My days were too full. I couldn't manage everything, the children, my work at the Institute, the correspondence for Radio–Canada, my pregnancy, this

194

business of Léandre's custody …When I gave my letter of resignation to my boss, Allister Sparks, he was not exactly pleased, but he understood my situation. The team gave me a nice party when I left. They gave me a plaque with the words, 'To Lucie Pagé, renowned teacher and television coach, wife with many portfolios, lifelong colleague of the IAJ'. My therapist tried to convince me that my resignation from the Institute was another reason to get out of the house, since my social life would otherwise be non-existent.

'What? Do you want me to go and stand in the street or in a bar with a sign saying, "I am looking for friends"?'

'There's no need to be sarcastic …'

'Anyway, I am happy on my own. I do not have the energy to find friends.'

'Because that would force you to settle down in South Africa and make a "real" life here?'

'Perhaps. But the main reason is that I work at home because I want to keep my job as a correspondent for Radio–Canada.'

'But you told me that that doesn't even cover your travelling expenses!'

'It doesn't matter. That's what I want to do. I don't care about the money. Anyway, Jay says he will come to live in Quebec soon.'

'Lucie …'

I had similar conversations with each of the three therapists I saw over several years in South Africa.

Yes, I believe that Jay will come to live in Quebec. Soon. He told me so himself. Yet, we seem to be the only two who believe it …

My social life is limited, but at the same time so precious! I still see my friend Colette and her son Duncan, with whom we lived when I arrived in Johannesburg. And several times a week we go to Omar's, to eat, to talk, to watch a film, always to laugh, no matter what's going on. Omar supports me in my struggle for custody of Léandre. But I do not follow his advice. According to him, I should keep Léandre and stay here. A wife stays with her husband. Children stay with their mother. That's it. He does not understand when I tell him that I do not want to deprive Léandre of his father.

I meet a lot of people at Omar's. The room that Omar chooses for the occasion usually determines the type of contact we will have. If we sit in the large lounge, the conversations are official. In the small family lounge, it's more relaxed. But when we sit on the soft couch in his bedroom, we no longer need to censor what we say.

It is on this couch that I meet the beautiful Terese. Such beauty should be illegal! She is coloured, but has Indian features and beautiful black hair, silky and thick, which falls to the nape of her neck. Terese is gentle and reserved in the big lounge, but so warm when you get to know her! We have laughed so much, she, Omar and I. For hours on end, talking about politics, society, feminism or racism. Her partner is Jack Coolen, a white South African of Dutch origin. We laugh about the cultural adjustments we have to make as part of a mixed couple. Terese is full of vitality. She has, or rather had, two sisters. One of them drowned. Her parents are still devastated, even though several years have passed since it happened.

My social life takes place almost entirely at Omar's. It is a meeting place for a number of people. Omar now lives alone, recently divorced. His three youngest daughters are still with him, even though their official residence is several streets away. He has bought a house for his ex-wife. For his daughters. For his little darlings, whom he spoils incessantly.

Omar says that I shouldn't work. That I have enough children to keep me busy. He doesn't understand: even with a dozen children, I would want to do what I am doing. Omar is sixty years old and a Muslim through and through. Despite his apparent liberalism, he likes to have his tea served by the woman in his life. Even though he knows perfectly well where the kettle is in the kitchen. These differences between us are not important. I adore him. And I know the feeling is mutual.

Jay agrees with my therapist: I must get out, meet people. My social life must expand beyond Omar's house. So, to help me, he offers me a wonderful gift: a one-year subscription to a fitness centre, the Health and Racquet Club. It's really only whites who are able to afford a subscription. I try to convince Jay to come with me. 'I would be the only black person training,' he replies. 'So what?' But I get nowhere; he doesn't want to come.

I go alone, for the swimming pool. Every morning, I leave my two boys at school and nursery school, then I go and swim a kilometre. I have always done this. I need it. This exercise helps me destress. In summer, in Quebec, I swim across the lakes; in South Africa I do lengths. But I don't meet any 'friends' at the pool.

I swim until the baby is born.

46

Shanti

Although I am devoted to journalism, I avoid journalists like the plague. Jay sometimes asks me to take part in a documentary about his life and family. I always refuse. Finally, he stops asking, after always meeting with resistance.

There are two exceptions, however. I agree to participate in two programmes. The first is hosted by Evita Bezuidenhout, or Pieter-Dirk Uys, an Afrikaans drag artist who uses his persona for political satire. White audiences adore him, which is odd, because his persona is a complete challenge to the white mentality, especially the Afrikaner mentality. Evita is superb. Shrewd in her interviews, funny enough to make you wet your pants, but very serious when she needs to be.

She is doing a portrait of Jay to discover the man behind the 'devil's eyes'. Her hypothesis: this fired-up activist, this goal-driven trade unionist, this serious man, must have a warm, human side.

In actual fact, that is all Jay is. Warm and human. But he doesn't let it show. He is hard, doesn't suffer fools, demands a lot from his employees, but has the reputation of getting the job done and being an extraordinary boss. All his close colleagues say they work like crazy with him, but that they prefer him to any other boss. Jay listens. He knows how to encourage people, how to congratulate them on work well done and how to trust teamwork. He likes to surround himself with strong people, women in particular. 'They are generally more peaceful, less competitive,' he says.

I have only a short interview with Evita, during which I ask her a riddle:

'Do you know why Jay was made Minister without Portfolio?'

'No, why?'

'Jay has a habit of losing everything. He loses his keys, his wallet, his cellphone, pens by the dozen. So when I told Mandela about this bad habit, he decided not to give Jay a portfolio; he would have lost it anyway!' The joke went around the country.

The other programme in which I agree to participate is hosted by Dali Tambo, son of Oliver Tambo. Dali is funny, eccentric, a born presenter. His show, *People of the South*, consists of fairly intimate interviews, where singers, comedians, politicians or business people usually reveal a secret side of their personality. Society's great names appear on the show, and sometimes even perform. Mandela has already sung a song on one of the shows.

I refuse to play along several times, until Dali himself comes to the house to convince me. His charm and sincerity win me over. I accept, warning him that my baby is due soon and that he should organise a replacement just in case.

In the studio a group of African singers and dancers welcome the guests and accompany them to the couch on the stage. My mother and Léandre are in the audience.

'How far along is your pregnancy?' Dali asks in opening.

'Nine and a half months. I hope to get through the programme!'

Everyone laughs.

Dali and I have prepared a surprise for Jay. I have brought along one of the many love poems he has written me. Dali asks him to read it. He is surprised and embarrassed, but agrees. The poem is beautiful. Jay has a way with words. Unfortunately I have since lost that poem, but he regularly writes me new ones ...

Three days later, our family is discussed on South African television once more.

It happens on 16 June 1995, an important day for South Africa, because, nineteen years before, hundreds of school pupils throughout the country were killed by the South African police. Everything started in Soweto, when youths protested against Afrikaans as a compulsory medium in schools. Up to 1993, 16 June was an unofficial holiday, but a holiday none the less. You saw nobody on the streets. Everyone would be gathered in stadiums or with friends to honour the memory of

Hector Peterson, the first pupil killed in Soweto, who became a celebrated martyr, the symbol of the day.

Since then, 16 June has become South Africa's day of remembrance, like Quebec's *Je me souviens* (I remember), which evokes the fact that French Canadians are different from English Canadians. A day that evokes the apartheid regime, a day in which one remembers tragic events so that they may never be repeated. A day that celebrates an awakening youth, hence the reason that it has been named Youth Day.

On 16 June 1995, Jay therefore takes the day off, partly because it's a public holiday, but also because he wants to spend some time with the family. My time of delivery is approaching. It is a lovely day, sunny but cold. The coldest day of the winter up to now. Getting up this morning, I realise that I do not have any photos of this pregnancy and of my big belly. We go into the garden to take some. I have Braxton-Hicks contractions, the normal contractions one has throughout a pregnancy. However, they are stronger than usual. Nothing to worry about, though. I have them fairly often.

At six-thirty that evening, the Braxton-Hicks contractions are even stronger, but I feel no pain. Just normal contractions. We call the midwife for advice. She recommends that we call her again if the contractions become regular, strong and painful.

Jay has only one appointment today. He has to participate in a live television programme with young people, to mark Youth Day.

Our friend Foxy as well as Omar and his daughters arrive. Five children in the house. Loulou starts preparing the meal. At eight everyone sits down in front of the TV to watch the sixty-minute programme in which Jay will answer the questions of twenty young people. The programme has barely started when I have a strong contraction. At a quarter past eight I have another, even stronger and very painful. Jay is on the air. He is talking and gesticulating as he gives a short history lesson on the show.

I go to my room. Eight eighteen. Another strong contraction. Serious this time. The time has come. I call the midwife. I call Jay. His driver has his cell. He has had orders to get Jay out of the studio if anyone calls to say I am having the baby. Eight twenty-five. This is serious. But I tell myself that perhaps it's still far off. Eight thirty. No, it's started! Jay is still on the screen. No one has given him the message! Loulou calls him again.

Eight forty. Jay is still busy talking on TV. He has no idea what is happening. Now it's Omar's turn to call. 'You get him out of there immediately!' Eight forty-five. The presenter announces, on camera, that I am having the baby and tells Jay he must go home!

Eight fifty. My waters break. This is really it. For twenty minutes it feels as though I am having one strong, continuous contraction. Omar comes into my room and asks if he can do anything. My trousers are soaked with my waters. As a good Muslim, he wouldn't dare remove them for me, but he does start to wonder how the baby is going to get out ...

Nine o'clock. The baby pushes. Loulou doesn't know what to do. She is panic-stricken. She is still busy serving the five children their food. And Omar, again because he is a good Muslim, will not interfere in the kitchen. I call my mother to tell her to put candles in the bathroom and to prepare the bath for the delivery. This is where I want to give birth to this baby. In water. The children are in the passage making an incredible racket. I cannot bear it. Loulou gets them to leave. She tends to me, and, secretly, she panics. Where are the midwives? Where is Jay? She runs around the house talking to everyone in French. She goes outside to tell the policeman at the gate to open up immediately and let the midwives in as soon as they arrive.

Five past nine. The baby pushes. Loulou calls the home of one of the midwives to find out when they left. She neither wants nor knows how to deliver a baby. Particularly her grandson!

Ten past nine. Jay arrives. At last. I feel the baby descending, it feels as though he's coming out, this little boy. My third boy ... I have had five months, since the ultrasound, to get used to the idea that I am not having a daughter. Not this time, at any rate. This baby has to come out. I tell Jay to roll up his sleeves and go and wash his hands. He will have to catch the baby. Too bad about the midwives. He looks at me, bewildered. My look tells him that I am very serious.

Nine seventeen. The midwives hurtle in (there has to be two of them for a home delivery). They put down their equipment. Sue Lee and Liz Harding, who delivered Kami, examine me. They tell me I'm dilated to ten centimetres ... I have known that for some time! They tell me to push. 'You can push. Push, Lucie. Push.' I am afraid of the pain. I don't want to push. 'Push, Lucie, push.' I push. On all fours on a shower curtain on the floor in my room I push.

Nine twenty-eight: out *she* comes. She! Yes, she! A girl. A dream! Realised at last! I can't get over it. I shout. Jay and I shout. A shout of life, a shout of intense joy. Peace. Blessed peace envelops me all at once. *Shanti*. Peace, in Hindi. I want peace. I have peace. A year of peace. Peace on 16 June.

On 16 June? Then it hits me – Jay has become a father on 16 June! Many people thought this was pre-arranged, that I'd induced the birth. Honestly! If it really had been up to me, I'd have chosen 24 June, the national day of Quebec.

The next morning, the telephone rings constantly. Several million people watched the television programme and know that I have given birth. 'A girl or a boy?' they want to know. Shanti has made her entrance in style. As the minister's wife, I smile for the cameras. Photographers arrive from all over. I have rings under my eyes. I am aching all over, but I have to smile. I am the wife of a minister! I say no to photos, but Jay insists. I want some peace, but his pride wins me over. 'Jay Naidoo delivers. And it's a girl!' the newspapers announce on Sunday.

I receive more flowers than I know what to do with. Dali Tambo, among others, sends some. The programme he has recorded with us is broadcast on 25 June, accompanied by the message, 'Dedicated to Shanti, a new person of the South'.

Nelson Mandela gets wind of the delivery. I had run into him scarcely six weeks before. He had pointed at my belly and asked how the baby was behaving. I had replied, 'This baby is Jay's RDP. His *reproduction* and development programme!' He had laughed heartily. And he used the joke later, on television and radio, when he talked about children being born ...

The day after that meeting, a rather funny thing happened. We were in Cape Town, more precisely in a squatter camp on the outskirts of the city, participating in the launch of the Masakhane Campaign, which means 'Let us build together'. The aim of this campaign was to reverse an established habit of boycotting payments for water, electricity and rent for houses belonging to the state. The new government wanted to put an end to this practice.

Mandela gave the main speech. Scarcely had he begun talking when Kami, at the turbulent age of two and a half, got up onto the podium and pulled at the President's trousers! I wanted to remove him from there, but with fifty or so cameras and microphones all around I gave up. Jay, who was seated with the dignitaries, looked at me, as if to say, 'What shall we do?' Mandela's bodyguard approached, but before he could touch Kami, Mandela picked him up. He put down the pages of his speech and sat him on the edge of the lectern, saying, 'So, you want to read my speech with me?' He read the rest of his speech like that. The journalists were in a state of panic because Mandela could no longer be seen! That evening, on television news, you heard extracts from Mandela's speech, but you couldn't see him because Kami filled the picture.

After Shanti's birth, Mandela called one of his colleagues to ask whether she knew the name of our new baby. She did not. So he sent me his autobiography, in which he had written, in his magnificent writing, 'To Lucie. Compliments and best wishes to a dynamic and wonderful lady. Congratulations for increasing our population!' Then he signed it 'Madiba', followed in brackets by 'N Mandela' and the date, 20 June 1995.

Since Madiba was the name he used among his familiars, he had just given me permission to call him that too. But I was never able to. I always said 'President Mandela'.

I finally leave for Quebec with the three children and my mother. Shanti is only a month old, but I have to appear in court for custody of Léandre. I am suffering from a bad case of post-natal depression.

When I arrive in Montreal, I have an appointment with my lawyer, then with a psychologist. My friend Louise Sarrasin has lent me her house so that the psychologist can come to 'analyse' us. But at the last minute the psychologist changes her mind. She would rather see me playing in a park with Kami and Léandre, Shanti at my breast, while she spends three hours analysing our relationships. I didn't feel that it was fair to make me prove myself as a mother in this way. I felt I wasn't making the grade. Then the psychologist interrogated me on my own. When Jay arrived from South Africa, it was his turn.

She also met Léandre, his father, his father's wife, who was also pregnant, and the latter's daughter, who is the same age as Léandre ...

Her report reached the same conclusion as the two previous ones: it would be in Léandre's best interests for him to be in his mother's home rather than his father's.

The day before the case, there is a dramatic turn of events: Léandre's father drops the case! He finally agrees to sign the agreement that I have proposed, which corresponds to what the psychologists think and what Léandre wants. The psychologist has mentioned that I have recorded all our telephone conversations over the past four years without his knowledge. Which explains his about-turn ...

Om Shanti! May peace be with you. Shanti's birth brought peace to the custody battle, after four years of hell and a debt of one hundred thousand rand. Peace, peace at last!

I have learned a lot from this experience. I have learned that what takes precedence above all else is respect for the child, respect for his relationships and his emotions, even when you are separated. Léandre is the one who has gained the most.

I return to South Africa with my three children, relieved, happy. Finally, peace. *Om Shanti.*

47

Betty

More than ever, I need help. The first months with three children are intense in terms of learning how to organise things. I thought I could trust Elizabeth. But she is fading away. I can no longer count on her.

A month before Shanti's birth, I asked her for her help in this period. She disappeared at the end of the week I gave birth. She only returned on the Monday morning: she came into my room to see the baby, didn't ask me how I was and went off to empty the dustbins. She didn't give me a cup of tea, a sandwich, or even a smile.

I felt betrayed. When Elizabeth had her baby, I rushed back from the Institute, where I was still working, and stayed with her at the hospital throughout the delivery. The attitude of the doctor, a white woman, had revolted me. Not once did she look at Elizabeth. Not once did she address her, except to say, 'Move your buttocks down.' She went as far as addressing the nurse in front of Elizabeth, 'This is my number thirty-two. Another eight and I pass my course.'

I stayed with Elizabeth, encouraging her at each contraction, wiping her forehead between each one. Push! Push! A little girl was born. After three boys, this is a gift from heaven. If the baby is wanted ...

For two months afterwards I served her meals. Good balanced dinners, with green vegetables. I bought her vitamins and iron. I gave her clothes, blankets, a nappy bag. I bought her nursing bras.

Her indifference was a blow to me in my time of need ...

Suddenly, my patience evaporated. I needed help more than ever with the three children, and she did nothing but wash the floors and the clothes. She even stopped doing the dishes. After three warnings, Jay also lost his patience and asked her to leave. She left with some of the crockery and bedding that belonged to me. I never saw her again.

I started looking for another domestic. Colette gave me the name of an agency that could recommend women with experience. With Jay as a minister, I was looking for someone reliable and, above all, for someone who could cook. From time to time I needed a break from the task of preparing twenty-one breakfasts, lunches and suppers every week!

So a representative from the agency arrives at the house the morning after my call, accompanied by a splendid woman, speaking five languages: Northern Sotho (her home language), Zulu, Xhosa, English and Afrikaans. She has a very soft, song-like voice. She has the body of an African woman who has grown up on *pap*: large breasts, large middle. In her African outfit, coloured dress and head scarf, she has an imposing presence.

Her name is Betty.

She seems shy. We put Shanti in her arms. And do the interview like that.

Betty has a great deal of experience, as shown by her curriculum vitae and supporting references. Can she cook? Ah! What a question! She has all the certificates for the appropriate courses, from puff pastries to lamb stews. Three children? No problem. She has three children herself! And no, she will not be having any more. Anyway, she says, she is in the process of divorcing her husband, who is a policeman.

We present her with a list of daily and weekly tasks to be completed, which she accepts without turning a hair. 'Is that all?' she seems to say, lifting her eyebrows and brushing the piece of paper aside with her hand.

We do not promise her a job, saying, without letting our feelings show, that we will call her tomorrow. But she has barely crossed the threshold when Jay and I look at one another with the same expression on our faces. Yes! We are definitely taking her!

This is how our beautiful Betty entered our lives. I believe she is here to stay.

48

From revolutionary to minister

Jay is full of secrets.

He has never learned to communicate his emotions. We are working on this in our joint-therapy sessions.

When he was a political activist, not expressing his emotions constituted a means of survival. He learnt that secrets save lives. Getting involved in political activism brings enormous risks, for yourself and for your family. Exposing your plans or secrets to your loved ones puts their lives in danger. Jay never told his mother exactly what he was doing. He wanted to spare her. Not that it prevented the police from arresting the poor old woman at over seventy years of age and interrogating her using methods that would wear out the soul of a twenty-year-old. She knew nothing. All she knew was that he was working for 'the cause'. By keeping his secrets to himself, Jay saved her life.

However, you need to develop different qualities and attitudes to grow from a political activist to a husband and father of a family. The role of the father is in his blood. You could say that he had a similar role in COSATU: the father of a large family.

He also practised with Léandre. Perhaps he was a little awkward when he first assumed the role, content to read him stories and to play construction games or soccer. Then, gradually, he gained confidence. He started, for example, giving Léandre a bath, not so simple when a child is not your own ...

When Kami was born, Jay took the little bundle and spent days rocking him and talking to him. Then one day, I said to Jay that I needed a break from everyone, from my husband and children. Just for a few hours. Kami was four months old. I expressed some milk and put it into a bottle. I prepared a nappy bag and then I sent Jay to the zoo with the two boys and Omar's two daughters, Haneefa and Yasmin, who were eight and twelve years old. Jay admitted that he was very nervous, because he had never given Kami a bottle.

But everything was fine. I had a few hours' rest and Jay had the opportunity to become better acquainted with his role as father, alone with the children. From that day, Jay has never been afraid of jobs relating to the children. He even tackles the 'unpleasant' jobs with pleasure: changing nappies full of poo, wiping snotty noses. He is always the one who cleans up after someone has vomited. Just the smell makes me feel ill, whereas for Jay it might as well be spilt milk. Jay prepares meals, washes the floor, and sings as he does it. He nurses the children and takes great pleasure in making up stories for them, playing each of the characters. Don't forget, he is an orator. He can keep one or more children – or fifty thousand people – on the edge of their seats with his amazing stories, which all offer lessons and insights.

The one area in which Jay is completely hopeless is organisation. If we go away for a few days, for example, I have learnt not to let him pack the bags. He has no idea of what to pack for a weekend or put in a nappy bag for one day. This is probably a 'male' weakness, although I have not seen any study on the subject yet.

Jay does not cut the children's nails either. This requires too much precision. On the other hand, I will never be able to match his ability to invent fantastic stories. I would gladly trade this talent for that of manicuring.

Jay does not fear failure. He has fears, but not of failure. He is living proof that it is possible to be humble and to have confidence in one's self at the same time. It comes from his mother, he says. Believing in yourself gives you an invaluable force in life. It is this I would like to be able to give my children as a legacy: the certainty that they are capable of great things. Do we all have a power, a gift? One thing is certain, we all have a passion. We just have to find it.

There is only one Jay – not Jay the minister and Jay in slippers in the lounge. Jay is a whole man. He would never, ever, betray the memory of his dear mother, who devoted her whole life to her children, to justice and to racial equality. But neither would he ever betray himself, his principles or his soul.

It is also quite an adjustment for Jay to move from being a political activist to a legitimate government politician. One evening when he was in a melancholy mood, he began to tell me one story after another, memories that no longer conjured up the fear which had originally accompanied the events, but rather evoked nostalgia in him. 'One evening,' he told me, 'we were printing Marxist-Leninist pamphlets by hand. I had borrowed Logie's car [his brother's car] to distribute them before daybreak. When the printing was finished and we went outside, the car had disappeared. I had forgotten to put on the hand brake. The car had rolled to the bottom of the slope and crashed right into the concrete wall around a house!' Logie and he regularly reminisce about this incident. They always laugh. The night's work was all for nothing because the authorities burned all the pamphlets the next day.

'Another evening,' continues Jay, 'I was in a car with Jayendra [Naidoo] and a white woman activist. We were discussing plans of action against the government. Three policemen noticed us. [For a white to be associated with two 'blacks' was quite unusual at that time.] They asked us to get out of the car. No doubt believing that we liked to do 'it' as a threesome, one of them said, 'Hey *Chilli Bites*, what are you doing with a whitey?' They were arrested and taken to the police station. They convinced the police that they were discussing their university studies and they were released.

Jay loves telling the story of his first trip outside the country. He was twenty-seven years old. He had gone to Amsterdam with colleagues, for a meeting with the Dutch trade unions. At the airport he saw a white shoe-shiner. 'We were so excited at the idea that a white person could clean the shoes of a black person that we all had ours cleaned.' They took photos and showed them with great pride to their friends and colleagues in South Africa.

That evening, reminiscing about 'the good times', Jay admitted his nostalgia: 'I miss the times when we chanted slogans in the street.' Then he added, 'It's much easier than building a country.'

The pressures of Jay's new job weighed heavily on our family life. And I thought I didn't see him much when he was General Secretary of COSATU! When Jay became a minister, he more or less disappeared from our lives. He was working all the time. Since parliament is in Cape Town, he often spent whole weeks in session there, only coming home on weekends, which he spent working madly as well.

Jay was very tense for his first few months, even for his first few years in government. Everything was new, even though he knew the country from top to bottom.

49

From South African to Indian

When Jay travels, everyone asks if he comes from India.

'No, I am African, South African.'

'Ah, but you were born in India.'

'No, I am South African.'

'Ah, but your parents come from India.'

'No, they are South African.'

'But you go to India regularly.'

'No, I have never been there.'

The Indians have been in South Africa for a hundred and forty years. The KwaZulu-Natal region cultivates sugar cane, among other things. From 1860 onwards, the British government, which controlled the region and possessed an empire in the Indies, encouraged the immigration of more than one hundred and fifty-two thousand Indians to alleviate the shortage of labour on the plantations. Today, more than eighty per cent of roughly one million South Africans of Indian origin live in KwaZulu-Natal.

The Indians were treated differently to the blacks. They were not slaves in the true sense of the word. They were indentured labourers, or labourers on contract. They were promised a piece of land after five years' work. The promise was not always kept ...

On 7 June 1893, only two weeks after his arrival in South Africa, Mohandas Gandhi, then a young lawyer on a legal mission at twenty-three years of age, was thrown off a train at Pietermaritzburg Station because of the colour of his skin. This injustice revolted the young lawyer, who was eventually to spend twenty-one years in the country fighting for the equality of his people and for justice. Mohandas Gandhi would become a 'mahatma', which means 'great soul'. He later said, 'I was born in India, but I was made in South Africa.'

Mahatma Gandhi had a great influence on the Indian population of South Africa, but also on the Africans themselves. The ANC, for example, adopted the policy of non-violence before resorting to the armed struggle.

Jay's great-grandmother emigrated to South Africa in 1864. She was not a Naidoo, but the origin of this name is quite amusing. When the Indians arrived, they had to give their name to the customs officer at the port. Now at that time, Indians did not have surnames as we know them. They had a first name to which was added 'son of so-and-so' or 'daughter of so-and-so'. The British, however, demanded a 'proper' surname, and so they gave the Indians names related to their geographical origin. Thus, an immigrant from the province of Tamil Nadu received the surname 'Naidoo'.

Jay now wishes to make peace with his origins and to accept them. He has come a long way in acknowledging this heritage since our first meeting. Together with the 'new South Africa', Jay began a profound personal transition.

Some women dressed in white, from the World Spiritual University of the Brahmas Kumaris, facilitated this transition. The Brahmas Kumaris were founded in India by the great Brahma Baba in 1936. Even though he is now dead, his spirit continues to direct them. This spiritual university is headed by women and claims to have more than three hundred and fifty thousand followers throughout the world. Although the Brahmas Kumaris have a religious character, their most important mission is the transmission of human, moral and spiritual values. Thus, members of all sorts of religions are found among their followers. 'Spirituality is the key to respect and confidence,' says the Brahmas Kumaris leader, Dadi Prahashmani.

Jay met a few of these missionary women in the context of his work. They devote special energy to recruiting political leaders. 'Power should be imbued with spiritual values,' they say. They have also met President Mandela on one occasion.

The Brahmas Kumaris offer meditation courses, relaxation sessions, yoga and reflective workshops on all kinds of subjects, and they regularly organise conferences with a social and political character at their headquarters on Mount Abu in Rajasthan in India or at one of their three thousand two hundred centres situated in seventy countries around the world.

Om Shanti, Om Shanti, Om Shanti (peace be with you), the Brahmas Kumaris say when they welcome people. They have been visiting us regularly since Shanti's birth, which coincides with Jay's first meeting with these women.

At around this time, I start talking openly to Jay about India. I repeat what I said when I met him, almost five years ago. 'You eat like the Indians, you think like them, you move like them, you practise yoga and meditation like they do.' Jay is intrigued. Yes, he practises the traditions and rites passed on by his family. But he is only now starting to recognise that he is a South African of Indian *origin*.

If I had to use an adjective to describe my marriage with an 'Indian', it would be 'peaceful'. I have no problem accepting the various rituals of his religion, like throwing a few drops of alcohol for the ancestors into the garden when opening a bottle. I also join in the prayers that Jay recites, after having prepared incense, fire, water, milk, freshly picked flowers and some fruit. He places them all on a silver tray, which carries a photo of his mother. He joins his hands, closes his eyes and prays. For me, it is a moment of reflection. It always does me good.

Jay does not expect me to adopt his religion, or even to conform to the rituals that accompany it. He has to cut his nails outside, over soil and in daylight hours, according to Hindu custom. This is exactly how it is done in India. But he does not say a word when I cut my nails and the children's in the house in the evening (even though he does not like it at all). On the other hand, he raises his voice if we kill a spider. You are not allowed to kill any living thing! You have to pick up insects and put them outside, gently, in their natural environment, and not crush them underfoot. Jay believes in reincarnation. He does yoga and meditates every morning. Jay is a very deep being who attaches a particular importance to the spiritual in all aspects of life, and I love that.

Among Indians, or at least in Jay's family, children have a remarkable respect for old people. The experience – and the wisdom – they have to pass on is valued. A god or goddess is always openly on display in their homes. Jay was brought up with the image, here and there in the house, of Sarasvati, the goddess of education. It is in fact rare to find non-educated Indians in South Africa. Under apartheid the Indians benefited from far better schools than the blacks, even if they were less well equipped than those of the whites. Parents are, generally, highly involved in their children's education and will make up for gaps in the system at home.

Jay does not impose his values, his religion or his culture on me. For my part, I accept every new ritual that he wants to practise. He does not expect the children to become Hindu. He would not be offended if they became Catholic. All that he asks is respect for the fundamental values of life.

The ceremony marking Shanti's birth, for example, was held according to Hindu tradition; it lasted about two hours and was accompanied by singing. Nisha, Jay's sister, carried out all the ritual steps, using incense, fire, water, fruit and milk that had been blessed. My favourite part was where we wrapped Shanti in a blanket and rocked her while singing a gentle, spiritual song. The Brahmas Kumaris also said some special prayers.

Jay, who has never visited India, now has to go there as part of his work and the Brahmas Kumaris invite him to visit their headquarters, at the top of Mount Abu. He accepts, because a return to his ancestral country is a spiritual process for him. For some time, Jay has been attending a number of meditation sessions with the Brahmas Kumaris. He is ready. He wants to discover his roots.

When I'm invited to accompany Jay, I do not hesitate for a moment: I want to go back to India. This country really fascinated me when I visited it in 1986. My falling in love with Jay had something to do with his culture.

So, we are leaving. I feel a bit guilty travelling at the state's expense and I fear people's comments, journalists' comments. However, the fact that the state pays my travel expenses is in line with ministerial regulations. We take Shanti with us, because I am still breastfeeding, but we pay for her ourselves.

The captain of the Air India plane comes to welcome us. It is an honour, he says, to welcome Jay Naidoo onto the plane that will take him to the country of his ancestors. Jay is well known and liked there.

Many Indians are proud that one of their own has been so actively engaged in the struggle against one of the worst political regimes of the century. They offer to put us in first class. Jay hesitates, then says no, thank you, he is fine in business class. I, however, who travel between Quebec and South Africa so often with the children in economy class, jump at the opportunity to be spoilt, for free! I nudge Jay a few times as if to say, 'Wake up, man. If you don't want to go, I'll go!' The captain insists, and so do I. 'What principle will be compromised if you go and sit in first class?' Jay finally gives in. It is a first for us both!

The journey is very comfortable and the members of the crew are friendly. One after the other, they come to see Jay in order to shake his hand, ask him for an autograph and cuddle Shanti.

When we arrive in New Delhi, Jay is whisked off to a whirlwind of meetings. I go walking with Shanti in this enormous metropolis. To walk through Delhi is to experience several eras at the same time and to see the different faces of India in one place. Between the donkeys, horses and sometimes even camels pulling carts, the dense crowd, the cows and other animals wandering down the roads, the motorised rickshaws and the cars, there is always something to catch your attention. Ten million people live in Delhi. The pollution there has become so bad that it is often difficult to breathe. I am glad that no one has organised a programme of activities for me, as they did in the Scandinavian countries. All that has been provided for me is a car with a driver, but I categorically refuse to use this service. I prefer to take the local taxis and rickshaws.

Jay is captivated. The first evening, after his meetings, we sneak out of the hotel (he doesn't want a bodyguard or a driver). We travel around in a rickshaw late into the night. It is the first time that Jay has set foot in a country where the majority of people resemble him physically! The Indian spectacle fills him with wonder ...

A few days later, we go to Mount Abu, in Rajasthan, to the Brahmas Kumaris. The journey is dreadful. Five hours in an old car without any suspension, at forty degrees, on winding roads blocked by cows and crowds of people ...

As we go deeper into Rajasthan, the colours intensify. The women wear brightly coloured saris. It is beautiful. The towns and villages blend into one another. There are no big uninhabited spaces between the towns, as there are in Canada. They are always packed with people. There are crowds everywhere.

At the top of Mount Abu, however, peace reigns. Everything is simple. The food is healthy and vegetarian. The Brahmas Kumaris are calm and always smiling. No one speaks loudly. Everything is gentle. I believe in the values that they advocate. The values of honesty, spirituality and truth, values that would change the world if everyone adopted them in daily life. The Brahmas Kumaris believe in God, or in a supreme force that they call Baba.

On Sunday evening, one of the Brahmas Kumaris leaders sits on a podium in front of three thousand people to meditate. She manages to get their God to talk before us. Her voice changes as the 'Great Baba', the supreme being, speaks to us! Personally, this aspect of the religion seems a little forced and annoys me. But I respect its rituals, apart from the fact that I am the only one, among three thousand followers, dressed in green. Everyone, Jay included, is wearing white. I had not purposely wanted to stand out, I simply had not thought of wearing white clothes, nobody had mentioned it.

We spend a few days in Mumbai (Bombay) and in Kovalam, in Kerala, where we meet a famous doctor. His body is enveloped in a simple piece of fabric (a *dhoti*) and he is wearing flip-flops. Jay, who is in the habit of meeting 'important' people wearing a suit and tie, is fascinated by the simple appearance of this doctor.

Besides, he also resembles Jay. Jay might be wearing shoes, but, in his head, he is walking barefoot, like this old Indian. Humility doesn't wear a particular outfit.

I think that this quality of Jay's is greatly appreciated in South Africa. He could walk around dressed in a simple *dhoti* and barefoot. People might talk, but it would not contradict his way of being in the world. And it is exactly like this that I imagine him, as an Indian sage, barefoot, shortly after our return from India.

❖ ❖ ❖

It happened on World Water Day. I went with Jay to the township of Alexandra, in Johannesburg. I wanted to be there because I like to listen to his speeches. After all, that is what he was doing when I first met him …

Alexandra is an extremely poor township. About a quarter of a million people live crammed into one square kilometre, most of them in shacks made of corrugated iron or cardboard, without water or electricity. Alexandra is a stone's throw from Sandton, one of Johannesburg's richest suburbs, adorned with trees, flowers and street-lights. These two suburbs were joined together in the last local elections. The same municipal budget now has to cover two entities. Fusing these two worlds represents quite a challenge. It will take several generations before the contrasts disappear.

Jay often goes to Alexandra. Today, on World Water Day, he is going to 'adopt' a school that he will visit on a regular basis from now on. Water is a rare commodity in Africa, and South Africa is no exception to this rule. Young people, especially those in the rich areas, need to be made aware of the value of this precious resource.

Just over eight hundred pupils are waiting for us. They have been preparing for this day for a long time. For a minister to come to a school is an event in itself, but the fact that this minister is Jay Naidoo is extraordinarily lucky. Jay is a popular hero and he is received as such. People want to touch him, to talk to him. The children have written songs in his honour and, between the various speeches, Jay accompanies them in their dances.

These eight hundred pupils share six taps. Every day, they literally fight for a few drops of water.

Throughout the ceremony, my heart swells with emotion. The songs are wonderful, and the hope that is evident in this welcome is intoxi-cating when you think of all the dreams that the revolution has made possible. The majority of these children are poorly housed. They sleep under cardboard or corrugated iron roofs, in community halls or even in churches. They are dirty. They are thirsty. But everything is forgotten today because Jay is visiting them.

Outside the school hundreds of people have gathered to see him. In the children's songs and poems, in Northern Sotho, we hear Jay Naidoo's name again and again, like a prayer, expressing a sort of vener-ation. And since I have come unexpectedly, they have added 'Mrs Naidoo' to their texts at the last minute.

I am given a gift: a hand-made broom. Jay takes it from me at once, explaining that he is the one who does the sweeping at home! Because he knows that, by his example, he can contribute to breaking the stereotypes that are still so strong here.

I leave moved. The children sing and dance in the street, in front of and behind our car, hanging onto it. They would like to keep Jay with them the whole day long. Jay is also moved. 'It is experiences like this that really thrill me,' he says to me.

50

It's Cape Town or Montreal

My beautiful friend Terese with the silky black hair, whom I meet from time to time on the couch in Omar's bedroom, whom I always laugh with, even at sad things, has not come to the airport to fetch her partner, Jack Coolen, who is returning from a business trip abroad. Yet he has let Terese know his time of arrival ...

Jack calls home. No reply. Perhaps Terese is caught in a traffic jam. She is never normally late. Jack waits. And waits some more. He starts to get worried and calls Terese's father. The latter says that he will immediately pop around to his daughter's place. Terese is not there. Her father goes to check at the small block of flats that belong to her.

Terese is there, in one of the flats. She hasn't answered her cellular phone because she has an axe planted in her head. The kitchen floor is covered with blood. Only a few years ago, Terese's father found his elder daughter, after she had drowned. And now he finds his second daughter, murdered.

A new tenant was about to move into one of the flats Terese owned and she had decided to repaint it. She was taking the cans of paint out of her small white Toyota Corolla when a man walked by.

'Poor madam! Let me help you with your brushes and your paint.'

'That's very kind of you! Thank you!'

When they were in the flat, he took an axe and split her skull with it. For her car. For her Toyota! That is all he wanted. The keys to her car!

Omar is still in shock when he gives me the news. I myself have just had my car stolen, a new Jetta. When Shanti had to spent four days in hospital with a bad virus, I left the car in a parking garage for the night, because I was still breastfeeding and therefore had to sleep with her. The following morning, the car had disappeared. I informed the authorities, who immediately posted an armed guard in front of Shanti's room. The last thing they needed was to have the minister's daughter kidnapped!

I lost my car. Terese lost her life for her car. The soft sofa in Omar's bedroom is in mourning. We are all in mourning. I say to Jay:

'It's Cape Town or Montreal!'

'What? What are you saying?'

'I don't want to live in Johannesburg any longer. I have had enough of the violence. I have had enough of the murders. I have had enough of always being afraid at a traffic light that someone is going to take my car, my children or my life. I am always afraid. And since you spend half your time in Cape Town, what difference would it make to us, except for improving our quality of life?'

'You're sure? You would really like to live in Cape Town?'

'Actually, I would prefer Montreal. But I leave the choice up to you.'

'It's true that the children would love Cape Town, with the sea, the beaches and the mountains. And school?'

'There is a French school. I have checked.'

It is essential to me that my children go to a French school. Firstly for the language, because I alone am not able to pass my language onto my children in a non-French environment. School and the language they speak with their mother offer an adequate balance for the environment, television, friends and the language they speak with Jay. In addition, the French School follows the northern hemisphere calendar, from September to June. Since Léandre sees his father at Christmas and during the two months of the North American summer, it is essential that I keep to the northern school year. If there was no French School in Cape Town, I would not even think of moving the family there.

'And your work?' asks Jay.

'Here or in Cape Town, what's the difference, since I spend ninety per cent of my time in my office at home. And now, with the Internet, I no longer need to go to the press archives.'

'Are you sure you want to move?'

'I can't bear Johannesburg any longer. I want to leave. I am sick of living weighed down by fear; I am even afraid in my bedroom!'

During the five years I have lived in Johannesburg since 1992, the cases of violence have multiplied around me. Colette has told me about people who were killed in the road, opposite her house, one night; about Spongi, her adopted daughter, who was raped; about her neighbour, who was raped by three men who then stole everything from her house. Our French neighbour and friend, Gilles Dirickx, the economic counsellor at the French Embassy, was kidnapped at his front door, taken away and tied up, but miraculously managed to get away. My friend Musa was stabbed in the eye – the last thing you need as a television journalist. A woman was tied to a tree, raped and left for dead. My friend Karen Lubbe was stopped by two men who wanted to steal her car. She screamed and begged them to leave her boys, who were sitting strapped in on the back seat. The robbers eventually let them go. All these victims of violence are in therapy today. The stories never end. Everyone has some horror to relate.

Johannesburg stresses me. The burglar bars, the alarms, the electric fences, the cars that are stolen at red lights, even with children inside, all haunt me. I have to lock a metal gate *inside* the house, separating the bedroom section from the rest of the rooms!

The violence is sapping my energy. I want to leave.

Cape Town is a more provincial city. Even though the murder and crime rates are also high there, the violence is, for the moment, confined largely to the coloured and black townships.

Ministers are entitled to a residence in Cape Town, because they have to attend sessions there on a regular basis. When we chose one, two years ago, it was only for Jay. We had the choice of a dozen houses, each one larger than the next, some with six bedrooms and two kitchens. We took the smallest – or rather, the least large. It has four bedrooms, a small family lounge, a large one for official receptions, a very small family dining room, a cubicle really – only large enough for a round table a metre and a half in diameter and six chairs set close together: intimate, which I like. The large dining-room, with a rectangular table several metres long, will be transformed into ... a playroom! With three children, you need a room where you can shut them up sometimes! We'll put the large table in the official lounge.

There is nothing exceptional about our house. The furniture is beige and brown; the curtains are beige and brown; the carpets are beige and brown. I hate beige and brown! But these seem to be the government's favourite colours.

In each room there is a button on the wall. It is for calling the domestic worker. It rings in the kitchen, where there is a panel of red buttons. A button lights up, indicating, in Afrikaans, the room from which the call originates. I promise Betty that we will never call her in this way. She has followed us to Cape Town. I was afraid of losing her, since her children live near Johannesburg. I give her two train or bus tickets each year to go and visit them.

Betty admires Jay and she is happy with us. 'No one else has ever treated me like you do,' she repeats constantly. Against Omar's advice, I have developed an emotional relationship with her. 'You must not do that, Lucie. It will cause problems.' He says this because he does not know Betty. Betty is pure gold. Everyone tells me how lucky I am. I hear all sorts of terrible stories on the subject of domestics, but I thank God for sending me Betty.

Betty hums all the time. She has a superb voice. With Shanti tied to her back with a towel, she hums African songs as she works. Even when she is on all fours cleaning the floor, Shanti follows her everywhere and has her naps according to the rhythm of the cleaning. Betty has never been to Cape Town. She has never seen the sea either ...

Although the house isn't beautiful, the gardens are. We stay in Groote Schuur estate, a collection of fifteen or so houses in which the presidents and deputy-presidents, as well as certain ministers, have always lived. It is an extraordinary place, green, full of flowers and alive. Everywhere we come across guinea fowl. Twice a year, the mother guinea fowl guide dozens of babies in single file, across our gardens, the little wood, the fields and the palm trees.

The estate is situated on one side of Table Mountain, and on the other side lies the city. In ten minutes we can be in the centre of town, at parliament, at the French School or at the market.

Ten minutes more takes us to the edge of the Atlantic. And fifteen minutes in another direction delivers us to the Indian Ocean. You can even smell the ocean in my bedroom. I sleep with the French doors wide open; the sea breeze lifts the curtains right up to the ceiling ...

Sleeping with the door open in South Africa? I am not afraid any more! I live inside the best guarded enclosure in the country, with Mandela as a neighbour! In Johannesburg, the doors have triple locks ... behind the double locks of the metal security gate. The windows were protected by bars. Here, I finally have an open view. I no longer feel like I am in prison.

I am, however, surrounded by policemen and gardeners who are human. And humans steal and rape. Deputy-president Mbeki's driver, for instance, allegedly raped the young daughter of a domestic. Will South Africa be safe one day? Without crime, this country would become one of the most attractive on the planet.

Since our arrival in Cape Town, we have had a few thefts. A bit of money, a hairdrier, a torch. Later it was Kami's bicycle from the garage, clothes and more money. Betty keeps telling me to keep the doors closed. The gardeners are under-paid, she warns me. 'If you leave the door open and your handbag in sight, they will come.' But I always forget to close *everything*. There must be at least a few dozen doors and windows in the house! And in summer it gets hot!

Kami and Léandre go to the French School. Kami, at four years old, is in the second year of nursery school. Léandre, at ten, is in the fifth year of primary school. The school is small, but its gymnasium is impressive, wood-panelling throughout, even the stage. It's like a country school, right in the city.

The school has about a hundred and twenty pupils of all nationalities, particularly French, but also from the West African countries, the island of Mauritius, and from Quebec, two of which are mine. The French make us pay higher school fees, because we are not French. One day, at a school meeting, I point out that this is discrimination. No, replies the principal, it is just the rule. Then Jay, irritated, gets up and talks about discrimination, which he does with a certain authority. Making Quebecois or Mauritians pay an extra ten per cent in school fees because they are not French nationals is, he says, discrimination. I go one step further and ask why, if the school wants to attract French-speaking pupils, are we classified in this way. Despite our intervention, the policy has never changed ...

Shanti will go to the small Montessori nursery school at the entrance to the Groote Schuur estate. What a wonderful coincidence, it's only twelve minutes by foot. Coming back takes a little longer, because you have to climb up the side of the mountain towards the house.

I start to get to know the policemen who guard the various entrances to the estate, which can be entered by four different roads. But, over the years, there are always new policemen who ask to see my ID. They insist on seeing my papers. One day I reply that I am the wife of Minister Jay Naidoo. 'You don't look like a Mrs Naidoo,' retorts the guard. My South African identity book does not help, since it says 'Non-South African'. But usually a little wave and a smile is enough to have the gates opened.

Astonishingly, visitors sometimes simply arrive on our doorstep. They could simply come in and kill us. At other times the policemen give our friends a hard time, call me to check their identity documents and accompany them right into my lounge. There is no consistency in the guards' work, and no discipline. But you must not talk about it, because it might give ideas to people wanting to knock off certain politicians ...

I feel completely safe, especially with Betty keeping watch. She keeps an eye on everything, tells me everything. She knows everyone's comings and goings, their visitors, even their mistresses. She informs me that one of the domestic workers she is friendly with has fallen pregnant by a government minister.

I do not miss Johannesburg and its urban stress in the least. I do, however, miss my den at Omar's. It is impossible to live our friendship over the telephone. We rarely see one another now, but our meetings are as intense as ever.

Contrary to what I expected, the children and I see even less of Jay after our move to Cape Town. Jay has to spend every second week, on an alternating basis, in Pretoria and Cape Town. When he has to attend sessions of parliament, it is always for as short a period as possible, because he has 'too much work to do' and has to get back to his main office, in Pretoria.

We lose touch with one another. I discover the beauty of the Cape on my own with the children. Jay only very rarely comes with us to the beach or the mountains. In addition, his ministry is being reformed. In fact, there is even talk of it being abolished.

Jay has always said that the aim of his job has been to get rid of his job, because the Reconstruction and Development Programme for which he is responsible should integrate into all the ministries. 'The shorter the period I hold this job, the better for the country, because my work is to change the priorities of the ministries, not to do their work for them.' But not everyone sees it this way.

If a programme fails in any way, or if an electoral promise is slow in execution, the blame is put on Jay. If a programme is successful or if a promise is kept, however, the minister responsible for the project in question is praised.

Jay eventually finds himself in a state of depression. He goes to see my therapist and takes anti-depressants for several months. No one knows, except Omar, our friend, Doctor Foxy, and myself. But Jay only tells us about this when he is over the depression. The pressure was too great, too sudden, he confides in us, when he realised the extent of the challenge 'to do a hundred and eighty degree turn with a country that has been drifting in the same direction for three hundred and fifty years'.

One day, President Mandela calls him into his office and informs him that there can no longer be any justification for his post as Minister without Portfolio and that he is now appointing Jay as Minister of Post, Telecommunications and Broadcasting.

After two years, Jay's post has been abolished. Despite this, the press still talks about its failure.

However, Jay recovers his health.

51

The Cape of Good Hope

Our exploration of the Cape takes us to some extraordinary places. The countryside is among the most beautiful I have ever seen, even after visiting more than thirty countries. The magic of Cape Town is in its mountains and in the two oceans that wash up along its innumerable beaches.

I find one, by chance, that must be three hundred metres wide and kilometres long, fading out of sight. Not a soul anywhere. The children love it. I read or doze while they build their sandcastles tirelessly. It's Noordhoek Beach, about twenty minutes from town, on the Atlantic Ocean. You have to drive over Chapman's Peak, where television networks from all over the world come to film scenes that take your breath away. To get to Chapman's Peak, you take a narrow, winding road that cuts through the mountain. On the right, there's a sheer drop to the sea. In the distance you see the small village of Hout Bay, which leads out onto a rocky islet populated by thousands of seals. The horizon leads to Rio ...

An hour's drive from Cape Town, passing through little fishing villages where the fish and chips are always the day's catch, we reach a national park, where the baboons have right of way. The ground is arid and there are low shrubs. A few kilometres from the end of the road, a board indicates that we have reached the south-western extremity of the continent. This is the Cape of Good Hope. Right at the end of the road, you climb a hundred steps on foot, to face the panoramic view of Cape Point, where, it is said, the Atlantic and Indian Oceans meet.

Right in front of us, there are in fact two streams of waves meeting to infinity on the horizon. You never tire of watching this marine border, it exceeds the imagination.

We often stop, on one beach or another, when we come to the tip of the continent. Some of the beaches have dunes. The children can spend hours sliding down them. We have often tried to have picnics, but it is far too windy.

Our other regular rendezvous with the sea is Camp's Bay. There are often lots of people on this beach, but it is so easy to go there, after dinner and before bedtime, to get some fresh air with the children. The sun goes down right in front of you. The twilight calms me. I close my eyes and breathe deeply.

The Cape also hides another treasure, the vineyards. Forty-five minutes from town, the vines stretch out between the mountains like a blanket. Going on the wine route takes you on a journey through the hills and mountains of Bilbo the Hobbit, whose author, Tolkien, is of South African origin.

It was in 1688 that the first vines were planted in the Cape by the Huguenots, French Protestants fleeing religious persecution under Louis XIV, who took refuge in South Africa. These French settlers found the climate and soil of the Cape suitable for viticultural development. The Rousseaus, Du Plessis, Marchards of South Africa remind me of the French influence in this country, yet most of these South Africans with French surnames no longer speak a single word of the language of Molière. The Huguenots were assimilated into the Afrikaner population.

My Québecois friend Laval Gobeil, sixty years old and the father of two daughters who attend the French School, helps me discover the wine route. Laval has just retired after working all over Africa for the Canadian government. His wife, Suzanne, a South African, also works for the Canadian government, in the consulate in Cape Town! Laval knows every last vineyard by heart. He takes all his visitors there, certain that they will be seduced by the beauty. At Franschoek (the 'French corner'), the little village near Stellenbosch, the names of the streets and the cafés witness the legacy of the Huguenots. From the terrace of the Petit Café to that of the Grand Bistro, Laval initiates me into the charm of good wine, making me taste specialities from various estates. I have not, until now, developed a taste for wine, this is a new world for me. Laval, however, knows the good wines and, in particular, knows why they are good. Exploring the wine route is always enjoyable. However, to be able to enjoy it to the full, it is strongly recommended that you have a driver you can rely on! Laval makes sure he does not drink too much.

For Sunday brunch, it is possible to come and picnic in the grounds of the different wine estates, to the sound of classical music played on the lawns by a small ensemble, reminding you of a scene from a Mills and Boon romance. I sometimes come to the Spier estate, in Stellenbosch, to have fun with the children, go walking, eat and listen to the concerts.

'What would you like for your birthday?' Jay asked me one day. 'I want to stroke a cheetah.' He wasn't entirely surprised. He knows how attractive I find these cats. The bigger they are, the more I like them. Spier has a centre for conserving and raising cheetahs. I spent fifteen minutes stroking a big male there. The fifteen rand seems a trifling amount for the enormous amount of pleasure I received. The big cat purrs with pleasure as I caress it – in fact my whole arm vibrates. I never knew that cheetahs also purred.

In the wine region, a railway line marks the border between this fairytale world and the hard reality of poverty, misery, hunger, violence, alcohol abuse and unemployment. In large part it is the coloureds who live on the other side of this 'border'. They are the ones who maintain the rich vineyards ...

It is also the coloureds who bring a rich diversity to Cape culture. On 2 January every year, the streets of the city are packed with people for the Coon Carnival. The first mention of one of these celebrations goes back to 1823. During the time of slavery, the first day of the year was the slaves' only day off in the year. When the British abolished slavery in 1833, the coloureds did not particularly want to celebrate a day that reminded them of their slavery so 2 January became *their* day for celebrating the new year, *die Tweede Nuwe Jaar.*

Towards the 1850s a new influence was incorporated into the celebrations of the Cape slaves, that of the Black-Face Minstrels, white singers and musicians disguised as blacks. The Cape coloureds have adopted the make-up of these 'minstrels' for their annual Coon Carnival parade. The word *coon* actually comes from *racoon*, referring to the black and white mask of this animal. Another typical Cape cultural tradition is that of the Muslim Malay choirs, which retain a marked Malaysian and Indonesian influence. The singers wear a kind of cap without a peak and play the banjo as they sing in a half-Asian, half-African fashion. But they are neither one nor the other, and their political and social situation reflects this ambiguity.

I did some radio training in Cape Town, at Bush Radio, an alternative community radio station that broadcast for a long time despite prohibitions. At one of the training sessions, I met the director of a community radio station in a coloured suburb where drugs and violence are the currency. She invited me to run a special programme on the role of radio in a community, where I would reply to listeners' questions. As an introduction, I mentioned that such a radio station should be at the service of the community and offer all types of resources. I eventually spent the hour talking to women who called in to find out if their husband had the right to beat them, to find out what to do with a son who was still wetting his bed at the age of twelve, to find out whether their daughter, raped by an uncle and a cousin, would get over it one day, to ask whether their child, who had been having nightmares since armed men broke into the house and killed his father and his two brothers, should see a psychologist ...

I spoke with passion against domestic violence, and emphasised the responsibilities of parents, the rights of children and the role of a community radio station in this hard and nightmarish life, especially for women. I touched on taboo subjects. The programme director stared at me, but did not interrupt.

This happened at ten in the morning. At ten in the evening I received a call at home. It was the director. 'The telephone has hardly stopped ringing.' The irony is that this radio station was the voice of PAGAD, People Against Gangsterism and Drugs, a group that was, officially, fighting against gangsterism and drugs but in reality using methods as violent as the Mafia, allegedly responsible also for the bombs set off in Cape Town as well as various murders. The government, and thus Jay, as Minister of Telecommunications, wanted to close down this radio station. But I had just given it a new vocation. Our professional paths – Jay's and mine – could not have been more opposed.

52

Racism

I have always been allergic to racism, particularly because my sister Tanya is coloured and her negroid features have sometimes caused her problems. I have neither Jay's patience nor his diplomacy, especially if anyone insults my children! An Afrikaner had already said to me, 'You have wasted the lives of two children by putting black blood in their veins when you could have made them a hundred per cent white.'

One day, at Johannesburg airport, when we were on the way to Jay's family in Durban, we were checking in to receive our boarding passes. Léandre was in Jay's arms, Kami was in mine. The official glared at us, mumbling something in Afrikaans. He purposely took his time giving us our boarding passes. Once on board the plane, we discovered that he had allocated us four seats separated from one another, scattered from one end of the plane to the other. Even little Kami's seat was miles away from us and his brother! Yet the plane was half empty. Without saying a word, the official had exercised his power of discrimination.

On another occasion, Jay and I were refused a table, on the pretext that they were all reserved. I had seen the register. It was not true. In another restaurant we were given a table, but we were never served! And this happened after 1994, when Jay was a minister!

One day, during a session of parliament, a National Party MP said to Jay 'Go back to where you belong', ordering him to go back to India, the country of his ancestors! This would be like telling a Québecois to return to France, or an Afrikaner to go back to Holland. The MP was obliged to give Jay a public apology.

On another occasion, a racist incident could have had more dramatic consequences. We were spending a holiday in Omar's flat at the seaside, in Umhlanga, near Durban. Enjoying our rare moments of relaxation as a family, I was building sandcastles with Kami while Jay's sisters, Nisha and Dimes, and my mother, Louise, were talking peacefully. Jay, Léandre and Omar were having a great time in the big waves. All of a sudden, I saw Jay get knocked over by a huge wave. Then he suddenly disappeared. I leapt up, worried. But he re-emerged from the water and crawled out onto the sand. He stood up with difficulty and staggered up to us. I thought he was playing the fool. But no, it was serious, as we discovered six hours later when Jay collapsed.

He was talking to Louise when he suddenly lost consciousness in the middle of a phrase. Omar panicked. Frozen, Kami and Léandre didn't say a word. I leapt to the telephone and called an ambulance. The first question I was asked was the following:

'What race is the patient?'

'I beg your pardon? What are you saying! What does it matter? My husband needs an ambulance!'

I looked at Jay, unconscious at my feet. I was very conscious of the consequences of my response. If I said that he was white, they would send an ambulance immediately. But by doing that I would compromise my principles!

'You have no right to ask me his race!'

I went on to say that the Interim Constitution, which had come into force just a few weeks before (in November 1993), stipulated that discrimination on the basis of race, sex, and so on was prohibited.

'It is illegal even to ask me such a question!' I added.

She wouldn't budge. An argument broke out. I refused to divulge the patient's race, despite the pleas of Omar and Louise, who could not understand why I had chosen this moment to have a political debate! We did not get an ambulance ... Omar instead phoned a paediatrician friend, Jerry Coovadia. He arrived 15 minutes later, with his emergency bag. Jay had regained consciousness. Jerry examined him thoroughly, then reassured us, 'I am sure it is the shock from the wave. Everything will be fine ...'

Kami was born under apartheid laws. When I went to register his birth, he had to be 'classified' in terms of the law about the racial classification of the population. On the form, I had to declare him coloured or Indian. But I wouldn't. I categorically refused to give his father's race. The official looked at Kami, looked at me and then said, giving a forced sigh, 'I am classifying him 'white'.' As the official, she had to make the decision ...

South Africa does not have the monopoly on racism, however. At Mirabel International Airport in Quebec, Jay was invariably stopped and searched. Every time! He was examined from head to foot, sometimes with no consideration. His passport was scrutinised in minute detail, as if the officials were looking for proof that it had been falsified.

One day, a customs official went too far. Doubting the authenticity of the diplomatic passport that specified that the holder was a minister of the South African government, and probably suspecting Jay of importing drugs, he took him into an adjacent room. Jay was subjected to an hour-long intensive interrogation. Then he was searched from head to toe, both his person and his baggage! All this time I was waiting on the other side of the barrier with our children. And if he had been a white South African minister?

Although Jay was patient, there are boundaries you simply do not cross. That day, furious at this unjustified suspicion, he exploded. Nothing annoys him as much as a lack of respect, whether it comes from a director of the World Bank giving a paternalistic monologue on what Africans should do, or from a customs official in Montreal, London or anywhere else, exhibiting dubious zeal. This time, the story got into the Canadian papers.

The airport authorities claimed that it was a routine check performed on about ten per cent of passengers, chosen at random. 'Completely random,' they insisted. But never, never, have I been searched at Mirabel, and I have passed through that airport dozens of times. I have, however, since observed the composition of the ten per cent in question. It's very coloured ...

But you have to know how to distinguish racism from other behaviour. Sometimes, certain remarks do not indicate racism. They are inspired simply by ignorance, or a healthy curiosity. I have on a number of occasions observed curiosity aroused by 'difference'.

At Lac-Mégantic, the village in which my mother was born, I was in the waiting room of the hospital with Kami. A woman stared at the two of us for a long while. Finally, she asked:

'Is that your child?'

'Yes, this is my son.'

'But his skin, well, it is a little dark.'

'Yes, his father is African.'

'Ah! I thought so!'

'A South African of Indian origin.'

'Oh I see!'

A silence followed. The woman stared into space. Then she wanted to know, 'What does a South African of Indian origin look like?'

The same day, the nurse who was taking Kami's temperature and weight said the same thing to me:

'His skin is a bit dark. Where was he born?'

'In Africa.'

'Ah! I thought so. Did you adopt him when he was very young?'

'He is my son. He came out of my belly.'

She said nothing further.

The following anecdote, an amusing one this time, took place at La Patrie, near Mount Mégantic. We had just done the shopping for Christmas Eve with Kami and Shanti. Jay had gone to fetch the car and I was waiting inside, with the shopping bags and the children. Two women looked at us for a long moment. Then, they came up to us and pinched the cheek of one child and stroked the other's hair. Unpretentiously, they made this remark to me:

'Their skin is quite dark!'

'That's because their father ...'

Just at that moment, Jay came in.

'Here is the father!'

And the women, seeing Jay, commented, 'Ah! But their skin is quite light!'

It wasn't racism. It was quite simply curiosity. That is healthy. Racism is learned, taught, transmitted. No one is born a racist. You acquire it. And this is the reason that it can be eradicated, no matter where it puts down its roots.

53

The whole truth and nothing but the truth

Here I am busy searching for the truth … I have decided to produce a major documentary for the radio and the press on the Truth and Reconciliation Commission. After spending more than two years pregnant and three years breastfeeding, I needed to take up the reins of my professional life again.

If the majority of journalists who came to cover the last elections have now left, it's not because there is no longer anything to report. On the contrary, a new country is being built. But first the old country has to be buried, and to bury the old country, you have to know what you are burying! There are chapters missing from the history of apartheid.

The Truth and Reconciliation Commission has been established by the Government of National Unity to shed light on the period between 1 March 1960, from the period when all the anti-apartheid movements were banned, and 10 May 1994, the date of Nelson Mandela's presidential inauguration. The Commission has two years to interview thousands of people, grant amnesty to those who comply with a number of set criteria and write a report – the missing chapter in the country's history.

The TRC was born of a compromise between what the National Party envisaged – forget everything, close the book, like in Chile – and what the ANC wanted – to punish the guilty. A Nobel Peace Prize winner, Archbishop Desmond Tutu, was selected to head this commission.

Only Inkatha and certain parties on the extreme right are boycotting the work of the Commission.

I am researching the subject in depth, or at least in enough depth to produce a solid synopsis. Thanks to a former work colleague, the journalist Sylvain Desjardins, I establish contact with the director of the Radio–Canada programme *Dimanche magazine*, Pierre Trottier. Pierre wants the story. And with the help of my friend Luc Chartrand, I also succeed in selling the story to the magazine, *L'actualité*.

I aimed high in the synopsis that I sent them, interviews with the TRC President, Archbishop Desmond Tutu; with retiring South African deputy-president and National Party leader, Frederik de Klerk; with the head of Inkatha, Mangosuthu Buthelezi; with the vice-president of the TRC, Alex Boraine; and with the principal actors in a psychological drama that has no equal anywhere.

Having obtained appointments for all the desired interviews, I catch a plane to go and met Frederik de Klerk and Buthelezi in Pretoria.

De Klerk is a small man, who reminds me of René Lévesque (the former premier of Quebec) physically. He has a cigarette in his mouth every waking moment. I have never met Frederik de Klerk privately, but have come into contact with him at banquets, official dinners and congresses. We will not be alone on this occasion either. Shaking my hand, he hastens to introduce his press secretary.

'There are some questions I will not answer,' he says straightaway, on the defensive. De Klerk, it must be said, accepted the establishment of the Truth Commission, but this does not mean that he does not run great risks, both personally and for his party, by participating in this perilous exercise. Certain security force chiefs have started to talk, revealing what the National Party government really did, exposing the secret war carried out by the forces of law and order.

I have spent days preparing for this interview. I have read everything I could get my hands on about De Klerk. I feel as if I have had tea with him, I know him so well.

I want to know if he is worried about his reputation. He says no, that he has done nothing wrong. Then I ask him if apartheid was a crime. He avoids replying, stating that the United Nations' declaration on the subject of apartheid is 'vague'. It does, however, affirm that 'apartheid is a crime against humanity'. Moreover, De Klerk defends the original idea of apartheid as wanting the 'races' to live separately, 'like the French in France and the Dutch in the Netherlands'. But the dream did not work in South Africa, he acknowledges.

'I could have continued as President,' he says. 'But there would have been a full-scale civil war.' What De Klerk is saying is essentially that he did not release Mandela out of moral conviction, but for economic reasons, because apartheid was quite simply no longer viable.

In releasing Mandela, De Klerk would have liked to negotiate a sharing of power for ten years, or even forever, if that had been possible. He wanted a right of veto for the whites and special laws and privileges ratified by the Constitution.

During our interview he explains that the struggle against the blacks was not really a struggle against blacks. The apartheid government was fighting Communism, he states. Communist countries were financing the activities of anti-apartheid groups. And when the Berlin Wall fell, there was no longer any reason to keep Mandela, the 'comrade', in prison.

Crimes had been committed by members of all parties. But De Klerk denies having sanctioned torture and killing. At this point in the interview, I read him a phrase from the minutes of a Security Council meeting at which he had been present and at which the *elimination* of the activist Matthew Goniwe was recommended.

De Klerk mumbles. His press secretary tries to intervene, but he lifts a hand to indicate to her that everything is fine. Then he scratches the top of his right eyebrow, a nervous tic he has. The press secretary scribbles a few words on a bit of paper, which she slides over to him. I am not able to decipher them. De Klerk immediately hides them under his pack of cigarettes.

'We were talking about eliminating the *conditions* that were favourable for the propagation of revolutionary thoughts,' he then explains. The activist Matthew Goniwe had, however, indeed been assassinated shortly afterwards. The policemen who executed him eventually admitted this crime before the TRC.

A year later, I met Frederik de Klerk on the occasion of a dinner with Kofi Annan, Secretary General of the United Nations, at parliament in Cape Town. I got into the lift with Jay. De Klerk was already inside. He recognised me. And then Jay, pretending to know nothing, introduced me. I blushed a beetroot red. I had been introduced, a year before, as a Canadian journalist. Nothing more. If he had known that I was Jay's wife, would it have changed anything? I don't know. In the lift, being a polite man, De Klerk said nothing.

I never saw him again. De Klerk resigned from the Government of National Unity and took all his ministers with him when the new Constitution was accepted in 1996, the main reason for his resignation being the fact that the ANC refused a permanent sharing of power. He made the headlines again the following year when he got divorced on Valentine's Day. He immediately remarried the wife of a good friend. For a Calvinist Afrikaner, this is rather paradoxical, because among the members of this community, the tradition of marriage is sacred. One could say that Frederik de Klerk challenged accepted conventions all his life ...

I meet Mangosuthu Buthelezi the same afternoon. I don my armour. He has a terrible reputation among journalists, whom he does not like at all. He gets worked up, I panic and cut the interview short. I am afraid of him. Only thirty seconds of the interview are usable.

Later, I see him again with Jay, on more than one occasion. I don't believe he remembers our interview. He likes to say, of Jay and himself, 'We are children of KwaZulu-Natal.'

An interview with Archbishop Desmond Tutu is like a good show and I would willingly pay the price of a ticket to attend. He is alive, passionate, and he gesticulates all the time. His body is just as expressive as his voice. I think it would be torture for him to have to keep his hands still while he talked. Despite his close relationship with the ANC, nobody doubts his impartiality and his integrity. For example, certain members of the ANC, among them Thabo Mbeki, declared that the crimes committed in the name of the struggle against apartheid should not be judged in the same way as the crimes committed to keep the regime in place. Tutu does not agree. 'A crime is a crime.' Tutu takes his mandate seriously. He is, I believe, incapable of injustice. He knows that his past might raise doubts about his impartiality and perhaps it is also for this reason that he is so hard on the ANC.

I met Desmond Tutu several times during the few hundred hours I spent at the Commission's headquarters, a stone's throw away from parliament. I went through more than a thousand hours of testimony with a fine-tooth comb. I had to go through both the transcriptions and the tapes in order to transfer sound clips to my own tapes. This enabled me to listen to astounding evidence, evidence that gave me cold shivers, even after I had listened to it ten times. And I was also able to follow everything on television, because the testimonies were broadcast live. The witnesses were seated on a platform and the commissioners at an oval table. In the centre of the horseshoe, Desmond Tutu presided over the sessions.

Tell the whole truth? Nothing but the truth? What a question! Zanele has been waiting for years to tell the truth. Right hand raised, left fist pressed against her thigh, Zanele tries to find her voice like the others who have given evidence before the Commission. 'I swear it,' she eventually articulates. Zanele's words fall heavily in the courtroom. This woman was arrested, tortured, sexually assaulted and detained for a year ... for nothing. On 17 June 1986 the police stormed into her house and dragged her to the police station. She was accused, she explains, of having killed a man. Her throat dry, she continues, 'They handcuffed me to the chair. They stuffed some papers and a piece of cloth into my mouth and then they covered my head.' Then she hesitates and the audience tenses. Her silence reveals the pain she still feels at the memory. 'They attached clips to my ears, both my ears, and they switched it on. I realised only then that it was some kind of an electric shock. They did this several times, up until my bladder couldn't take it.' Zanele no longer has a dry throat; her voice is completely strangled. She can't breathe. 'They started smacking me, pushing me around also. They unbuttoned my blouse and pulled my breasts out of my bra.' Zanele grips her handkerchief between her fingers, which soon disintegrates. 'They emptied out a drawer and crushed my breasts in the drawer several times ... until a white sticky substance burst out of my nipples.'

The narrator who read the translation of Zanele's testimony for my radio documentary was also choked with emotion.

'The truth hurts, but silence kills,' reads a sign behind Desmond Tutu. He spent the first sessions of the Commission holding his head in his hands. And crying. He says that even though he 'knew' that atrocities had been committed, he was unaware of the details, the magnitude, the extent of the horrors. 'We knew, but in a general way. Now everything becomes specific. Statistics talk, statistics cry, statistics become real, and that is devastating.' Today, for the first time, millions of South Africans are learning the truth. While there is a grotesque fascination with the Commission hearings – Radio Zulu, one of the sixteen state radio stations, broadcasts a special programme each week that draws over a million listeners! – the interest is particularly strong among the blacks. The blacks want to know. But the whites, in contrast, avoid staring their guilt in the face. 'Many whites feel guilty, either of having voted for the party responsible for these crimes, or for having done nothing to prevent them. They pleaded that they didn't know, and now that they know they are nervous and fearful,' says Alex Boraine. 'The whites remained in ignorance because of the media, which collaborated with the apartheid regime,' explains Desmond Tutu. A survey reveals that sixty-four per cent of white South Africans (compared with thirty per cent of blacks) do *not* have any confidence in the Truth and Reconciliation Commission. 'The Commission is simply going to create more division,' thinks Professor Hermann Giliomee, but he admits that the Commission has succeeded in 'exposing the whites to the realities of apartheid. I believe that whites have a rather rosy view of what apartheid meant for blacks.'

A new witness is on the stand. A white. An Afrikaner. A real Boer. 'In your view, were politics and religion related in some way?' asks a commissioner. 'One hundred per cent. And to be more precise, the National Party and the Dutch Reformed Church.' It is Dirk Coetzee talking, a former security force commander. A man who never had any contact, of any sort whatever, with blacks throughout his childhood (apart from his domestic worker). Coetzee decided to confess before the Commission (a total of just over seven thousand people followed his example). The two main criteria for obtaining amnesty are the admission of your crime and the establishment of a political motive for the crime. Anyone who has not submitted a request for amnesty by the end of the Commission, in June 1998, is open to judicial prosecution. Coetzee has a trial awaiting him next year. He is hoping to obtain amnesty before it starts ... He does not want to find himself behind bars with his colleague Eugene de Kock, also a former security force member. De Kock was found guilty of six murders and eighty-three other crimes, fraud and corruption among them. His sentence: two life sentences plus two hundred and twelve additional years' imprisonment!

De Kock is a scapegoat, up to a certain point, believes Desmond Tutu. 'He is an adult. He is responsible for his actions. But he was part of a system.' He hesitates, then adds in a grave tone, 'If we had had a different system of human values, it would not have been possible to live in an atmosphere like this where you eat your braai while bodies burn beside you and you believe, in everything you do, that you are protecting your country.'

Tutu is talking about the braais at Vlakplaas, the mere mention of which sends shivers down one's spine. De Kock and Coetzee were both commanders at Vlakplaas, a beautiful country house in a bucolic setting near Pretoria. Coetzee, in a surprisingly calm manner, enumerates his tasks while he was there, in 1980 and 1981, as a policeman working for a 'special section' of the South African security forces, 'stealing cars, blowing up houses, assassinating people, blowing up railway lines, harassing people, anything but legal police work'. In short, he was the head of a death squad.

Dirk Coetzee pleads guilty. He admits having served a system, like a good soldier. 'I was prepared to die and to kill for my country.' He'd certainly seen a lot of bodies, even smelt them. 'A body that is burning smells like meat on a braai.' In the same calm way, but with a hint of regret in his voice, he describes the scene, 'We were sitting around the braai, drinking beer.' His team had just eliminated Sizwe Khondile because he had been suspected by the security forces of being an activist. They drugged him, shot him and threw his body onto a wood fire.

'A body takes about seven hours to burn to ashes completely. And while that was happening we were drinking and even having a braai next to the fire. And the chunks of meat, especially the buttocks and the upper part of the legs, had to be turned frequently during the night to make sure that everything burned to ashes. And the next morning, after raking the rubble to make sure that there were no big pieces of meat or bone left at all, we all went our own way. Now, I am not saying this to show how brave we were; I am saying this to show the Commission how callous we were and to what extremes we went in those days.'

Coetzee apologised several times during his testimony, which lasted for days. 'We were made to believe that we were God's own people. The country was the last Christian territory in Africa and we were threatened by a Communist revolutionary onslaught from the North, which, if it succeeded, would plunge the southern tip of Africa into chaos.' Dirk Coetzee began to fill out his curriculum vitae in the former Rhodesia – 'I burnt and buried the bodies of guerrillas' – before arriving at Vlakplaas. To white South Africans, the black revolutionaries had taken on the colour of the 'red threat' – *die rooi gevaar* as it was known in Afrikaans. South African soldiers had their fingers on the trigger in Angola, Mozambique, Rhodesia, Namibia. They were fighting *die rooi gevaar*.

'Apartheid was not the only cause of the conflict,' Frederik de Klerk also maintains. 'The revolutionary movements had fallen into the hands of a world power that had expansionist plans for southern Africa. We were fighting against Communist control of the whole of southern Africa.'

Kader Asmal, Minister of Water Affairs and Forestry and co-author of the book *Reconciliation Through Truth*, accuses the former leaders of having used the word 'Communism' as 'a catch-all directed against all forms of opposition to apartheid. They waged war against the blacks on the pretext of a war against Communism.'

General Constand Viljoen, a member of parliament and leader of the ultra right Freedom Front, who was head of the South African armed forces between 1980 and 1985, flies off the handle at the suggestion that Communism was simply an excuse for waging war. 'Certainly not! The liberation movements had the support of the USSR and China. We were fighting Communism, which wanted to take over southern Africa. I am particularly proud that we were able to keep Communism out of southern Africa and also very proud of having contributed to the international fall of Communism.'

Kader Asmal is familiar with this argument. Tapping his cigarette in the ashtray, his head slightly bent, his eyebrows raised to the top of his forehead, he declares, 'I must say that, even leaving room for exaggeration, I find this statement remarkable! That the whole struggle against apartheid was a Communist conspiracy, led by Moscow? Well, if there are people who still believe that, I fear they have not understood the evils of apartheid.'

'Apartheid was a mistake,' De Klerk says in correction. Blurring the lines between a mistake and a crime is to blur the moral distinction between the crimes committed against apartheid and those committed in the name of apartheid. The TRC makes no moral distinction between the crimes committed on either side. 'Moral' is not the same as 'legal'. 'The struggle against apartheid was morally just and noble,' says

Tutu, 'but,' he hurries to add, his eyes wide, 'war is bad, war is evil. And those who fought for a noble cause were not necessarily noble themselves.' He is speaking of supporters of the ANC ...

Nombulelo Delato was burnt alive by ANC 'comrades'. (Four hundred and seventy-seven people were burnt alive by the 'comrades' in 1986 alone, the year the state of emergency was imposed.) Her daughters, Thomzana and Busiswe, give evidence before the oval table. Nombulelo was killed because she had bought meat when the ANC had organised (or imposed) a boycott. Thomzana tries to tell her story while struggling for breath, gathering up her courage, her voice choked with sobs, 'She could not run. She was walking slowly. Her clothes were burning ... the comrades prevented us from helping her.'

The former soldiers of Umkhonto we Sizwe, the armed wing of the ANC, are panicking. The state attorney is preparing indictments for thirty-five murders committed by members of the ANC. An Umkhonto we Sizwe soldier declared to the South African press (8 December 1996), 'We were fighting a system that was recognised by the whole world as being a crime against humanity. I sacrificed my life, and my education, for the freedom of this country. And then I'm expected to confess to violations of human rights? It's a farce!'

'The ANC thinks it is the Holy of Holies,' maintains the head of Inkatha and Minister of Home Affairs, Mangosuthu Buthelezi. In an interview, Buthelezi talks with his eyes closed. 'The ANC believes it is like Moses, who freed the children of Israel from Egypt,' he grumbles. In his view, the Truth Commission is not the cure for the problems of South Africa. On the contrary, he predicts that the Commission 'is simply going to bring things to a head. Fourteen thousand members of my party, four hundred of them leaders, are dead! And neither Mr De Klerk when he was president nor Mr Mandela has lifted a finger to prosecute those who are guilty! The Truth Commission is just a witch-hunt of the enemies of the ANC,' he concludes.

De Klerk puts it a bit more gently. 'The Commission naturally has to investigate crimes committed by the security forces. But, and I am not attacking it,' he explains, 'it needs to look at things a little more closely from the other side.'

'De Klerk is probably right,' admits Alex Boraine, vice-president of the TRC, 'but we hear so many atrocious stories about the crimes committed by the members of the security forces that that becomes our agenda.' The impartiality of the Commission is constantly questioned. Even though Desmond Tutu insists that 'all the political parties participated in the process of selecting the commissioners', he admits that he has had to reprimand commissioners several times for remarks exhibiting partiality towards the ANC. And if those guilty of crimes in the ANC do not come to testify? 'We will send them a subpoena to appear,' Boraine cuts in without hesitation.

'We knew that we were above the law,' says Dirk Coetzee.

'Different rules apply during war,' admits De Klerk. 'And yes, I knew about secret operations. But we established rules and we certainly did not ask our people to commit serious violations of human rights like assassination, murder or rape.'

'We had an eleventh commandment,' says Coetzee, 'never get caught. *Never* get caught.' Coetzee and his team eliminated every trace of bodies, more often than not by blowing them up with dynamite. 'The orders to eliminate an activist were usually given by a wink or a nod of the head, or by saying "Make a plan with so-and-so",' relates Coetzee. Then he takes care to add that, even if they had been caught, 'It wasn't really a big problem. It would be awkward for the police. But in the end, everything would be arranged. And I have examples, Mr Commissioner.'

Themba Khoza is one such example. This Inkatha leader received one hundred and fifty firearms plus ammunition from Eugene de Kock, who was the Vlakplaas commander from 1985 to 1989. Khoza was arrested (4 September 1990) in possession of this arsenal. It was the police who put up his bail of ten thousand rand.

General Johan van der Merwe, a former Police Commissioner who fulfilled several functions related to state security under De Klerk and Botha, sits up very straight before the commissioners, like a soldier. 'They [the police] reached a point where it became difficult for them to distinguish between legal acts and illegal acts.'

Adriaan Vlok, Minister of Law and Order under De Klerk and Botha, had visited Vlakplaas. During his trial, De Kock accused former president Botha and Vlok of having been directly implicated in the crimes. Van der Merwe confirmed these revelations before the Commission, 'Vlok gave me an order that came directly from Botha's mouth: "Bomb Khotso House"'. Khotso House was bombed. It was the headquarters of the South African Council of Churches, suspected of serving as a secret meeting place for the ANC. A culprit had to be found. The government lottery chose Shirley Gunn, a white Umkhonto we Sizwe activist. She was arrested, tortured and detained for a period of two months with her sixteen-month-old son. Then, they took away her son, Haroon, whom she was breastfeeding. 'Haroon could sense my distress and he started to cry. They pulled him out of my arms and he started screaming, reaching, shouting for me. I was absolutely desperate,' she recounts in a tone that makes you feel as if it happened two hours ago rather than seven years ago. She was then made to listen to record-ings of Haroon crying 'Mama, mama, mama'. Shirley today suffers from post-traumatic stress syndrome. She is not ready to forgive, unlike the majority of the victims who are giving evidence. She has opened a case against Vlok, but he has requested amnesty.

De Klerk insists, 'I'm not prepared to endorse non-authorised criminal acts. If they [the policemen who are confessing] believe that the National Party is going to support them, I'm afraid that they have misunderstood us badly.'

'We are not looking for culprits. What we are really trying to do, in a very calm, deliberate way, is look for acknowledgement. That's the heart of it – the acknowledgement. And leaders fail when they don't want to do this,' Kader Asmal, Minister of Water Affairs and Forestry, reminds everyone. But he adds, 'If De Klerk says that he didn't know about Vlakplaas when he was president, that he didn't know about the death squads, even in 1993 – not even in the 1980s! – he is exercising a very selective memory.' And Tutu states, 'It seems strange that the President would not be completely informed about atrocities committed. If he did not know, then he must have been incompetent. If he knew and did nothing to put a stop to it, then he is an evil person … And he knows that he is caught between these two explanations.'

De Klerk claims to be astonished by certain revelations made before the Truth and Reconciliation Commission. Tutu, Boraine, Asmal, Viljoen, the media and the public are surprised to learn certain facts. The wife of a policeman who has just admitted committing forty murders over seventeen years is also surprised: she thought her husband worked for an insurance company! Among other national surprises there is the existence of the Sanhedrin and of TREWITS, the Afrikaans acronym for the Counter-Revolutionary Target Information Centre, two state bodies that deliberated on the life and death of a revolution and its revolutionaries. They drew up lists of 'targets' to be destroyed, inside the country and elsewhere in the world. The Sanhedrin presented a monthly report on its activities to the State Security Council.

The past has not finished surprising people in South Africa. In the short term, the success of the Truth Commission rests on the approval, by the various political parties, of its final report. But its real success, professes De Klerk with a big smile, will be achieved if it manages 'to replace the accusing fingers with hands that are joined and that advance, together, into the future'. 'This Commission is risky and delicate,' warns Tutu. 'But it represents the only means of healing and reconciling our seriously wounded beautiful country.' So that, once and for all, apartheid can be done away with.

54

How many beddy-byes till you come back to Quebec, Mama?

At the end of 1996 Jay falls seriously ill. We have to make an emergency return from Mauritius, where we are spending Christmas. Arriving in Durban, Jay collapses. He is burning hot. His face starts to swell up. He is immediately taken to hospital.

The diagnosis is clear: Jay has an abscess on his tonsils. But the doctors are not able to explain why his face is swollen. His cheeks are like tennis balls. The doctors warn us that an abscess could be dangerous. It could burst and infect the whole system. There is therefore a risk that Jay might die. They need to operate urgently.

Kami is frantic. He has left his papa on a stretcher in hospital. We are staying with Jay's brother, Logie, and his wife Corona. Practically the whole family is there: Dimes, her husband Vasen and their daughter Roshanthi; Iyaloo and his wife Kamala; Nisha and Sagaren. Only Pat and Popeye are missing. I explain Jay's condition to Kami as well as I can. I make him a drawing of the throat, representing the tonsils as small balls, and show him what the doctor is going to cut with his scalpel. 'But it won't hurt Papa, because he'll be sleeping. And when he wakes up, everything will be better and his little balls will be gone.'

After the operation, at the hospital, the whole family is gathered around Kami, who wants to be the first to speak to Jay. His father's voice is no more than a fine thread. He even has difficulty swallowing and dribbles like a baby.

Kami asks his question, 'Papa, did it hurt when they cut your balls off?'

Jay chokes. The family standing around the bed burst into laughter. Kami doesn't understand what's going on.

The mystery of the swollen cheeks remains. I say to Jay that it looks like mumps. The doctors think this unlikely, in view of Jay's age and the fact that Kami would undoubtedly have caught the virus since they had just spent a month together. They do all sorts of tests. The results of the blood tests arrive from Johannesburg five days later.

The doctor comes into the hospital room looking serious. He says to Jay that he has good news and bad news.

'The good news is that we've eliminated all other possibilities because we've just received a positive result for mumps.'

'And the bad news?'

'I have to tell you, Mr Naidoo, that in four per cent of adults, mumps can cause sterility.'

'Only four per cent? In fact we were talking about a vasectomy recently ...'

Jay was very ill. But the tonsillectomy has solved one problem for me: Jay no longer snores. What a relief!

Jay began 1997 in hospital. Soon after, it would be my turn ...

Léandre is coming back from a month's stay in Quebec, where he has spent the Christmas holidays. The returns are always difficult, I know. Léandre cries at night when he goes to bed. Discreetly, as quietly as possible, he cries. It destroys me. I go in to him. He tries to hide his feelings. And I try to reassure him by telling him that he has the right to cry because he is missing his papa, that I do not think badly of him for missing his papa because he loves him, that I will not be cross if he expresses his love for him, that I understand what it means to love someone and that the absence of the other person always leaves a pain in our hearts, that he can cry in my arms, that he can rely on me, that we will talk to his papa, write to him, send him things, that he is going to see him again in a hundred and eighty beddy-byes ...

I ask him questions. I want to know what makes him laugh, what makes him sad, what makes him angry or full of despair.

'I am happy here, Mama. I am fine here with you, with my family. But I still miss Papa. I want to go and live in Quebec when I am twelve. I want to start high school there.'

We'll see, my darling. We'll see. But I know that is what will happen in the end. His desire is too great. He is ten years old. One day I will have to let him go. In fact, I let him go when he was born. There is a deep love between Léandre and I. I don't need to see him or hear him to know that. I will have to let him go one day. But for the moment he is here, in my arms.

'I love you, Mama,' says Léandre. 'I love you, Papa,' he says as well. I understand. I know that it hurts. I know all about this heartbreak, this cul-de-sac, this non-choice. I know that it is impossible to choose. I know, my love, because it is with you that I have experienced this emotion that ties my stomach in a knot, that only tears can relieve.

'What would you like most in the world, my love?'

'What would I like? I would like you and Papa to get together again and for us to live in the same place. In Africa or in Quebec, that doesn't matter. But in the same place.'

'If your papa and I live together, what is going to happen to Jay?'

Léandre looks at me wide-eyed, the truth shining out.

'No, I don't want Jay to go.'

'So?'

'So that's how it is.'

'Yes, my darling, that's how it is.'

'How many beddy-byes until you come and live in Quebec, Mama?'

That question again! The one everyone keeps asking me. Every summer, when I go to Quebec, *everybody* asks me, 'When are you coming back, Lucie?' I always reply 'soon'. It will be soon. One day. I don't know ...

Léandre has learnt to live with these 'non-choices'. He cries for a week and then it's better. He has his friends, school, tennis, swimming and basketball. He has the mountain and the sea, the beach, his bike, rollerblades that he can use quite safely within the estate. He has a computer with games, he has a 'taxi' at the door, with his mama driving, or Peter, Jay's chauffeur, taking him to a friend on the other side of Cape Town. He has his grandmother Loulou, here for another six-month visit. Léandre has everything he needs. Except his father.

If Jay could follow us to Quebec, it would be so simple ...

In therapy, this is a question that we explore at almost every meeting. And then this one, 'Do you regret your decision to come to South Africa?'

All my therapists have asked me that question. At first it threw me. I said I would think about it.

Jay, Kami and Shanti are the products of my dreams. I have been spoilt by heaven. But I have no miraculous solution to release myself from this feeling of a divided life.

Today, 18 January 1997, it is nice and hot. It is a beautiful summer's day in Cape Town, with a slight sea breeze blowing. Louise and I have organised a treasure hunt to celebrate Léandre's tenth birthday with ten of his friends. We have set out five different trails in the forest behind the former presidential residence, Groote Schuur, built by Cecil John Rhodes, Prime Minister of the Cape Colony, in the 1890s. This house has served as the official residence of the country's prime ministers and presidents. De Klerk was the last president to stay there, as Nelson Mandela finds it too ostentatious. The bath in the main bedroom cost one hundred thousand rand! Mandela lives next door, in the house reserved for the deputy-president. Behind these buildings two little paths run on either side of a stream that flows down from the mountain. About three hundred metres into the woods, the path opens out into a small clearing under the palms. Here there is a braai, a wooden table, and two mini-amphitheatres with wooden benches.

Today, eleven children are running around under the palms and the banana trees. Eleven identical treasures are hidden somewhere in this forest. And with the hot, sunny day we are having, I couldn't have made a better choice than hand-shaped water pistols, the index finger pointing forward.

Léandre laughs. He is fine here, now. We will never live in ideal circumstances, but I can at least offer him the first thing that every child needs: unconditional love. The two words are inseparable, my therapist told me. Their 'inseparability' says everything. They say, quite simply, 'I love you, my darling, because you are who you are, with your good points and your bad, your passions and your desires, which are not my own.' I love you, Léandre. How I love you! How many beddy-byes until I go back to Quebec? I don't know. In the meantime, I love you. I love you forever. Happy birthday, dear Léandre.

I know that his twelfth year is approaching. He will leave. But today, we are having fun. We are enjoying the pleasures life has to offer us.

55

Sound trip to Robben Island

I could 'hear' the report in my head throughout my visit to the prison of Robben Island. I heard each sound: that of the metal gates closing, the clicking of the locks, the sound of water running … I could even hear snatches of the interviews that would make up the report.

I had just conceptualised a sound trip to Robben Island, the prison that became famous when so many leaders of the anti-apartheid struggle were imprisoned there, including Nelson Mandela, of course.

For four centuries this island – five and a half kilometres long by one and a half kilometres wide – housed the men and women that South African authorities judged undesirable. It was an island that was dreaded and feared. In 1617, two British prisoners were given the choice of death by hanging or life-long exile on Robben Island. They chose Robben Island, but soon after begged the authorities to hang them. During the centuries that followed, the island was used as a prison for Khoikhoi accused of petty theft, Xhosa chiefs who opposed British imperialism, criminals, the mentally ill, lepers, prostitutes … and those the authorities wanted to silence and forget: political prisoners. In 1964, the Rivonia trialists, political prisoners who included Nelson Mandela, were sent to Robben Island. They were separated from the other one and a half thousand prisoners because the authorities feared they would exercise too great an influence on them. They were right. Several of the Robben Island prisoners in time became MPs, ministers, councillors, prime ministers, professionals and even president.

It is February 1997. We have come to Robben Island as a family, together with a group of South African politicians. Two months ago, the island gave up the last of its prisoners; the prison is going to be transformed into a museum. We make the forty-five-minute boat journey in the same boat that used to transport the prisoners. I find myself sitting next to Mangosuthu Buthelezi. We talk for a long time, about KwaZulu-Natal, children, family, Canada.

We tour the island in the bus that used to take the prisoners – criminal and political – to the forced labour camps. We visit the prison and the cell where Nelson Mandela spent eighteen of his twenty-seven years of imprisonment. His cubicle measures one comma eight metres by two and a half metres. There are about twenty cells for solitary confinement, arranged on either side of a narrow corridor lit by neon lights, which make an awful racket and which, since the start of the sixties, stayed switched on twenty-four hours a day. The humming of these lights forms part of the sound memories of all the prisoners.

Lionel Davis acts as our guide. This former Robben Island prisoner has become a guide on the island on which he suffered for so many years! 'It's my therapy,' he says. He describes each corner of the prison to us as if he is showing us the house he has lived in for years. 'This mark on the wall was made when a prisoner talked back to a guard and the guard hit him with his truncheon.' Further on, he tells us, 'This is where Nelson Mandela buried his manuscript …' The guide supplies us with an enormous amount of detail. I have to get it all down on tape!

Lionel describes the cells in which Nelson Mandela, Walter Sisulu, Ahmed Kathrada and Govan Mbeki stayed. When he opens the door of Mandela's cell, I hear the creaking noise on my imaginary soundtrack. I sit down on the bed. I hear the squeaking of the springs, I hear the humming of the neon lights, I hear the blows of the truncheon, the shouts of the jailers, the freedom songs of the prisoners in the lime and stone quarries ringing with the sound of their picks. Without knowing it, Lionel has given me an idea for a unique radio documentary. After this sound trip to Robben Island, I know, immediately, instinctively, that this diplomatic visit to the island has just opened a new chapter in my professional life in South Africa. Several documentaries result from this first sound visit.

But once again I have to find someone to sell the idea to …

I need someone to say to me, 'Good idea! Do the report!' As if I need an excuse to work and legitimise what I myself want to do. It's a way of making up for past mistakes in other documentaries. It's always the same.

'Have you ever been satisfied with your work?' my therapist Dr G asks.

'That is what motivates me, what pushes me to complete these projects, the fact that I am never completely happy with the previous one.'

'So you are never satisfied ...'

'No, never.'

'There's a difference between accepting one's weaknesses and the imperfections of a piece of work, and not being satisfied. Are you satisfied with the effort that you have put into it?'

'Oh, yes, definitely! In fact I always put in too much effort, because I'm always afraid of not putting in enough.'

Pierre Trottier, the director of *Dimanche magazine*, likes the idea. I suggest thirty minutes to him. The documentary eventually makes forty-five.

I spent two whole days on the island during the month of May 1997. As luck would have it, I was accompanied by my dear friend Philippe Le Blanc. Philippe has been my hairdresser for twenty years. He came over to visit me for three weeks. Philippe is gay. When he is asked how many brothers and sisters he has, he replies, 'There are five girls in the family. I have four sisters.' That's what I like about him; he is not afraid of himself. He is my confidante, my 'girlfriend', in fact. Yes, that's what he is. Philippe is my closest girlfriend. We can chat, discuss things and sleep in the same bed.

Within two days of arriving in Cape Town, Philippe had checked out the gay bars, the gay travel agencies and the gay cafés. In his view, it was perfect. Cape Town is an African San Francisco. Publicly, homosexuality is denounced; socially it is tolerated.

Philippe is reliable and meticulous, and makes an outstanding assistant on Robben Island. I have two tape recorders and two types of microphones: one is unidirectional for interviews, and the other is omnidirectional for recording ambient sounds.

'Philippe, you are going to follow me everywhere, wearing headphones. I will tell you what sound to record and you must try your best to record only that sound. I am officially nominating you as my assistant while we produce my documentary on Robben Island!'

'No problem.'

'It's a voluntary job …'

'No problem.'

My plan is simple: the bulk of the report will have no journalistic commentary. The journey will be explained by the witnesses. Into this I will insert the sounds of chains, cries, tears, the scratching of pen on paper, a tennis ball bouncing, the sound of thousands of spoons being washed, guitar strings being plucked, the voices and shouts of children that prisoners hear only in their dreams, the sound of someone digging, the steps of silent prisoners in the courtyard, the sound of doors banging, songs intermingling with the sounds of picks and shovels, the blows of a truncheon, footsteps in the corridor, icy rain falling, keys clanking.

As soon as we cast off I bump into a group of young black men. They are trade unionists, making a pilgrimage. Six of them are playing cards, despite the cold, the wind and the freezing spray thrown up by the waves. They are talking, laughing and singing. How fortunate – I need a freedom song sung with passion to create an atmosphere for my documentary. I explain my project to them. No problem! They start singing two songs, one after the other, while they play cards, paying no attention at all to my microphone.

The longest road on the island is two and a half kilometres in length and separates the prison zone from the village where the guards and their families once lived.

Ahmed Kathrada, Mandela's fellow prisoner for twenty-six years and today one of his political advisors, recounts how apartheid continued behind those walls:

> *'When we arrived here, it was a very cold June morning. Cold and wind and rain and all. As you find in Cape Town in June. The first thing we had to do is to change into prison clothes. Now, I was the only Indian among the Rivonia prisoners who came here. So I was allowed to wear 'normal' clothes: long trousers, a shirt, a jersey, socks, shoes. All my colleagues were given short trousers. Right through winter, they had to wear short trousers. African prisoners were not given socks. They were given sandals, the kind made from motorcar tyres. But after much agita-*

*tion and hunger strikes over three or four years, we managed to
standardise the clothing issue.*

*There was also food discrimination. In the morning, we had the same
food: a dish of porridge and a mug of coffee. But the African prisoners were
given less sugar than we were. In the evening, African prisoners were just
given porridge again, with soup, while we were given bread – a quarter loaf
of bread. African prisoners were not given bread. It's an uncomfortable
feeling and instinctively, you want to reject it. But then, President Mandela
and Walter Sisulu in particular, persuaded us that it would be wrong, politically, to reject what we had. Our fight should be for equality on a higher
level, not a lower level. [...] Eventually, we all managed to get equal
portions of the same food. Of course, whites were given the best but they
were not [...] kept here. There were no women prisoners either. It was just
African, Coloured and Indian prisoners. All the warders were white.*

*As things relaxed, they allowed us to play sports. [Sports facilities]
were built in about the mid-seventies and then we played volley-ball here
and tennis. The President played tennis – he was quite good at it.*

*You see this long wall, we had a garden along this wall. And when the
President wrote his autobiography, the original manuscripts were buried in
the garden here. Then suddenly one day they came and started building
this wall and they discovered some of the plastic containers in which we
had hidden the originals. And for that, three of us were punished.'*

But the manuscript was retranscribed and part of Mandela's autobiography, *Long Walk to Freedom*, was written right here, in his cell, where
there was no bed for fourteen years. The political prisoners slept on the
floor, on a mat woven from sisal. 'It was very cold,' says Kathrada.

Govan Mbeki, the father of Thabo Mbeki, eighty-six years old and
vice-president of the Senate, recalls the death cries of the new prisoners.

*'When our young chaps got beatings from the warders, we had to warn
them: "The Boers will kill you. Cry when they start beating you. Bellow,
make a lot of noise." Then [the other prisoners] would start making a lot
of noise throughout the jail to get [the warders] to stop the beatings.'*

Ahmed Kathrada recalls:

*'These cells were our homes. You did everything here. Slept here. Ate here.
Exercised here. Studied here. It's hard to believe that we spent 18 years*

in a little place like this. I would stand on a chair here and look outside. And in the afternoons, after they locked us up and it was quiet, we would see animals out there, buck, ostriches and so forth.'

Singing played a crucial role in the prisoners' lives, as Walter Sisulu testifies at eighty-five years of age, with twenty-six years of imprisonment behind him, eighteen of them on Robben Island:

'Whistling, singing were not allowed. Now, singing, take my case, if there is anything that has kept me alive, it is singing. Singing in my cell, talking in my cell, moving up and down in my cell, that is what really gave me confidence. Let's see. [Sings] This was a way of saying, "We are going to be in Parliament, these are the men who will represent you".

At first we used to sing when we dug in the lime quarry. Singing creates harmony. It gives you strength. So when they noticed that we were enjoying it, that we were inspiring each other, they stopped it.'

Govan Mbeki explains how Nelson Mandela loved to dance:

'Musical instruments were not allowed at first. But, later on, we were allowed to buy them. I chose a guitar and I used to play. We all enjoyed it. It was wonderful. And some of the others, especially Nelson, loved to come and dance around us as we played. And in the main section — you know Robben Island has seven jails — they had a band — just beautiful — they played saxophones and drums and so on. It was beautiful!'

There were many hunger strikes on Robben Island. They were the only form of pressure that did not result in a beating! Ahmed Kathrada explains:

'We had quite a few hunger strikes here, and we decided among ourselves, that the older people, and the people who were not well, should be exempt from the hunger strikes. But even there, President Mandela and Sisulu never wanted the exemptions. They took part in all the hunger strikes and took the punishments as they came.'

The worst atrocities were committed in the stone quarries. Hundreds of political prisoners worked there. Sometimes, under the guise of punishment, the jailers would attach them to a post by their hands and leave them there all day. It is also here that they would bury them up to their necks in the sand and then urinate on their heads. 'This was a hell-hole, this quarry,' says Lionel Davis.

Then Ahmed Kathrada concludes:

'The harshness of the apartheid system, the suffering, the hardship, those are all part of history, part of reality. But in my opinion, the main message from Robben Island should be one of triumph, a message of victory. Because Robben Island was identified by the enemy at the time as the place where they were going to crush the leadership and the activists of the movement. And the political prisoners took up that challenge and did not allow themselves to be subdued by the authorities. And in the end, I say, it was a triumph, because from Robben Island and from other prisons, our people got into parliament and into government – President Mandela, for instance. You can say the whole negotiation process – in fact the genesis of the negotiation process – started in prison. They couldn't stop the movement that began here. In the end, it was a victory for the movement.'

My computer is not powerful enough to run a digital editing pro-gramme, which is in any case rather expensive. So I work in the old way. I spend entire nights editing, with scissors and a razor blade, cutting and pasting my tapes in a studio kindly lent to me by Zane Abrahams, manager of the community radio station Bush Radio. In return, I offer him a free broadcast of the documentary. In fact, he can broadcast it as often as he likes!

The Robben Island Museum has bought the rights to the documen-tary. The cassette is now sold in the tourist office on the island. I ceded my author's rights for almost nothing. I have never known how to negotiate, but I console myself with the thought that it's for a good cause. This island and its monuments must be preserved at all costs.

The museum wanted the audio tape and a video as well. The marketing manager decided to adapt the documentary for the Cape Town Planetarium as well. Seated in armchairs tilted towards the ceiling, you are able to view images of the prison on the three-hundred-and-sixty-degree screen that normally reflects the heavens. Some seventy-five slide projectors and a few dozen video machines project images onto the vaulted screen as you hear the soundtrack of the documentary. But I was unpleasantly surprised by the final product, completed in my absence, during one of my trips to Quebec in the summer of 1997. And to think that the company that undertook the video part of the project received nine times my fee!

After the viewing, I got up furious. Everything had been done in a hurry. The images did not correspond to the soundtrack. I told the marketing manager of the museum and the team that had produced this visual section that I refused to have either my name or my documentary associated with this project unless major changes were made. The official launch was planned for the following week. My changes would take too much time, they protested. But I did not give in.

The changes were made, and there were also further changes after the official launch. I was ashamed of the result. But we finally managed to put together a show that ran for five months in Cape Town.

One Sunday afternoon I visited Walter Sisulu. He had asked me to keep him company and have a cup of tea with him. I invited him to come to the planetarium and he accepted. We phoned the planetarium to warn the staff we were coming. Obviously the management immediately called the press. A crowd was waiting when we arrived. Walter requires support when he walks. We chatted right up to the viewing room, ignoring the cameras and microphones. The following day Walter's outing was reported in the papers, because his public appearances were becoming more and more rare.

The museum organised two launches. On both occasions, I was invited to say a few words beforehand. I shook like a leaf, even after all the years I had spent teaching others how to make a speech! The first launch was on 24 September 1997, Heritage Day. The first part of the museum's inauguration had taken place on the island, and had been attended by Mandela. But he wasn't able to come to the second part because of an official engagement.

Not long afterwards, I went to a large dinner attended by Nelson Mandela and Bill and Hillary Clinton. While talking to an American diplomat, I mentioned that I would particularly like to meet Hillary Clinton to talk to her about the situation of women in South Africa. This subject interests her and she was keen to go and look at projects initiated by South African women.

No sooner said than done. I congratulated Mrs Clinton on her interest in the plight of women. I talked to her about my videos. Then about my work on Robben Island. I gave her a cassette I had in my pocket. She seemed really thrilled to receive this little gift.

She introduced me to her husband. He took my hand and, without letting go of it, asked me what combination of circumstances had led to a French-Canadian journalist being 'on assignment' in South Africa for so long. I replied that it was because I had done an interview and then decided to marry my interviewee. He laughed heartily, still holding my hand. Bill Clinton is a tall, charismatic man. He looks you straight in the eye, with a penetrating gaze, not common among politicians ...

A few months later, a large yellow envelope arrived at the house. Léandre saw it first.

'Mama! You've received a letter from the White House! But that's the president of the United States, isn't it – the White House?'

'Yes, it's from the White House. What could it be?'

'Why have you received a letter from the White House?'

Léandre was impressed. So was I. I opened the envelope in front of him. It was from Hillary Clinton, thanking me for the tape on Robben Island. She had listened to it. 'It is a wonderful reminder of a very special part of my visit to South Africa.'

56

Drowned

My boat capsized and sank. I almost drowned. One part of me died. Another needed to be born.

I have just spent two months in Quebec. Two months of strained relations with Jay, who did not come over. Not even for a week, not even for two days …

'I have too much work. I am a minister, Lucie.'

Too much work. Married to another woman – South Africa! Since we moved to Cape Town, we hardly ever see Jay any more. He is always away. At a meeting, in Cape Town, in Pretoria, or somewhere else in the world, but absent. I am a 'happily married single mother,' I say. But 'happily' doesn't ring true anymore …

Love is not the problem. It's there. Strong. Powerful. As if we had spent twenty lifetimes searching for one another.

'When you met me,' Jay tells me constantly, 'you knew I was deeply involved in the politics of this country.'

No, I didn't know what it would mean in everyday life, with children, shopping lists, dentist appointments and parents' meetings. I didn't know what it would mean to live with a man that everyone knows, but who is never at home for more than a few hours at a time, at night, tired … but, of course, totally devoted to his country! To his wife also. To his children, obviously. The love he feels for us has nothing to do with his availability.

'What do you want, Lucie?' asks my therapist.

'My husband at home, having dinner with us from time to time, say four times a week.'

In six months, Jay has had dinner with us only twice. But when he is at home, sometimes on the weekend, he gives us his full attention. He has this capacity to close the political door in his brain and open the family door.

'You are all precious to me. You are my life. You are my priority,' he says.

He doesn't stop telling me this ... on the telephone!

I live with Jay through the television, the press, the radio and the telephone. I say, half joking, that when I want to see him, I turn on the television!

I have the impression that Jay has difficulty fully accepting the 'Canadian' part of our marriage. Sometimes, I get the impression that he blames me for the fact that the children are more Québecois than South African. This is the subject of numerous discussions, both at home and in therapy. However, it is not possible for me to take Jay's place. I cannot transmit either Indian or African culture, traditions or beliefs to my children on his behalf. My childhood memories revolve around a lake and a canoe, while his have a township on fire where the sound of AK-47s replaces the sound of birds at night. It is never easy to marry two cultures. Shanti is living proof of this – she doesn't speak English. She was born when Jay was already a minister, when he had already started to disappear ...

'We could get a second domestic to help you,' proposes Jay.

'It's not a matter of help. Betty is quite good enough. It's a husband I want.'

My therapist insists, 'You absolutely have to make friends, Lucie.'

I find Peta Wolpe. Sue Sparks introduces us, as she did the blind couple. She phones me one day to suggest that I call this 'very lovely girl', a South African with two children attending the French School. Eventually it is Peta who calls, after Sue has urged her do so.

Peta is the daughter of a Communist anti-apartheid activist named Harold Wolpe, a white Jewish South African who risked his life and the lives of his three children by fleeing across the country, across the border, and finally to London, where the Wolpe family lived, in exile, for almost thirty years. They all returned to this country when Nelson Mandela was released. Harold died shortly after Mandela took power.

Peta Wolpe became an intimate friend. But this friendship did not alleviate my distress …

My boat began to sink during that summer, in Quebec, after a row with my father. We are so similar: both pig-headed. But he has always stood two hundred metres tall in my eyes. We have never talked enough. This time we talked, but it came out wrong. On that day, at his home on Lake Labelle, in the Laurentians, he said some things that really hurt me. My father has difficulty putting up with children, especially when they are worked up. Now, my little Kami, being very active, couldn't stop moving. My father criticised his behaviour, but at the same time raised questions about my parenting abilities. I flew off the handle. The argument degenerated, other subjects were dragged in …

We were outside, on the lawn on the edge of the lake, tearing each other to pieces. Kneeling on the grass, shouting and crying, I poured out thirty-five years of history in five minutes. So did he. I threw my beer glass into the bushes. We said things to one another that wounded both of us deeply. Some things just came out badly. But what I couldn't swallow was his criticism of my role as a mother – the most important part of my life was about to collapse in the twinkling of an eye. I have spent my life trying to prove my worth to my father. Any criticism would have hurt, but this one killed me.

I took the car and drove like a madwoman, at two hundred kilometres an hour on the twisting road along the shores of Lake Labelle. I was going to commit suicide. Heading towards the sheer drop at the side of the road, my foot hesitated between the accelerator and the brake. I thought of Kami, Shanti and Léandre, who were with my father. I braked and stopped two millimetres from the edge. The skid marks are probably still there. I vomited. I sat and cried. I looked at the water in the lake. I wanted to drown myself in it.

I went back to my father's two hours later. I packed my bags and told the children to get into the car. My father tried to stop me. I saw the sadness in his eyes. Mine were swimming. In the depths of my being, I know that it is for him that I write and make documentaries. To prove my worth to him. But it's not working. I am still not good enough. In my eyes.

I left in tears.

In the very deepest part of my being, I felt that I was dead.

Returning to Cape Town, I cracked. I cried constantly. Between radio reports, I cried. I could not manage to take a bath or make myself a cup of coffee. Jay wasn't there. I didn't have anyone.

One day, I stopped eating. I hid myself in the woods behind the house; it was night and it was pouring with rain. I was barely conscious, curled up in the woods on the damp ground.

Betty was looking after the children. I was no longer capable of doing so. She didn't understand what was going on. Nor did the children. Nor did I.

I phoned Jay in Johannesburg, desperate, only half-conscious in this nightmarish dream-reality. I no longer knew what I was doing. I was afraid of myself. I was afraid for the children. I wanted to take them with me, to the 'other side', where nothing would hurt any more. Jay leapt onto an aeroplane. He was also afraid.

We met in the rooms of our family doctor. In addition to an orthodox training, he was also a homeopath and a naturopath. He believed in the 'holistic' healing of the body. The body and the spirit form one entity, he said. He was right. Because my spirit was no longer alive, and my body was collapsing.

He immediately prescribed some sedatives and arranged an appointment with one of the best psychologists in the country ... who happened to be his wife.

And Dr G was a gift from heaven.

I believe that even if I had spent my whole life in Quebec, I would have collapsed like this. Perhaps South Africa was simply a catalyst to lead me to this therapy. One thing was for certain: I could no longer – all at the same time – be the wife of a minister, a freelance journalist, a mother torn between two continents, a wife for very brief periods, a solitary worker, a French-speaking person, a white Catholic married to an Indian of the Hindu faith. I could no longer live married, but alone. I had to build a new relationship with my father, whom I love deeply. And above all I had to stop hating myself.

Dr G is beautiful. Her silky white hair folds into the nape of her neck: it glitters like so many diamonds. Her face is young, without wrinkles, but full of experience, which keeps you guessing about her age. She could be forty or fifty years old. Her look is penetrating: it awakens something in you. She has a gift.

You have to go to hospital, she says. I refuse. The children, my work, Radio-Canada – I cannot just abandon my normal life like this. And I have just started a big project: a radio biography of Walter Sisulu. Walter was the first ANC activist to broadcast an anti-apartheid message on the radio, from a secret studio, in the early sixties. I want to get my hands on the extract where he calls the people to revolution. I should also spend a full week recording with him, while we walk and take tea. There's no opening for a stay in hospital in my diary.

To me, going to hospital would be a symbol of failure.

So I refuse, but agree to take some medication; I do want to undergo psychotherapy, but insist that I have to keep up my daily activities, no matter what kind of state I am in.

'Depression is an illness, Lucie,' Dr G explains. 'It is not a flaw. Depression can be treated.'

'But not flaws?'

They prescribe Zoloft. But I suffer terrible side effects from this antidepressant. I feel as if I'm definitely going crazy. I have anxiety attacks. I can't stop moving. I feel like tearing my hair out. I lose control. After two weeks, the side effects – migraines, thirst, insomnia – are too much and I stop taking the medication. The effect is devastating. I don't know who I am any more. I'm losing it, I can feel it, but I can't do anything about it. I feel completely powerless, out of control. My heart is beating at a rate of one hundred and seventy beats a minute.

I am admitted to hospital urgently.

I take a single room; I cannot bear the idea of seeing anyone else. I get special permission to close my door – after a search to make sure that I am not hiding any knitting needles or scissors to slit my veins.

In fact this isn't really a hospital. It is a rehabilitation centre, a refuge for broken people, crushed by drugs or mental illness. Sitting in the cafeteria, eating cold toast and porridge that is too salty, I realise how vulnerable I am. I take refuge in a corner, my back to everyone else, embarrassed, ashamed, my eyes swollen from the constant flow of tears over the last few hours, the last few days and weeks. There are a large number of cocaine addicts in detoxification programmes here. There are also schizophrenics and manic-depressives. And me in my corner. We are all living with failure. At least I am not alone.

In the evening, I line up at the medication counter, head down, shredding a crumpled tissue between my fingers. Here I am in *One Flew Over the Cuckoo's Nest* queuing up to receive my little container of pills and to swallow them in front of the nurse. Like a child.

I also obtain special permission not to attend daily group therapy. The word is to leave the minister's wife alone. This time I do not rebel against my privileges. I spend my days in my room. I have books and a television set. But I cannot read or concentrate on anything at all. It is as if I am suffering from a complete breakdown. I feel like a city hit by a huge natural disaster. My infrastructure has collapsed. Everything needs to be rebuilt. I can no longer function in the same way.

Dr G comes to see me almost every day. She has accepted my case partly because of Jay, in whom she believes even though she has never met him. She is employed by the government and her speciality is treating the families of people in the military. Hardly surprisingly, this is an environment with a great deal of emotional disturbance. After meeting me, Dr G knew she could help me. I am the daughter of a military man. Dr G knows the lives of military personnel.

'You are strong,' she says. 'I am confident. You'll need to do a lot of work and it won't be easy, but I know that you will come out of it okay.'

Her words hit a wall. I do not hear them. I do not even see how I will ever be able to pack my bags and leave here. I leave going to the toilet until the last minute because getting there seems to require too much effort. I have figured it out: I stop drinking. In this way, I can spend a whole day in bed, staring at the ceiling.

The medication knocks me out. Eventually they prescribe another antidepressant, Serzone, which takes six weeks to start working. I do not experience the same side effects. I feel dazed, but not nauseous.

I ask Jay to phone Gilles Le Bigot at Radio-Canada and tell him that I am 'temporarily unavailable'. I am afraid to phone him myself. In fact I have no idea how to tell him what is happening to me. It would have come out in tears. Gilles calls me. He understands, he says. I am surprised that he understands. I am surprised that anyone can understand, because I don't understand.

I need a massage. For eighteen years now I have paid for a massage at least once a month. It's a need, like the need to swim. Jay finds a masseuse, Lynn Millard, who comes to the centre. As she massages me, Lynn asks me what colour I associate with my current state. I answer 'red'. I hate red, but at the moment this is all I can see. And what colour would make me feel better? Green. Blue. Turquoise … Then Lynn asks me to imagine a hole in the top of my head, to imagine green and blue light filtering in from a supreme power, and replacing the red, which is flowing out through my extremities, my fingers, my feet. For a year I have massages with Lynn's colours.

Jay and the children come to visit me. I want to leave with them, go back home, which is only five kilometres from here. I have told the children I have a problem with my liver. I would love to tell them the truth, but I am afraid that Léandre's father will use this new argument to try and take my child away from me again. I will tell them the truth one day. I will make them understand their mother isn't superwoman, that she is weak and fragile, like everyone else, even if children think their mothers are invincible.

This morning, I said hello to someone. It's the first word I have uttered in three days. I had to try a couple of times because my voice was rather hoarse. A nurse invited me to a therapy session that was about to start. I shook my head and started to cry. I rushed up to my room and stayed there for the next three days with the door closed. Except when Dr G arrived.

Two and a half weeks later, I can bear it no longer. Jay is struggling with the children and his crazy schedule. Shopping, Shanti's hair, homework, the house; it is his turn to experience family life as a single parent. 'I had no idea,' he admits one evening, still out of breath from the supper-homework-stories-bath-teeth-bed routine.

I feel ready to leave. I promise to relax. The medication will start working soon anyway. Dr G hesitates. I insist.

I should have listened to Dr G.

57

Miscommunication

As soon as I get out of the rehab centre I phone Walter Sisulu. He is my neighbour, living a hundred metres away. On the other side, a hundred metres in the other direction, lives Nelson Mandela. Higher up, two hundred metres away, is Govan Mbeki, the deputy-president of the Senate, and next door, his son Thabo Mbeki, the deputy-president. I live in South Africa's powerhouse.

I spend two full days with Walter Sisulu (who was born in the same year as the ANC, 1912), during which he tells me about the smallest details of his life. He adores his wife Albertina, but doesn't sleep with her any more. 'In prison, where I spent twenty-six years, the lights were left on day and night. I can't get out of the habit and the light disturbs Albertina.' He laughs. A breathing problem makes him clear his throat often.

I ask him how he feels about having spent his life in Nelson Mandela's shadow. He looks at me with surprise, even though people must have asked him this question a thousand times. After recruiting Mandela, training him and encouraging him throughout his life, Sisulu spent his life in his student's shadow. 'I don't think I have lived in his shadow. He is who he is and I am who I am. We worked as a team.'

Walter Sisulu is not at all power-hungry. Fortunately. He does not have Mandela's charisma, but he has the same principles and has lived the same hopes. He is incorruptible. Walter has a generous soul. In prison, he never hesitated to give his bar of soap or his writing material to a companion who needed them. 'And when he no longer had anything to give, he would give other people's things!' Ahmed Kathrada, his prison companion for twenty-six years and later the president's advisor, tells me one day.

The cassettes on which I taped my conversations with Walter Sisulu are still in my drawer. My project to do an audio biography of Walter Sisulu has once again come up against a wall of depression.

Only five days after my release from the rehab centre, I fall into the abyss again, more deeply this time. I am completely crushed. This time, it's off to hospital, the real one.

Jay phones Loulou urgently in Notre-Dame-des-Bois, Quebec. 'Come quickly. We need you. Lucie is in hospital and I can't cope with the children and my work.' Loulou arrives in Cape Town forty-eight hours later and stays for a month. She takes charge of the house. You need a mother for that.

I am in Constantiaberg Hospital, in the suburbs of Cape Town. Everything has a hospital smell, even the food. Once again, I have a private room. But I am not allowed to close the door.

They have decided not to listen to me anymore. I am here for as long as is necessary. My dose of Serzone is doubled. Dr G sees me more often, as often as her schedule permits.

The nurses take my blood pressure, my temperature and my pulse every four hours, day and night. I have a fit. I tell them that they are using the wrong instruments to measure my despair. Finally, they leave me in peace.

Dr G gives me homework to do. If someone gives me something to do, I do it. I find this work very difficult; the advanced statistics course I did at tech was far easier! The first thing I have to do is to prepare a résumé of my life, in three pages, and then list the major events. Then comes the crunch.

'Now make a list of your successes.'

'There aren't any.'

'Everyone has some. What about your children? Aren't you a good mother?'

'Well, yes, but ...'

'That's a success. Success is not necessarily measured in percentages or in numbers of reports. What about your documentary on Robben Island?'

'Well, yes, but there were so many flaws in the final product …'

'Are you not happy to have done it?'

'Yes, but …'

She is the defence lawyer. She makes me see my weaknesses, but also what is good in me, so that I can look at it there, on the page, with her.

'Didn't you mention to me that you have done some trekking in the Himalayas?'

'Yes. So what?'

'Didn't you reach the peak of an important mountain?'

'Yes, the summit of Mount Gokyo.'

'How high is it?'

'Five thousand eight hundred metres.'

'Without an oxygen tank?'

'Without oxygen.'

'That's a success.'

It is not difficult to make a list of such successes, as minimal as they may be. The challenge is to see these accomplishments as successes.

'Just because there is room for improvement in a report doesn't mean it is no good.'

'Can you really speak of success?'

'Yes.'

Dr G gives me more tasks. Every day. I feel as if I am clearing the hard disk of my internal computer. Some files have to be erased. Wherever it is, I have to eradicate the virus that is infecting the other files, those that hold my memories, my consciousness, my dreams. Dr G is my anti-virus software.

I want to get out. I have been hospitalised for almost three weeks and I can't take any more. Dr G fears my return home. She suggests that I spend a few days, perhaps a week, in a 'halfway house'. This is actually a little chalet set in the forest surrounding Cape Town. The area is peaceful, but there is a big dog there. I'm afraid of dogs. 'It's psychological,' says Dr G, 'Come on, we'll exorcise this fear too!' (No success here; I am still afraid of dogs.)

Loulou and the children come to visit me. Dr G comes also, to continue the therapy sessions. I feel better. But I know that I am still very, very fragile.

I make a big decision: I want to discover myself, get to the person living inside my body. My greatest difficulty is accepting myself for who I am. And I have fears that I have repressed all my life.

'How tall is your father?'

'Five foot, seven and a half inches.'

'And in your mind?'

'Two hundred metres.'

'How about we reduce him to five foot seven and a half in your mind?'

'How?'

'Write him a letter. You don't have to send it to him. But write down what you'd like to say to him.'

I write for two months. The formulation of this letter appears crucial to me. I don't want to alienate myself from my father. Because I love him dearly. I don't want to accuse him or blame him, because he has his own problems, starting with his relationship with his mother. But we have a communication problem. He sees my despair as an accusation and goes on the defensive as soon as it comes up. I openly admit to the wonderful memories I have of my childhood. The problem is that something other than the wonderful memories has plunged me into the state I now find myself in. I am afraid of myself. I am ashamed of myself. I am afraid to tell Papa that I have always been *afraid* of him. I think that I was afraid of the 'soldier' in him.

Soldiers … That reminds me of a story.

I was twenty-one years old. I was working as a monitor at the Lac Mégantic summer camp, in the sailing school run by my uncle, Claude Grondin, my mother's brother. He and I are great friends.

That summer, I swam across the lake every morning at seven o'clock. Almost two kilometres.

One fine day some soldiers from the Canadian army arrived and set up their tents. Flexing their biceps, I could see they were interested in me, the little monitor, the only 'chick' in the camp. Sitting quietly on the edge of the lake, I decided to challenge them casually, 'I think I'll swim across the lake.' They burst out laughing, but quickly took the bait. The next morning at seven we met on the edge of the lake. The faint rays of the sun hadn't yet helped the mist to evaporate from the surface of the lake. The guys had celebrated around the fire the previous night and got to bed late. They dipped a toe into the water and declared, 'No problem.' But the way their nipples hardened when they touched the water told a different story.

Three, two, one, go! Twenty minutes later I reached the other side of the lake and turned around. I overtook them, one by one, on the way back. Two gave up and the third one almost drowned. He had to be picked up in a boat. Soldiers … only too human.

My father was human, but I was afraid of the soldierly aura that surrounded him.

I have always been ashamed of myself, without ever knowing how to explain it. How do you express this feeling when you are five or ten years old? Or fifteen or twenty? I'm thirty-five and I still don't know. What I do know for the first time in my life, is that I am determined to 'put it into words'.

For two years, nothing would make me miss my biweekly, then weekly, meetings with Dr G.

After a few months I started to notice the progress I was making. I saw myself reacting differently to certain situations without having to tell myself, 'This is how I must react.' I saw myself changing. I still don't understand how words uttered in a therapy session can change or heal a person, but I know that it does happen.

All of a sudden, my father has assumed human proportions. Even my mother has grown smaller and I hadn't even realised that she was too big! I know that my father has always loved me. He has always told me so, but we didn't speak the same language. There was a miscommunication.

I was eventually able to leave the halfway house. I arrived home the day before Kami's birthday, 22 November 1997, the day he turned five.

That day, the house was full of kids, four and five year olds, and mothers staying for tea and cake. I looked a wreck. I felt weary and fragile. But I felt that I was on the road to recovery.

Betty had prepared everything. Hot-dogs, hors-d'oeuvres, little sugared dainties, and three cakes. What would I do without Betty?

After the past few months, I need a break from everything, with my children. I can't wait for Christmas! I want to go to Quebec, to the cold and the snow. I need to refresh my ideas. We all leave, Jay as well, for Notre-Dame-des-Bois. I spend these holidays on my skis in the forest on Mount Mégantic. I ski like a maniac, stopping only to relax with my family.

Then, disaster strikes, literally … We experience the devastation of the Quebec ice storm of January 1998. In the one-hundred-and-fifty-year-old log house in Notre-Dame-des-Bois, we manage the power failures because we still use wood for heating. From the lounge windows, we count the trees that fall one after the other. 'Oh, no, not that one!' Crack! There it goes. All our trees were affected, three-quarters of them seriously damaged.

One night, at midnight, we put on head lamps and go tobogganing in the enormous field behind the house, on the crust of frozen snow, up to our neighbour's place, six hundred metres away. The slope is gentle, but you can slide down the strange surface easily enough. For a few days, the icy layer makes walking in the forest easy too. The trees, the shrubs, the ground, the branches, the twigs, everything glistens with colour in the rays of the sun. I have never seen such a beautiful natural disaster!

I regain a positive view of life.

58

The voice of the violin

The sun is setting. It is starting to get cold. The musicians are tuning their instruments. I haven't brought the right jersey for an open-air show. Jacques Sellschop lends me his jacket. He has invited me here this evening, to a classical music show on the Spier estate in Stellenbosch. The concert is being held in an outside amphitheatre, set among the vines. Jacques Sellschop, marketing manager of MTN, one of the two cellular phone companies in the country, is rich, white and upper-class. While waiting for the concert to start, he shows me some photos of a musical 'adventure' – meeting Yehudi Menuhin, who, at eighty-two years of age, came to South Africa to give a concert. Unfortunately he had to leave for the US before the event could take place, because his mother was dying. Menuhin had the time to do a little work, though. And to leave three hundred violins for the underprivileged. Together with MTN, the famous violinist established the Violins for Africa project, as he'd already done in China.

'Look, Lucie, isn't it beautiful?'

In the photos Jacques shows me, black children, violin in hand, grinning from ear to ear, play proudly beside Yehudi Menuhin.

'That's a first – poor underprivileged children playing the violin. Do you know, that changed their lives?'

I look into Jacques' eyes. The lights go out. The concert begins. I whisper into his ear, 'By showing me those photos you have just given me a lot of work. There's one hell of a story there!'

I immediately knew I was going to throw myself into a report on the Violins for Africa project. I had 'heard' the music, just by looking at the photos. It was beautiful. I had to record it.

Throughout the concert I thought about the violins of these children. During the sonata, I dreamt of their sonata. At the end, I repeated to Jacques that I wanted to put together a report. 'Call me on Monday,' he replied. 'I'll give you the names of some people to contact.'

But what is so unusual about children playing the violin? These children come from poor areas, from squatter camps, where there is nothing to do but hang around the streets and get up to no good. As they grow up, so their mischief can become quite serious – Cape Town suburbs have some of the highest incidents of murder in the world …

The story of the violins is about poor, but ordinary children with a thirst for learning, for trying something new, for having a goal in life.

I have to interview Yehudi Menuhin. Jacques organises it. I do the interview by phone, with Menuhin in London and me in Cape Town, in French and English, because I intend doing this report in both languages, so that it can be broadcast both here and in Canada.

Pierre Trottier of *Dimanche magazine* on Radio-Canada accepts the proposal.

I get hold of Ronnie Samaai, the director of the project and a long-time violinist himself. Now retired, he works for next to nothing. 'I have never worked as hard in my life!' he says. 'And it's the most wonderful work I have ever been given!' All day long Ronnie does what he loves best: plays the violin and teaches this noble art. Ronnie is always smiling. He believes in the soul, in music, in dignity, in equality, and in making dreams come true, even for the poor. 'I was not able to play for the Cape Symphony Orchestra for the pure and simple reason that I didn't have the right skin colour. I want these children to have the opportunity, the competence and the possibility to merit, with dignity, a place in the Symphony Orchestra, if that is what they desire.'

I met several children from different poor areas in Cape Town: Khayelitsha, Guguletu, Sarepta and Kuilsrivier, townships on the outskirts of Cape Town, areas where the legacy of apartheid is most apparent, in the dust, disease and poverty of blacks and coloureds. However, being black and poor does not tally with the prestige and elitism of the violin.

One parent told me:

'To me the violin is not any instrument. It's not the type of instrument you can go around the corner and buy like a recorder that costs only a few rand. So there is a meaning attached to it for me, and that is that my child is learning not only an expensive instrument but an elite instrument. It's a big step forward. Our country has changed. Our kids have been taken out of the dust and given a chance in life. I never dreamed that my son would play a musical instrument, never mind a violin. The only thing we could play was the radio!'

To Yehudi Menuhin and Ronnie Samaai, music is a basic need. Yet there are so many basic needs to be satisfied in South Africa. More than half the population lives below the poverty line. Almost fifteen million South Africans do not even have access to potable water.

Should any available money not be spent on more urgent basic needs like housing, electricity, health and education?

'Oh, I love that question!' cries Ronnie Samaai. 'There are basic needs. Music is one of the basic needs, I believe, in any person's life. If you look at the amount of money that is injected into sports these days, it is unbelievable! The child [who has mastered an instrument] has developed a certain degree of self-esteem, self-worth, self-confidence. Isn't that what we want for our children?'

'Music is the key to life!' exclaims Yehudi Menuhin when I put the same question to him. 'It doesn't only allow you to communicate, to express yourself, it also allows you to attain a more complete balance because it absorbs your frustrations, your suffering, and it gives rise to a profound joy and a satisfaction that eliminates any desire for revenge.'

Tembisa, twelve years old, was limping through school. At home, her six brothers and sisters were managing, with difficulty, to eat reasonably well in their corrugated iron shack, small, dirty, but nonetheless full of life. Tembisa did not do her homework, had no friends and did not play any sport at school. I waited for her for two hours on the morning of the interview. She arrived in tears. Her mother had disappeared. She had not come home the day before. The seven children were in a state of confusion. They would find out that their mother was in prison for selling meat without a permit …

I look Tembisa in the eye and wipe away one of her tears, others have already soaked her school uniform, which is dirty, torn, and worn. I see a toe peeping out of a hole in her shoe. Even socks are a luxury she cannot afford. In silence, I take her violin case, and give it to her as if it were a baby. I ask her, 'Can you tell me about this? What happens when you let your bow slide across the strings?'

Tembisa looks at me, at the school principal and at Ronnie. She takes the case. She handles it as gently as a new-born baby, 'The violin helped me change. If I have worries from home, I forget all my problems when I play the violin.'

Then she takes out her 'baby', shiny, so small yet so powerful.

'Since I started with this violin,' explains Tembisa, 'I have become a respectful person and I am now very interested in sport and my school-work. I feel very happy and something happens inside me, even when I practise at home alone.'

In fact, Tembisa is now among the top three pupils in her class. She has made friends. She plays soccer. And when things are going badly at home, she takes out her violin and uses it to bring back the calm.

'It is important to give young people a voice,' says Yehudi Menuhin. 'The violin can be a voice. It satisfies the child's desire to have something near to it, an instrument that responds to the need for expression. A true life companion, something the child can hold and love wholeheartedly. For poor children, a violin is a friend and a voice.'

I asked the children how they would react if someone took their violin away from them. Here is the reply a little ten-year-old girl, Yunus, gave me:

'I would cry! I would cry because I like it. I don't want it to stop. Because when I'm alone, I just take my violin out and play. And the loneliness disappears and I feel, quite simply, very happy. It's my friend. It's my best friend now.'

I dined with Yehudi Menuhin when he returned to Cape Town to give the concert that had been cancelled a year earlier. He was smiling. He was happy. And, thanks to him, the eyes of a large number of children are shining more brightly than ever.

Yehudi Menuhin died a year after this report. It gave me quite a shock.

I sent my cassettes and reels to Pierre Trottier by way of a Canadian, who was returning to Canada. The arrangement was that he would post the parcel in Quebec. Not receiving any news, neither criticism nor thanks, I got worried and wrote to Pierre Trottier. What if the cassettes were lost?! I sent him two, three, four emails. I phoned and left messages. At first I thought that my tapes had not arrived. Then I thought he hadn't liked them. Or worse, that he'd hated them. I listened to the report once again. Sure enough, I found it was full of faults! I immediately regretted having sent it to him. I rushed off to Dr G.

Finally I received a two-line email from him, two little lines, with my name in inverted commas, which said it all, as far as I was concerned. 'Yes, "Lucie", I have received the tapes.'

I was bothering him, I could tell from the tone of this laconic email. But I never found out whether the report was OK or not. I never disturbed Pierre Trottier again. And I never did another report for *Dimanche magazine*. I learnt much later that he had been away on vacation. I had misinterpreted his silence …

SABC radio liked it, though. They broadcast it twice with the sponsorship of EMI Records. I was interviewed on the show *Women Today*. After the broadcast and interview, the station received loads of calls from people wanting to donate money and violins for the children. One woman called from the Netherlands. She had heard the report during a stay in South Africa. She sent her violin, forgotten in the attic and worth a fortune. Someone else gave Tembisa a violin worth fifteen thousand rand!

For a year I received other calls, sporadically, from various people who wanted to talk to me about violins and music and tell me how they can save someone's life. Yes, music can change a person's life.

Over a period of a year, I had collected enough evidence to prove that music can even save a country …

59

Freedom songs

Archbishop Desmond Tutu had already said, 'Without music, my life would be grey. Without it, the heart of life would be missing.'

Desmond Tutu, the missionary 'sent from heaven', has always expended all his energy for justice. Even in the most difficult moments of the struggle against apartheid, especially during the eighties, he expressed his hope by singing, 'Without any [freedom songs], our struggle would have been a great deal longer, a great deal bloodier, and perhaps not even successful.'

This statement says a great deal about the role of South African songs in the country's liberation.

I want to produce a long radio documentary on these songs. Nothing has been done on the subject, despite the fact that in nearly all reports and documentaries on South Africa broadcast anywhere in the world, you hear or see crowds singing.

The songs were exceptionally powerful in mobilising the masses. When ten thousand people start singing, the force can strike you dumb.

There is no authoritative work on the subject. The songs haven't even been transcribed, they are part of an oral tradition. I would like to put a little bit on tape. I would like to get Desmond Tutu to sing for me. In fact, I would like to get everyone I interview for this documentary to sing. I therefore choose them carefully; they have to be expressive.

Tutu seems completely absorbed by the subject:

'And with us blacks, South Africans, you know ... we sang when we were weeping, we sang when we were joyful, we sang at weddings, we

sang at funerals. We sang and we sang. We sang when we were reminding ourselves that although the enemy seemed to be strong, God was stronger. And that Satan represented all the forces of evil, injustice and oppression.'

Then, without my even asking him, he starts to sing. He knows what I want. I recognise the song from political gatherings and I am surprised to learn its origins. It is a religious hymn. It talks about God choosing us and giving us hope.

The first freedom songs were in fact born in the church. 'Alleluia' appears in several. God was the only source of hope.

One of the most popular freedom songs, *Nkosi Sikelel' iAfrika*, asks God to bless Africa. Composed by Enoch Sontonga in 1897, it was the ANC's official anthem for decades, and later, in 1994, it became part of the South African national anthem.

Clearly, for Desmond Tutu, this song is the very symbol of the liberation:

'Nkosi Sikelel' is the cream of our songs. Because in the end, as it were, we start where we began, with God, because we are saying we want our freedom.'

Baleka Mbete, deputy speaker of the National Assembly, talks to me about this same hope.

'I'm a politician. In the struggle, music played such an important role that I just don't see how we would have endured all those years, here or in exile, without the support of music and song.'

Baleka agreed to grant me a 'singing' interview. With all my interviewees, I would spend about fifteen minutes describing my project and explaining the special requirements for recording for a radio audience. I asked them to sing rather than to refer to the songs by name. I tell them not to be embarrassed, that I will stop the tape recorder if it is no good. It is not easy to sing in front of a microphone, alone, in the presence of a stranger, without music, without encouragement, without a crowd to get you going.

After trying for several months, I finally managed to find a choir that agreed to sing several songs free of charge, precisely because nothing had yet been done to preserve them. Other choirs wanted to charge me between four and twenty thousand rand, and I simply couldn't afford this amount. I am therefore deeply grateful to the choir of the Western Cape Democratic Teachers' Union. I went to Guguletu, Cape Town, to record them. They sang fifteen songs. It was exquisite. Élizabeth Gagnon, from the programme *Des musiques en mémoire* (Musical Memories) on the cultural channel of Radio-Canada, who broadcast the documentary, had a few CDs pressed for me; I gave one to Desmond Tutu, another to the choir and I kept one for myself.

These freedom songs, as they were known under apartheid, from 1948 to 1994, will disappear. That is the price of victory. These songs, which make it possible to trace the outlines of the history of apartheid, emerged in exile and in popular gatherings. But once the goal was achieved, you gradually stopped hearing them.

There are other reasons for their disappearance too. Umkhonto we Sizwe's anthem, for example, contains the words 'Let's kill the Boers'. Now eighteen months ago a large number of Boers – white farmers – were killed. They were the targets in a wave of murders. For this reason, the political leaders decided not to sing this song at the recent funeral of an Umkhonto we Sizwe commander, although this was the ANC tradition. For Baleka Mbete, it was a painful decision, as it marked the beginning of the end, the death of freedom songs …

The Deputy Minister of Defence, Ronnie Kasrils, gave me a captivating account. First of all he told me that he would not be able to sing during the interview, because it would be too embarrassing. But as the interview progressed, I kept asking him 'For example?' when he referred to a song. He hesitated, then he asked me to stop my recorder. 'I am going to have a scotch; after that, perhaps I will be able to sing.'

Ronnie does not like microphones. But he adores singing. He sang out of tune, but very expressively. He told me a story that will remain with me forever.

He talked to me about Vuyisili Mini, a black anti-apartheid activist and trade unionist from the Eastern Cape. Vuyisili Mini was a gifted writer and composer who wrote a large number of South African freedom songs, the best known of which is entitled *Nanzi Indoda Emnyama Verwoerd*. It contains the words, 'Beware, Verwoerd, the black man is coming. Beware, Verwoerd, the black man will get you!'

Vuyisili Mini and two of his colleagues were hanged on 6 November 1964, under the government of the architect of apartheid, Hendrik

Frensch Verwoerd, who was prime minister from 1958 to 1966. Verwoerd, the man who was to invent the system, and refine and impose the most severe apartheid laws, was a native of the Netherlands. He was assassinated in 1966, at the National Assembly, by a white who thought his policies were too lax!

The day before his hanging, Vuyisili Mini wrote a reply to the government's offer of pardon. If he gave up two other comrades who were active in the ANC's armed struggle, his death sentence would be commuted. He had the choice between death or denunciation. Two names for his freedom, or his life! 'Never!' Mini said before being executed.

In actual fact, Vuyisili Mini was hanged because he had become too powerful – his freedom songs had the ability to unite crowds, even a whole people, and to communicate a common goal. *Nanzi Indoda Emnyama Verwoerd* …

You can kill a man, but you cannot silence his voice. Mini's voice resounded and still resounds in South Africa. On 6 November 1964, when the jailer asked him, sarcastically, whether he was going to sing right up to the gallows, Mini began to sing his most popular song, together with the one thousand five hundred other prisoners in that prison in Pretoria and all the activists in all the ANC camps scattered across the African continent. *Beware, Verwoerd, the black man will get you. Beware, Verwoerd, the black man is coming.* Vuyisili Mini sang right up to the gallows.

Ronnie Kasrils told me this story in a very emotional fashion, repeating several times '*Nanzi Indoda Emnyama Verwoerd*', beware, Verwoerd, the black man will get you.

Although his songs are well known, Vuyisili Mini himself is not. He is one of the country's forgotten martyrs. However, it was he who refined the formulation of political slogans, endlessly repeated by crowds, 'Get out, Verwoerd', 'Don't be afraid', 'We are not far from freedom', 'We will get there with grenades, bazookas and AK–47s', and also 'Watch out for informers' and 'We will never lose hope'.

How can music and singing become not only a tool, but a political weapon? Is some music 'dangerous'? Ronnie Kasrils replies:

'Absolutely. In South Africa, we didn't defeat apartheid by out-shooting [the government]. They had a very, very powerful army. They were extremely well equipped.'

Ronnie Kasrils knows what he's talking about. He formed part of the group, with Nelson Mandela, that founded Umkhonto we Sizwe in December 1961. They were fully aware that they would never be able to expel the apartheid government by force of arms. It would have to be a 'negotiated revolution'. The armed wing could destabilise the country, create agitation, but it would never be able to overthrow the government through a coup d'état:

'There were only a few of us, we weren't well equipped, we had to create propaganda to inspire the people. That was our strongest weapon. And the mobilisation of the masses through song and toyi-toyiing featured as a weapon. That is what inspired people, inflamed people and was very much part of this massive avalanche that eventually buried apartheid.'

Singing, a weapon? Desmond Tutu, with his big eyes and his wriggling fingers, leans forward in his chair. As a man of faith, he hesitates to use this word:

'The crowds that were singing scared the living daylights out of our enemies ... Whenever they heard it, it sent shivers down their spines. Because many of them actually didn't understand the words, they just heard the sound. Oh, it's a tremendous sound. It's a tremendous sound! And if you were on the wrong side of that sound, you feared the advance of the hordes!'

At popular gatherings, the crowd would go into a trance and become one. They *believed* it was all-powerful; it filled them with the hope of crushing the enemy.

The freedom songs were a source of energy and of courage. Baleka Mbete was a woman soldier, participating in the ANC's training camps. She explains:

'Early in the morning, our people would be singing. Deep in the Angolan bush, depression can kill you. The songs kept us alive. We sang to stay alive. So, in fact, it became a weapon precisely because it pulled us together. It focused us. It energised us. So I don't think we would have pulled through without the freedom songs. I really don't.'

As the struggle gained momentum, the songs began to incorporate the symbols and heroes of the struggle – Mandela, Sisulu and Albert Luthuli, Nobel Peace Prize winner in 1960 and ANC president for fifteen years. The words became more and more direct. Those of the song *Somlandela uJesu* ('We will follow Jesus everywhere'), for example, became 'We will follow Luthuli everywhere'.

Among the prisoners on Robben Island, singing was crucial. All those I talked to highlighted its importance. Walter Sisulu even maintained that singing saved his life!

16 June 1976 marked a change in tone. Soweto was in flames. School pupils were demonstrating against Afrikaans as the compulsory medium of instruction. And the rage born that day would echo right through the eighties, the darkest years of apartheid. The songs became imbued with this rage.

In contrast with the previous, largely submissive generation, the youth of the eighties believed themselves invincible. *'Thina silulutsha, asinakubulawa,'* they sing. ('We are the youth. We cannot be destroyed.') After 1976 the young people leave the country en masse, in their hundreds, their thousands, their tens of thousands. Rage in their hearts, they become involved in the armed struggle and join the training camps scattered across Africa, Europe and Russia. They depart with the freedom songs of the sixties and return with those of the eighties, far more aggressive, even more powerful, capable of uniting any crowd.

With this new generation a popular dance suddenly makes it appearance, the toyi-toyi, born in the camps of Zimbabwe.

Ronnie Kasrils remembers having sung and danced like that in a military training camp in the USSR.

'The Soviet citizens used to watch us in wonderment as we used to march through the snow singing our African freedom songs. They had their own songs of course, but these didn't provide a tenth of the strength and the morale that ours did. And the officers, the Red Army officers who had defeated Hitler's troops at Stalingrad, used to say to us, 'You have impressive morale, it comes out in your singing.'

The toyi-toyi was just another, astonishing dimension of the freedom song.

Desmond Tutu often found himself in front of crowds shouting 'Viva the AK-47!' inside his church, which posed a moral dilemma for him.

'I remember that they had a song, Sizowadubula ngombayimbayi, or something like that. It was about shooting [the whites]. It was difficult to

know how to stop them. I didn't usually sing that, because I thought it was very bloody and belligerent. But sometimes, it was a way of allowing people to let off steam. You know, it was like a valve enabling them to release some of the anguish and the built-up anger that they had inside ... it was better to sing it than to actually use an AK-47.'

I read the uneasiness in Desmond Tutu's body language, but I press him for more information. He goes on:

'Sometimes the alliance [with the supporters of violence] might be uneasy, especially when the songs called for blood. But we were saying, "We can't continue in this way forever, our people can't be doormats for others to wipe their boots on. That can't be what God wants." And therefore, there was that alliance. We had to channel the anger and the energies of the people.'

Desmond Tutu is silent. He looks at me, looks upwards, then, as if he had just confessed a truth, he mutters:

'Even if the freedom songs made the church a bit too radical, the church in turn made the songs less bloodthirsty.'

Then he laughs. With his beautiful deep laugh, Tutu lets go.

'I think, there's no doubt that they instilled courage. [They said] "We are going to Pretoria" or "We are going to open the doors of the jail, Mandela is going to come out and we are going to be free". Or for those going to see Tambo in exile, "Come back. Bring the boys and make sure this government is overthrown." I think you'd be naïve if you said it wasn't something that changed the attitude of people.'

The freedom songs effectively changed the attitude of a people, saved this people. You can stop a people working, you can stop them studying, travelling, moving, taking care of themselves, even eating and drinking. But you cannot stop them singing. The apartheid laws and canons did not succeed in destroying the one true, indestructible weapon: the soul of the people.

60

You are free to go, my child

Léandre wants to leave. Should I let him go? I have legal custody of him until he comes of age. I call the shots. But no, I don't call the shots when it comes to deciding my child's fate.

Léandre wants to be in Quebec to start secondary school in September 1998. He wants to know what it will be like to live with his father. He is used to spending the summer and Christmas holidays with him, but he doesn't know what 'real life' will be like: day-to-day living, taking out the rubbish, bedtime, doing the dishes, homework.

I know, I can sense, that I have to let him leave. But I get advice nonetheless. I talk about it to Dr G. I talk about it to a psychiatrist and a child psychologist. They all know my case. They all know Léandre. They all say more or less the same thing. First, that a mother knows what's best for her child. Secondly, that if the environment in the other family is healthy, if the father is good and attentive to his needs, if there is no form of abuse, a boy on the threshold of puberty has a natural desire to spend more time with his father. They all agree that letting Léandre leave will not harm his development, but they also say his life will be equally fulfilling with his mother!

The decision tortures me for months. Obviously I want Léandre to stay with me.

Those around me, my friends, Omar, tell me to keep him. But if I listen to them, Léandre will bear me a grudge forever. I care about his well-being. Léandre will be twelve in six months' time, and he wants to live with his father. He wants to get to know Quebec. He wants to celebrate Halloween and go skiing. I am the last person he needs to convince about his need to be in Quebec.

Jay is also devastated to see me, and his son, both devastated.

This morning, there are several rainbows around the mountain. I take the children to school. Léandre is silent, sad, even. I want him to be happy.

'Would you like to have supper with me on the weekend? Just you and me?'

'Why?'

'Because I think we need to have a talk, on our own, just the two of us.'

'Okay.'

He knows what we are going to talk about. I have made my decision. I am on the road to freedom. The freedom songs have been ringing in my head for months now. I owe Léandre, my son, his freedom. The freedom to know and to love both his parents. The freedom to choose where to live without this being interpreted as meaning 'I don't love you' or 'I don't want to stay with you any longer, Mama'. I owe him the freedom to express his desires without feeling guilty.

I have chosen my favourite Thai restaurant. Situated in Constantia-berg forest, the restaurant has managed to create an Asian atmosphere in Africa. The atmosphere is friendly. The lighting, subdued. The ideal spot for a tête-à-tête. It's a hideaway for Jay and me. The food is excellent, and Léandre has developed a taste for Asian food.

'You know that I love you very much, don't you?'

'I know.'

'You know that I only want you to be happy?'

'I know.'

'You know that I only care about your well-being?'

'I know.'

Léandre doesn't say much, that's how he is.

'I know that this African adventure, which has lasted for seven years, hasn't always been easy, for you, for me, for all of us. I have tried to do my best; I believe I have made good decisions in relation to you. The decision to come to Africa was not easy to make. Not at all.'

I pause, but Léandre remains silent.

'But I do not regret my decision. I love Jay. We are a couple and we are together 'for life'. At least, that's what we hope.'

'I know.'

'There have been difficult times, but there have also been many, many wonderful moments. We have done so many great things together. Just the fact that you've learnt English will be an asset for you throughout life. You've travelled to Europe, Africa and Australia. We've done some great things together, haven't we?'

'Yes, we have!'

'Are you happy with us? Do you like living with us?'

'Yes!'

'Have you enjoyed your African experience, so far?'

'Of course!'

'What do you like?'

'I like living here.'

'But what else? What do you like here?'

'Everything. The beach, the country, the things you can do.'

'Do you like your school? Have you enjoyed your primary school in South Africa?'

'Yes.'

'Why do you want to go and live with your father?'

'Because it appeals to me. I feel like doing my secondary schooling in Quebec.'

'You know that it won't be a holiday. It will be school and all that.'

'I know.'

'Do you get on with your father's girlfriend, and her daughter?' (She has a daughter six months younger than Léandre.)

'Yes. I also want to see Guillaume, my brother.' (His father has had another child with his partner.)

'Yes, I know. And I know that you love your papa very much. And I respect that. I think it's a good idea to try and live there. And I will be coming back to Quebec soon!'

'When? That's what I'd really like, for you to live in Quebec. I'd really like you to come back!'

'I know. But I can't leave right now. I want to wait at least until the next elections, in a year's time. After that, I'll see. Do you understand why it is important for me to stay until the next elections? Because then

I will have covered the whole Mandela era for my job, from the year he was released from prison up to his departure from public life. Do you understand that?'

'Yes.'

'What would you like most in the world?'

'For you to come to Quebec.'

'I know. I want you to understand something: your room will always be here for you, with us. Wherever you are, you will have a room, a family, a home. If at any time you realise that you are not happy, you can come home. This will always be your home. You will always have a place with us.'

'Even if I wanted to come back in December?'

'I think it would be better not to break the school year. I think we should evaluate the situation in a year's time, after your first year in secondary school.'

'But what if I'm really, really unhappy and I can't go on?'

'Of course, my darling! You can come whenever you want. But let's say the ideal would be to wait a year.'

'Okay.'

'Let's try one year at a time.'

'Yes.'

'Are you OK with that? Is there anything else you're worried about?'

'No, I think it'll be fine.'

He eats in silence, digesting our conversation. He doesn't seem relieved or excited.

I change the subject. I tell him about some of the crazy experiences Jay and I had in Durban, when I first arrived in South Africa. Léandre was still in Quebec, Kami was not yet born, and we were living at Logie's (Jay's brother's) house. Logie and Corona had insisted that we sleep in their bed while they were away. Jay and I had said that there was no need for us to use the main bedroom, that the children's one would be fine. After insisting some more, they left. That night, at bedtime, I got into the children's bed. I waited for Jay, but he did not come. I said to myself that he was taking a very long time to brush his teeth. I heard nothing in the house. Eventually I called him, and he replied … from the other bed, Logie and Corona's, where he was waiting for me!

Léandre laughs wholeheartedly. I like laughing. I like seeing him laugh. I want him to laugh. But I would like to see him laugh every day, with my own eyes. This evening, I have decided to let him laugh. And it hurts me. Because I will no longer see him every day, as I should.

'You know that I am going to miss you very, very much. You know I love you.'

'Me too, Mama.'

'Can I ask you a personal question? You don't have to answer.'

'What?'

The question burns on my lips. I know I should not ask him, but I do, all the same.

'If I had said to you this evening that I was not letting you go and live with your father, that I wanted you to stay with us, what would you have said?'

He replies without hesitation. And his reply throws me completely.

'I would have accepted your decision.'

As simple as that.

'You have the choice between living with us and living with your father. Is your choice to live with your father?'

'Yes.'

'You know that you will always have a room with us, a home …'

'I know, Mama!'

'I want to be sure that you understand that you don't have to ask to come and live with us. You can just come.'

'Thank you, Mama. I love you very much too.'

I feel relieved, very relieved. Sad too. Happy. I don't know. Is this what letting go means? Does it hurt so much? But it's for his own good …

First-born children are special. All children are special, of course, but with your first-born you learn and you discover. I am letting my son go.

Léandre and Betty have a very special relationship. They form a perfect couple in the kitchen. Léandre adores cooking. At the age of nine, he already knew how to prepare a meal for six, Chinese chicken or meat pie. We have cooked together since he was very small. And then I started buying him recipe books for children, incredibly well put together and beautifully illustrated. He wanted to try everything. He often gives us a treat on Sunday morning – preparing pancakes with maple syrup. He gets out all the ingredients, organises everything meticulously – not at all in the way he does his homework! He adjusts his recipe book on the plastic stand and throws himself into the preparation with such concentration that it is almost impossible to talk to him while he is cooking. A true chef.

Léandre's eyes are just at the level of Betty's middle. When she takes him and hugs him in her arms, his head gets lost in her ample bosom. Léandre has great times at Betty's side, wooden spoon in the air. They share a beautiful love story. Betty is going to miss Léandre, and he her.

Léandre wants a photo with Betty and Peter, Jay's driver. Peter and Léandre are as thick as thieves. Since our dinner at the restaurant, Léandre has been quite open about what he will miss. As much as he looks forward to leaving, he has to get used to the idea.

Kami and Shanti are heartbroken. Léandre is Kami's hero, his best pal ('My brother can do this, my brother can do that, na-na-nanana-na'). Léandre is Shanti's humble, but protective servant, a precious darling.

'Me don't want "Eandre" to go.'

'Shanti, Léandre doesn't have the same papa as you. He has to go and see his papa for a while. He will come back to us later.'

Kami is starting to understand what it means for his brother to have another father. He is also fascinated by the idea that Léandre can have another brother!

June 1998: Léandre is ready to leave. He will fly on his own. He prefers to travel alone. He has done this since the age of eight. Nearly twelve hours to Amsterdam, then a twelve-hour wait in a room set up for children – electronic games, computers, books, beds, hamburgers and chips. No wonder he likes travelling alone! He's made this trip so many times!

'Bye, Léandre. A new stage of your life is starting. Just remember, I love you very much and you will always have a room with us …'

'Mama! Stop it! I know. And I love you too, Mama.'

He can't tell me often enough …

61

Mrs Jay Naidoo

'Oh! You work? But why? Aren't you a minister's wife?'

I see red every time someone asks me this question, especially if it's a woman! The opposite would never happen. If people meet the husband of a female politician, they'll ask, 'What do you do for a living?'

However, you don't have to be married to a minister to experience this kind of discrimination. Just being a married woman is enough. Being the wife of a minister adds a very specific dimension to the battle for equality of the sexes, though. It's a daily battle for independence. Sometimes I feel that I'm getting nowhere, that I'm always starting from scratch. People tend to think of me in relation to Jay, as though I have no identity of my own.

When I'm asked whether I'm involved in politics, I say no. But if they want to know whether it's hard being married to a man who is a politician, I can answer readily. When I give my opinion on government policy in the field of telecommunications, people will often say, 'Oh! But your husband said something else! You must be mistaken …' They believe I think what Jay thinks, that I am simply an extension of his brain, that I have no opinion of my own.

What really upsets me too is when people try to obtain favours because I'm married to Jay. People, even from Quebec, will try to use me to get a meeting or an interview with Jay, with another member of parliament, or even with Mandela! It's infuriating, I always tell them off! This is the reason that, in an almost provocative manner, I always reply, without hesitation, 'I do not work with Jay. I sleep with him. You can call his secretary if you want a meeting.'

Because I am the wife of a minister, certain things are expected of me. It is presumed that my personal and consumer habits are linked to my status. For example, everyone supposes that it is obvious that I drink wine, as a representative of the Wine Foundation did when she phoned me:

'Mrs Lucy Naidoo?'

'No, it's Lucie Pagé.'

'Can I speak to Mrs Naidoo?'

'Speaking. It is Mrs Pagé.'

'I would like to speak to the wife of Jay Naidoo.'

'That's me, but my name is Lucie Pagé.'

'Oh! Mrs Naidoo?'

Grrrrr.

'I am from the Wine Foundation and I am preparing an article. I would like to know what you think of wine.'

'I don't think anything. I drink beer.'

'But you must drink wine from time to time?'

'Almost never. I prefer beer.'

'But what is your perception of wine?'

'What do you mean, my perception?'

'How do you perceive wine?'

'I do not understand your question.'

'But what is your PERCEPTION OF WINES!'

'I do not have any perception. I am a beer-drinker, through and through.'

'But what do you offer your guests when they come to your home for a meal?'

'I tell them to bring their own wine, since neither I nor my husband drink wine; we know nothing about it. In fact, my husband drinks water.'

A perplexed silence at the other end of the line ...

'But you are the wife of a minister! You *must* drink wine. All the ministers' wives have answered our questionnaire!'

'I drink beer, madam. I like beer. I am mad about beer. Especially red beer. Can I talk to you about beer?'

She hung up, offended.

A woman from M-Net phoned me in May 1996. She was looking for a TV host for a weekly fifteen-minute programme aimed at raising awareness about several social issues. The idea was to associate my image with the programme, for me to join in discussions now and again, to try to convince the rich to make financial contributions to centres for abandoned babies, centres for battered women, and so on.

But why me?

'Because you are the wife of Jay Naidoo,' she replied. Not because of my documentaries on rape or battered women. Not because of my work. Not because of my spirit, because of what I think or do, but because of Jay! Even if it is for a good cause, I do not want to do it, I cannot play the role of 'the wife of'. If I need my husband's name to accomplish a task, if mine is not enough, this is tantamount to a form of submission in my eyes. I would gladly associate my name with a project if it was motivated by my own qualities and efforts. But in this case, I would have been presented as Mrs Jay Naidoo and not as Lucie Pagé.

I replied in writing, suggesting that if they were looking for a 'personality' they should approach my husband. 'There is a tendency in South Africa,' I added, 'to label women according to what their husbands do. I am not "Mrs Jay Naidoo". I am Lucie Pagé. And I am a long way from being a "personality".'

Without Jay's name, mine would have meant nothing to the producers in charge of the show. End of story …

Another incident involves Krisjan Lemmer, a satirical columnist in the *Mail & Guardian*. It occurred in 1999, when the report of the Truth and Reconciliation Commission (TRC) was published. The man responsible for the TRC's website, Steve Crawford, found himself embroiled in a clash between the publishing company, Juta, which published the more than three thousand pages of the Commission's report, and the Commission itself. Juta wanted to prevent the TRC from selling a CD-ROM containing the report and the thousands of pages of testimony for two hundred rand. Juta wanted to keep the rights and sell the report on its own, without the testimony, for seven hundred and fifty rand. Steve Crawford was up in arms at this injustice. He accused Juta of wanting 'to make money with the history of the people' and launched an Internet petition in protest.

I signed the petition. In the 'comments' box, I wrote, 'The TRC report is the collective memory of a nation. It is part of history and history means nothing if it is not accessible to all. There is no price to history, and selective memory – which the TRC fought against – should be opposed in every possible way. Charging seven hundred and fifty rand is encouraging selective memory.'

A few weeks later, I read Krisjan Lemmer's column in the *Mail & Guardian*. He outlined the dispute between Juta and Steve Crawford, then reproduced the full text of my Web message, saying that one petitioner had summed up the situation very well.

Up to this point it was fine. No problem. It was his last phrase that made me fly off the handle.

'Nicely put. Not surprising since the petitioner, Lucie Page, is the wife of communications chief Jay Naidoo.' Would it have been surprising if I had not been married to Jay? In other words, I don't have an independent mind because I am the wife of Jay Naidoo …

One day, Nelson Mandela called Jay into his office. He had seen an article giving the hundred most popular bachelors in the country, and Jay was among them! 'Call Lucie before she sees it herself!' Mandela recommended to Jay. Mandela is very 'pro-women'. He openly supports the bill on abortion. 'I am convinced that this is the only path to follow,' he has already said on this subject. He likes 'strong women'. Thus, on 18 July 1998, he married Graça Machel, on the day he celebrated his eightieth birthday! Graça, who was Minister of Education in the Mozambican government, is the widow of the former president of Mozambique, Samora Machel, who was killed by members of the apartheid regime; she is the only woman in the world to have been First Lady of two countries. Mandela has more women than men among his employees. One hundred and fifteen as against ninety-two. Fifty-two black men and forty-five black women. Eighteen coloured men and twenty-nine coloured women. Five men and seven women of Indian origin. Seventeen white men and thirty-four white women. He is surrounded by women …

Of course, I do not refuse to 'play' the role of minister's wife in certain situations. I am Jay's wife and proud of it! And when the time comes to accompany him to official receptions, I never go as a journalist. When I request an interview, I never mention Jay's name. He is the father of my children, he is my husband, he is the man with whom I share my life, but he is not a work colleague, and definitely not a ticket for obtaining favours.

Nonetheless, it is thanks to my status that I have the privilege of meeting all sorts of personalities at receptions, meals and meetings, some official, others not. This is how I ended up sitting next to the former prime minister of Canada, Pierre Elliott Trudeau, who was on a personal visit to witness what he had boycotted all his life: apartheid. The Canadian High Commissioner, Chris Westdall (the one who left when my mother made the 'fleur-de-lys' speech at my wedding), who had invited Jay and myself to dinner, placed me next to Pierre Trudeau. When I sat down, I introduced myself as 'Lucie Pagé, from Quebec', even though I was born in Nova Scotia, in the English part of Canada. He smiled. We talked about my children, my life together with Jay, and South Africa. After a few drinks, I explained my somewhat cheeky introduction, explaining that as a child I had been given beatings at times, in school, in parks, in class, in Nova Scotia, in Manitoba, in Ontario, as a result of my 'Québecois character'. I was constantly reminded that I was 'not the same'. *French Frog, French Frog, you're just a French Frog* … Then I asked Trudeau why, damn it all!, he had sent the army into the streets in 1970? He almost choked on his mouthful of wine, then replied that his version of events had never been made known to the general public, that the media had slaughtered it. And that the meal we were enjoying together was not a suitable occasion for a history lesson.

'But it would afford me great pleasure to offer you a history lesson on the Quiet Revolution if you should come to Montreal,' he added. (The Quiet Revolution (1960 to 1966) was a period when Quebec asserted its autonomy in the social and political spheres.)

'Are you serious?'

'Absolutely.'

'If I call you in Montreal and say to you "I am coming for the lesson", you will really receive me?'

'Absolutely,' he repeated.

I never called him …

It was also owing to my status as a minister's wife that I ate at the same table as the president of Cuba, Fidel Castro, and chatted all evening, in Spanish, to one of his advisors. Castro gave a fiery speech on apartheid, on Mandela and on what 'freedom' really means. Even those who did not understand Spanish had shivers running down their spines, he spoke so passionately.

And again it was this status that allowed me to have a drink with the famous South African jazz pianist Abdullah Ibrahim, also known as Dollar Brand. We attended a concert by Yehudi Menuhin together and we talked about the crucial role of music in life. I asked him what he thought of the Montreal Jazz Festival, in which he had participated. He replied, without hesitation, 'It is the best jazz festival on the planet.' He dreams of producing something along the same lines in Cape Town, where he was born.

It is also because I am Jay's wife that I had tea with the Dalai Lama, the president of Argentina Carlos Menem, with the French president Jacques Chirac, the president of Libya Muammar al-Gaddafi, with Bill and Hillary Clinton, with the violinist Yehudi Menuhin and the film producer Costa-Gravas, with the Secretary General of the UN Kofi Annan, and with Queen Beatrix and Prince Claus from the Netherlands. My world changed when Jay became a minister. I began to move in another society. And there was absolutely no way I could mix my professional and my personal lives.

Of all these meetings, there is one that is particularly dear to me. On a November afternoon in 1998, I spent some time in the company of a master of music, David Helfgott, the real-life hero of the film *Shine*. Without music, David Helfgott would be dead, it's as simple as that. Music is his life. He had an extremely difficult childhood, ruled over by an authoritarian father, and spent a whole decade in a psychiatric hospital. He got over it. Well, almost. He does what he loves and what fills him with passion: he plays the piano. Despite his illness. 'The doctors don't really understand his illness,' his wife Gillian told me. 'They can only control the symptoms.' David is able to play a piece of music, hold a conversation with someone and listen to two other conversations all at the same time. Afterwards he is capable of repeating to you what everyone said. His brain functions at a phenomenal speed. It is as though he is driving five cars at the same time.

I showed him the piece *Berceuse* (Lullaby), composed by the Québecois pianist André Gagnon, because I was learning it at the time. He played it on my old rented piano, from start to finish, without any hesitation, as if he had played it all his life, with all the emotion it required. And while chatting and commenting on it at the same time! He played the piece several times, saying that it had something special, beautiful, gentle about it. Then he stopped at one passage where, he said, there was a small mistake. He changed the notes, declaring it an improvement, and then he played the piece again … perfectly.

When we receive visitors at home like this, it is Jay who prepares the tea and biscuits. I obstinately refuse to play the role of a 'domesticated' minister's wife. Jay does not expect that anyway. He does not expect anything from me in this regard, except, perhaps, a little diplomacy …

From time to time, when I bring up rather sensitive subjects in front of guests, Jay glares at me or kicks me under the table! Like the day we went to dinner with the Canadian Human Resources Development Minister, Pierre Pettigrew. When the conversation came round to the subject of violence against women in South Africa, I mentioned that this country had the highest rape rate in the world among countries that were not at war. Jay was furious that I had talked about violence and not about a positive aspect of his country. I was sorry, but in support of the cause of women I would even present my views to the Pope! One cannot be silent about the fact that women, who make up a little over half of the world's population and who do two-thirds of the work, although they receive only a tenth of the pay and own only a hundredth (one per cent!) of the assets, are the main victims of violence. Any diplomacy that wants to keep this quiet is sick!

Finally, it was in Finland that I experienced an absolute nightmare in my role as a minister's wife. When we were welcomed at Helsinki airport, we were each given our respective programmes, as is customary. Mine included visiting museums and cathedrals, having tea with dignitaries, a lunch at which I would be the guest of honour. As usual, I discreetly nudged Jay as a signal to have my programme cancelled, because I prefer to walk the streets on my own, popping into cafes and shops to explore the country in my own way.

Jay managed to cancel everything except the lunch in my honour. I told myself it was the price I had to pay for being a minister's wife and for having the right to a plane ticket, even though no job description for me is laid down in the ministerial regulations.

On the day of the lunch, a driver comes to fetch me at the hotel. I have nothing special to wear. A pair of black pants and a white blouse. A few pieces of jewellery from the flea-market. Worn shoes. Too bad. Finding the driver sympathetic, I tell him that I do not really like these ceremonies for ministers' wives and that I would far prefer to go walking in town. He listens attentively and, hearing this last phrase, gives me a smile in his rear-view mirror.

We arrive at the home of the South African ambassadress in Helsinki. There are about fifty women – only women! – waiting for me. As I get out of the car, the driver touches my arm discreetly and says that he will come back in an hour to see if I am ready to leave. So understanding!

The hostess introduces me as 'Mrs Jay Naidoo', and I repeat, each time, that my name is Lucie Pagé. The ambassadress gives me a little smile as if to say 'Yes, yes, alright'. And then continues to call me Mrs Jay Naidoo! We go into the kitchen, which is almost as big as my house in Africa. The ambassadress has a South African cook brought in especially to prepare her daily meals. Today, in my honour, a leg of lamb is being carved and prepared. The South African taxpayers would be outraged to see where their money goes.

The presentation lasts an hour, during which I feel very uneasy. I do not really understand the relationship between my presence and the elaborate preparation of lamb in the company of fifty or so wives of diplomats from a variety of countries.

As they serve up the food, I announce that I am vegetarian. Purely from a desire not to be assimilated by these society women, I boycott the lamb! I engage in a few polite, but senseless conversations. I have no desire to be in this place and I have been smiling for more than an hour, through clenched teeth. No one has asked my opinion or my permission to attend this useless show.

If I had been invited to a get-together of fifty women to discuss useful things, women's projects or community projects, for example, I would have gone with pleasure. And among the women present there are undoubtedly some who would have preferred a different scenario.

I notice the driver. I slip out! Thank you! Goodbye! They perhaps found me rather abrupt, but I hate wasting time.

The driver takes me to see the town. He explains how Helsinki tricked the Germans during the war. They lit lights in a field, to simulate an alternate location of the town for the Germans, and the Germans fell for it. They destroyed the non-existent town. This is the reason that Helsinki is packed with historical treasures, preserved by cleverness.

A little later, the driver drops me at my meeting place with Jay, to whom I give an account of the afternoon. He laughs until he cries.

'You're not angry?'

'Not at all, Lucie. You did well. I fully agree with you. It's a waste of time and money.'

'I left a little hastily. I did not have time to repair my reputation. I think I left it in a thousand pieces on the carpet.'

'I'm not worried. You did well. Come! Let's go and have some dinner, since neither of us have had anything to eat!'

And we went off to enjoy … lamb chops.

62

Third wedding: India

Jay has to go to India on a business trip, two weeks of conferences in which he'll have to build relations in the field of telecommunications. He is also fired up by a personal project close to his heart. Since his therapy sessions with Dr G, he has wanted to retrace his genealogical roots and return to the village where his great-grandmother was born.

After the two weeks of work, the whole family will join him in India, including Léandre and Louise, who will come from Quebec.

Jay has also cooked up another plan.

'Will you marry me?'

It is difficult to say no to a proposal from your husband!

'Again?'

'We will be married according to the Indian tradition, according to the tradition of my ancestors, of southern India.'

I am thrilled.

This third wedding will have a spiritual dimension: it will unite the continents that represent Jay, myself and the children. Our family consists of descendants from four continents. Jay has ancestors in Asia and in Africa. I have French, Irish, Amerindian and Québecois blood from Europe and America. It will be a wedding in which we celebrate our love – intense, powerful, fiery – and we unite our destinies, this time more deeply conscious of our commitment to each other, with the three children. It will also show that we accept our fate, torn between two continents.

The preparations are extremely complicated. We have to coordinate Jay's schedule – in India – with Léandre and Louise's arrival from Quebec, with that of Kami, Shanti and myself from Cape Town, while Nisha, Jay's sister, and her husband, Sagaren, who have never been to India, arrive from Johannesburg a few days later. We also have to plan how the eight of us will travel (with our mountain of luggage!) in this enormous country for three weeks. I have to have the family immunised against a host of diseases. It is a logistical nightmare. But we eventually all fly off.

✽ ✽ ✽

India is another world.

From north to south, from east to west, from the big cities to the smallest rural villages, we travel the country by car, camel, elephant, rickshaw, taxi, bus, train, plane, foot, most of the time completely amazed at the spectacle of Indian life.

Our journey begins in Mumbai (Bombay), where Louise, sitting in the back seat of the car following us, experiences three motor accidents in two days, all of them bumper bashings. The cars don't have safety belts. They don't have side mirrors either, because they drive pressed up against one another. In addition, it is not uncommon to see cars with scratches along the length of their bodies. Only cows, wild boars, donkeys, goats, camels, elephants, dogs, hens and buffalo appear safe on the road.

Because Jay is a minister, the Indian authorities want to ensure his safety and that of his family. Indian history is littered with political assassinations. We often end up sleeping with soldiers at our doors, armed with a weapon capable of killing a camel. We also have official cars and drivers at our disposal. We need two cars to cart us around.

The only things that you can really drink in India are tea and Coca-Cola. The locals give me a funny look when I take out a towelette to wipe the top of a bottle. I don't want to insult them, but nor do I want my children to ingest what is now on my towelette … which has turned brown and dirty.

One evening, in Mumbai, we attended a show by Sivamani, an extraordinarily talented percussionist. He has slightly African features, but is an Indian through and through. As fate will have it, he has just married an Indian from Cape Town.

Sivamani makes sounds with all sorts of things. He has more than a hundred pieces of equipment: instruments, sound boxes and even different-sized jars filled with water to different levels. The sounds he draws out of them are new to our ears. The show is held under the Gateway of India, the British triumphal arch in India, next to the beach. Hundreds of people gather. What an irony to celebrate the wealth and triumph of Indian culture under this colonial monument!

At Bangalore, right in the centre of India, we are greeted with a magnificent show of Indian music and dance. The women's bodies are adorned with jewels; they wear brightly coloured costumes, which shine brilliantly.

Once again I find out that everyone knows Jay. Some people even worship him because they see him as a compatriot who has triumphed over injustice in Africa. People regularly recognise him in the street, ask for his autograph, want to touch him and talk to him. Indians are proud of him because he is Indian. Jay has always rejected this type of recognition before. But, in the course of this journey, he discovers his Indian pride.

During our stay in India, we celebrate Jay's forty-fourth birthday, on 20 December 1998. He first goes to see Saï Baba, five hours from Bangalore by road. Saï Baba has a reputation for great wisdom; he is an intensely spiritual person. Hundreds of thousands of people from all over the world come to India to see him, and, if possible, to touch him. The temple town where he lives accommodates ten thousand people at a time. Saï Baba is also an excellent magician. He asks to see Jay, and makes a precious stone appear in his hand. Then he transmits to Jay the words of the 'Almighty', with whom he appears to be speaking.

When Jay returns to our rooms, a birthday cake is waiting for him. Léandre has thought of the perfect present: a brick. Jay used to tell the children the same story again and again, 'Count yourselves lucky, children. When I was a child, I only had a brick to play with and I pretended that it was a car in the sand.' We found a brick with the initials 'NB' on top, which was immediately baptised 'Naidoo Brick'. Jay insisted on bringing it back to South Africa. The gift touched him deeply.

Jay and I marry in Bangalore. We choose this town in Karnataka because our friends Devaki and Lakshmi Jain live there. Lakshmi was the Indian High Commissioner in South Africa and his wife, Devaki Jain, is an author, economist and feminist. An extraordinary, humble couple, motivated by compassion. Both are passionate about justice and human dignity.

On the Monday morning, 21 December, Louise and I dress the children. Kami and Léandre both wear an Indian outfit: a long shirt reaching the knee, cotton pants gathered at the ankle and sandals. No complications here. The beautiful Shanti looks like a little princess in Indian attire. As an unmarried woman, she wears a black dot on her forehead. I, as a married woman, wear a red dot.

The doorbell rings. Two young girls arrive with large bags containing my sari, flowers that have been blessed for my hair and heavy gold jewellery, rather flashy for my taste. The girls are timid and extremely polite. They have magnificent bodies and are exquisitely beautiful. I recognise them as the dancers who welcomed us on our arrival in Bangalore.

I slip a dozen bracelets on, one after the other. While one of the young girls puts on my make-up, the other envelops me in the long piece of mauve silk fabric with gold edges. A gift from Devaki …

The procession is waiting for us. We have to go to the temple.

Jay looks like a prince, a maharajah, a mahatma even! He is wrapped in a *dhoti*, fabric that has been wrapped around the body in the same way for thousands of years. At the temple, he is asked to take off his cotton shirt – his torso must be bare. He carries two enormous grey feathers, one resting on each shoulder. The ritual involves us first walking around the temple, barefoot, three times. Then, a group of musicians, playing instruments that I have never seen before, follow us up to the altar, where an enormous Ganesha, a protective god with the head of an elephant, decorated with flowers, incense, fruit and milk that has been blessed, guards the ancient temple. The interior, which is very simple and rather empty, is spotless. The scent of incense wafts on the air. At the front of the main hall is an altar decorated in thousands of colours.

The *swami* or priest officiating doesn't speak a word of English, but we communicate easily in his deep gaze, in fact one could drown in his eyes. He smiles.

I ask him, through an interpreter, what people think of a white person marrying an Indian person. He replies that the Indians are very proud when a stranger marries their culture, or at least accepts it. At our side, a journalist from the local paper sent to cover Jay Naidoo's marriage takes notes all the time.

The ceremony becomes more solemn. The priest has us make several ritual gestures, blowing here, sprinkling petals there, sipping water ... Prayers, some of them sung, follow. The atmosphere that reigns in the temple is difficult to describe. You feel peaceful and serene there.

The priest asks Jay to repeat some words in Sanskrit, sacred words that only the husband (hmmm!) has to say, which he does for a good ten minutes, arousing ripples of laughter from the priest and the congregation, because Sanskrit is not easy, especially for an Indian from Durban! Next we exchange rings, which have to be put on our toes, according to an exact and symbolic ritual, each of us on our knees in front of the other in turn. Then it is the turn of the garlands, which are wrapped three times around our necks. It is more than two hours since the ceremony began, yet everyone, including the children, seems intoxicated by the music and the singing. The crowd grows as the rumour of a wedding spreads in the streets. In the end, there are several hundred people in the temple.

Next I slip the sacred *mangalsuthra*, made of gold, around my neck. This is a pendant hung on the end of a long chain, that must fall between your breasts and over your heart. Devaki bought it for me. The *mangalsuthra* is the equivalent of the Christian wedding ring. 'You must never take it off, even when bathing or sleeping,' the priest tells me seriously. 'You must always keep it around your neck.' Whether I wear it around my neck or not, my *mangalsuthra* is worth its weight in gold to me.

To end with, the priest asks us to sit facing one another, for the ritual of the games with a coconut and with bunches of flowers, which are thrown between the partners. These matrimonial games were invented a very long time ago, when children were married off from the age of about ten. Today the tradition endures in adult marriages. We throw the bunches of flowers and the coconut to one another three times. Actually, we have to roll the coconut on the ground towards each other, but we do have to throw the flowers. For fun, when it is time to return the coconut, I make as if to throw it. There are stunned gasps from those present. Jay and the priest laugh wholeheartedly. The journalist wrote that the priest was offended, but this wasn't true.

Then all the people present have something to eat, sitting cross-legged in long rows. Many of them, particularly the old women, stare at us as though we come from another planet. Everyone is served a large banana leaf bearing a cup of dahl, a little rice and a small portion of sugared rice as dessert. The food, which you eat with your fingers, using your right hand, is absolutely delicious, worthy of the best Indian restaurant. Thus the ceremony ends, after three hours.

This third wedding was grandiose, unforgettable, symbolic. It was a more lucid, enlightened way to seal our destiny. Léandre, Kami and Shanti will understand the importance of this event in time. Louise, the only person to have attended all three of our weddings, found it moving once again. Nisha was also close to tears. Nisha and Sagaren are conservative in their traditions, but open to life, to everything that is different. 'What is, is.' We all thought that day of *Aya*, which means grandmother, or Grand Mother, Jay and Nisha's mother. Jay would so much have liked her to be there …

After the wedding, we travelled to Chennai (Madras), in the state of Tamil Nadu. When we reached our lodgings, we had to brush strange insects and white ants off the grey bedcovers. The beds carried the hollows of a thousand resting bodies. We put the three children under one sheet, on filthy cushions on the floor. The sheet was supposed to protect them from the hundreds of thirsty mosquitoes, perhaps also infected with malaria. The place stank of shit and urine. There was no toilet paper, no hot water, no drinking water. It was a government guesthouse. India – the real India – was greeting us!

The next day we left for Pondicherry, a former French colony. It took four hours to travel the hundred and sixty kilometres to our destination. Fields and fields of basmati rice. On the 'highway', grains of rice lay out to dry in large rectangles protected by stones, forcing cars to drive around them, while trying to avoid a head-on collision. Nonetheless, the road was littered with car wrecks …

The crime rate in India is very low, even though there are a billion inhabitants and millions of poor people. Perhaps because of their culture, which teaches the essential values of life, like respect, even for grains of rice drying on the highway.

Jay goes to Gollipalli, near Vellore, with Sagaren, another ten hours by road, while we, the women and children, wait for them in

Pondicherry, wandering peacefully along the colourful streets. Gollipalli is the village from which his great-grandmother departed in 1864. Jay wants to go back to his roots. He needs to know where he comes from. He discovers that he belongs to something besides politics. He belongs to himself. But who is he? He searches. He finds. He finds the plot on which his ancestral home stood. The foundations of the house are still there. A few hectares still belong to him, according to Indian family tradition.

The villagers are afraid of him at first. They think he has come to reclaim a few hectares of land! No, he assures them. Realising that his return is spiritual, they end up welcoming him with open arms. He meets one very old lady who remembers her own grandmother speaking of Jay's great-grandmother. Lucky find! They take him to the old temple, which his grandparents undoubtedly frequented. He prays there. He reconnects with his ancestors, with himself. He brings back a handful of soil and a stone from the remains of his ancestral home.

What are we without history? Who are we without our roots? On the way back to Pondicherry, the driver tells Jay that this journey has changed the way he views life. He has realised that he has not appreciated his parents as he should. He has thought of his mother the whole way and wants to go and see her straight away, to tell her that he loves her, that he now sees everything she has done for him.

63

Vijay

At Pondicherry, French is read, heard, spoken, tasted and smelt – all tinged with the Indian culture. A sweet mixture. Exquisite, especially for a Québecois! We walked for hours in the town, on the beach, morning, noon and night.

We also visited the Aurobindo *ashram* (a monastery, in India), founded by Sri Aurobindo, an Indian guru. Two thousand people live there permanently. Sometimes, ten thousand gather there! The school at this ashram, which takes children from pre-primary to the end of their secondary schooling, is unique. The teachers, who come from all over the world, are volunteers. The education is free. All the sciences, from mathematics to computer science, are taught in French. History, geography and other subjects are taught in English. The children select their own timetable and subjects, but physical education, music and art are compulsory. Even though the graduates receive no diploma, the requests to study there far exceed the number of places available. We met some of the 'products' of this school, young people who are succeeding in life, who have developed real self-confidence, who are open and resourceful and, at the age of twenty-five, already well placed in some profession or other. At the Aurobindo school they teach the verb *to be* before the verb *to have*.

We celebrated Christmas peacefully in our rented guesthouse. You have to take off your shoes when you enter. It is calm, quiet and smells good. The people are always smiling. They greet you by joining their hands and saying *Om Shanti*. Surgi Murti, who manages this spiritual

B&B, is dressed in white cotton, and is always barefoot. The children are calm, as though the pure simplicity of the ashram calms them naturally.

We meet Vijay, the director of the Aurobindo ashram. Vijay is also a great expert in child education. I don't yet realise that this meeting will change my life and, indirectly, those of Shanti, Léandre and, especially, of Kami …

We have been invited to tea with Vijay. He is sitting, barefoot and cross-legged, on an old sofa, covered in clean, white cotton.

Kami is in a bad mood and refuses to come into the room. Vijay asks me if I have something to say about Kami. I am surprised by his question. And then he talks to me a bit about spirituality, about children … All of a sudden I feel the need to talk to him one on one, about Kami. Kami is difficult, full of pent-up anger. I think that it's my anger, which I transmitted to him while I was pregnant with him. I was not ready to welcome him. He came much too early. And then he was a boy. An 'other'. Men leave, they leave you …

Because I took months to bond with Kami, I still feel guilty today. I would do anything to undo the wrong I might have done him. Vijay sees everything, simply by analysing Kami's and my behaviour. He understands everything, without my saying a word …

That evening, Jay and I return to see Vijay.

In less than two minutes I am telling him the story of Kami, of his birth, his first few months, the initial years that he spent crying, and I am crying my eyes out too. I cry and cry. Vijay remains calm. Jay is surprised. He never knew that I was carrying such a burden of guilt, this shame, these regrets, this hurt. Hurt that I have always hidden, that I even try to hide from myself.

Kami was born in my anger.

Vijay talks to me calmly. He suggests ways for us to deal with Kami. He makes me realise that I am too impatient with him. Too demanding even. I start to follow his advice straight away. At Pondicherry I learn how to tame Kami, my own son. Vijay simply explained how. The greatest lesson was to realise that anger gets you nowhere. Vijay explained to me that I must channel Kami's energy, his curiosity, his intelligence, his frustration and his anger. Kami is determined, like me. Pig-headed, like me. I often feel that I am looking at myself when I look at Kami. Since then, I have been communicating regularly with Vijay by email. I write to him in French and he replies in English. He has helped me discover Kami. His main message is the following, 'Anger gets you absolutely nowhere. Be firm, but calm …'

It is this impression of calm that stays with you when you think of India and its culture. This is what I love about Jay. His calm.

After Pondicherry we head for the Indian jungle. From Khujurao we leave in an Ambassador, those old British cars that they still make here, with springs in the seats that bounce you up to the roof without any effort at all. It's hell! Eight hours on the road to travel one hundred and sixty-seven kilometres! If you can call it a road …

At Satna, halfway through our journey, our driver knocks over an old man. There's a big bump! And then it feels as though we've driven over something. After two unsuccessful attempts to move the car forward, our driver manages to reverse. Bump and bump again! I am with Léandre and Shanti – the others, in the front car, have not noticed anything. The crowd attacks our car. When someone knocks over or kills someone on the road in India, the driver is often killed, sometimes burned in his car. The people open the door and try to pull our driver out of the vehicle, which is still moving – with no one at the wheel! His body is hanging out, but he still has his foot on the accelerator. He is negotiating with the passers-by. I am screaming at the top of my voice, which spurs the driver to make a quick recovery. He manages to get the upper hand and steps on the accelerator. We succeed in getting away. I never found out if the poor old man died, but everyone said that our driver made the right decision to save himself. If he had not, he would be dead. This is an aspect of Indian culture that escapes me …

When we eventually reach the Indian jungle, where you find all the characters from *The Jungle Book* (we already travel with two little Mowglis and a Hindu princess), after a whole day in the car and still shaken by the incident, we have to get into another vehicle, a jeep.

It is cold. I get the children ready. I take out all the warm clothes we have. They won't be enough. We drive fifteen kilometres into the bush to meet up with 'our' elephants. Seven of us get onto one elephant, sitting on a small platform. All around us there is silence, mountains and nature. In this jungle there are peacocks (India's national bird), deer, monkeys, eagles and vultures, bears, snakes and thousands of other types of animals and insects, but they are not our main objective. We are looking for tigers. There are only two thousand tigers left in India, fifty-seven of them in this Bandhavagarh Nature Reserve. Darkness falls and we haven't spotted any yet. We have to leave. We are freezing. The temperature has fallen to almost zero. Then suddenly, whoosh! We get a glimpse of the stripes of a large male – just for a few seconds.

The next day we get up at five-thirty. Again. Almost every morning we have to get up at an ungodly hour. After breakfast (bananas and cold toast), we leave. Shanti has diarrhoea, so her granny Loulou stays behind with her. I leave with Jay, Kami and Léandre. We visit some caves, sculpted hundreds and hundreds of years ago. Then our guide receives a call on the jeep's CB. Quickly! A mother tiger with her three twelve-month-old cubs has just been spotted not far from here! We drive as fast as we can on the dirt roads, in the cold rays of the rising sun, to a partic-ular location in the jungle. There, an elephant is waiting, ready to receive us on its back. We climb up and move through the jungle, our mahout sitting on the elephant's neck, tickling its ears with his feet and shouting orders at it (an elephant can understand up to four hundred commands!). We suddenly come upon the unique sight of four cats. One of the young tigers, already very large at twelve months, majestic, magnificent, is washing his paw with his big tongue, getting ready to go to sleep for the day. Our guide immediately decrees that 'Mother-in-law must see this'. Another guide is sent to fetch Loulou and Shanti. So we all see the tigers. We stay there for over an hour, on the elephant's back, walking around the four cats. The tigress is huge and magnificent, and seems almost docile. Elephants and tigers have a mutual respect for one another, and our presence on the back of the elephants doesn't seem to bother the little family at all.

The following morning, we retrace our steps, except that we break the hundred and sixty-seven kilometre journey in two. Four hours the one day and four the next. Hell, nonetheless.

Next we see the desert, on camels. Shanti says, 'I would like a camel at home. But just one.'

We saw beauty at Agra: the Taj Mahal. So grandiose and majestic that I can't find the words to describe what you feel before this tomb, which took twenty thousand people twenty-two years to build. After the visit, we sit for an hour as the sun sets, admiring this work of art, this masterpiece, this wonder of the world. The Taj Mahal has the perfect curves of a woman. Your eyes do not tire of looking at it. Kami is now thoroughly familiar with the story of Mumtaz Mehal, the wife of Emperor Shah Jehan, who died giving birth to her fourteenth child. Madly in love with her, her husband had this mausoleum erected in her memory. He then wanted to build an identical mausoleum for himself, but in black, on the other side of the river, facing the first one – mad with love he was. His own son had him put in prison, so that he would not waste money on this folly. For seven years until he died, he admired the Taj Mahal through the bars of his cell.

On 5 January, Léandre leaves us. He is returning to Montreal, via London. At the age of twelve, he is crossing the planet alone. I cry every time I have to leave him at the airport. But this time, I cry from panic.

In Delhi, only those with a plane ticket are allowed into the airport. I am therefore not allowed to go in with Léandre. I explain that he is my son and that I cannot leave him alone, that he would not know where to go in this enormous building. I am told that I need a special pass from the manager. At this stage, it is one o'clock in the morning. But nonetheless, Jay goes off to look for someone. Léandre is crying. He is scared. So am I. The guard looks at us without any compassion.

Léandre finally obtains permission to be accompanied by his mother 'only', it is clearly stated. I go to the counter … which is closed! The moment we get there, the neon lights above the counter switch off.

'Too late. Come back another day.'

Incredulous, I stare at the employee who has greeted me with these words.

'But my son's ticket is confirmed, he cannot miss the plane. It's not our fault that no one wanted to let me enter the airport!'

'That's not my problem. Come back another day.'

Léandre is in tears. I am furious. I can't take this any more! Then a light goes on in my head. I had paid for Léandre's ticket using points that Jay had accumulated. And as the only available seat was in business class, I had to take it.

So I shout, 'But he is in business class!'

Hierarchy is extremely important in India. The caste system is still respected there. The words 'business class' launch the employee into action. He checks his computer, takes Léandre's passport and gives us his boarding pass. A woman arrives immediately and takes Léandre, without even giving me a chance to kiss him goodbye. In tears, I cry, 'Just a moment! You can quickly let me kiss my son!' I give him a hug and whisper into his ear, 'Everything will be fine. I am with you. I love you.' I wait until he has disappeared through the doors. He throws me one last look. A tear is rolling down his cheek. I see everything in his eyes. They say, 'I love you, Mama, but I'm scared.'

He manages fine.

64

The greatest journey on earth

I am finally realising a project that has been close to my heart for a long time. My long-standing friend and colleague, with whom I have made several long documentaries, the director Jean Leclerc, is starting a new television series: *Les Plus Belles Routes du Monde (The Greatest Journeys on Earth).*

This series will uncover the history of a country by following a particular route, geographical and historical, cultural and touristic. The series is being heavily financed by the hotel group Relais & Châteaux. The silent partnership comes with one condition: an indirect publicity slot for their company *in* the documentary. I oppose this way of doing things – in vain. We have to interview a member of Relais & Châteaux, to promote the quality of the wine …

I had met with Jean for two hours in Montreal the previous summer. He had asked me to find a route that we could follow to discover South Africa geographically and historically, but one without political connotations! Difficult …

We eventually decided to trace the history of the country, from its beginnings, using the freedom songs of the different peoples, blacks, whites, Indians and coloureds. But these songs would not be limited to those created to protest against apartheid.

After seven months of research and preparation, my file contains more than a thousand pages! The journey has been mapped out. We will cover more than eight thousand kilometres in three weeks, visiting all the large towns in the country and a good number of rural areas, from caves containing rock paintings to the village where Mandela spent the major part of his childhood, from the Kalahari Desert to the palace of the Zulu king, Goodwill Zwelithini. The filming is difficult to organise. I have to coordinate almost five hundred people all over the country, for twenty days. A logistical nightmare! If one domino falls, what will happen to the three or four hundred behind it?

If only I could interview Nelson Mandela in this documentary …

I met him and his wife recently. They were at my neighbour's house, the Speaker of the National Assembly, Frene Ginwala, who was celebrating her mother's ninetieth birthday. I chatted a bit with Mandela. He asked how my 'little one in Canada' was doing. I spent more time with Graça, talking about my documentary. She thought it was an original idea to discover the country through its freedom songs and told me I should do the same for her country, Mozambique. Then she asked me if I was going to interview her husband. 'I have been on the waiting list for eight years, but I hope so.' She replied simply, 'I will try to convince him.'

I know that Mandela already knows about the documentary. Two weeks ago, when I arrived in Johannesburg, my cellphone rang as soon as I switched it on. A woman's voice said, 'Just a moment, the president wishes to speak to you.' The contacts for my documentary included the president of a choir, the president of the Khoisan Association and the president of a theatre group. I did not know which was calling me. All of a sudden, I hear, 'Hallo, Lucie. How're you?' It was Mandela! 'Oh! Hi, President Mandela!' I said, surprised. The people around me on the airport moving walkway looked at me, shrugging and sighing, as if to say, 'Who does she think she is?' So I got off the moving walkway and went into a corner. Mandela and I talked about children, life, work, Graça, and he told me he would like me to come and have tea with him. Since he was about to hang up and I was trying to obtain an interview with him, I asked whether he knew about my project. 'Lucie, I can hardly hear you on the phone. Come and see me in Cape Town so that we can talk.' Yes, he knew about it. That is why he called.

A week later, I am invited to go to Mandela's house at five-thirty in the afternoon, with Loulou, Betty and the children. At five, we are all ready and I have rehearsed a proposal to obtain the interview a thousand times in my head, when … the telephone rings. It is Ella, the head housekeeper, who says, 'He is returning from Germany and has other things to do.' Meeting cancelled. I wonder if I will ever have this famous cup of tea with him or, even less likely, the interview.

Tuesday 2 March 1999. The team arrives: the director, Jean Leclerc, the cameraman, Richard Hamel, a colleague on a Radio–Québec programme *Visa Santé (Visa Health)* ten years ago, and the producer, Guy Bonnier.

We've been planning this baby for years. Jean and I have been talking about it for almost five years. We've thought out and refined the commentary down to the last detail.

I would not have been able to make this documentary when I first arrived in South Africa. I needed these years of experience, but after all this time, experiencing solitude, mingling with the crowds, preparing hundreds of reports, I am ready. A year's research for a ninety-minute radio documentary on freedom songs will serve as a framework for this TV documentary. I am ready for 'The greatest journey on earth'.

Jean, Richard and Guy are on their first trip to South Africa. I hardly ever have people from Quebec stay with me, but it's always a pleasure.

The first shoot: a boat tour of Robben Island. It's a historical re-enactment: we plunge into the end of the eighteenth century. In 1795, with various European countries falling to the French troops of Napoleon Bonaparte, an English squadron of warships sails ten thousand kilometres across the Atlantic to accomplish a mission that will change the course of South African history. Its destination: the Dutch colony of the Cape of Good Hope. Its orders: to seize the territory. The motive: the lucrative trade with the East Indies is under threat following the defeat of the Dutch monarchy at the hands of Napoleon's troops.

In two ticks, Jean and Richard transform a bland space into an extraordinary film set. With the hired costumes, you can really imagine yourself on the ocean in 1795!

When we get home, there is a fine dinner waiting for us: chicken curry and rice with vegetables, prepared by my precious nanny, Betty. She is very proud to be able to look after and spoil these men. She has been waiting for them for days.

Richard is ill. I take him to hospital. He goes reluctantly, his only frame of reference are the emergency rooms – if you can call them that – at the hospitals in Quebec. 'I don't have six hours to spend in a waiting room!' But this is a private hospital. We only wait for two minutes before he is examined and some antibiotics are prescribed.

We have the house to ourselves. The children are away on school holidays with their grandmother. My visitors transform the house, release new energy as they open their suitcases, offer anecdotes and ask questions. I rediscover South Africa through their questions. I see myself eight years ago. If I had had someone to answer my questions as I am answering theirs, perhaps I would have felt less lost. All their questions are interesting and pertinent. 'Is apartheid really dead? Are the whites afraid? Do the blacks want revenge? Why is there so much violence? Do you like South Africa?' They arrive with their quota of South African myths and legends from the reports, articles and documentaries of journalists from all over the world. South Africa is crime, blood, violence. This is the message that is broadcast clearly all over the world. Despite this, we are not involved in any incidents (although we come close a few times!), even with the equipment that is worth hundreds of thousands of rand and the characteristically Québecois naiveté of the team as far as security is concerned. Not too bad for a country that is supposed to be violent!

In the first few days of filming, the guys ask me, 'For the love of God, what are you doing in South Africa?' It is an opinion rather than a question, and I have heard it more than once over the years. By the time the shoot is over, they've discovered the answer for themselves, 'South Africa is magic.' As I tell Richard, I have not spent all these years in South Africa as a masochist. There is something here that does the soul good. You can easily find *the light* here if you have an open heart.

One afternoon, we are heading towards a dicey neighbourhood, in an industrial park in the suburbs of Cape Town. On the other side of a wide road, where it is not at all advisable to stop, a man goes by, sitting in an armchair on top of the roof of an old car wreck being drawn by a horse. 'Make a U-turn,' say Richard and Jean who think it's worth shooting. This was only the first of many, many stops. You need images like this to create a portrait of a country.

The next afternoon, after a long day of filming images of pre-history in caves three hours north of Cape Town, we arrive at a lodge for a well-deserved rest. The telephone rings. Urgent! Nelson Mandela is expecting us at six! Hit the road, guys! We must leave, it is four o'clock.

Impossible, we won't make it. We need at least three hours. The roads are dangerous. We travel at what seems two hundred kilometres an hour, and the journey is spent counting down the minutes and the kilometres.

We eventually arrive, at six-fifty. But we have missed Mandela. I meet Graça, his wife, though. She is very supportive about the documentary and says that she will organise ten minutes with the big boss. But not a minute longer! When? Who knows …

65

Security Studies 101

The following day, we go to Bredasdorp, an Afrikaner bastion three hundred kilometres south of Cape Town. Very, very white. The blacks have to sit outside to eat leftover sandwiches, all from the same plate. These blacks will play the roles of slaves in our re-enactment of the Great Trek, the great migration that took fifteen thousand Afrikaner families north. They left in 1835, with their slaves. Our black actors take to their roles so well that you could easily mistake them for real slaves! Their 'owners' look bewildered when I invite them to come and eat with us in the house afterwards.

The period of the Great Trek has left its mark on the history of South Africa. The migration of these slave owners, fleeing to retain their freedom and their convictions, symbolised the Boers' spirit of independence and gave birth to white nationalism. These Voortrekkers – pioneers – also sang freedom songs as they moved into unknown territory. We are here to reproduce these songs.

The filming has required an enormous amount of coordination, particularly with six imposing bulls, which have been transported along with the film set, in an enormous trailer. And then we have to find a field without any power lines or houses, just a field with mountains in the background. Our efforts are rewarded. The grey sky is perfect. So are the actors. One of the Afrikaners, who says he would do anything to return to apartheid times, lets off his musket during a scene that restages the 16 December 1838 clash between the Boers and the Zulus, as though he were actually living the moment.

The origin of the clash lay with Dingane, the Zulu king, the half-brother of the famous king Shaka, the Zulu warrior who became known as the 'African Napoleon' in the nineteenth century because of the enormous territories that he conquered. Dingane, who seized the throne in 1828 by assassinating his half-brother, had five hundred Boers on the Great Trek assassinated, among them their leader Piet Retief, who had come to negotiate with him in an effort to obtain some land. The incident led, on 16 December 1838 at Blood River, to one of the bloodiest battles to take place during the Great Trek.

The previous day a Boer commando of four hundred and sixty-four men, armed with rifles and cannons, had headed towards the Ncome River, known today as Blood River, on their way to meet the Zulus. Having camped there for the night, they got up at dawn to find themselves surrounded by a powerful Zulu army ten thousand strong. The four hundred and sixty-four Boers threw themselves at their adversaries. Three thousand Zulus were killed, while only three Boers were injured. This miraculous victory was interpreted by the Boers as a divine sign: God had chosen them to lead South Africa. The Boer songs reflect this belief.

We made use of this pool of white actors to shoot other scenes as well, among them that of the discovery of the first diamond. In 1866, in Hopetown, near Kimberley, Louisa and Erasmus Jacob were playing with some shiny pebbles they had found on the neighbour's farm, near the mountains of the Orange River. A travelling salesman, John O'Reilly, immediately recognised the true value of the 'pebbles' and took them with him. A small, twenty-one carat stone eventually ended up in the hands of the Colonial Secretary of the Cape, who declared, 'This diamond is the rock on which the success of South Africa will be built.'

From one day to the next, this discovery transformed the countryside, the population and the history of South Africa as a whole. The country, with its widely scattered population, its modest exports of wool, ivory and ostrich feathers, a country without roads, railway lines or banks, suddenly started to attract adventurers from all over the world. This pebble, baptised Eureka, led to the birth of Kimberly, 'the town that sparkles' in the space of only one season. Fifty thousand diamond prospectors from all over the world descended on the bars, brothels and hastily erected hotels.

After this part of the filming, we go to Johannesburg. Here I am, back in this metropolis, which moves at two hundred kilometres an hour, colourful and fascinating despite the crime. I say nothing to the guys about my fear of travelling inside a kombi – a popular choice for thieves – with our equipment, valued at hundreds of thousands of rand, in full view. I remind them of the precautions they should take, in a very nonchalant way. I say nothing to them about Terese, of whom I think every time I land here.

No one seems to agree on the origin of the city's name: Johannesburg. But the most logical account seems the following: in the wake of the adventurers fighting about diamonds, gold-diggers invade South Africa. In 1886 George Harrison, an Australian prospector, eventually discovers gold. Johann Joubert and Johannes Rissik, two government officials, are sent to the area with the mandate to choose the site of the future mining village. This is how the city of Johannesburg was born.

Although everyone rejoiced at the discovery of gold, its exploitation soon led to conflict between the Boers and the British. The Boer War, which followed between 1899 and 1902, was relentless. The Boers waged a guerrilla war in the countryside against the powerful English army, which was well equipped and highly trained. For every Boer action, the English reprisals against the civilian population were terrible. They destroyed farms and crops, took goats, cattle and sheep, anything that could feed the resistance. Finally, they took women and children and put them into what they called refugee camps, but which were in fact the first concentration camps in history. Twenty-six thousand Afrikaner women and children died of disease and negligence in the camps. The blacks were condemned to forced labour. But, unlike the whites, they were hardly ever given food. Fourteen thousand blacks died – something the history books often forget to mention. Today, one hundred years after the Boer War, gold capital of the world and the heart of the country's economic activity, Johannesburg is an enormous metropolis. But it is to the adjacent black town of Soweto that we make our way …

I adore Soweto. But I am afraid of Soweto – black and risky, beautiful and ugly, gentle and captivating, brutal and murderous. Soweto shows us a different face every few seconds. One camera is not enough for Richard. His head turns like a weathercock. And Jean finds that he needs to be able to turn more than three hundred and sixty degrees to see everything.

Mandla and Max accompany us. Mandla is Jay's bodyguard and Max is his driver. I have 'borrowed' them. We are paying them well. Mandla is sitting next to me. He has a lump under his waistcoat around the height of his belt … I am driving. Max is following us in the other car.

At one point, we stop on the main road. Jean and Richard are filming with Mandla. I am with Guy and Max. Two men, in a kombi full of holes (from bullets, not rust!), stop when they notice our equipment. Dollar signs gleam in their eyes. They are discussing – just a few metres away from us – the contents of our vehicle and what price they can get for it. Max walks over and tells them to clear off. Which they do. They were armed, Max tells me afterwards, information that I keep to myself to avoid adding any further wrinkles to Jean's face. We leave at once.

At the next stop, in front of the largest hospital in the southern hemisphere, Baragwanath (since renamed the Chris Hani Hospital), we drop off Mandla, Jean and Richard, who go off on foot to do some filming. Max stays with Guy and me. We stop at the side of the road. Max parks his car facing the wall. I would simply have left mine parallel to the road, but I do the same as him. Max gives me a quick safety lesson, 'Always park facing the wall. Put as many obstacles as possible in the way of a quick get-away for thieves.' His long years of training in camps in Russia, Tanzania and Angola have earned him the position of ensuring the safety of a minister. Max and Mandla would do anything for Jay Naidoo. Anything at all. And the last thing they would want is for the minister's wife to be killed. So I feel safe …

Max continues his 'Security Studies 101' course. Body language is crucial, he says. 'Your body language must be offensive. If you adopt a defensive attitude, it's always more difficult to get out of a situation. So it was better to go up to those chaps who were eyeing our equipment and tell them to clear off immediately, with my body straight and upright, my head up, one hand on my hip, which means, "I'm armed too" '. Max and Mandla are former Umkhonto we Sizwe soldiers. South Africa is full of soldiers. From one day to the next, or so it seems, the majority of these soldiers found themselves out of a job, untrained for anything except fighting a war. Today this generation is lost, frustrated. And armed.

Richard and Jean could spend hours in Soweto, but we have to get back to Johannesburg. We are going to have dinner in Sandton City, where the social scene has changed of late. It is no longer rare to see blacks walking up and down, briefcases in their hands, cellphones to their ears, well dressed, in this underground labyrinth of top-class shops, restaurants and offices. Just a few years ago, this scene would have been surprising, in the same way that the white beggars on the roads surprise people today.

We are in the economic heartland of Johannesburg. Jean asks me where he can film whites walking down the road. The snag is there aren't any. Jean doesn't believe me. The whites shut themselves up. They enter their offices through underground parking garages and leave in their cars, with their doors locked, and head for their homes, which crouch behind enormous walls. Although you don't see them, the whites are here, in the shopping centres, in the ultra-protected office blocks, in the well-guarded restaurants. My friend Luc Chartrand was also taken aback when he left a restaurant one evening. The guard unlocked the door and checked that all was clear before letting him out ...

So, not a white in sight! And yet the pavements are crammed with people! It is rush hour, in the middle of a business district. Yet the whites remain hidden. There are only blacks in the street. The whites are suffering from their past. They have built themselves a prison, with bars of gold, but a prison all the same.

We also go to Gold Reef City, in Soweto, an enormous theme park. It is built on a gold mine, which has been transformed into a tourist attraction. Here it is possible to descend more than a kilometre into the earth. The hard and dangerous work of extracting the gold inspired a kind of liberation music among the miners. These labourers, who came from all over, speaking different languages and dialects, used their rubber boots as musical instruments to communicate with one another. This type of dancing, born three kilometres underground and known as gumboot dancing, is still very popular. Five men, who do daily shows for the tourists, dance for us. After a week in South Africa, this is the first time the team is experiencing true African culture. A culture that vibrates with passion. A culture that colours life and stirs your soul.

The 'African' journey is just beginning. We spend a day in an

Ndebele area before moving into Zulu territory. We go to the heart of KwaZulu-Natal, to Nongoma, to the residence of the Zulu king, His Majesty Goodwill Zwelithini.

We have an appointment with the king at eleven o'clock, and we arrive at eleven sharp. The king's aide-de-camp congratulates us on our punctuality. As for His Majesty's, it could be improved … We are asked to wait in a small lounge, where they bring us sandwiches. The big hand goes all the way around the clock once. It is one of the privileges of royalty to make their guests wait. The less important you are, the longer you wait! But if we had been five minutes late, our meeting would probably have been cancelled!

King Goodwill Zwelithini arrives two hours later … in a suit and tie. I ask his assistant if His Majesty could change into the traditional costume of the Zulus: a leopard skin around his waist, a crown of leopard skin on his head, a bare torso, a feather on his head. We wait another hour in order to have an 'authentic' Zulu king.

According to protocol, you do not interrupt a king. The result: three questions and a forty-five minute response! I left the fourth question out …

His Majesty King Goodwill Zwelithini is a descendant of the father of Shaka. He was crowned king of the Zulus in 1971. For him, singing and dancing are vitally important to Zulu culture. And the freedom of the Zulu people, according to His Majesty, is protected by their king. He explains to us, passionately, the role, the place and the evolution of the freedom songs in Zulu history. Then he dances and sings to us, with thirty other Zulus, artists whose profession it is to perform for the king and his guests when the king so desires.

When we are finished, I ask the king whether I could have a photograph taken with him. He accepts with pleasure and, as he turns around to stand next to me, he accidentally pricks my leg with his spear. I pretend not to notice, because according to custom, when a king does this to a woman, he wants her as a wife …

The next day, while we're filming a reconstruction of the life of King Shaka, my telephone rings. It is Betty. Her nineteen-year-old daughter, who lives in Johannesburg, has just been raped. For an hour, between the Zulu songs, I call all my old contacts at a women's centre, a hospital, a clinic, and I get hold of a forensic surgeon, a psychologist, a social worker. I organise all sorts of appointments for her. And then I call Jay.

'Jay? Have you heard? Betty's daughter ...'

'I know! I've heard! It's dreadful. These damn men! What a curse ...'

Jay is in Johannesburg. He will take some money to Betty's daughter and ask his driver to take her to the various appointments.

I call Betty.

'Go to Johannesburg. Your daughter needs you.'

'But I don't have any money, Lucie.'

'You will have a plane ticket tomorrow morning. Pack your bag. I will pay for the ticket.'

'Thank you, Lucie! Thank you. I don't know what I would do without you.'

'Go and look after your daughter. She needs you.'

Betty is in a state. I too am panicking. I am worried that Betty's daughter may have contracted the HIV virus.

66

The president's song

I have fifty Xhosas in front of me. I want them with bare torsos and bare feet. I want them passionate, I want them full of life. This is the day that has worried me from the beginning. Because today is the day we are filming the scene illustrating the freedom song that has been ringing in my ears for a year. *Nanzi Indoda Emnyama, Verwoerd* (Beware, Verwoerd, the black man will get you), sung by Vuyisili Mini when he was hung on 6 November 1964. He was born in the Eastern Cape, as were Nelson Mandela, Steve Biko, Walter Sisulu and so many other famous South African political activists. The Eastern Cape is considered to be the cradle of the struggle against apartheid.

We are in the Lock Street Jail in East London, a prison that has been converted into a museum, built in 1880 for executions by hanging. The gaping hole, three metres deep, above which prisoners swung, is still there. In reality, Vuyisili Mini was hanged in Pretoria, but I wasn't able to get permission to film there. We are therefore going to simulate a hanging here. Craig Nancarrow, head of tourism, has agreed to open the doors of this establishment to us. I had to choose my words very carefully to convince him to 'sell' the province with a hanging!

I also had to convince Jean, because the series we are working on is supposed to be apolitical. In writing the script, I nonetheless insisted on placing a scene with a political hanging right at the beginning. I had to fight to keep the scenes portraying crucial aspects of the country's liberation from being cut from the documentary. I couldn't simply hide the reality of the nation to humour Relais & Châteaux! Jean has to defend this decision to the broadcaster.

The choir is silent. A group of about fifty workers have managed to get a day off for the filming. We have only a few hours to film this complicated scene, the most important in the whole documentary, in my view. They need to understand its importance. In two minutes, I describe what I'm looking for. With passion, we can achieve it. As if by magic, the obstacles turn into wonderful challenges.

They all know Vuyisili Mini and his songs. I ask them to imagine that they are there with him on 6 November 1964, singing with him at his death and passing on his legacy. I ask them to sing what is in their hearts, what they would like to say to the apartheid government that assassinated so many of their comrades, but with their hearts and their voices. I think the message is clear …

They sing from the depths of their hearts. The hanged corpse swings above the pit as the 'detainees' sing and walk around and around the hole. The room vibrates. Craig Nancarrow shows me the hairs standing up on his arms. A white South African with gooseflesh … *Nanzi Indoda Emnyama, Verwoerd* …

I think once again of what Desmond Tutu said to me about the power of the songs. They disconcerted the police and the soldiers. Hearing them sent shivers down their spines. A song was a weapon. In the proper sense of the word.

'Cut!' Jean and Guy are in tears. I hug them in a corner of the room. The freedom songs are like a drug. You always want more.

I am all fired up. I shout out in the way that people do at gatherings, '*Amandla!* (Power!)'

The others yell, '*Ngawethu!* (To the people!)'

'*Amandla!*'

'*Ngawethu!*'

'*Viva Vuyisili Mini! Viva!*'

'*Viva!*'

'*Viva East London! Viva!*'

'*Viva!*'

'*Viva South Africa! Viva!*'

'*Vivaaa!*'

Their last cry lasts several seconds. Its deep echo, in this chamber of death, gives us all gooseflesh. Their cry comes spontaneously, like a true cry from the heart. And these men, with their naked torsos, look at me, a silent smile on their lips, as the echo fades in the depth of the pit.

The documentary would be really complete if, in addition to this sequence of the hanging, it included an interview with Nelson Mandela! We haven't stopped trying to obtain a meeting with him. Personally, I have been trying for eight years already. Eight years of facsimiles, emails, telephone calls, meetings. In vain. Too busy. 'He's already given an interview to CBC (the English channel of Radio–Canada). Translate it,' I had already been told.

I wrote the script as though Nelson Mandela would not appear in the documentary. Because he had said so in his stories and in his interviews, I wrote that 'music, singing and dancing held a very important place throughout his life. In his struggle against apartheid, and during his twenty-seven years in prison, Mandela sang, like so many other black prisoners, one of the most popular of all the South African freedom songs, composed by Vuyisili Mini'. I am absolutely certain that Mandela sang Mini's song. *Nanzi Indoda Emnyama, Verwoerd* or *Strydom* or *Botha*. The words were adapted to the political reality of the period in question. 'Beware, head of state, the black man is coming.' Everyone sang it.

But we still have no news from the president, even though we are so close to him …

We are in Qunu, a little village lost in the far reaches of the Eastern Cape province, which is not even on the map! Qunu is, however, well known among journalists. They have often visited it with their television cameras, to collect images of 'Mandela's home', which you can just distinguish behind the walls, bars and barbed wire. This residence, which he recently had built, is a replica of the house that served as his prison for the last five years of his detention. Mandela was born in Mvezo, but his family moved to Qunu when he was still a tiny baby. It is here that he spent the major part of his childhood.

We have to find images of daily life, moving images, images that speak to you, images worth a thousand words. We find them, one after another. The grain that was ground using a large stone by a Xhosa woman from the Thembu people – Mandela's people. A woman singing a song. The crowd following suit. The village singing.

The big mama disappears, then returns with a plastic bowl, in which she washes her dishes, her clothes and her children. This receptacle becomes a drum. The rhythm of life takes form and unfolds, before us, for us, for our camera, which steals a little part of this life. The mama beats her bowl. An old man wearing a white blanket, a carved and varnished stick in his hand, a hierarchical symbol, moves to the centre of the group of women and dances. A communal trance unites them. The village might not exist on a map, but it pulses with life.

The villagers have arranged a small round hut to resemble the classroom that existed seventy-five years ago. I had told them that we wished to do a historical reconstruction of the young Rolihlahla receiving the name of Nelson on his first day at school. The classroom is full of boys and girls. A descendant of Mandela, who also carries the name Mandela, plays the future president.

Nelson Rolihlahla Mandela describes his first day at school as follows in his autobiography:

'On the first day of school my teacher, Miss Mdingane, gave each of us an English name and said that thenceforth that was the name we would answer to in school. This was the custom among Africans in those days and was undoubtedly due to the British bias of our education. The education I received was a British education, in which British ideas, British culture and British institutions were automatically assumed to be superior. There was no such thing as African culture.

Africans of my generation – and even today – generally have both a Western and an African name. Whites were either unable or unwilling to pronounce an African name, and considered it uncivilized to have one. That day, Miss Mdingane told me that my new name was Nelson. Why she bestowed this particular name upon me I have no idea. Perhaps it had something to do with the great British sea captain Lord Nelson, but that would be only a guess.'

All the inhabitants of the village then follow us to the river. About fifteen small boys bathe in the nude. As Mandela did seven or eight decades ago, right here, on these banks of reddish sand.

Rolihlahla Mandela played *thinti*, a game in which you try to hit a big piece of wood stuck into the ground with a long stick that you throw from a few dozen metres away. Mandela still has a scar on his leg as a souvenir from this game. The young Mandela proved to be talented at this game.

A woman who was the leader of the village had asked to see me, so I use the opportunity to hand over to her the small sum we have set aside in our budget for the school and the children of the village, and I thank her profusely. She in turn thanks me warmly.

We return to Qunu the next morning to film the women smoking their long pipes, a privilege they acquire at menopause. How our hormones change our lives!

% % %

We still have several thousand kilometres to cover. We move on to the north, to the Kalahari Desert, where people wear T-shirts saying, 'I survived 52 degrees'. There we film a scene with some San people singing and dancing to call the rain. And rain it did …

Returning to Cape Town, I leave my cellular phone on all the time, even during filming, because Graça Machel has informed me that I will eventually have ten minutes with her husband, at twelve-thirty. 'Someone will call you to confirm,' she promised me. Tomorrow is our last day of filming. Then it's all over.

It is midday. Graça said twelve-thirty. Ten past twelve – no news. At twelve-thirty, sitting in a small café in my suburb, five minutes away from Mandela's home, we are ready to leap up the moment we are called. At one, the phone rings.

'Nine o'clock tomorrow morning. Just ten minutes!'

'Is there a possibility that the meeting may be cancelled?'

'That is always possible with a president.'

The next morning, we are ready to leave at eight-thirty. Thank God, no one has phoned to cancel! I revise the three-minute summary I intend to give Mandela to explain our project a thousand times.

We arrive at Mandela's. It is only a hundred metres from my home, but seems a long way when you are going to do an interview! It is the first time I am going to his house. A bodyguard, standing as stiff as a soldier in a corner of the large lounge, observes the team's every movement. I am surprised to see that he is white …

These last moments are agonising. We are ready.

Ten minutes past nine; the atmosphere in the room changes. Nelson Mandela makes his entrance.

'Hello, Lucie! Nice to see you here!'

'Hello, President Mandela. It's nice to see you too! How are you keeping?'

We embrace, giving one another a warm hug. He smells so nice. I say to him, 'Can I keep my nose in your neck?'

He laughs.

He notices that I am wearing a Xhosa outfit, which I bought in Qunu, made by the village women. An outfit from his village, his people. I introduce him to the members of the team, Richard, Jean, Guy, and Louise (who has accompanied us purely because she wants to see him again). He remembers my mother and embraces her warmly.

We sit down. The camera rolls. Mandela does not like talking about himself. But he doesn't have to be asked twice to talk about the role of singing and dancing in his life. 'Singing and dancing have been present throughout my life,' he says.

I ask him to sing his two favourite freedom songs, as I have warned Graça I am going to do. 'You know, Lucie, I was told that you wanted to hear my two favourite freedom songs. Well, I only remember this one.'

And, out of the hundreds or perhaps thousands of freedom songs that exist in South Africa, he sings the very one I have chosen as the thread throughout the documentary, Vuyisili Mini's song as he walked to the gallows. We all got gooseflesh at this unusual coincidence.

The version he sings has a variation, though, *Nanzi Indoda Emnyama, Strydom.* (Beware, Strydom, the black man is coming.) He mentions Strydom rather than Verwoerd. He explains that Strydom was one of the apartheid prime ministers. Then he talks to us about Vuyisili Mini, a hero of the people, in his view. He reminds us that human beings, all over the world, but especially in Africa, long before the era of colonisation, used to sing and dance, and that they are still singing and dancing today. And that the apartheid freedom songs galvanised the people and united them to pursue the same objective.

We could not have asked for a better ten minutes from him. In fact, we get twelve minutes and six seconds. The bodyguard is tapping his watch with his finger.

Leaving, I find Jean Leclerc in the car, frozen like a block of ice. He turns slowly towards me and says' 'I am so happy that I feel like crying.' Then he gets quietly out of the car, without saying a word.

67

The African Connection Rally

Two days after my freedom song journey ends, I leave to meet up with Jay in Tunis. I sleep soundly on the plane. I am welcomed at the airport by two officials from the South African embassy, a driver and a bouquet of flowers.

I will be Mrs Naidoo for a few days.

Jay is not at the hotel, but he has left his mark on his room. I see where he has set up his meditation corner. His socks are lying on the floor. The lid has not been put back on the tube of toothpaste. The bath towel is not properly folded, and it's damp. I have stopped getting upset about this type of thing. He does make an effort when I'm around, though.

A bouquet of roses welcomes me. A note says that I am expected for a massage.

A short time later, I hear the door open and Jay immediately shouts, 'Lucie? Lucie? Are you here, Lucie?' Seeing me, he takes me in his arms. He kisses me, makes a fuss of me, laughs, tells me he loves me. He undresses me, in gentle haste, and doesn't stop telling me that he loves me, that he is happy I am there, that he needs me, my strength, my energy. Jay is happy. We enjoy a tender moment of love before going for a mudbath. Every day for the next four days, at different times of the day, we have wonderful health treatments, all sorts of baths and massages. Jay has spent the last six months training, following a strict diet, meditating and, now, pampering his body, in order to be able to survive twelve hours' driving per day for the twenty-one days of the formidable rally he is preparing to undertake.

Jay, Minister of Telecommunications of the most visible government in Africa, is also the chairman of the committee of telecommunications ministers on the continent. Their mandate is to sensitise Africa, and the world, about the need to 'connect' the continent. Jay takes the project very seriously. He wants to promote new hope for the continent: liberation through communication. He wants to do it himself, physically, on the ground, from north to south. Christened 'The African Connection Rally', the project aims to emphasise the necessity of creating a 'highway in the sky', to link Africa with the rest of the world. Jay will be driving a Pajero 4x4, with Geoff Dalglish, a motoring reporter who has completed dozens of rallies in his life. But for him this is the equivalent of what Mount Everest would be for a climber. Navin Kapila, an Indian (from India) whose thirty-nine-day round-the-world rally is entered in the Guinness Book of Records, and two mechanics will go along in another jeep. Above their heads, a helicopter and a cargo plane, transporting spares and several dozen journalists, will follow them.

Some say that this rally is a publicity stunt in preparation for the next elections, which are two months away, on 2 June 1999. They do not understand this campaign. Jay really dreams of connecting Africa. He has a message for the Tunisians, the Egyptians, the Somalians, the South Africans, white, black, Indian and everything else, 'We are all Africans.'

He is being led by his soul. This is not a political marketing ploy, because he wants to get out of that world. He has spent the last year preparing to do so. But Dr G, our therapist, and I are the only ones who know about it. He intends keeping it secret until the elections, because, he says, 'the ANC needs me'. He wants to carry this campaign through Africa, a physical and spiritual journey that will crown his political life.

Today, in Tunis, I am accompanying my husband in his mission. I sometimes dive into his world, but generally I stay in mine, alone, with my children. I look at Jay and I wonder what powerful force guides him and makes him act. Why does he not come and live with us, in Quebec, for a while? But do we choose a mission in life or are we chosen for a mission? Will we ever know the answer to this question?

My depression released in Jay a need to find himself internally. He realised that he could not keep the little coloured bottles of emotion that he has always kept tightly sealed within himself closed forever.

Jay is torn. Torn between his mission and his family. Albertina Sisulu was right to say, at our wedding, that I was Jay's second wife, that he was married first of all to his country, like her husband, Walter. Jay only comes home to change his shirt once in a while. I am hardly exaggerating. Naturally, I support him in his projects. But I do not have the marriage I dreamed of. Only the husband.

And my mission – what is that? 'Our missions are intertwined,' says Jay.

Here I am now in Bizerte, at the most northerly point on the African continent, a stone's throw from the Mediterranean. Jay needs me, at this moment. I am his pillar of moral strength. 'I need your energy.' He is leaving in a few minutes …

During the speeches, I hold Jay's arm, sitting next to him on the stage. I think of this enormous continent that he is about to cross, following an itinerary that no vehicle has ever attempted before: across the sands of the desert, across mountains and rivers. The five men will cross several regions at war and countries ravaged by crime. I am afraid, but I am confident as well.

'When I turned on the ignition of that vehicle,' Jay would later say, 'I had only one goal in mind, to get myself to the other end in one piece. Cecil Rhodes wanted to construct a railway line from the Cape to Cairo, with the aim of subjugating the continent. Now, we want to construct a technological highway from the Cape to Cairo, with the aim of liberating the continent.'

Jay would like every school, every clinic, every village, no matter how remote, to be linked to the world. In every town or village where he stops, Jay tries to communicate his passion by saying that 'the realisation of this dream will catapult us into the twenty-first century, towards sustained development, towards the social enrichment of the population and towards the freedom that can come only from knowledge and information.' He always explains that 'on a continent of more than seven hundred million people there are only forty million telephones. This is the lowest telephone density in the world. There are more telephones in Tokyo or New York than on our entire continent!' Then his voice surges and his body language becomes more expressive. 'Millions of people on our continent have never watched television (only five per cent of the population have access to it), or have even listened to the radio (twenty per cent have access to a radio). Only forty million Africans can use a telephone. And the majority of these 'fortunate' people live in towns.' He always pauses before adding, 'Half of humanity has never made a telephone call in their lives!' This journey is also a journey of African unity, an African renaissance. Because the struggle against apartheid has animated a new continental consciousness. The information highway is simply one instrument of this awakening.

Jay makes dozens of speeches. When he talks to a crowd, he burns with passion. And his charisma inflames the audience. I miss seeing him address the crowds. It was in this role that I first got to know him, the first time I ever saw him. Jay has the ability to captivate a crowd, whether there are a hundred or a hundred thousand people there. He has a gift, a power ... When a crowd of a hundred thousand got out of control at a Whitney Houston concert in the Ellis Park stadium in Johannesburg, they called Jay to calm the people down.

Today he is talking in Tunisia. Then it will be in Libya. He bridges the border between Sudan and Egypt, after a five-year crisis between the two countries resulting from an attempted assassination of Egyptian President Mubarak. Jay reunites the ministers of telecommunications of the two countries and the three of them, arm in arm, launch a new era 'because communication is the only viable route'. He helps release Libya from its worldwide isolation through the use of telecommunications. He is welcomed by dozens of thousands of people all along his journey, simple, ordinary people who believe in his dream and would like to bring it to fulfilment, with him, for the good of everyone.

I was choked with tears when the grey Pajero left. The television cameras were trained on me. I barely had two seconds to wipe my cheeks. Karen Lubbe – the girlfriend of Geoff Dalglish, Jay's co-pilot – was clinging to my arm, sobbing wildly. But I had to get a hold of myself, having accepted the role of 'Mrs Jay Naidoo' and the related media responsibilities of such occasions. I returned to Johannesburg after a few interviews.

Ten days later, I go to Kenya with Karen Lubbe to meet up with our 'men' halfway. They arrive in Nairobi a day late, having suffered some damage from bad fuel. The two mechanics accompanying the team have a tough time repairing the damage.

While waiting, I stay in the hotel. It appears that, as far as crime is concerned, Nairobi has become even more dangerous than Johannesburg. A member of the rally planning team has been threatened with a knife at her throat.

It is late evening when we are told, by means of police walkie-talkies, that the procession is on its way. I go down to the street in front of the hotel. The Kenyan Minister of Telecommunications follows me. 'I'm staying at your side, because I know that he will come straight to you!' Which is what happens. Getting out of his car, ignoring the crowd of journalists, cameras, photographers, ministers, officials and spectators, Jay rushes into my arms. Then we have to surrender ourselves to rounds of speeches, an official dinner and media conferences before we finally meet back at our hotel room, in the early hours of the morning.

The group is back on the road early the next morning. 'If you knew how much I needed these few hours with you. I don't think I would have been able to keep going without the thought of them,' Jay whispered in my ear before leaving.

Ten days pass quickly and Jay finally arrives in South Africa. I am able to follow everything on the Internet site [africanconnection.org], which posts new photographs of the rally's progress every day. In addition, SABC Television is covering the rally and gives a five-minute report every morning. I was interviewed in Nairobi, at dawn, live by satellite. They also managed to make contact with Jay using a portable satellite telephone, and we spoke to one another, live on air. Jay admitted that he was lost deep in the bush. I asked whether that was his excuse for not having phoned me the day before ...

The end of the rally is spectacular, because Jay is in his own country. The normally very quiet little village of Cape Agulhas (the village where, in April 1996, a restaurant refused to serve us because of the colour of our family) is crawling with people; a helicopter flies over the tip of Africa, where we are all waiting, in a howling gale. Singing and dancing welcome the guys when they finally reach the most southerly tip of this sacred continent. Jay is relieved. That's an understatement. But the journey is not yet over. The cavalcade has to continue to Cape Town, another three hours' driving. Jay gets into the Toyota Previa with me and the children.

It was a great moment. It was a great adventure. I worked closely with Sue de Villiers, one of the project coordinators. At times we had to deal with the crises. The public only saw the smiles and promises of communication. Mandy Woods and Joan Nowak, Jay's press and administrative secretaries, worked like maniacs, following him everywhere, preparing everything as they went, sometimes at the last minute. Around a dozen people worked day and night for more than two months to make this project a reality. And Jay is conscious of this, even if today the glory is his.

A few days later, at a great banquet, one of the two Pajeros that had made the journey was put on display in the hall of the banquet venue. The vehicle was dirty, covered in mud, as if it had come out of the jungle. According to Jay, the vehicles were never that dirty. The one on display had been intentionally muddied.

The whole family, except Léandre, attends the celebration, even Betty, who is dressed as though she is attending the wedding of a king.

Sue de Villiers and I have arranged a little surprise for Jay: I am going to make a speech during the banquet. Jay knows nothing about it. The master of ceremonies, a TV personality called Bobby Brown, is in on the plan. First of all there are the speeches by, among others, Minister Kader Asmal, standing in for Deputy-President Thabo Mbeki, the presidents or chief executive officers of the three large companies that have sponsored the rally – Siemens (technology), Vodacom (cellular) and Telkom (telephone) – and the Deputy Mayor of the City of Cape Town. Then, by video, the Secretary General of the Organisation of African Unity, Dr Salim Salim, congratulates Jay on the great mission that has been accomplished.

Then it's my turn. The sheets of paper on which I have written what I am going to say will not stay in place on the lectern. I cling to the lectern like a lifebelt in the middle of the ocean. I can see nothing in front of me; the spotlights are too powerful. Neither, fortunately, can I see the giant screen behind me, which seems to magnify the smallest sign of nervousness. Certain dignitaries who took my communications courses are in the room. I must put into practice what I taught them! It is not easy! I told them, among other things, not to read, but to speak directly to people. I, however, am incapable of doing so without my papers in front of me.

I start off in French, 'Monsieur le vice-maire, ministres, dignitaires, mesdames et messieurs, bonsoir (Mr deputy mayor, ministers, dignitaries, ladies and gentlemen, good evening).' Then I change over to English:

'That's another African language [the French], but I will continue in English, because even Jay, after eight years of living in a French-Canadian household, doesn't really speak French. When I moved here in 1991, my four-year-old son, Léandre, didn't speak a word of English. Two months later, Léandre was perfectly bilingual, with the English Indian Durban accent and everything, and Jay could say, 'Bonjour, comment ça va?' Then came Kami. He said, 'With Kami at least I'm starting from scratch.' At three years of age, Kami was perfectly bilingual, and Jay? Not really. Then came Shanti. So he said, 'Okay, now for sure, I'll learn French.' She's three now and bilingual. Jay still doesn't really speak French. So I said, 'Jay, you're almost there. I know, let's make another child and you'll really speak French.' He said, 'No, no, no, its OK. I'll go and buy a CD-ROM course!'

He went and bought a CD-ROM course and started learning at home on the computer. The computer, which is part of the furniture, like the Internet, email, fax, and, of course, the phone, has become one of our basic needs. Our three children, twelve, six and three years old, all use the computer, for games of course, but also to communicate and to learn. Léandre surfs the Web and does a lot of his school research on it. Kami and Shanti send electronic postcards to their grandparents in Quebec. You can say it has become a staple to us.

About two years ago, Jay came home one night after having a real boy's talk with Navin Kapila, one of the drivers of this rally and the Guinness Book of Records holder for a rally around the world, and he asked me, 'What would you say if I did a rally across the African continent?' I said, 'You're crazy. What for?' He said, 'Because the majority of the children on this continent don't have the opportunities that our children have.' That was the seed that he planted that night. He said it was not just a car rally, but a rally in the full sense of the word: to rally people around one cause. A rally to open telecentres, to install phones, faxes, the Internet and email, so that all children could have a place in our future. A rally to market a continent that often carries a disturbing image to people: 'Don't come here unless you really have to.' Because when we talk about Africa abroad, it's always to say, 'Africa? Now what's the problem?'

And Jay went to bed that night with a dream – a dream of discovering the other Africa that nobody talks about; a dream of connecting Africans among themselves, and Africa to the world. A dream of connecting the children of today to the future of our planet.

I'm sure some of you know or have heard of Marshall McLuhan, a Canadian writer who was the most famous communications theorist of his time. McLuhan is best known for coining the phrase 'the medium is the message', which became popular in the 1960s. His unorthodox theories on communications sprang from his conviction that electronic media themselves have an impact far greater than the material they communicate. He argued that technology transforms the basic structures of society. McLuhan was also the first to predict that every part of this planet would be electronically connected and would eventually produce a huge 'global village'. This of course includes Bizerte and Cape Agulhas, Botlokwa, Sirte, Alexandra and Alexandria, Wadougane, Yabelo, Morogoro, Mzuzu, Chipata and Hadar, and of course, all African towns.

Ironically, the single most frustrating thing during this rally was that there were no phones to get into contact with Jay. It's a disempowering feeling not being able to use a phone when and where you want to. Since Jay is a minister, that's usually the way we do our pillow talk – I put my phone on the pillow. A phone fulfils the basic need of wanting to say, 'Hi, how's it? I'm with you. I love you.' Jay and I wouldn't be together today if it wasn't for the phone. Our courting was done across two continents. He'd phone and I'd answer. That's how a phone can change people's lives. It can even save lives. With 'telemedicine', for example.

The first time I had a real telephone conversation with him during the rally without getting cut off or having to shout was last Friday when the rally entered Malawi. He was tired and exhausted, but in good spirits. After a good fifteen minutes' conversation, I asked him, 'Jay, are you happy?' He said, 'Oh, it's a logistical nightmare and this is difficult and …' I said, 'No, no, Jay. Are you happy, inside, in your guts, with yourself?' There was a three-second silence, then he said, 'Lucie, I believe in what I am doing.'

I think that says it all. And I think the African Connection Rally is a first step to giving full meaning to what Marshall McLuhan said more than 30 years ago. Because the global village means nothing without Africa!

I would like to ask a true African, in heart and in spirit, Minister Jay Naidoo, a man I believe in, to please come and share a few words with us. Thank you.

This was the last speech I made in South Africa. It was different from the others. I was not a journalist this time, but a wife. Jay said that this speech was the best present he could ever have wished for. And his, which followed, was electrifying. 'I have a good teacher, as you can see,' he said.

His political mission is complete. A new mission is starting: that of connecting Africa. Is it possible to do so from Quebec? Because for me the moment of return is approaching. I want to live near Léandre, who is living in the Outaouais region in Quebec. With or without Jay, I will be leaving. As soon as the elections have passed, in two months' time, I will complete the 'mandate' I had given myself: to cover the Mandela era, from his release from prison to his retirement from public life.

When I get home that night, a woman who also has 'a mission' calls me. Her voice is weak. Sue Sparks is very ill. Her cancer has now attacked her liver. She thanks me for everything and tells me that she is proud of Jay and that she believes in him. She asks to speak to him. She wants to speak to my mother as well.

The next day, 28 April 1999, I call her to tell her that I'm coming to see her the following Saturday, 1 May. She turns fifty-five on 8 May and I want to see her before that. 'I am coming to have lunch with you.' Despite her illness, despite her weakened state, I need her strength, her energy, her positive spirit.

Twenty-four hours later, Allister phones me. Sue has just passed away. The following Saturday I go to her funeral. Up to this point, it hasn't really hit me. All her friends are there, everyone except her. I cry when I see her coffin.

Sue has prepared everything for her own funeral, down to the smallest detail. She left us a few words that I will keep forever. In them, she quotes a French psychologist, 'It is not faith, but the depth of living that you leave behind you that allows you to abandon yourself to the arms of death.'

Then she adds, 'I hope that this does not sound like self-satisfaction, but I believe that my life has not lacked meaning. I feel privileged to have met people of integrity and great stature and to have been influenced by them, but I have learnt just as much from poor, disadvantaged people for whom daily life was a struggle, but who triumphed in spite of everything and became heroic.'

Allister told me later that two weeks before Sue died, President Mandela had called her. He knew that she was ill. He was in the area. 'I will be there in ten minutes,' Mandela said.

Allister and Sue welcomed the entourage. Nelson Mandela spent an hour with her on the terrace. They talked a lot. As if there was only an hour to say everything. Then he left.

Sue had an African soul. She believed in the philosophy of *ubuntu*, a word that means 'a person is a person through other people'. A sort of antithesis to individualism. As a result of the way she lived, because she believed in *ubuntu*, she will live forever, through the lives of the people that she changed and influenced.

68

The hidden camera

The telephone rings. It is Jay. He is in Johannesburg, campaigning for the elections.

'Lucie, I am busy closing all my files and I need to sort out the money that I gave you in Kenya, do you remember, the dollars.'

'Yes, I remember. Don't worry.'

In Nairobi he had entrusted me with his allowance for expenses. He doesn't like to carry cash around with him. He prefers a credit card. When I returned to Cape Town, I hid the notes away with my own cash. Three thousand dollars altogether, most of it money I was saving, in an envelope in the bottom of a drawer in my bedroom, a place no one would look. Even Betty, discreet as she is, does not clean out these drawers.

Putting down the phone, I nonetheless go and look through the drawer to assure myself that the money is still there.

Catastrophe! The envelope is no longer there! I am on my way out and I can't afford to be late. I go to look for Betty in the kitchen. My knees are trembling. Three thousand dollars is a lot of money. It's almost as much as Betty earns in a year. I start doubting myself. Perhaps I hid the notes somewhere else.

I ask Betty if she has seen a white envelope with a lot of money in it. She says no. And then she starts to panic with me. She says she will go and look for it, I mustn't worry, the money has to be somewhere in the house. I search my office, then go back to my bedroom and call Jay back. I shout at him, in front of Betty, 'But why did you entrust that money to me? I have lost it! I have lost it!' I am in tears.

Louise gets up, woken by the racket. Kami and Shanti don't understand what is happening. I ask them whether they have seen the envelope. 'What envelope, Mama?' They have not seen it. I see it in their eyes. Louise looks at Betty and says dryly, 'I hope it's not you, again.' What? An insult! How dare she accuse Betty? Immediately suspect she's guilty just because she's a black domestic?

I am annoyed with my mother for being so short with Betty, who now has tears in her eyes. 'But it's not her fault! I'm the one who's lost the money! It's my fault! Everything is my fault!' Then I leave the house, asking Betty to empty *everything* in my room, to look everywhere, in every corner, even among the socks and underclothes.

I get to my massage appointment exhausted and embarrassed at the scene I have caused. I shouted at Louise, Kami and Shanti. Liz, the masseuse, tells me to let the tears come, to let it all out. I close my eyes. I tell myself that it's only money, after all. Only money. A lot of money. We are always short of money. I need it to work. I need it for my children, for housekeeping, for my return to Quebec. But it's only money.

Two hours later, I return home. My bedroom looks like it has been hit by a tornado. My mother has emptied out all the drawers and cupboards. 'I told Betty I would do it,' she says, examining each item of clothing.

'Nothing?'

'Nothing.'

'Lucie … I have my doubts about Betty. The two suitcases that she put in the entrance hall last week … She hasn't stopped talking about them.'

Betty had put two suitcases next to the front door. They stood there for two weeks, locked. My colleague from Radio–Canada, Sylvain Desjardins, and the assistant he had employed, my friend Karen Lubbe, had promised to take them to Johannesburg for her and drop them off at Betty's sister's place. She would thus have less luggage to carry on the bus when she went back home. We were moving soon and I did not see anything fishy about it.

Louise and Betty spend several hours a day chatting.

'She never stopped saying to me last week that she hoped you didn't think she was leaving with anything that belonged to you.'

The thought hadn't even crossed my mind.

'Betty wouldn't steal anything from me, Louise. Never. Not Betty.'

Louise knows my affection for Betty. She also knows that Betty adores us and that she would never do us any harm. It is so easy to accuse someone weaker than yourself, especially, I tell myself, someone who has been oppressed all her life. But then, not only would Betty not do something like this to me, but she would be even less likely to do it to Jay, the man who has spent his whole life fighting for the rights of workers, of blacks, of the poor, of women.

Nonetheless, the more Louise says, the more I start to doubt.

'You think that the money could be in her cases? We can set our minds at rest about that.'

I call Karen in Johannesburg to ask her where she has taken the cases. I want her to get them back and open them. She interrupts me.

'Lucie, I'm sorry, the cases are still here. I haven't had time to take them yet.'

'What? They are still with you? Open them!'

'But they are locked!'

We need Betty's permission to open them. We have to go by the book in case our evidence becomes unusable. A rapist recently went free on a technicality – a policeman had not followed the prescribed procedure when collecting evidence.

If Betty has stolen this money, it would be the most dreadful betrayal after everything we have done for her. But I don't want to believe that she is guilty. I cook up a plan to prove to everyone, myself included, that Betty is not a thief.

I shut myself in my office, telling Louise and the children that I have work to do, reports to prepare. Which is true. But I also want to execute my plan: hide my video camera in the office and film Betty. She comes in here every morning when I leave to drive the children to school. When I get back, my office is tidy, my papers are in order.

I will leave my handbag here. Thieves, real thieves, compulsive thieves, cannot stop themselves from stealing. Or at least checking whether there is anything to steal.

On Monday morning, 31 May, we follow our usual routine. I have not slept very well, but I don't let anything show. I feel like a traitor towards Betty. Her words come back to me, 'I will never work for any other family after working for you. It's paradise working for you. Everyone envies me!' she always says. 'I will be changing your children's nappies one day,' she tells Léandre. I feel awful putting her to the test. I hate suspecting her. But Louise trusts her instinct and money has been disappearing. 'Beware of the gardeners, Lucie,' Betty constantly tells me. 'You leave the doors open too often.'

This morning, before I leave, I turn the camera on. I leave my bag in the office, after marking every note in my wallet with a tiny red dot.

I drop the children at school. Betty is undoubtedly in my office. I told her I was going to the gym, so she won't feel rushed … I know the tape will tell me the truth. If she doesn't even look in my handbag, I'll be almost certain she is innocent.

I return home, butterflies in my stomach. I can't go to my office straight away. My routine is to go to the kitchen, make myself a cup of coffee, read the front page of the paper, chat with Betty about my work, about this evening's dinner, about Jay's suit that needs to be cleaned.

Calmly, with my usual smile and a few words of encouragement, which I lavish on Betty every morning, I leave the kitchen, my stomach in a knot. I want to explode, but I act as if this Monday morning is like any other Monday morning.

Entering my office, I nervously put my cup of coffee down on the corner of my desk. I spill a few drops. I am trembling! To betray or be betrayed – both are terrible.

I climb onto a chair to get the camera down from where it is hidden among books and documents. I rewind the cassette. This is the moment of truth.

I sit down at my desk, pick up my cup of coffee. A mouthful. It's hot. I open the little screen and press PLAY.

The scene that unfolds before my eyes crushes me. Not only does Betty rifle through my handbag and my wallet (she counts the money without taking any), but she opens my diary and studies my appointments. She looks through every little compartment in my handbag. She takes out my shopping slips and examines them before replacing them in *exactly* the same place. Then she cleans the office, reading all my papers in the process. She opens the drawers, examines the things inside, takes out the papers and glances through them. You can hear her picking up cassettes – I have hundreds of recordings – and putting them back.

She comes within a hair's breadth of looking right into the lens, but she doesn't see it. A hair's breadth and all would have been lost. Her cleaning isn't finished, but I stop the camera. I collapse! Sobs rack my whole body. I don't believe it. I don't want to believe it. I call Jay, still in tears. I describe my plan and its results. And I tell him about the suitcases.

Jay is dumbstruck. 'But I treated her better than a member of my own family all these years!' He is still in the middle of the election campaign – the elections take place in two days' time. 'I'm coming with the suitcases,' he says, still incredulous. And he drops all his activities, his appointments, his speeches, to jump onto a plane. Jay has no pity for thieves. 'Don't let on that anything's wrong,' Jay warns me. 'Don't say anything. Act normally.'

An hour later, I come out of my office, the camera in my hand, and I bump into Betty. It's not at all unusual for her to see me carrying a camera. It's part of my work. She often sees me with headphones on my ears or a mike in my pocket. I give her a big smile to tell her that the elections are nearly here, that she will be able to vote for the second time in her life. I go into Louise's room and play her the section of tape where Betty spends a good fifteen minutes rummaging through my things. Louise turns pale, 'I knew it.'

I have a report to prepare, my mind is elsewhere. I go to fetch the children from school. For them, life couldn't be more normal. But mine has just come up against a brick wall. It's incredible how much energy you have to summon up to pretend that everything is fine. I am exhausted. Dinner must take place normally. Fortunately, the children are there. Louise and I get them to talk, to lighten the atmosphere, so that we can take refuge in silence, which requires less energy. Betty comes to play with Shanti for a few minutes during the meal as she usually does. Jay should arrive soon. With the suitcases. 'Tell Betty she has made a nice supper, Shanti.' Is the money inside the suitcases? 'Have you done your homework, Kami?' The phone rings. 'Hello, may I help you?' says Betty, in that gentle, polite, respectful tone of voice that once seduced me. It's Radio–Canada. No, not to ask me for a story; there's another journalist looking for a South African who can speak French.

Jay eventually arrives. He puts the suitcases in the garage, where Betty is not likely to see them.

We put the children to bed, then Jay and I meet in my office to plan our strategy. He wants to question Betty – without telling her that we have the videotape. He wants to get her to confess. If she confesses, we will ask her to write a letter of resignation and to disappear from our lives.

Just the previous week, I had said to her once again that I would take care of her to the end of her days. I had given her various things as gifts – my mixer, my toaster, the sewing machine I had bought for Louise, clothes, sheets and blankets, games, a bike, lamps, a radio – in part to relieve my guilt about abandoning her after her four years of service. I had also planned something to thank her for her devotion: a bouquet of flowers and a bonus of several thousand rand.

We are ready. Jay asks me to go and fetch Betty. I go to the kitchen, where she is tidying up the dishes from dinner, and tell her that Jay wants to see her in my office. She nods to indicate that she has understood. I think that she has noticed the tension in the air. She is not singing in the kitchen this evening, as she normally does.

At Jay's request, I have set up my tape recorder in the office. It is on. We want evidence.

Fifteen minutes, twenty minutes, thirty minutes go by. Betty is still in the kitchen. This is not like her. She 'obeys' immediately when Jay asks her to do something. Jay, who is waiting nervously in the office, cultivating further doubts about Betty's guilt (she didn't take anything from my wallet, according to the videotape), becomes impatient and demands that she come at once. I am too nervous to face Betty again. I delegate the task to Louise. She goes into the kitchen and, in a firm voice, says that Jay is waiting for her *now*.

Betty leaves her pots and pans and, moves towards my office at a snail's pace. Louise and I are in the little lounge, nervous, not knowing what to expect.

The door remains closed for fifteen minutes.

'Have you ever taken money in this house?'

'No, never.'

'Have you ever looked through Lucie's handbag?'

'No, never. I would never do that.'

'Have you ever opened Lucie's wallet without her permission?'

'No, never. I would never do that, Jay. I love you. You are my family.'

'Do you deny having stolen any money or looked through Lucie's things, her handbag?'

'I deny everything. I would never do that.'

Betty leaves the office without saying a word. She goes to her room and leaves the kitchen in a mess, which is not normal for her.

Jay is devastated.

'She denies everything.'

'Everything?'

'She denies ever having looked through your bag. She denies having taken any money. She denies having taken the three thousand dollars. She denies everything.'

We don't know what to do now. We don't have enough evidence of her guilt, because she didn't take anything when I filmed her this morning.

It's at this point that I mention to Jay that I watched the whole hour and a half of the videotape and that on it Betty makes some telephone calls, first one in English, then a second in Northern Sotho, her mother tongue, using the other line, the one for the computer modem. Jay finds it odd that she changes lines.

We play the tape again. In the English conversation, Betty talks about a dangerous atmosphere in the house. She says she thinks I have set a trap for her by leaving my handbag in the office, something I never do. Why would she use the word 'trap' if she wasn't in the habit of looking through other people's bags? A handbag left in plain sight would not constitute a trap for anyone who did not rummage through other people's things. Now I know why she hasn't taken the money in my bag: she suspected it was a trap.

In this conversation she also reports that I have announced my intention to call the police if I do not find the stolen money. She mentions that she now has another adversary, Louise, whose attitude has changed and who no longer talks to her; that my mother is on my side …

About a quarter of an hour later she comes into the office again and picks up the telephone for the modem to make the second call in her mother tongue. Later, we would find out that she was speaking to her sister, her accomplice. It was at her home that Karen was supposed to drop off the suitcases …

The story becomes more complicated. What worries us – Jay especially – is that she switches lines for the second call. This is not normal behaviour. It reminds Jay of the precautions taken in the underground, at the time of the struggle against apartheid. Jay is a minister today. Could Betty be a spy? Jay always has important files with him. Even if he doesn't have anything to hide, he often has confidential files with him.

'We have to call the police, Jay. This is too serious. What if it's more than a simple theft? What if our security is at risk? Yours, mine, the children's?'

'You're right. I'll make a call.'

Jay has 'friends' everywhere. He calls the brother of one of his colleagues. Let's call him 'Joe'. This man is one of the top officials in the South African intelligence services. Jay wants his opinion before taking any legal action, before making any accusations.

'Joe will come over tomorrow,' says Jay, putting down the receiver. 'Let's go to bed. It's late.'

'Where are the suitcases?'

'In the garage. Betty won't find them.'

'Shouldn't we look inside them?'

'We need to think a bit. Let's go to bed, Lucie.'

That night we go to bed with our heads full of questions without answers. Who is Betty? Who is this woman we have been living with for four years? I still have doubts. I am still hoping that there is another explanation for our evidence and that Betty will be found innocent.

69

The confession

The following morning, we have to continue pretending nothing is wrong. Betty doesn't know about the videotape. But the tension is palpable. Louise is very tense. Betty obviously hasn't slept a wink – she is pale and has dark rings under her eyes.

Shanti gets up.

'Hello, Betty! Are we having pancakes this morning?'

'Of course, my love.'

Shanti adores Betty's pancakes. Shanti was born with Betty. Betty is her nanny, her friend, someone she trusts. I can leave my children with two people without worrying about them: my mother and Betty.

Kami enjoys his pancakes. 'Your pancakes are delicious, Betty,' he tells his nanny. The family goes about its business as usual.

The elections will take place tomorrow. They mark the end of the era of Mandela, who, as he promised in 1994, is retiring at the end of his term in office. The end of the Mandela era marks the end of a period of my life in South Africa. And I have so many reports to do before I leave! Jay is theoretically still running for election.

Joe will not be coming before dinner time. He is snowed under with security concerns surrounding the elections. But he will come this evening because Jay is involved.

Betty cleans the house as usual, but without humming. I spend the day in my office reading the papers, listening to news bulletins and writing reports for Radio–Canada. Work is the best remedy against worry.

Betty must be starting to wonder what we are cooking up. Everything is too calm, as if nothing has happened. It's possible that she thinks I've simply had a panic attack because of the disappearance of the money, and that Jay has questioned her simply to reassure me. Betty is intelligent. Very. And cunning as well. Too cunning.

Dinner passes normally. The children tell us about their day at school. We talk about tomorrow's elections. With the meal finished, it's time for the children's baths, and at precisely that moment Joe rings the front doorbell. Louise takes care of the little ones. Betty is cleaning up the kitchen. Jay and I sit down with Joe in the main lounge where we receive our guests. I have lit a fire in the grate. It is cold. I am trembling, from cold or from fear, I am not sure. Jay outlines the events, then we go into the office to view the video cassette. Joe is staggered. And impressed with my idea of hiding the camera. 'We have enough material to open an investigation. I'll call my colleagues at once and get them to do the initial interrogation.'

Joe is not a policeman in the true sense of the word. To follow legal procedure, he therefore has to call the police for the interrogation.

Thirty minutes later, the doorbell rings again. It is the police. They are excited to be meeting Jay, but also concerned, since the matter relates to his security.

The four men sit down at the large table at the end of the lounge. They prepare the interrogation, discuss their strategy and then view the cassette. They agree that they have never seen anything like this.

I am getting ready to go and comfort Louise when Jay calls me.

'Go and fetch Betty.'

'Is everything ready?'

'Yes, we're ready. Go and fetch her.'

I go out through the kitchen door that leads to Betty's room. I knock and, without waiting for her to open the door, say:

'Jay wants to see you at once.'

I cannot look her in the eye.

Betty goes into the main lounge and sits down at the end of the table. Joe and the two policemen thank us and tell us they will call us in a while.

We close the two doors that give access to the main lounge and sit down in the small family lounge. Louise smokes one cigarette after another. She recalls all the occasions on which she has 'lost' money. She tells us how one day she caught Betty holding Jay's wallet – wide open. 'I found it on the floor,' was her immediate excuse. 'Why didn't you tell me this before?' I ask Louise. The smallest incidents we can remember now become suspicious. Jay and I can both think of times, in Johannesburg and in Cape Town, when money disappeared.

It is after ten. We are exhausted. But we are all a bundle of nerves.

I hear the main lounge door close. Are they finished? I go to see. Betty has gone. I call Jay. We all sit at the large table.

'She denies everything.'

'Everything?'

'Everything.'

They looked at the video cassette with her and despite that she continues to deny it! I do not understand.

'She would pass a lie detector test without a problem. This woman has exceptional self-control.'

And I thought I could get her to sign a letter of resignation this evening! I would have liked her to leave in the morning, first thing, for Johannesburg. I was ready to pay for her bus ticket in order to get her out of our lives.

'I can't do anything more,' says Joe. 'It's now up to the police to open an investigation and follow procedure.'

Jay agrees and thanks the men.

I shout, 'Wait! Give me a few more minutes. You need a confession, don't you?'

'A confession in writing and signed, yes.'

'Can you give me ten minutes with Betty? I will get you your confession!'

They are sceptical. Jay looks at his watch, but I look at him insistently. They indicate that they agree.

'Come with me, Jay. I need your support.'

We both sit down in the small family lounge. I send Louise to fetch Betty.

'Do you really think you can get her to confess?'

'Leave it to me. I know Betty. I know what to say.'

Betty comes into the lounge, her head not quite as high as in the presence of the policemen. Jay is nervous. I have never seen him so tense! I am trembling myself. All this seems like a bad dream.

Betty sits down on the couch. I give her a little smile. And I drop my little bombshell.

'Betty, I know that you take money out of my wallet now and again. We all have good and bad points. I have learnt to live with your weaknesses, just as you have learnt to live with mine. I know that you need money and that you have three children you adore, and I know that you do your best. I know that you need money for them because you want to give them the best. So I have learnt to turn a blind eye to this petty theft. But lately ...'

She interrupts me. I wasn't expecting that.

'Yes, Lucie, I admit that I take the odd twenty-rand note from your wallet now and again.'

I am flabbergasted. Absolutely staggered. Her words ring in my head – *I admit that I steal now and again.* I am still hoping she will protest her innocence; that my wonderful gentle Betty – who has carried Shanti on her back for years, cooked us delicious meals every evening, hugged me to tell me how happy she was with us – has not betrayed us. One day, Betty had said to my mother, 'Lucie didn't even wash the sheets when I had to sleep in her bed. I don't know any other white person who would do that!' Betty, my friend beyond barriers of race or class. *I admit that I steal now and again ...*

She continues,

'But the American money – never! I swear it, Lucie! I would never steal so much money! It wasn't me. I swear it, it wasn't me.'

I want to believe her. I do believe her. Then I start to doubt. One minute I trust her, the next I doubt her. A pendulum that is driving me mad! Jay suddenly gets up and leaves the room. He is shattered. He had not expected this confession either. He can't deal with the emotions aroused by this betrayal.

'Betty, this is really difficult for me. But the police are not joking. These men are serious. They are doing their job. They are going to arrest you and put you in prison.'

'But I can't go to prison! I have children. What will happen to my children? Lucie, I beg you, help me. I beg you, Lucie!'

'I am helping you because you have children. That's the only reason I am helping you. I have children and I know their lives would be ruined if I went to prison.'

Silence.

'I've done everything for you, Betty! Everything! I don't understand how you could have done this to us. But I am going to help you. Listen. I know for a fact that if you cooperate with the police, it will be much easier for you. If you tell them what you have done, write a confession for example, it will show your goodwill and be easier for you.'

'Okay. What must I write?'

'Wait here. I'll be right back.'

I go back to the men, who all look at me enquiringly, including Jay.

'She is going to write a letter and sign it. What must she write?'

The men look at one another. They don't ask me how I got the confession. They take off their jackets and sit down. The matter has just taken a new turn. I put a few logs on the fire, then go and make some coffee. It could be a long night.

Jay gets up to go and call a lawyer friend to advise him on what the confession should look like in case it needs to be used in court one day.

It is past eleven. Betty is still waiting, sitting passively in the lounge. I signal her to come with me. We sit down at the small round table in the family cubicle where we have our meals. Jay sits down without saying a word. He is no longer in control of his emotions. He no longer knows how to stifle them. I am the one who has to ensure that things are done as required. I explain to Betty that she has to write a confession and ask her what she wants to confess. She says she will write that she has stolen money and that she is resigning from her job.

It takes a long time. Betty writes in capital letters. She is not able to write in cursive. Letter by letter, she writes her confession. In black and white, I can read her betrayal. I don't let it get me down. I have to be strong. I have to show Betty who has the power. I keep calm. I lift my head. I watch her write without a trace of hesitation the words 'I admit having stolen money from the Naidoo-Pagé family … I hereby also tender my resignation to the South African government, my employer …' We had to go to so much trouble to get her this job! I even paid an extra fee for her.

She signs and dates it at the bottom of the page.

'That's all for the moment. Go and wait in your room. I will call you later on.'

She gets up quietly, calmly. Betty has always been so calm, in all circumstances. But her calm takes on an entirely different meaning today. Her calm is suspicious.

I return to the men, who are not showing any signs of impatience, despite the late hour. The elections will be taking place in a few hours! I give them the confession. They are amazed. Then the three men go through the handwritten confession. Joe and the two policemen look at one another. Their look says it all.

'If she admits this, she's hiding a lot more. This is just the tip of the iceberg.'

How can they be so certain? Because criminals with their backs to the wall will confess to a minor crime if they think their confession offers a way out. Experience has taught police that a confession of a minor crime generally hides a mountain of secrets.

We call in the man responsible for the maintenance of the ministerial housing. He is in fact Betty's immediate boss. He arrives within a few minutes, since he lives only about a hundred metres away. We inform him of Betty's confession and her resignation.

'You realise that if she resigns she keeps all her social benefits and will receive a pension? If she is guilty, she must be fired. Then she loses everything. You are being very nice to her by not dismissing her.'

'I don't care about the money,' I say. 'I simply cannot live with her in my house any longer. She must leave tomorrow morning.'

The procedure for firing a domestic worker employed by the government is a long one. The real irony is that Jay is the reason for this, because he fought for their union protection!

'I will keep the letter until tomorrow morning, but you need to think carefully about your course of action,' says her boss.

'What do you know about Betty?' asks Jay.

'I know that she has been receiving large parcels lately, almost every week.'

'What kind of parcels?'

'Things she has bought by catalogue. Crockery, all sorts of things.'

He leaves, followed by Joe and the two policemen.

Jay closes the door behind them and takes me in his arms.

'Wait! I forgot something!' I run outside and catch Joe, 'There's one more detail.' I suddenly remind myself of Lieutenant Colombo, the famous television series detective, who always comes back for one last detail.

'What is it?'

'It's just that I recently wrote Betty a letter of recommendation, since we are leaving the country. I said in the letter that Betty's integrity is beyond compare, that she is honest and that I would strongly recommend her, even for President Mandela!'

Joe stares at me, incredulous. Then he says, 'You have to find that letter.'

'Must it be destroyed?'

His look answers my question. It must be destroyed, and at once!

I go back into the house. I had informed Jay a few weeks before that Betty had asked me for a letter of recommendation. I reveal the contents of the letter to him. Jay's face falls.

'We have to lay a charge,' I say, 'and start court action.'

He shrugs his shoulders.

'Aren't you the first to say that you would not hesitate to lay a charge against someone who steals, even ten cents?'

'Yes, but against Betty … She's like a member of the family. I didn't know that this betrayal would have such an effect on me. I don't want to see her again.'

'Come, let's have a little brandy and we'll discuss it with Loulou.'

70

The suitcases

Jay and I join Louise in her bedroom. The room is full of smoke. It is almost midnight. While Jay and Louise are discussing the matter, I go out without saying anything. I must find that letter. To think that I had even made her four copies! Perhaps they are in the suitcases.

I go into the garage to fetch the two cases, slipping quietly past Betty's room. The light is still on inside. It is late. I have a heavy day of work tomorrow. Jay and I both have a lot to do for the elections.

I return to Louise's room with the suitcases. The one is very big and heavy; the other is smaller, but almost as heavy, as if it contains documents or books. The small one is fastened with a type of plastic belt, which is easy to undo. I heave them, one by one, onto Loulou's big bed.

We look at the cases for a good ten minutes. We discuss the consequences of opening them. We discuss strategy. But now, things have changed. She has confessed to petty theft and we all have very strong suspicions that she has stolen the envelope of money. I am surer than ever that the answer is in these suitcases somewhere. And I must also find and destroy that letter of reference!

Eventually, I unfasten the plastic belt, managing to get it through the teeth of the clasp without leaving any marks.

First of all I find a lot of new clothes, several pieces of underwear, bras and panties. The price tags are still attached. Very sexy pieces.

'A hundred and sixty rand for a bra! Even I can't afford that!'

At the bottom of the case is a pile of documents. This is what I'm looking for.

Betty is meticulous, like me. Everything is filed in an orderly fashion. All sorts of documents have been slipped into plastic sleeves. I meticulously take the contents out. If I can find that letter – the four copies – I will be able to sleep peacefully, for the few remaining hours before dawn.

Page by page, I go through the documents. Legal documents, life assurance policies, lots of life assurance policies.

'But what's she doing with all these life assurance policies?'

'She's been talking a lot about travelling recently,' says Louise. 'She even bought a new set of suitcases.'

'But why so many life assurance policies?'

I continue my inspection of the documents. Finally, I come across the letters I am looking for.

'Burn them!' says Louise.

'I must also erase the file on the computer! Don't touch anything. I'll be right back.'

I run into the office to delete the file in question. There is no longer any trace of my text. Then I go outside and burn the letters. The ashes fly up into the starry sky.

Breathless but relieved, I return to Loulou's room. Nothing has been moved. I get back to work, continuing to check the contents of the plastic sleeves. Apart from the life assurance policies, I find no evidence that might link Betty to the theft of the American dollars.

I am not satisfied. Betty is methodical. There must be bank receipts or something somewhere.

I open other files. I find a notebook. I recognise Betty's writing. I go pale and start to read it aloud. Jay and Louise stop talking.

'How to make letter and parcel bombs.'

'Let me see that!'

Jay panics and snatches the notebook from my hands. He flips through it quickly and hands it back to me. He looks dismayed.

At the top of another page there is a heading: *Secret service military training*. It looks like the name of a course Betty may have taken. It explains how to make bombs, all sorts of bombs, among them small ones that you can hide among the personal effects of victims. There is a chapter on weapons, on electronic bugging, on other spying techniques, on examining the contents of rubbish bins. Suddenly, something occurs to me.

'Do you remember, three years ago when we moved to Cape Town and Betty wanted to go and fetch our mail? She insisted on having the key to our post box. She used the excuse that it would force her to go for a walk every day.'

I had thought it a good idea and even encouraged her to get the exercise, since she suffers from diabetes and obesity. I had given her the key to the post box and for the last three years, she had brought the mail home. Faithfully ...

If Louise could smoke two cigarettes at the same time, she would. She looks as though she's seen a monster.

The discoveries are not over. I come across a certificate confirming that Betty has, 'successfully', completed a course on how to handle firearms. Another document is attached to it with a paperclip. It is a certificate of ownership and a licence to carry a firearm.

'She has a firearm.'

'What?!'

'And she knows how to use it. It's a revolver.'

71

Hidden microphones

Silently, I enter the main lounge to fetch the bottle of brandy that has survived three moves in eight years. It will not survive tonight! I make a detour via the kitchen, lift the curtain above the sink, and look out over the little courtyard towards Betty's room. I see a ray of light under her door. She is still awake. That is not normal. Has she got her revolver with her?

I pour glasses of brandy for Jay, Louise and myself and then continue my exploration of the documents. I find a few invoices, but nothing out of the ordinary.

Suddenly something clicks, 'Something's missing …'

'What?'

'I don't know. Something is missing. I am going to go through the contents of the folder again.'

'Lucie, stop playing Colombo,' says Jay. 'Go to bed.'

'No, something is missing.'

I pick up the folder containing the plastic sleeves again. I haven't examined the contents of the first and the last pockets properly, because they are protected by a piece of cardboard. I look at them more closely.

There it is! I find what I have been looking for right from the start. Receipts. Receipts for the purchase of a new stereo system, pots, a television set, a lounge suite and a set of kitchen furniture. I also find receipts for bank deposits, one of them into the account of her sister in Johannesburg. I add up the receipts, which are all dated in the week of my return from Kenya, just a few days after I put the envelope in the drawer in my bedroom. The total is equivalent to the amount that was stolen, give or take a few rand. Finally, I have what seems to be proof. Betty will have to do some fast talking to explain how she got hold of a year's salary in one week!

We cannot take in any more. It seems that the more we find, the less we want to know, but the more we need to know. And the big suitcase? We'll see tomorrow. We decide that Betty will have to open her suitcases, in front of us and in front of the police, if she wants to leave tomorrow.

Jay is too tired to think any further. He is shattered.

'Let's go to bed,' he says. 'I will call Joe in the morning.'

Louise does not sleep all night. She is too afraid. She puts the chains on all the doors in the house. She wedges chairs up against some of the inside doors. She goes around the whole house checking all the windows are properly closed. In so doing, she discovers that one of the sliding doors in the main lounge has been delicately removed and replaced, off its rails! We don't understand anything any more. This reminds me of the incident that occurred last year: while we were in Quebec, someone had searched the house, particularly the office, which Jay and I share, and the bedroom. They had switched on my computer. Nothing had been stolen. But everything had been checked out.

I lay my head on the pillow, trying to think of the elections. I have to do a report in a few hours' time.

Jay and I curl up together and fall asleep in a silent embrace, the only remedy against despair. There is nothing more to say, no words can express the hurt we are feeling.

The next morning the nightmare has not faded. The more of Betty's secrets we discover, the less we recognise her.

Betty is not aware of any of our discoveries. This morning she is not in the kitchen preparing porridge, pancakes or cereal as usual.

'Where's Betty?' ask Kami and Shanti.

Jay and I have agreed to tell them the truth once Betty has departed from our lives.

'She has gone to vote.'

Betty clearly hadn't slept a wink all night. I caught sight of her through the kitchen window as she came out of the bathroom.

She was coming back from the polling station.

Jay and I drop the children off at school. It's always a big event for them when we both take them. Kami is proud to walk into school with his father.

Returning home, I go to see Betty to tell her what the situation is. Jay cannot face her. He, who has never been afraid to risk his life for his work, is incapable of telling Betty what is in store for her.

Joe, alerted by multiple messages from Jay, arrives at the house.

'Why didn't you call me last night?' he exclaims when Jay brings him up to date on the rest of the story. 'Your life may be in danger!'

Jay says he did not want to disturb him after the long evening they'd had.

'But this is serious!'

Joe gets up, a bit edgy, and takes out his cellular phone. He makes several calls, some in Afrikaans, others in English, then announces that his colleagues are on their way.

Jay went to vote this morning at seven. I have some reports to prepare. Radio–Canada will definitely not accept my taking leave today! Joe and Jay beg me to go about my business. They have a lot on their plates today. But Betty's case has just been classified a 'national priority'.

As I am writing my report, I hear cars pulling up. It seems to me that there are several, but I don't have time to go and check. When my first report is complete, I come out of my office. There are more than fifteen policemen in the house and almost as many cars in the drive! I hadn't expected such a turnout. Jay informs me that Betty is going to be formally arrested.

I am making my way through the crowd of policemen and secret agents when two plain-clothed agents come in with two large cases. Joe signals them to go into the main lounge. 'Sweep the house,' he tells them. The two men put on headphones and start searching for hidden microphones.

I have gone back to work in my office when one of the technicians knocks at the door.

'Excuse me, Mrs Naidoo. Can we come in here for a few minutes?'

'I have work to do. Can it wait ten minutes?'

'We won't disturb you, I promise!' he says, coming in and ignoring my request. 'Go on working.'

He comes in with his assistants. He puts down one of the large cases crammed with electrical equipment. I am fascinated by what is inside. It reminds me of the show *Mission Impossible*. He undoes one of the plugs for the telephone and attaches some wires to it.

'You can go on working,' he insists, squatting on the ground, a screwdriver in hand.

A few minutes later, I return to the lounge. There is no one in sight! All the equipment has been taken outside, into the courtyard.

'What's going on?'

Joe signals me to be quiet, his finger to his lips. He invites me to go out with him. Outside, he asks me:

'Can you describe to me in detail the problems you have had with your telephone?'

'Well, for a few years, the line has been disconnecting in the middle of conversations, after a clicking sound. Sometimes I hear people talking in Afrikaans. They seem to be conversations between policemen.'

'What do you hear when the communication is interrupted?'

'Less than a minute after we start talking, I hear a little click and then the line disconnects. That's all.'

'We found two hidden microphones in your telephone plugs. The click that you hear and the break in communication are the result of interference between the two microphones.'

Hidden microphones, phone bugs in my office! They're telling me that my telephone conversations have been listened to and that my emails have been read, even the tender exchanges between Jay and myself. I ask Jay whether they have found any microphones in our bedroom. But I'm horrified by the very idea, so before he has a chance to reply, I say, 'If you know, I don't want to know. Ever!'

Something suddenly comes back to me. I tell Jay and Joe about it. A few months after we moved in, three years ago, two Telkom employees arrived to do some repairs. I told them we hadn't called anyone. But, without thinking, I let them in and they fiddled with one of the plugs in my office. I found that a little odd and asked them for some identity. They showed me a crumpled piece of paper, dated the previous year. Joe is stunned at my naiveté.

So many memories now take on a new meaning. Last year, we were planning a party for Shanti's third birthday. Jay and I discussed it on the phone. The following morning, Jay was still in Johannesburg when a policeman called me and wanted to know how many people would be at the party. I was flabbergasted. How could he have known we were going to have a party? We hadn't mentioned it to anyone.

They ask me to be present when Betty's suitcases are opened. I will finally be able to see what is in the big bag. I am afraid. What if there's a firearm inside? What if she grabs it and starts shooting, like a madwoman, like they do in schools in the United States, like they do in the streets of Soweto to steal a car or kill someone?

A policeman and policewoman lead me into Betty's room. I have to ask her whether she agrees to having her suitcases opened. There has to be a witness. Everything has to be done according to the rules.

'Do you agree to having your suitcases opened in front of us?'

She agrees. She has some nerve. I've stopped being surprised. We all go to the garage. There are a dozen of us around the suitcases: Betty, the police officers, Joe, Jay, Louise and myself. The conversation takes place in Afrikaans, a language Betty speaks fluently. This detail, which I had never paid any attention to, now seems suspicious to me.

Betty opens the small suitcase. The policewoman signals me to take out the contents. I take the objects out one at a time, clothes, photos, ornaments and documents. Betty doesn't know that the folder is no longer there. She goes through the documents. She's looking for the folder now, as she replaces her things. But she remains extraordinarily calm. She opens the second suitcase, the large one. Right on top I discover a large plastic bag. Inside I find the leather Khoisan outfit that I had had made for the filming of *The Greatest Journeys on Earth*.

'But that's mine!'

The policewoman jumps. Betty retorts, 'But it was in the garage. I thought you were throwing it out.'

'You could have asked me!'

A policewoman confiscates the evidence and gives the outfit to a colleague. I continue the search. I find the African hat I bought last month at the market at the Waterfront.

'That was not in the garage! It was in my cupboard!'

For the first time, Betty's face reveals a little emotion. She knows she has hurt me. The policewoman takes this second piece of evidence and passes it to the same policeman, who is writing in his notebook. I empty

362

the suitcase: a set of new saucepans with gold-plated handles, lots of new clothes … I discover my Opium perfume box. It is full of photos. The bottle isn't there. It disappeared a week after Jay brought it back from a trip for me. I obviously never suspected Betty.

In an inside pocket of the suitcase, I find a diary in which she keeps a little journal. I open it and read everything I can as I page through it quickly. On one page, in the month of March, she admits, 'I'm tired of being a thief in this house.' Elsewhere, 'Louise is now an enemy.'

The cases are empty. I take refuge in my office. I don't want to know any more! I have to mourn the loss of my children's nanny, my child-minder, my confidante, a friend. Something has died.

Betty has finally been arrested and taken away by the police. They have all left. At last.

Jay and I have decided to tell the children the truth as soon as they come home from school. They have to know. They will find out everything one day. And the fact that Betty left without giving them a kiss or a hug requires an explanation.

'Kami, Shanti, listen to me. Betty stole some money and the police have taken her to prison.'

'Mama, stop making jokes. Where is Betty?'

'She is in prison, Kami, because she stole some of our money.'

'Mama, stop it! Betty would never do that. Where is she?'

'I promise you, it's true. Betty is in prison.'

'Mama, you're not funny. It's not nice to do that to Betty. Where is she?'

They cannot believe their ears. Shanti laughs and tells me I'm very funny with my jokes. Kami says that it's not funny to play jokes like that.

We talk about it all evening. It's an opportunity for a good lesson in life. We will talk about it for days. The children need time to assimilate this news. I don't know how to break the news to Léandre. He has a photo – a precious one – of himself and Betty. He has spent a great deal of time with her in the kitchen. When he hears the news, he will be completely crushed.

What still remains unanswered is this question: Who was Betty working for? A political party? The far right? The business world?

Later I found out that Betty admitted everything, at least as far as the theft was concerned. Beyond that, it's impossible to know where the investigation led.

Ten days after her arrest, as Jay and I were getting ready to attend a banquet with Colonel Gaddafi and President Mandela, the phone rang. I answered. Someone asked if I would accept a reverse-charges call from a Betty Monisi. I froze, then said yes. Betty was calling from prison.

'Please, Lucie, help me.'

She was crying.

'I am suffering here. I am suffering terribly. It's dirty. It's cold. My children need me.'

'But you betrayed us!'

'I'm sorry, Lucie. I promise I will never do it again. I'm really sorry. I will never do it again. I promise you!'

She was begging me. I said I would see what I could do and I hung up, without any intention of helping her.

Later I heard that she had been released on bail that same day. I wasn't able to find out who paid her bail. Perhaps Betty thought that her release was the result of my call!

I never heard mention of Betty again after that. They had told me that I would have to give evidence at her trial, in September 1999. I was never summoned. I still don't know whether she was spying on us, and if so, for whom. I don't know where she is. I don't know anything. She still haunts me.

72

The decade

On 16 June 1999, Shanti's fourth birthday, only two weeks after our 'Bettygate', I go to Pretoria to cover the major event of the decade: the end of the Mandela era. This was the final date I had set for my return to Quebec. I have been preparing for years, because I would like to finish my journalistic coverage with a bang. I am happy and sad at the same time; happy to have had the privilege of living through and covering the Mandela era as a journalist; sad to be leaving my work as a correspondent for Radio–Canada, a job that has been my umbilical cord to Quebec. I have always imagined this day differently. I saw myself, enthusiastic, talking about the crowd – one hundred thousand people are massed on the lawns of the Union Buildings – talking about the gathering of political leaders from all over, about Nelson Mandela resigning with a proud and happy smile. He said, 'Now I want to garden and play with my grandchildren.' But the spectacle before me wasn't getting through to me. I was emotionally exhausted. Because of Betty. I did not have the energy to fully savour this moment, marking the end of my stay in South Africa.

I did my last report weighing every word and every comma, because I knew that these seventy seconds were my last. That hurt. After terminating the communication with the Radio–Canada newsroom, I collapsed. I didn't know whether to laugh or to cry, to celebrate or to go into mourning.

I wrote a letter to the people at Radio–Canada to thank them for having been there, having listened to me, having believed in me, in the information I delivered to them all these years. But I received no acknowledgement of receipt. Not a word. Not a phone call. Day after day Jay said, 'Just wait, they will reply.' Nothing.

My letter remained pinned to the noticeboard in the Radio–Canada newsroom for a while. Like an autumn leaf, it was eventually swept away. While within me, the need to tell the story of this experience, to weigh up this decade – or almost a decade – spent in South Africa, became urgent, became more acute than ever. This is the reason I have written this book.

I was in a hurry to leave. Shanti had already been in Quebec with her granny Loulou for two weeks. The boxes had gone. I was living out of two suitcases. But the departure had to be delayed because Kami fell seriously ill and ended up in hospital with pneumonia. A reaction to having to leave his country of birth? He says he is looking forward to discovering Quebec, though. He is eager to see his brother again. I am also missing Léandre, terribly. I have a son I adore on one continent and a husband I adore on another. What can I do?

I returned to Quebec with my children, without Jay, hoping up to the last minute that he would leave with us. But he couldn't. Everyone told me so. I hoped all the same. A good friend, Sam Pitroda, summed up the situation well, 'It's impossible, Lucie. His mission is in Africa. He is African. And Africa needs him.'

Sam tells me that I am dreaming. My therapists all told me I was dreaming. Everyone says I am dreaming. *Jay was born with a mission.* But he, on the other hand, continues to affirm, 'One day, Lucie, soon. Soon, one day.'

I am still waiting. I still believe him. Jay has always kept his promises …

I was so keen to return, but I am lost in Quebec. The adjustment to a totally different life is difficult for us all. Jay is on the other side of the world. 'How many beddy-byes until Papa comes?' That eternal question is reversed now. It is Kami and Shanti who want to see their father. But when he comes, it's never for more than a week or two at a time, every couple of months. The reply is still the same, 'Soon, my sweethearts. Soon …'

Six months after moving back to Quebec, I almost left everything, abandoned everything. I called Jay. I asked him the fateful question,

'If you had to choose, would it be me and the children, or your mission in Africa?' He did not reply. He waited. I didn't say anything. And then he whispered, 'It would kill me to leave Africa.'

I don't want Jay to have to choose between his work and his family. We have a love that is sure, a love that is deep. But for the time being I have to be here, in Quebec. As for Jay, together with Jayendra Naidoo he has established a company, in Johannesburg, with the objective of installing modern technology in Africa. Their company is called *J and J*. Jay has also been appointed Chairperson of the Board of the Development Bank of Southern Africa by the South African Cabinet. Then the office of the Secretary General of the United Nations, Kofi Annan, asked him to be part of a team to advise him on telecommunications in developing countries. It is difficult to criticise Jay for wanting to devote himself to all these noble causes ...

He comes to visit us, but is always gone in a flash. In the calm that follows, his absence is difficult to bear.

I have returned with two children, to join the third, who left a year ago. I have returned to build myself a new dream, and to put on paper what I experienced over nine years. I need to empty it all out. I need to extract this African decade, this era of Mandela, that I experienced torn between two continents. I need an autumn. I dream about one. I need the snow, to glide through the forest on my skis, without diplomatic protocols or rules. I need to feel close to my family and my friends; I need the winter, the lakes and Mount Mégantic. I want Kami and Shanti to know the other half of their heritage, of their culture, even if they already speak French with a Québecois accent, as if they were born here, even if they have eaten pancakes with maple syrup since they were tiny. I would have liked to share the beauty, the peace, the tranquillity of this country with Jay. But that's impossible. In any case, it's not something we can do right now ...

Even though I find the continual absence of Jay too heavy to bear, I would not be capable of leaving him. Because I love him, despite his absence. The fact that he is a leader is also exciting. It's like living out a fantastic novel every day. He travels all over the world, talks to me about the challenges of the planet, calls me to tell me that Mandela says hello, that he has to go to New Delhi, that Africa is a jewel. He writes to me to tell me that he has turned down a job that pays several hundred thousand dollars a year, when we have difficulty making ends meet. 'I refused it because I want my work to mean something to ordinary people,' he says. Nothing is ever boring with Jay. He is merciless in the war for justice for all. My desire to see him home at five-thirty every evening, and 24/7 over weekends, goes against my desire to see him in action, working and fighting for justice. A leader does not work from nine to five.

Mama, how many beddy-byes until Papa comes?

Soon, my sweethearts. Soon …

While we wait, we communicate every day, by telephone or by computer.

Johannesburg, 20 August 2000

Hello my love

What emotions you must have gone through to see a fast rewind of the last decade! It must have been exhausting, my darling. But another week and you can send it off to the publisher. I pray for you and send a mountain of energy and goodwill. You are on a river of life. There have been obstacles. You have sometimes had to divert into a tributary. But your determination always drives you back to the main stream. And now you can see the estuary. You have travelled a long and testing journey. You have faced momentous challenges. And now you will soon see a beautiful sight. Yourself coming towards you. Confident, smiling, happy with yourself. You will look into your eyes and see peace. And you will smile inside.

I will be there to hold your hand, as you will be when I embark on my journey. We have been born of the same spirit. Our souls are intertwined in the history of time. And we have much more to share. Draw from your strength within. And draw from our love. It is inexhaustible. A source of passionate energy. I love you, sweetie pie.

I must leave you. The night has fallen. Solitude bites. I must close the curtains.

Your husband

This story is far from finished …

Gatineau, Quebec, 1999–2000

Epilogue

This book was first published in Canada in 2001, in French. Following its publication, I travelled the length and breadth of Quebec, visiting book fairs and giving talks on South Africa and Africa, on women, on journalism, and on relations between developed and developing countries. Canadians were hungry for information on Africa and South Africa in particular. I realised that all the work I had done as a reporter in the 1990s in South Africa was just a drop in the ocean for people who wanted to learn more about this beautiful country and continent. People want to know about Africa, the *forgotten continent,* and have had enough of the news about wars and blood, about violence and poverty. I have had hundreds of letters from people thanking me for taking the time to write about South Africa and the 'miracle' this country has achieved, saying that seventy-second radio reports and the odd newspaper article were not enough for them to understand the situation in South Africa. I have never been so close to Africa and have never talked so much about South Africa as I did in this period in Quebec after writing my book.

And I waited and hoped and prayed that Jay would come and 'live' in Quebec for some time, for a few months, for a few seasons, for a year. But he didn't come. I spent three years hoping and waiting. Three years of seeing my husband ten days out of every two months. It was beginning to be a strain on our relationship. In the end, the relationship was barely surviving, but the love we have for each other could not be thrown away. So I had to take the agonising decision to leave my son Léandre again, to leave my mother and father and friends and work and to separate Kami and Shanti from their brother to be with Jay. I moved back to my not-so-favourite city, Johannesburg, in August 2002. Since returning, I have been writing articles and doing radio reports again for Canada on South Africa.

In South Africa I am scared of crime and rape, I am outraged by racism and corruption and even though tremendous progress has been achieved, I pray every day that the 'political miracle' translates into a real social and economic one, where fear is not part of our lives. I miss my own country badly, as well as my son and family. I have slowly come to accept that I will have to share my life between two continents. Thirteen years ago, I met Jay. I am still working on having him come and live in Quebec one day, even though 'he is already married to South Africa' as Albertina Sisulu said at our wedding. But he married me too. Three times! So if I do steal him away from South Africa one day, don't be angry. Instead, thank him for having given up most of his life for his country. And congratulate him for taking care of his wife and children, for letting himself be loved by a woman who believes in him and in South Africa. We do not have a normal relationship. But we do have an extraordinary one.